# REFERENCE
# LIBRARY
# OF
# BLACK
# AMERICA

# REFERENCE LIBRARY OF BLACK AMERICA

## Volume II

Edited by

**Kenneth Estell**

**Distributed by Afro-American Press**

*Reference Library of Black America* is based upon the sixth edition of *The African American Almanac*, published by Gale Research Inc. It has been published in this 5-volume set to facilitate wider usage among students.

Linda Metzger, *Senior Editor*

Kenneth Estell, *Editor*

Monica Hubbard, *Contributing Editor*

David G. Oblender, *Associate Editor*

Victoria Coughlin, Paula Cutcher-Jackson, *Contributing Asociate Editors*

Janie Wilcox, *Contributing Assistant Editor*

Simon Glickman, Joyce Harrison, Carmen Johnson, Michael Knes, *Writers*

Beth Baker, Kimberly Burton Faulkner, William J. Moses, David Sprinkle, *Copyeditors*

George Hobart, *Photo Researcher*

Jeanne Gough, *Permissions Manager*

Margaret A. Chamberlain, *Permissions Supervisor (Pictures)*

Barbara Wallace, *Permissions Assistant*

Sandra C. Davis, *Permissions Supervisor (Text)*

Michele M. Lonoconus, *Permissions Assistant*

Victoria B. Cariappa, *Research Manager*

Maureen Richards, *Research Supervisor*

Donna Melnychenko, *Editorial Associate*

Mary Beth Trimper, *Production Director*

Evi Seoud, *Assistant Production Manager*

Mary Kelley, *Production Assistant*

Cynthia Baldwin, *Art Director*

Barbara J. Yarrow, *Graphic Services Supervisor*

Mark C. Howell, *Cover Designer*

Mary Krzewinski, *Page Designer*

Willie F. Mathis, *Camera Operator*

Nicholas Jakubiak, *Desktop Publisher*

Sherrell L. Hobbs, *Desktop Publisher*

Benita L. Spight, *Data Entry Supervisor*

Gwendolyn S. Tucker, *Data Entry Group Leader*

Nancy K. Sheridan, *Data Entry Associate*

*10/94*

The paper used in this publication meets the minimum requirements of American National Standard for Information Sciences—Permanence Paper for Printed Library Materials, ANSI Z 39.48-1984. ∞™

Printed in the United States of America
for distribution by Afro-American Press

# Advisory Board

# Contributors

**Stephen W. Angell**
Associate Professor of Religion, Florida A&M University

**Robin Armstrong**
Adjunct Lecturer, University of Michigan, Dearborn

**Claudette Bennett**
Bureau of the Census, United States Department of Commerce

**John Cohassey**

**Allen G. Harris**
President, Air Force Association,
General Dainiel James Chapter

**Hayward Derrick Horton**
Assistant Professor of Sociology, Iowa State University

**George Johnson**
Professor of Law, Howard University School of Law

**Faustine C. Jones-Wilson**
Professor of Education, Howard University; Editor, *The Journal of Negro Education*

**Donald Franklin Joyce**
Director, Felix G. Woodward Library, Austin Peay State University

**Kwame Kenyatta**
Detroit Board of Education; New African People's Organization

**Mark Kram**
Sportswriter, *Philadelphia Daily News*

**Marilyn Hortense Mackel**
Associate Professor, Western State University College of Law, Judge Pro Tempore,
Los Angeles County Superior Court, Juvenile Department

**Ionis Bracy Martin**
Lecturer, Central Connecticut State University


**Dan Morgenstern**
Director, Institute for Jazz Studies, Rutgers University


**Wilson J. Moses**
Professor of History, Pennsylvania State University


**Richard Prince**
National Association of Black Journalists


**Nancy Rampson**


**Michael D. Woodard**
Director, Los Angeles Institute for Multicultural Training;
Visiting Scholar, UCLA Center for Afro-American Studies

# Contents

Contents

**Volume III**

Contents

# Introduction

*The Reference Library of Black America* is based upon the sixth edition of *The African-American Almanac*, first published in 1967 as *The Negro Almanac* and since cited by *Library Journal* as an outstanding reference work.

## New Features in This Edition

All material was extensively reviewed by the editor and a board of prominent advisors and, where appropriate, updated and/or expanded. For example, the expanded chapter on national organizations now includes a history of black organizations in the United States and provides biographical information on leaders of major associations, past and present. The chapter on fine art now includes coverage of the applied arts—architecture, industrial design, fashion design, and graphic art—and a directory of museums in the United States.

Some chapters which appeared in the fifth edition were totally rewritten to focus on issues facing contemporary African-Americans. In particular the chapters on law, employment and income, the family, and education, were rewritten to reflect new and changing concerns within the black community regarding such issues as racism in the criminal justice system, factors in employment and unemployment, family structure and stability, and African-centered education.

Several completely new topics were added to this edition, including: a chapter on Africans in America since the first arrival of Africans in the Western Hemisphere through the Civil War and Reconstruction; a chapter on black nationalism covering the history of cultural nationalism and Pan-Africanism in the United States; a chapter on popular music covering contemporary music forms, including rhythm and blues, soul, gospel, rap, and country music. In addition, an appendix listing African-American recipients of selected major awards is new to this edition.

While many chapters have been expanded, others which appeared in the fifth edition have been incorporated into new or existing sections of the book. For example, biographical profiles included in the chapters on women and on prominent African Americans have been absorbed into existing chapters.

## Content and Arrangement

Information in this edition of *The Reference Library of Black America* appears in twenty-seven subject chapters. Many chapters open with an essay focusing on historical developments or the contributions of African Americans to the subject area, followed by concise biographical profiles of selected individuals.

Although the individuals featured in this edition represent only a small portion of the African-American community, they embody excellence and diversity in their respective fields of endeavor. Where an individual has made a significant contribution in more than one area, his or her biographical profile appears in the subject area for which he or she is best known, and cross references in other chapters lead the user to the profile.

In order to facilitate further research, a bibliography and list of publishers is provided. The bibliography has been divided into two major divisions: "Africana" and "African Americana." Within these two divisions titles are arranged alphabetically by author under categories indicative of their subject matter.

More than eight hundred maps and illustrations aid the reader in understanding the topics and people covered in the work. A name and keyword index provides access to the contents.

# 5

# *Africa and the Western Hemisphere*

# 5

# *Africa and the Western Hemisphere*

A Brief History of Africa ■ The People of Africa ■ Blacks in the Western Hemisphere
■ Country Profiles

## ■ A BRIEF HISTORY OF AFRICA

In recent years archeologists have come to believe that early humans, Hominidea, originated in Africa some two to three million years and migrated to other continents.

By the Middle Stone Age, three distinct groups had evolved—Bushmanoid, Pygmoid, and Negroid. Only a few Bushmen, and related Hottentot people, are still found in parts of the south-west portion of the con-

Cyrille Adoula, Jomo Kenyatta, and other members of the Pan-African Movement for East and Central Africa meet, 1962.

| | | |
|---|---|---|
| Libya | December 24 | 1951 |
| Sudan | January 1 | 1956 |
| Morocco | March 2 | 1956 |
| Tunisia | March 20 | 1956 |
| Ghana | March 6 | 1957 |
| Guinea | October 2 | 1958 |
| Cameroon | January 1 | 1960 |
| Togo | April 27 | 1960 |
| Mali | June 20 | 1960 |
| Senegal | June 20 | 1960 |
| Madagascar | June 26 | 1960 |
| Zaire | June 30 | 1960 |
| Somalia | July 1 | 1960 |
| Benin | August 1 | 1960 |
| Niger | August 3 | 1960 |
| Burkina Faso | August 5 | 1960 |
| Cote d'Ivoire | August 7 | 1960 |
| Chad | August 11 | 1960 |
| Central African Republic | August 13 | 1960 |
| Congo | August 15 | 1960 |
| Gabon | August 17 | 1960 |
| Nigeria | October 1 | 1960 |
| Mauritania | November 28 | 1960 |
| Sierra Leone | April 27 | 1961 |
| Tanzania | December 9 | 1961 |
| Rwanda | July 1 | 1962 |
| Burundi | July 1 | 1962 |
| Algeria | July 3 | 1962 |
| Uganda | October 9 | 1962 |
| Zanzibar (part of Tanzania) | December 10 | 1963 |
| Kenya | December 12 | 1963 |
| Malawi | July 6 | 1964 |
| Zambia | October 24 | 1964 |
| Gambia | February 18 | 1965 |
| Botswana | September 30 | 1966 |
| Lesotho | October 4 | 1966 |
| Mauritius | March 12 | 1968 |
| Swaziland | September 6 | 1968 |
| Equatorial Guinea | October 12 | 1968 |
| Guinea-Bissau | September 10 | 1974 |
| Mozambique | June 25 | 1975 |
| Cape Verde | July 5 | 1975 |
| Comoros | July 6 | 1975 |
| Sao Tome and Principe | July 12 | 1975 |
| Angola | November 11 | 1975 |
| Seychelles | June 29 | 1976 |
| Djibouti | June 27 | 1977 |
| Zimbabwe | April 18 | 1980 |
| Namibia | March 21 | 1990 |

Independence dates of African countries.

tinent, while a few isolated Pygmy groups have survived, mainly in the Congo forests. However, it was the Negroid group which became dominant on the continent.

Sophisticated societies developed in early Africa, among them the Kush, between 700 B.C. and A.D. 200 and the ancient Ghana, Kanen, Mali Songhai, and the Haissa states. In the Congo, the Kingdoms of Lunda, Lula, Bushong, and Kongo were founded, proba-

A Malian woman pounding grain.

bly between the sixteenth and eighteenth centuries. On the Guinea Coast, the city states of Benin, Ite, Oyo, Ashanti, and Yoruba date back to the fifteenth century. These states traded extensively in gold, ivory, salt, and livestock.

Trade with Europe began around the fifteenth century, with the slave trade an important part; an estimated ten to thirty million people were sold into slavery by the mid-nineteenth century. The interior of Africa was first exposed to Europeans in the eighteenth century by missionaries, traders, and adventurers. Reports of the continent's resources eventually spurred European conquest and direct control of virtually all of Africa. By 1900 only Ethiopia and Liberia remained free of European control.

In 1910 the British granted dominion status to the Union of South Africa. However, independence for the black-dominated regions of Africa, did not come until some forty year later. In 1957, independence movements started with a rush in Kenya, Ghana, and Guinea. By the late 1960s most of Africa had achieved independence.

## ■ THE PEOPLE OF AFRICA

### Population

The African population is most heavily concentrated in Nigeria, southern Ghana, along the Gulf of Guinea, Benin and Togo, the Nile Valley, in northern Sudan, the East Africa highlands of Ethiopia, Kenya, and Tanzania, eastern Zaire, the eastern and southern coasts, and the inland High Veld of South Africa. The desert and mountain regions are largely uninhabited.

In recent years the population of African has grown rapidly. In 1950 the total population was estimated at 281 million; by 1990 the population had reached 817 million. No

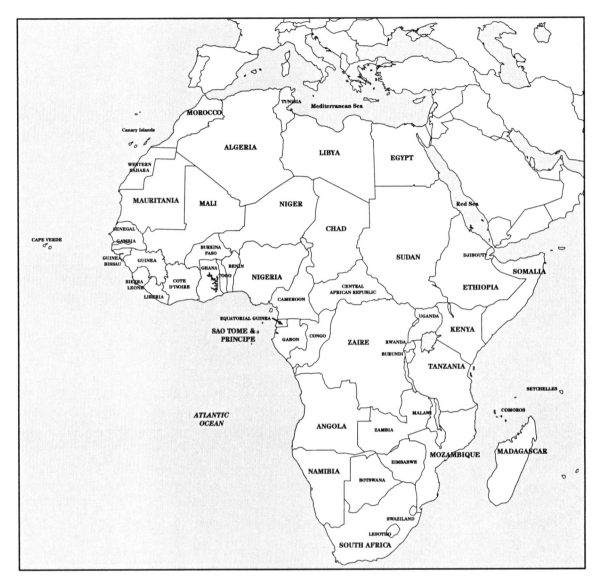

Africa.

African nation has developed an effective population control program, and such practices as having multiple wives and early marriages continue. By the year 2020, the population of Sub-Sahran Africa alone is expected to reach 1.2 billion.

Until recently, almost ninty percent of Africa's population lived in rural areas. African cities with populations exceeding one million include Accra, Ghana; Addis Ababa, Ethiopia; Cape Town and Johannesburg, South Africa; Cairo, Egypt; Maputo, Mozambique; Ibadan and Lagos, Nigeria; and Kinshasa, Zaire.

In addition to indigenous Africans, about 5 million people are of predominantly European descent, and 1 million are of Asian descent.

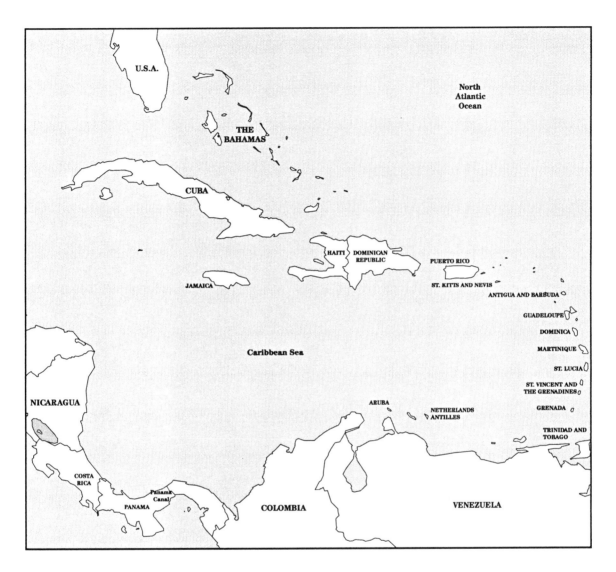

The Caribbean.

## Language

The diversity of Africa's people is underscored by the existence of more than 2,000 languages and dialects, including africanized forms of English, French, and Portuguese. Some fifty major languages are spoken by groups of one million or more people. The major language groups include Arabic (spoken mainly in north Africa), Fula, Hausa, Lingala, Malinke, Nguni (which includes SiNdebele, Xhosa, and Zulu), SeTwana-SeSotho, Swahili, and Yoruba.

## Health

Diseases which have been successfully monitored and controlled in Western na-

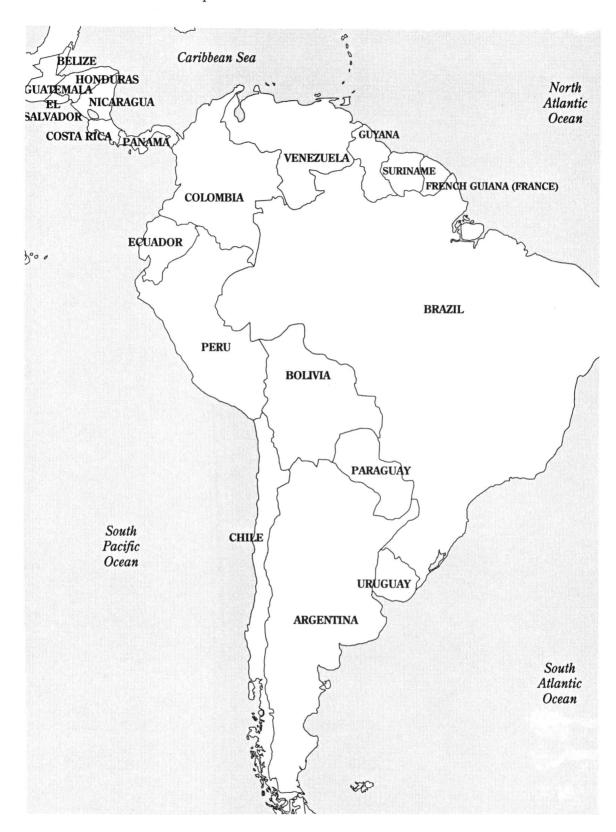

South America.

tions (diphtheria, measles, pertussis, polio-myelitis, tetanus, and tuberculosis) continue to be a problem in many parts of Africa. Diarrhea and tuberculosis account for one-half of all deaths in children.

The emergence of Acquired Immune Deficiency Syndrome (AIDS) has had a devastating effect on the continent. In 1990 there were an estimated 1.2 million AIDS cases, including some 400,000 cases in children under the age of five.

## ■ BLACKS IN THE WESTERN HEMISPHERE

The black population of the Caribbean and much of South America, like that in North America, is descended from African slaves who were transported to the New World to work on European settlements. On many islands of the Caribbean persons of African descent make up the majority of the population; on Barbados and Jamaica, blacks are the overwhelming majority. In other areas, notably on the continental mainland from Mexico south to Argentina, Africans have been largely absorbed into the mainstream of the population. In South America, the black population consists of a mixture of Africans and Indians, known as Zambos. Those who are primarily a mixture of Caucasian and American Indian are known as mestizos, and those who are a mixture of Caucasian and black are, as in the United States, referred to as mulattoes.

In recent years, the Caribbean basin has been a source of black immigration, with immigrants primarily from Jamaica and Haiti entering the United States in search of work. In 1980, the *Mariel* boatlift was successful in bringing Cuban refugees to the United States. More recently, thousands of Haitians have attempted, with little success, to immi-grate to the United States, since the September 1991 coup that ousted President Jean-Bertrand Aristide.

## ■ COUNTRY PROFILES

### Africa

**Algeria**
Official name: Democratic and Popular
   Republic of Algeria
Independence: July 5, 1962
Area: 918,497 sq. mi.
Population: (1991 estimate) 23 million
Ethnic divisions: Arab and Berber
Religious groups: Sunni Muslim
Languages spoken: Arabic (official), Berber
   dialects, French

Since the fifth century BC, the area that makes up what is now Algeria has been populated by indigenous tribes who have been progressively pushed back from the coast by invaders. As a result, the country boundaries have shifted during various stages of the conquests. Nearly all Algerians are Muslim, of Arab, Berber, or mixed Arab-Berber stock.

French colonization began in 1830 and continued until 1954, when the indigenous population staged a revolt on November 1. The revolution was launched by a small group of nationalists who called themselves the National Liberation Front. Negotiations led to a cease-fire signed by France and the National Liberation Front on March 18, 1962; France declared Algeria independent on July 3.

**Angola**
Official name: People's Republic of Angola
Independence: November 11, 1975
Area: 481,351 sq. mi.
Population: (1991 estimate) 8.6 million

Ethnic divisions: Ovimbundu 37%, Kimbundu
  25%, Bakongo 15%, Lunda-Chokwe 8%,
  Nganguela 6%, Haneca and Humbe 3%,
  Ovambo 2%, mestizo and European 2%,
  other 2%
Religious groups: Roman Catholic,
  Protestant, Traditional belief
Languages spoken: Portuguese (official),
  tribal languages and dialects

Angola's boundaries were formally established by the Berlin West Africa Congress of
1884 to 1885. Following World War II, Portuguese interest in colonizing Angola increased. Here, the Portuguese established a
slave trade and a strict and harsh colonial
rule.

Discontent over Portuguese unwillingness to concede eventual independence led
to the formation of the Popular Movement
for the Liberation of Angola (MPLA), the
National Front for the Liberation of Angola

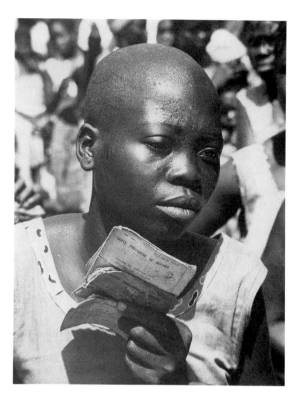

The Bakongo people of Angola are concentrated in
the northwest part of the country, adjacent to the
Congo and Zaire.

Angolans celebrating independence from Portugal.

(FNLA) and the National Union for the Total
Independence of Angola (UNITA). In January 1975, the Portuguese and the three liberation movements worked out a complicated
agreement—the Alvor Accord—which provided for a transitional government composed of all three groups and for elections in
preparation for independence in November
1975. Since 1976, Angola has been politically
unstable because of civil war and repeated
incursions by South African forces operating from Namibia. The United States does
not maintain diplomatic relations with Angola, but since 1978 the two countries have
had frequent contacts to discuss regional
and bilateral matters.

Angolans are almost entirely Bantu of various ethnic subgroupings. The Ovimbundu,
in central and southeastern Angola, are the

largest group, consisting of about thirty-seven percent of the population. The Bakongo, concentrated in the northwest but also living in areas adjacent to the Congo and Zaire as well as Cabinda, constitute about fifteen percent. The Kimbundu, about twenty-five percent of the population, are concentrated in the area around Luanda and out toward the east.

## Benin

Official name: People's Republic of Benin
Independence: August 1, 1960
Area: 43,483 sq. mi.
Population: (1991 estimate) 4.8 million
Ethnic divisions: Fon, Adja, Bariba, Yoruba
Religious groups: Traditional belief 61%,
    Christian 17%, Muslim 12%
Languages spoken: French (official)

During the precolonial era, Benin was a collection of small principalities, the most powerful of which was the Fon Kingdom of Dahomey. By the seventeenth and eighteenth centuries, first the Portuguese and later other Europeans established trading posts along the coast. From here thousands of slaves were shipped to the New World, primarily to Brazil and the Caribbean—this part of West Africa became known as the Slave Coast.

In 1892, the King of Dahomey was subjugated and the country organized as the French protectorate of Dahomey. It remained a French colony until independence in 1960, when the name was changed to the Republic of Dahomey. In 1975, the name was finally changed to the People's Republic of Benin.

The population of Benin comprises about twenty sociocultural groups. Four groups—the Fon, Aja (who are related), Bariba, and Yoruba—account for more than half of the population.

## Botswana

Official name: Republic of Botswana
Independence: September 30, 1966
Area: 224,710 sq. mi.
Population: (1991 estimate) 1.3 million

The Fon constitute one of the largest groups in Benin.

Ethnic divisions: Tswana 55%-60%, Kalanga 25%-20%, Kgalagadi, Yei, Herero, Mbukushu, Basarwa (Bushmen), Khoi (Hottentots), whites about 1%

Religious groups: Traditional belief 50%, Christianity 50%

Languages spoken: English (official), SeTswana

Europeans made first contact with the area in the early nineteenth century. In the last quarter of the century, hostilities broke out between the Botswana and the Afrikaners from South Africa (Transvaal). Following appeals by the Botswana for assistance, the British government in 1885 proclaimed "Bechuanaland" to be under British protection. In 1909, despite South African pressure, inhabitants of Bechuanaland, Basutoland (now Lesotho), and Swaziland demanded and received British agreement that they not be included in the proposed Union of South Africa. In June 1964, the British government accepted proposals for a form of self-government for Botswana that would lead to independence. Botswana became independent on September 30, 1966.

In 1977, the Botswana Defense Force was formed, largely in response to the Rhodesian conflict, which was affecting Botswana. Facing a threat of overt or covert military raids from South Africa directed against believed African National Congress targets, Botswana has embarked on modernization and expansion of the BDF. The nation remains opposed to South Africa's policy of apartheid and maintains no formal diplomatic relations with that country. In part because of its geographic location and reliance on South African transportation systems and goods, Botswana, nevertheless, maintains a pragmatic working relationship and close economic ties with South Africa.

Some fifty to sixty percent of the country's population is made up of the Tswana tribe (Botswana), which is divided into eight subgroups: Bamangwate, Bakwena, Batawana, Bangwaketse, Bakgatla, Bamalete, Barolong, and Batlokwa. The Kalanga, Herero, Bushmen (Basarwa), Yei, and Kgalagadi are minorities.

## Burkina Faso (formerly Upper Volta)

Independence: August 5, 1960
Area: 106,000 sq. mi.
Population: (1991 estimate) 9.3 million
Ethnic divisions: Mossi, Bobo, Mande, Fulani
Religious groups: Traditional belief 45%, Muslim 40%, Christian 15%
Languages spoken: French (official), More, other tribal languages

Until the end of the nineteenth century, the history of Burkina Faso was dominated by the Mossi, who are believed to have come from central or eastern Africa in the eleventh century. When the French arrived and claimed the area in 1896, the Mossi resisted but were defeated when their capital at Ouagadougou was captured. After World War II, the Mossi renewed their pressure for separate territorial status; Upper Volta became an autonomous republic in the French Community on December 11, 1958 and achieved independence on August 5, 1960.

The majority of the population belong to two major West African cultural groups, the Voltaic and the Mande. The Voltaic are far more numerous and include the Mossi, which make up about one-half of the population. The Mossi are still bound by the traditions of the emperor, the Mogho Naba, who holds court in Ouagadougou.

## Burundi

Official name: Republic of Burundi
Independence: July 1, 1962
Area: 10,747 sq. mi.
Population: (1991 estimate) 5.8 million
Ethnic divisions: Hutu 85%, Utusi 14%, Twa 1%

Religious groups: Roman Catholic 62%,
    Traditional belief 32%, Protestant 5%,
    Muslim 1%
Languages spoken: Kirundi and French (both
    official), Swahili

Prior to the arrival of Europeans, Burundi was a kingdom with a highly stratified, feudal social structure. Rulers were drawn from princely dynastic families (ganwa), from whom a king (mwami) was chosen.

European explorers and missionaries began making brief visits to the area as early as 1858; however, Burundi did not come under European administration until the 1890s, when it became part of German East Africa. In 1916 Belgian troops occupied the country; the League of Nations mandated it to Belgium in 1923 as part of the Territory of Ruanda-Urundi, now the nations of Rwanda and Burundi. Burundi became independent on July 1, 1962.

Burundi's population is made up of three ethnic groups—Hutu, Tutsi, and Twa. Hutus, who make up eighty-five percent of the population, are primarily farmers whose Bantu-speaking ancestors migrated into Burundi 800 to 1,000 years ago. The Tutsi, who make up fourteen percent of the population, are a pastoral people who apparently migrated from Ethiopia several hundred years later.

**Cameroon**
Official name: Republic of Cameroon
Independence: January 1, 1960
Area: 183,568 sq. mi.
Population: (1991 estimate) 11.7 million
Ethnic divisions: More than 200 groups
Religious groups: Christian, Muslim,
    Traditional belief
Languages spoken: English and French
    (official), more than 200 tribal languages

The earliest inhabitants of Cameroon were probably Pygmies, who still inhabit the southern forests. However, Bantu-speaking people were among the first to invade Cameroon from equatorial Africa, settling in the south and later in the west. The Muslim Fulani from the Niger basin arrived in the eleventh and nineteenth centuries and settled in the north.

Europeans first made contact with the area in the 1500s. For the next three centuries, Spanish, Dutch, and British traders visited the area.

In July 1884, Germany, the United Kingdom, and France each attempted to annex the area. A 1919 declaration divided Cameroon between the United Kingdom and France, with the larger, eastern area under France. In December 1958, the French trusteeship was ended; French Cameroon became the Republic of Cameroon on January 1, 1960.

Cameroon has about 200 tribal groups and clans, speaking at least as many languages and dialects.

**Cape Verde**
Official name: Republic of Cape Verde
Independence: July 5, 1975
Area: 1,557 sq. mi.
Population: (1991 estimate) 386,000
Ethnic divisions: Creole (mixed African and
    Portuguese), African, European
Religious groups: Roman Catholic,
    Protestant
Languages spoken: Portuguese (official),
    Crioulo (national)

Located in the north Atlantic Ocean, the Cape Verde archipelago remained uninhabited until the Portuguese visited it in 1456, and African slaves were brought to the islands to work on Portuguese plantations. As a result, Cape Verdeans have mixed African and Portuguese origins.

In 1951, Portugal changed Cape Verde's status from a colony to an overseas province. In 1956, the African Party for the Inde-

Cameroonian women husking corn.

pendence of Guinea-Bissau and Cape Verde (PAIGC) was organized to bring about improvement in economic, social, and political conditions in Cape Verde and Portuguese Guinea. The PAIGC began an armed rebellion against Portugal in 1961. Acts of sabotage eventually grew into a war in Portuguese Guinea that pitted 10,000 Soviet bloc-supported PAIGC soldiers against 35,000 Portuguese and African troops.

In December 1974, the PAIGC and Portugal signed an agreement providing for a transitional government composed of Portuguese and Cape Verdeans. On June 30, 1975, Cape Verdeans elected a National Assembly, which received the instruments of independence from Portugal on July 5, 1975.

The official language is Portuguese. However, most Cape Verdeans speak a Creole dialect, Crioulo, which consists of archaic Portuguese modified through contact with African and other European languages.

Central African woman preparing a meal.

## Central African Republic

Independence: August 13, 1960

Area: 242,000 sq. mi.

Population: (1991 estimate) 2.9 million

Ethnic divisions: More than 80 groups including, Baya 34%, Banda 28%, Sara 10%, Mandja 9%, Mboum 9%, M'Baka 7%

Religious groups: Traditional belief 35%, Protestant 25%, Roman Catholic 25%, Muslim 15%

Languages spoken: French (official), Sangho (national)

The first Europeans to settle in the area that is now the Central African Republic were the French. In 1889, the French established an outpost at Bangu. United with Chad in 1906, the outpost formed the Oubangui-Chari-Chad colony.

In 1910, it became one of the four territories of the Federation of French Equatorial Africa, along with Chad, Congo (Brazza-

ville), and Gabon. However, a constitutional referendum of September 1958 dissolved the federation. The nation became an autonomous republic within the newly established French Community on December 1, 1958, and acceded to complete independence as the Central African Republic on August 13, 1960. The first president, revered as the founder of the Central African Republic, was Bathelemy Boganda.

The Central African Republic is made up of more than eighty ethnic groups, each with its own language. About seventy percent of the population comprises Baya-Mandjia and Banda, with approxiamtely seven percent M'Baka. Sangho, the language of a small group along the Oubangui River, is the national language spoken by the majority of Central Africans.

## Chad

Official name: Republic of Chad

Independence: August 11, 1960

Area: 496,000 sq. mi.

Rural farmers in Chad.

Population: (1991 estimate) 5.8 million
Ethnic divisions: More than 200 groups
    including, Toubou (Gourane), Arabs, Fulbe,
    Kotoko, Hausa, Kanembou, Bagirmi,
    Boulala, Zaghawa, Hadjerai, and Maba;
    about 2,500 French citizens live in Chad

Religious groups: Muslim, Christian,
    Traditional belief
Languages spoken: French and Arabic
    (official); 200 tribal languages

The region that is now Chad was known to Middle Eastern traders and geographers as far back the late Middle Ages. Since then, Chad has served as a crossroads for the Muslim peoples of the desert and savanna regions and the animist Bantu tribes of the tropical forests.

The Sao people populated the Chari River basin for thousands of years, but their relatively weak chiefdoms were overtaken by the powerful chiefs of what were to become the Kanem-Bornu and Baguirmi kingdoms. At their peak, these two kingdoms and the kingdom of Ouaddai controlled a good part of what is now Chad, as well as parts of Nigeria and Sudan.

Children studing at a Koranic school in Chad.

The French first made contact with the region in 1891. The first major colonial battle for Chad was fought in 1900 between the French major Lamy and the African leader Rabah. Although the French won that battle, they did not declare the territory until 1911; armed clashes between colonial troops and local bands continued for many years thereafter. Although Chad joined the French colonies of Gabon, Oubangui-Charo, and Moyen Congo to form the Federation of French Equatorial Africa in 1910, Chad did not have colonial status until 1920.

In 1959, the territory of French Equatorial Africa was dissolved, and four states—Gabon, the Central African Republic, Congo (Brazzaville), and Chad—became autonomous members of the French Community. In 1960, Chad became an independent nation under its first president, Francois Tombalbaye.

Chad is made up of more than 200 ethnic groups. Those in the north and east are generally Muslim; most southerners are animists and Christians.

## Comoros

Official name: Comoros Federal Islamic
  Republic
Independence: July 6, 1975
Area: 838 sq. mi.
Population: (1991 estimate): 476,000
Ethnic divisions: Antalote, Cafre, Makoa,
  Oimatsaha, Sakalava
Religious groups: Sunni Muslim 98%, Roman
  Catholic 2%
Languages spoken: Shikomoro (a Swahili-
  Arab dialect), Malagasy, French

Located off the northwestern coast of Madagascar, Portuguese explorers visited the archipelago in 1505. In 1843, the sultan of Mayotte was persuaded to relinquish the island of Mayotte to the French. By 1912, France had established colonial rule over the islands of Grande Comore, Anjouan, and Hoheli and placed the islands under the administration of the governor general of Madagascar. After World War II, the islands became a French overseas territory and were represented in France's National Assembly. On July 6, 1975, the Comorian Parliament passed a resolution declaring unilateral independence. However, the deputies of Mayotte abstained; as a result, the Comorian government has effective control over only Grande Comore, Anjouan, and Moheli—Mayotte remains under French administration.

The Comorians inhabiting the islands of Grande Comore, Anjouan, and Moheli (about eighty-six percent of the population) share African-Arab origins. Islam is the dominant religion, but a substantial minority of the citizens of Mayotte (the Mahorais) are Catholic and have been influenced strongly by French culture. The most common language is Shikomoro, a Swahili dialect. French and Malagasy are also spoken.

## Congo

Official name: People's Republic of the
  Congo
Independence: August 15, 1960
Area: 132,000 sq. mi.
Population: (1991) 2.4 million
Ethnic divisions: 15 main groups, 75
  subgroups; largest groups are Bacongo,
  Bateke, M'Bochi, Sangha
Religious groups: Traditional belief 48%,
  Christian 47%, Muslim 2%
Languages spoken: French (official), Lingala,
  Kikongo

Early history of the Congo is believed to have focused on three tribal kingdoms—the Kongo, the Loango, and the Teke. Established in the fourth century AD, the Kongo was a highly centralized kingdom that later developed a close commercial relationship

A rural village in Congo.

with the Portuguese, the first Europeans to explore the area.

With the development of the slave trade, the Portuguese turned their attention from the Kongo Kingdom to the Loango. By the time the slave trade was abolished in the 1800s, the Loango Kingdom had been reduced to many small, independent groups. The Teke Kingdom of the interior, which had sold slaves to the Loango Kingdom, ended its independence in 1883, when the Teke king concluded a treaty with Pierre Savorgnan de Brazza, placing Teke lands and people under French protection. Under the French, the area became known as Middle Congo.

In 1910, Middle Congo became part of French Equatorial Africa, which also included Gabon, the Central African Republic, and Chad. A constitutional referendum in September 1958 replaced the Federation of French Equatorial Africa with the French Community. Middle Congo, under the name Republic of the Congo, and the three other territories of French Equatorial Africa became fully autonomous members within the French Community. On April 15, 1960, it became an independent nation but retained close, formal bonds with the community.

## Côte d' Ivoire (Ivory Coast)
Independence: August 7, 1960
Area: 124,500 sq. mi.
Population: (1991 estimate) 12.9 million
Ethnic divisions: More than 60 groups
Religious groups: Muslim 55%, Traditional belief 25%, Christian 20%
Languages spoken: French (official), tribal dialects

The first Europeans, the French, made their initial contact with Côte d'Ivoire in 1637, when missionaries landed at Assinie near the Gold Coast (now Ghana) border. However, these early contacts were limited.

In 1843 and 1844, France signed treaties with the kings of the Grand Bassam and Assinie regions, placing their territories under a French protectorate. French explorers, missionaries, trading companies, and soldiers gradually extended the area under French control, until 1893 when Côte d'Ivoire was officially made a French colony.

In December 1958, Côte d'Ivoire became an autonomous republic within the French community. Côte d'Ivoire became independent on August 7, 1960.

Côte d'Ivoire's more than sixty ethnic groups usually are classified into seven principal divisions—Akan, Krou, Lagoon, Nuclear Mande, Peripheral Mande, Senoufo, and Lobi. The Baoule, in the Akan division, are probably the largest single subgroup, with perhaps twenty percent of the overall population. The Bete, in the Krou division, and the Senoufo in the north are the second and third largest groups, with roughly eighteen and fifteen percent of the national population, respectively.

## Djibouti

Official name: Republic of Djibouti
Independence: June 27, 1977
Area: 9,000 sq. mi.
Population: (1991 estimate) 541,000
Ethnic divisions: Somalis (Issas), Afars,
    French, Arab, Ethiopian, Italian
Religious groups: Muslim 94%, Christian 6%
Languages spoken: French (official) Somali,
    Afar, Arabic

The region which now makes up the Republic of Djibouti was first settled by the French in 1862, as a result of growing French interest in British activity in Egypt. In 1884, France expanded its protectorate to include the shores of the Gulf of Tadjourah and the hinterland, designating the area French Somaliland. The boundaries of the protectorate, marked out in 1897 by France and Emperor Manelik II of Ethiopia, were affirmed further by agreements with Emperor Haile Selassie I in 1945 and 1954.

A July 1967 directive from Paris formally changed the name of the territory to the French Territory of Afars and Issas. In 1975, the French Government began to accommodate increasingly insistent demands for independence. In June 1976, the territory's citizenship law, which had favored the Afar minority, was revised to reflect more closely the weight of the Issa Somali. In a May 1977 referendum, the electorate voted for independence, and the Republic of Djibouti was inaugurated on June 27, 1977.

The indigenous population of the Republic of Djibouti is divided between the majority Somalis (predominantly of the Issa tribe with minority Ishaak and Gadaboursi representation) and the Afars and Danakils.

## Egypt

Official name: Republic of Egypt
Independence: February 28, 1922
Area: 386,650 sq. mi

Population: (1991 estimate) 54.8 million
Ethnic divisions: Egyptian, Bedouin Arab,
    Nubian
Religious groups: Sunni Muslim 90%, Coptic
    Christian
Languages spoken: Arabic (official), English

Egypt has endured as a unified state for more than 5,000 years, and archeological evidence indicates that a developed Egyptian society has existed much longer. In about 3100 BC, Egypt was united under a ruler known as Mena, or Menes, who inaugurated the thirty pharaonic dynasties into which Egypt's ancient history is divided—the Old and Middle Kingdoms and the New Empire.

In 525 BC, Persians dethroned the last pharaoh of the 26th dynasty. The country remained a Persian province until the conquest of Alexander the Great in 332 BC. After Alexander's death in 323 BC, the Macedonian commander, Ptolemy, established personal control over Egypt, assuming the title of pharaoh in 304 BC. The Ptolemaic line ended in 30 BC with the suicide of Queen Cleopatra. The Emperor Augustus then established direct Roman control over Egypt, initiating almost seven centuries of Roman and Byzantine rule.

Egypt was invaded and conquered by Arab forces in AD 642; a process of Arabization and Islamization ensued. The French arrived in Egypt in 1798. An Anglo-Ottoman invasion force drove out the French in 1801, and following a period of chaos, the Albanian Muhammad Ali obtained control of the country.

In 1882, the British occupied Egypt and declared a formal protectorate over Egypt on December 18, 1914. In deference to growing nationalist feelings, Britain unilaterally declared Egyptian independence on February 28, 1922.

The Egyptian population is fairly homogenous—Mediterranean and Arab influences appear in the north, as well as some mixing in the south with the Nubians of northern Sudan. Ethnic minorities include a small number of Bedouin Arab nomads dispersed in the eastern and western deserts and in the Sinai, as well as some 50,000 to 200,000 Nubians clustered along the Nile in Upper Egypt.

## Equatorial Guinea

Official name: Republic of Equatorial Guinea
Independence: October 12, 1968
Area: 10,820 sq. mi.
Population: (1991 estimate) 360,000
Ethnic divisions: Fang 80%, Bubi 15%, other 5%
Religious groups: Roman Catholic 83%, Protestant, Traditional belief
Languages spoken: Spanish (official), Fang, Bubi, pidgin, English, French, other tribal languages

The first inhabitants of the region that is now Equatorial Guinea are believed to have been Pygmies, of whom only isolated pockets remain in northern Rio Muni. Bantu migrations between the seventeenth and nineteenth centuries brought the coastal tribes and later the Fang people to the area.

The Portuguese, seeking a route to India, landed on the island of Bioko in 1471. The Portuguese retained control until 1778, when the island and adjacent islets, were ceded to Spain. From 1827 to 1843, Britain established a base on the island to combat the slave trade. Conflicting claims to the mainland were settled in 1900 by the Treaty of Paris.

In 1959, the Spanish territory of the Gulf of Guinea was established. In 1963, the name of the country was changed to Equatorial Guinea. In March 1968, under pressure from Equatoguinean nationalists and the United Nations, Spain announced that it would grant independence to Equatorial Guinea. In

Equatoguinean children.

September 1968, Francisco Macias Nguema was elected first president of Equatorial Guinea, and independence was granted in October.

The majority of the Equatoguinean people are of Bantu origin. The largest tribe, the Fang, constitute eighty percent of the population and are divided into about sixty-seven clans. Those to the north of Rio Benito on Rio Muni speak Fang-Ntumu, and those to the south speak Fang-Okak, two mutually intelligible dialects. The Bubi, who form fifteen percent of the population, are indigenous to Bioko Island. In addition, there exist several coastal tribes, who are sometimes referred to as "Playeros," and include the Ndowes, Bujebas, Balengues, and Bengas on the mainland and small islands, and Fernandinos, a Creole community, on Bioko. These groups comprise five percent of the population.

An Ethiopian market.

### Ethiopia

Official name: People's Democratic Republic of Ethiopia

Area: 472,000 sq. mi.

Population: (1990 estimate) 51.3 million

Ethnic divisions: Oromo 40%, Amhara 25%, Tigre 12%, Sidama 9%

Religious groups: Muslim 40%-45%, Ethiopian Orthodox Christian 35%-40%, Traditional belief 15%-25%

Languages spoken: Amharic (official), Tigrinya, Orominga, Arabic, English

Ethiopia is the oldest independent country in Africa and one of the oldest in the world. Herodotus, the Greek historian of the fifth century BC, describes ancient Ethiopia in his writings; the Old Testament of the Bible records the Queen of Sheba's visit to Jerusalem. Missionaries from Egypt and Syria introduced Christianity in the fourth cen-

Haile Selassie

tury AD. The Portuguese established contact with Ethiopia in 1493.

In 1930 Haile Selassie, was crowned emperor. His reign was interrupted in 1936 when Italian fascist forces invaded and occupied Ethiopia. The emperor was eventually forced into exile in England despite his plea to the League of Nations for intervention. Five years later, the Italians were defeated by British and Ethiopian forces, and the emperor returned to the throne. After a period of civil unrest, which began in February 1974, the aging Haile Selassie I was deposed on September 13, 1974.

Discontent had been spreading throughout Ethiopian urban elites, and an escalating series of mutinies in the armed forced, demonstrations, and strikes led to the seizure of state power by the armed forces coordinating committee, which later became the Provisional Military Administrative Council (PMAC). The PMAC formally declared its intent to remake Ethiopia into a socialist state. It finally destroyed its opposition in a program of mass arrests and executions known as the "red terror," which lasted from November 1977 to March 1978. An estimated 10,000 people, mostly in Addis Ababa, were killed by government forces.

Ethiopia's population is highly diverse. Most of its people speak a Semitic or Cushitic language. The Amhara, Tigreans, and Oromo make up more than three-fourths of the population, but there are more than 40 different ethnic groups within Ethiopia.

**Gabon**

Official name: Gabonese Republic
Independence: August 17, 1960
Area: 102,317 sq. mi.
Population: (1990 estimate) 1.2 million
Ethnic divisions: Fang, Myene, Bapounou, Eschira, Bandjabi, Beteke/Obamba
Religious groups: Christian, Muslim, Traditional belief
Languages spoken: French (official), Fang, Myene, Bateke, Bapounou/Eschira, Bandjabi

Gabon's first European visitors were Portuguese traders who arrived in the 15th century. The coast became a center of the slave trade. Dutch, British, and French traders came in the 16th century. France assumed the status of protector by signing treaties with Gabonese coastal chiefs in 1839 and 1841. In 1910, Gabon became one of the four territories of French Equatorial Africa, a federation that survived until 1959. The territories became independent in 1960 as the Central African Republic, Chad, Congo (Brazzaville), and Gabon.

Almost all Gabonese are of Bantu origin. Gabon has at least forty tribal groups, with separate languages and cultures; the largest group is the Fang. Other tribes include the Myene, Bandjabi, Eshira, Bapounou, Bateke/Obamba, and Okande.

Gambian President Dauda Jawara addresses local authorities.

## Gambia

Official name: Republic of The Gambia

Independence: February 18, 1965

Area: 4,361 sq. mi.

Population: (1991 estimate) 874,000

Ethnic divisions: Mandinka 36.1%, Fula 16.8%, Wolof 13.4%, Jola 9.2%, Serahuli 7.3%, other 1.4%

Religious groups: Muslim 95%, Christian, Traditional belief

Languages spoken: English (official), Mandinka, Wolof, Fula, other tribal languages

Gambia was once part of the Empire of Ghana and the Kingdom of Songhai. When the Portuguese visited in the fifteenth century, it was part of the Kingdom of Mali.

By the sixteenth century, Portuguese slave traders and gold seekers had settled. In 1588, the Portuguese sold exclusive trade rights on the Gambia River to English mer-

Cattleherders in rural Gambia.

chants. During the late seventeenth century and throughout the eighteenth, England and France struggled continuously for political and commercial supremacy in the regions of the Senegal and Gambia Rivers.

In 1807, slave trading was abolished throughout the British Empire, and the British tried unsuccessfully to end the slave traffic in Gambia. An 1889 agreement with France established the present boundaries, and Gambia became a British Crown Colony. Gambia achieved independence on February 18, 1965, as a constitutional monarchy within the British Commonwealth. In 1970, Gambia became a republic.

## Ghana

Official name: Republic of Ghana
Independence: March 6, 1957
Area: 92,100 sq. mi.
Population: (1991 estimate) 15.6 million
Ethnic divisions: Akan, Ewe, Ga
Religious groups: Christian 42%, Traditional belief 38%, Muslim 12%, other 7%
Languages spoken: English (official), Akan 44%, Mole-Dagbani 16%, Ewe 13%, Ga-Adangbe 8%

The first contact between Europe and the Gold Coast dates from 1470, when a party of Portuguese landed. For the next three centuries, the English, Danes, Dutch, Germans, and Portuguese controlled various parts of the coastal areas.

In 1821 the British government took control of the British trading forts on the Gold Coast. In 1844, Fanti chiefs in the area signed an agreement with the British. Between 1826 and 1900, the British fought a series of campaigns against the Ashantis, whose kingdom was located inland. By 1902, the British had succeeded in colonizing the Ashanti region.

On March 6, 1957, the United Kingdom relinquished its control over the Colony of the Gold Coast and Ashanti, the Northern Territories Protectorate, and British Togoland. The Gold Coast and the former British Togoland merged to form what is now Ghana.

Most Ghanaians descended from migrating tribes that probably came down the Volta River valley in the thirteenth century. Ethnically, Ghana is divided into small groups speaking more than fifty languages and dialects. Among the more important linguistic groups are the Akans, which include the Fantis along the coast and the Ashantis in the forest region north of the coast; the Guans, on the plains of the Volta River; the Ga- and Ewe-speaking peoples of the south and southeast; and the Moshi-Dagomba-speaking tribes of the northern and upper regions.

## Guinea

Official name: Republic of Guinea
Independence: October 2, 1958
Area: 95,000 sq. mi.
Population: (1991 estimate) 7.4 million
Ethnic divisions: Foulah, Malinke, Soussou, 15 smaller groups
Religious groups: Muslim 85%, Christian 10%, Traditional belief 5%
Languages spoken: French (official), tribal languages

The empires of Ghana, Mali, and Songhai spanned the period from about the tenth to the fifteenth centuries.

French military penetration into the area began in the mid-nineteenth century. By signing treaties with the French in the 1880s, Guinea's Malinke leader, Samory Toure, secured a free hand to expand eastward. In 1890, he allied himself with the Toucouleur Empire and Kingdom of Sikasso and tried to expel the French from the area. However, he was defeated in 1898, and France gained control of Guinea and the Ivory Coast (now Cote d'Ivoire).

Guinea became an independent republic in 1958, and voted against entering the French community.

Guinea consists of four main ethnic groups—Peuls (Foulah or Foulani), who inhabit the mountainous Fouta Djallon; Malinkes (or Mandingos), in the savannah regions; Soussous in the coastal areas; and Forestal tribes in the forest regions.

## Guinea-Bissau

Official name: Republic of Guinea-Bissau
Independence: September 24, 1973
Area: 14,000 sq. mi.
Population: (1991 estimate) 1 million
Ethnic divisions: Balanta 27%, Fula 23%,
    Mandinka 12%, Manjaco 11%, Papel 10%,
    Biafada 3%, Mancanha 3%, Bijagos 3%
Religious groups: Traditional belief 65%,
    Muslim 30%, Christian 5%
Languages spoken: Portuguese (official);
    Criolo, tribal languages

The rivers of Guinea and the islands of Cape Verde were one of the first areas in Africa explored by the Portuguese in the fifteenth century. Portugal claimed Portuguese Guinea in 1446. In 1630, a "captaincy-general" of Portuguese Guinea was established to administer the territory. With the assistance of local tribes, the Portuguese entered the slave trade, exporting large numbers of Africans to the New World via Cape Verde. The slave trade declined in the nineteenth century and Bissau, originally founded as a fort in 1765, became the major commercial center.

In 1956, the African Party for the Independence of Guinea-Bissau and Cape Verde (PAIGC) was organized by Amilcar Cabral and Raphael Barbosa. Despite the presence of more than 30,000 Portuguese troops, the PAIGC exercised influence over much of the country; the Portuguese were increasingly confined to their garrisons and larger towns. The PAIGC National Assembly declared the independence of Guinea-Bissau on December 24, 1973; Portugal granted de jure independence on September 19, 1974, when the United States recognized the new nation. Luis Cabral became president of Guinea-Bissau and Cape Verde. In 1980 Cape Verde established its independence from Guinea-Bissau.

The population of Guinea-Bissau comprises several diverse tribal groups, each with its own language, customs, and social organization. The Fula and Mandinka tribes, in the north and northeast of the country, are mostly Muslim. Other important tribal groups are the Balanta and Papel, living in the southern coastal regions, and the Manjaco and Mancanha, occupying the central and northern coastal areas.

## Kenya

Official name: Republic of Kenya
Independence: December 12, 1963
Area: 224,960 sq. mi.
Population: (1991 estimate) 25.2 million
Ethnic divisions: Kikuyu 21%, Luhya 14%,
    Luo 13%, Kalenjin 11%, Kamba 11%, Kisii
    6%, Meru 5%, Maasai, Non-Africans 1%
Religious groups: Traditional belief 26%,
    Protestant 38%, Roman Catholic 28%,
    Muslim 6%
Languages spoken: Swahili (official),
    English, tribal languages

The Cushitic-speaking people, who occupied the area that is now Kenya around 1000 BC, were known to have maintained contact with Arab traders during the first century AD; Arab and Persian settlements were founded along the coast as early as the eighth century AD. By then, Bantu and Nilotic peoples also had moved into the area. The Arabs were followed by the Portuguese in 1498, by Islamic control under the

285

Imam of Oman in the 1600s, and by British influence in the nineteenth century. In 1885, European powers first partitioned east Africa into spheres of influence. In 1895, the British government established the East African Protectorate.

From October 1952 to December 1959, Kenya was under a state of emergency, arising from the Mau Mau rebellion against British colonial rule. The first direct elections for Africans to the legislative council took place in 1957. Kenya became fully independent on December 12, 1963. Jomo Kenyatta, a member of the predominant Kikuyu tribe and head of the Kenya African National Union, became Kenya's first president.

### Lesotho

Official name: Kingdom of Lesotho
Independence: October 4, 1966
Area: 11,718 sq. mi.
Population: (1991) 1.8 million
Ethnic divisions: Basotho
Religious groups: Roman Catholic, Lesotho
    Evangelical, Anglican
Languages spoken: English, Sesotho

Until the end of the sixteenth century, Basutoland, now Lesotho, was sparsely populated by bushmen (Qhuaique). Between the sixteenth and nineteenth centuries, refugees from surrounding areas gradually formed the Basotho ethnic group.

In 1818, Moshoeshoe I, consolidated various Basotho groupings and became king. During his reign from 1823 to 1870, a series of wars with South Africa resulted in the loss of extensive lands, now known as the "Lost Territory." Moshoeshoe appealed to Queen Victoria for assistance, and in 1868 the country was placed under British protection.

In 1955, the Basutoland Council asked that it be empowered to legislate on internal affairs, and in 1959 a new constitution gave Basutoland its first elected legislature. On October 4, 1966, the new Kingdom of Lesotho attained full independence.

### Liberia

Official name: Republic of Liberia
Area: 43,000 sq. mi.
Population: (1991 estimate) 2.7 million
Ethnic divisions: 5% descendants of freed
    American slaves, 95% indigenous tribes
    (the largest of which are Kpelle, Bassa,
    Gio, Kru, Grebo, Mano, Krahn, Gola,
    Gbandi, Loma, Kissi, Vai, Mandingo, and
    Belle)
Religious groups: Traditional belief 65%,
    Muslim 20%, Christian 15%
Languages spoken: English (official), more
    than 20 tribal languages of the Niger-
    Congo language group

It is believed that the forebears of many present-day Liberians migrated into the area from the north and east between the twelfth and seventeenth centuries. Portuguese explorers visited Liberia's coast in 1461, and during the next 300 years, European merchants and coastal Africans engaged in trade.

The history of modern Liberia dates from 1816, when the American Colonization Society, a private organization, was given a charter by the United States Congress to send freed slaves to the west coast of Africa. The United States government, under President James Monroe, provided funds and assisted in negotiations with native chiefs for the ceding of land for this purpose. The first settlers landed at the site of Monrovia in 1822. In 1838, the settlers united to form the Commonwealth of Liberia, under a governor appointed by the American Colonization Society.

In 1847, Liberia became Africa's first independent republic. The republic's first 100 years have been described as a "century of

A Maasai tribesman.

survival" due to attempts by neighboring colonial powers (France and Britain) to encroach on Liberia.

### Libya

Official name: Socialist People's Libyan Arab Jamahiriya
Independence: December 24, 1951
Area: 679,536 sq. mi.
Population: (1991 estimate) 4.3 million
Ethnic divisions: Arab and Arab/Berber 80%, Berber 15%, Touareg, and Tebous Arab
Religious groups: Sunni Muslim 97%
Languages spoken: Arabic

In the seventh century AD, Arabs conquered the area that is now Libya. In the following centuries, most of the inhabitants adopted Islam and the Arabic language and culture. The Ottoman Turks conquered the country in the sixteenth century. Libya remained part of their empire—although at times virtually autonomous—until Italy invaded in 1911 and, after years of resistance, incorporated Libya as its colony.

King Idris I, Emir of Cyrenaica, led a Libyan resistance to Italian occupation between the two World Wars. Under the terms of the 1947 peace treaty with the allies, Italy relinquished all claims to Libya. On November 21, 1949, the United Nations General Assembly passed a resolution stating that Libya should become independent before January 1, 1952. Libya declared its independence on December 24, 1951.

## Madagascar

Official name: Democratic Republic of
    Madagascar
Independence: June 26, 1960
Area: 228,880 sq. mi.
Population: (1991 estimate) 12.1 million
Ethnic divisions: 18 Malagasy tribes, small
    groups of Comorians, French, Indians, and
    Chinese
Religious groups: Traditional belief 55%,
    Christian 40%, Muslim 5%
Languages spoken: Malagasy (official),
    French

Located east of the African mainland in the Indian Ocean, Madagascar is home to people who arrived from Africa and Asia during the first five centuries AD. Three major kingdoms ruled the island—Betsimisaraka, Merina, and Sakalava. In the seventh century AD, Arabs established trading posts in the coastal areas of what is now Madagascar. Portuguese sighted the island in the sixteenth century, and in the late seventeenth century, the French established trading posts along the east coast.

In the 1790s, the Merina rulers succeeded in establishing hegemony over the major part of the island including the coast. The Merina ruler and the British governor of Mauritius concluded a treaty abolishing the slave trade, which had been important in Madagascar's economy, and in return the island received British military assistance. British influence remained strong for several decades. The British accepted the imposition of a French protectorate over Madagascar in 1885. France established control by military force in 1895, and the Merina monarchy was abolished. The Malagasy Republic was proclaimed on October 14, 1958, as an autonomous state within the French community. A period of provisional government ended with the adoption of a constitution in 1959 and full independence in 1960.

Madagascar's population is predominantly of mixed Asian and African origin. The largest groups are the Betsimisaraka (one million), the Tsimihety (500,000), and the Sakalava (500,000).

## Malawi

Official name: Republic of Malawi
Independence: July 6, 1964
Area: 45,747 sq. mi.
Population: (1991 estimate) 9.4 million
Ethnic divisions: Chewa, Nyanja, Tumbuka,
    Yao, Lomwe, Sena, Tonga, Ngoni Asians
Religious groups: Protestant 55%, Roman
    Catholic 20%, Muslim 20%, Traditional
    belief
Languages spoken: Chicewa and English
    (official), tribal languages

Hominid remains and stone implements, dating back more than 1 million years, have been identified in Malawi; early humans are belived to have inhabited the area surrounding Lake Malawi 50,000 to 60,000 years ago.

Malawi derives its name from the Maravi, a Bantu people who came from the southern Congo about six hundred years ago. By the sixteenth century, the two divisions of the tribe had established a kingdom stretching from north of today's Nkhotakota to the

Zambezi River in the south and from Lake Malawi in the east to the Luangwa River in Zambia in the west.

The Portuguese first reached the area in the sixteenth century. David Livingston reached the shore of Lake Malawi in 1859. By 1878 a number of traders, mostly from Scotland, formed the African Lakes Company to supply goods and services to the missionaries. In 1891, the British established the Nyasaland Protectorate. Nyasaland joined with Northern and Southern Rhodesia in 1953 to form the Federation of Rhodesia and Nyasaland.

Throughout the 1950s, pressures were exerted within Nyasaland for independence. In July 1958, Dr. H. Kamazu Banda returned to the country after a long stay in the United States (where he had obtained his medical degree at Meharry Medical College in 1937), the United Kingdom, and Ghana. He assumed leadership of the Nyasaland African Congress, which later became the Malawi Congress Party (MCP). In 1959, Banda was sent to Gwele Prison for his political activities but was released in 1960.

On April 15, 1961, the MCP won an overwhelming victory in elections for a new Legislative Council. In a second constitutional conference in London in November 1962, the British government agreed to give Nyasaland self-governing status the following year. Dr. Banda became prime minister on February 1, 1963, although the British still controlled Malawi's financial security and judicial systems. The Federation of Rhodesia and Nyasaland was dissolved on December 31, 1963, and Malawi became fully independent on July 6, 1964. Two years later, Malawi adopted a new constitution and became a republic with Dr. Banda as its first president.

The Chewas constitute ninety percent of the population of the central region; the Nyanja tribe predominates in the south and the Tumbuka in the north. In addition, significant numbers of the Tongas live in the north; Ngonis—an offshoot of the Zulus who came from South Africa in the early 1800s—live in the lower northern and lower central regions; and the Yao, who are mostly Muslim, live along the southeastern border with Mozambique.

## Mali

Official name: Republic of Mali

Independence: September 22, 1960

Area: 474,764 sq. mi.

Population: (1991 estimate) 8.3 million

Ethnic divisions: Mande (Bambara or Bamana, Malinke, Sarakole) 50%, Peul 17% Voltaic 12%, Songhai 6%, Tuareg and Moor 5%

Religious groups: Muslim 90%, Traditional belief 9%, Christian 1%

A Bamana artist.

Malian men on camels.

Languages spoken: French (official) and Bambara (spoken by about 80% of the population)

Mali is the cultural heir to the succession of ancient African empires—Ghana, Malinke, and Songhai—that occupied the West African savanna. The Ghana empire, dominated by the Soninke people and centered in the area along the Malian-Mauritanian frontier, was a powerful trading state from about 700 to 1075 AD. The Malinke kingdom of Mali, from which the republic takes its name, had its origins on the upper Niger River in the eleventh century. Expanding rapidly in the thirteenth century under the leadership of Soundiata Keita, it reached its height about 1325, when it conquered Timbuktu and Gao. The Songhai empire expanded its power from its center in Gao during the period 1465 to 1530. At its peak under Askia Mohammad I, it encompassed the Hausa states as far as Kano (in present-day Nigeria) and much of the territory that had belonged to the Mali Empire in the west. It was destroyed by a Moroccan invasion in 1591.

French military penetration of the area began around 1880. A French civilian governor of Soudan (the French name for the area) was appointed in 1893, but resistance to French control was not abrogated until 1898 when the Malinke warrior, Samory Toure, was defeated after seven years of war. In January 1959, Soudan joined Senegal to form the Mali Federation, which became fully independent within the French Community on June 20, 1960. The federation collapsed on August 20, 1960, when Senegal seceded. On September 22, Soudan proclaimed itself the Republic of Mali and withdrew from the French Community.

Mali's population consists of diverse sub-Saharan ethnic groups, sharing similar historic, cultural, and religious traditions. Exceptions are the Tuaregs and Moors, desert nomads, who are related to the North African Berbers.

## Mauritania

Official name: Islamic Republic of
    Mauritania
Independence: November 28, 1960
Area: 419,229 sq. mi.
Population: (1991 estimate) 1.9 million
Ethnic divisions: Arab-Berber, Arab-Berber-
    Negroid, Negroid
Religious groups: Muslim
Languages spoken: Hassaniya Arabic
    (national), French (official), Pular, Wolof,
    and Soninke

Archeological evidence suggests that Berber and Negroid Mauritanians lived beside one another before the spread of the desert drove them southward. Migration of these people increased during the third and fourth centuries AD, when Berber groups arrived seeking pasture for their herds and safety from political unrest and war in the north. The Berbers established a loose confederation, called the Sanhadja. Trading towns were established to facilitate the trade of gold, ivory, and slaves.

In the tenth century, conquests by warriors of the Soudanese Kingdom of Ghana broke up the Berber confederation. In the eleventh century, the conquest of the Western Sahara regions by a Berber tribe decimated the Ghanaian kingdom and firmly established Islam throughout Mauritania. However, these people were defeated by Arab invaders in the sixteenth century.

French military penetration of Mauritania began early in the twentieth century. However, the area came under French control until about 1934. Until independence, the French governed the country largely by relying on the authority of the tribal chiefs, some of whom, such as the Emirs of Trarza and Adrar, had considerable authority. Under French occupation, slavery was legally abolished.

Mauritania became a French colony in 1920. The Islamic Republic of Mauritania was proclaimed in November 1958. Mauritania became independent on November 28, 1960 and withdrew from the French Community in 1966.

Moors, heterogeneous groups of Arab-Berber people who speak Hassaniya dialects, make up an estimated three-quarters of the population and are traditionally nomadic pastoralists. The country's black population—the Toucouleur, Soninke, Bambara, and Wolof—are mainly cultivators and are concentrated along the Senegal River.

## Mauritius

Independence: March 12, 1968
Area: 720 sq. mi.
Population: (1991 estimate) 1 million
Ethnic divisions: Indo-Mauritians 68%,
    Creoles 27%, Sino-Mauritians 3%, Franco-
    Mauritians 2%
Religious groups: Hindu, Muslim, Roman
    Catholic
Languages spoken: English (official), Creole,
    French, Hindi, Urdu, Hakka, Bhojpuri

Portuguese sailors first visited Mauritius in the early sixteenth century, although the island was known to Arabs and Malays much earlier. Dutch sailors, who named the island in honor of Prince Maurice of Nassau, established a small colony in 1638, but abandoned it in 1710. The French claimed Mauritius in 1715, renaming it Ile de France. In 1810, Mauritius was captured by the British, whose possession of the island was confirmed four years later by the Treaty of Paris. After slavery was abolished in 1835, indentured laborers from India brought an additional cultural influence to the island. Mauritius achieved independence on March 12, 1968.

Twenty-seven percent of Mauritians are of mixed European and African descent, tracing their origins to the plantation owners and slaves who were the first to exploit the island's potential for growing sugar. Descendants of the Indian immigrants constitute 68 percent of the population and are the principal laborers in the sugar industry.

### Mayotte (Mahoré)

Independence: n/a (overseas territory of France)
Area: 375 sq. km.
Population: (1992 estimate) 86,628
Religious groups: Muslim 99%; remainder Christian (mostly Roman Catholic)
Languages spoken: Mahorian (a Swahili dialect), French

Part of the Comoros archipelago, Mayotte shares its history with the Comoros Federal Islamic Republic. When Comoros declared independence in 1975, Mayotte voted to remain an overseas territory of France. Although Comoros has since claimed Mayotte, the French have promised the islanders that they may remain French citizens for as long as they wish.

### Morocco

Official name: Kingdom of Morocco
Independence: March 2, 1956
Area: 173,413 sq. mi.
Population: (1991 estimate) 26.1 million
Ethnic divisions: Arab-Berber
Religious groups: Sunni Muslim
Languages spoken: Arabic (official), French, Berber dialects

Arab forces began occupying Morocco in the seventh century AD, bringing with them Arab civilization and Islam. Morocco's location and resources led to early competition among Europeans in Africa, beginning with successful Portuguese efforts to control the Atlantic coast in the fifteenth century. France showed a strong interest in Morocco as early as 1830. The Treaty of Fez (1912) made Morocco a protectorate of France. By the same treaty, Spain assumed the role of protecting power over the northern and

Dancers from Morocco.

southern (Saharan) zones. The Kingdom of Morocco recovered its political independence from France on March 2, 1956.

From 1904 until 1975, Spain occupied the entire territory, which is divided into a northern portion, the Saguia el Hamra, and the southern two-thirds, known as Rio de Oro. Calls for the decolonization of these territories began in the 1960s, first from the surrounding nations and then from the United Nations.

Morocco's claim to sovereignty over the Western Sahara is based largely on the historical argument of traditional loyalty of the Saharan tribal leaders to the Moroccan sultan as spiritual leader and ruler. The International Court of Justice, to which the issue was referred, delivered its opinion in 1975 that while historical ties exist between the inhabitants of the Western Sahara and Morocco, they are insufficient to establish Moroccan sovereignty.

### Mozambique

Official name: People's Republic of Mozambique
Independence: June 25, 1975
Area: 303,769 sq. mi.
Population: (1991) 15.1 million
Ethnic divisions: Makua, Tsonga, Makonde, and other tribal groups

Religious groups: Traditional belief 50%,
   Muslim 30% Christian 15%
Languages spoken: Portuguese (official),
   tribal languages

Mozambique's first inhabitants were Bushmanoid hunters and gatherers, ancestors of the Khoisani peoples. During the first four centuries AD, waves of Bantu-speaking peoples migrated from the north through the Zambezi River Valley and then gradually into the plateau and coastal areas. When Portuguese explorers reached Mozambique in 1498, Arab trading settlements had existed along the coast for several centuries. Later, traders and prospectors penetrated the hinterland seeking gold and slaves.

After World War II, while many European nations were granting independence to their colonies, Portugal clung to the concept that Mozambique and other Portuguese possessions were "overseas provinces." In 1962, several Mozambican anti-Portuguese political groups formed the Front for Liberation of Mozambique (FRELIMO) which in September 1964 initiated an armed campaign against Portuguese colonial rule. After ten years of sporadic warfare and major political changes in Portugal, Mozambique became independent on June 25, 1975.

The ten major ethnic groups living in Mozambique are divided into subgroups with diverse languages, dialects, cultures, and history; the largest are the Majua and Tsonga.

**Namibia (formerly South West Africa)**
Official name: Republic of Namibia
Area: 320,827 sq. mi.
Population: (1991 estimate) 1.5 million
Ethnic divisions: Black 87%; White 6%;
   mixed race 7%
Religious groups: Predominantly Christian,
   Traditional belief
Languages spoken: English (official),
   Afrikaans, German, tribal languages

In 1878, the United Kingdom annexed Walvis Bay on behalf of Cape Colony, and the area was incorporated into the Cape of Good Hope in 1884. In 1883, a German trader, Adolf Luderitz, claimed the remainder of the coastal region after negotiations with a local chief. German administration ended during World War I, when the territory was occupied by South African forces in 1915.

On December 17, 1920, South Africa undertook the administration of South West Africa under the terms of Article 22 of the Covenant of the League of Nations and a mandate agreement confirmed by the League Council. The mandate agreement gave South Africa full power of administration and legislation over the territory as an integral part of South Africa. During the 1960s, as other Afican nations gained independence, pressure mounted on South Africa to do so in South West Africa.

In 1966, the United Nations General Assembly revoked South Africa's mandate. Also in 1966, the South West Africa People's Organization (SWAPO) began guerrilla attacks on Namibia, infiltrating the territory from bases in Zambia. In a 1971 advisory opinion, the International Court of Justice upheld United Nation authority over Namibia, determining that the South African presence in Namibia was illegal and that South Africa therefore was obligated to withdraw its administration from Namibia immediately. In 1977 the United Nations approved Security Council Resolution 435, calling for, among other things, the holding of elections in Namibia under United Nations supervision and the cessation of hostile acts by all parties. South Africa agreed to cooperate in achieving implementation of Resolution 435. Nevertheless, in December 1978, in defiance of the United Nations proposal, it unilaterally held elections in

Namibia which were boycotted by SWAPO and other political parties.

Intense discussions between the concerned parties continued during the 1978–1988 period. In May 1988, an American mediation team brought negotiators from Angola, Cuba, and South Africa and observers from the Soviet Union together in London. On April 1, the Republic of South Africa agreed to withdraw its troops. Implementation of Resolution 435 officially began on April 1, 1989. The elections held November 7–11, 1989, were certified as free and fair by the special representative, with SWAPO taking fifty-seven percent of the vote; the Democratic Turnhalle Alliance, the principal opposition party, received twenty-nine percent of the vote. By February 9, 1990, the constituent assembly had drafted and adopted a constitution. March 21 was set as the date for independence.

Namibia's indigenous Africans are of diverse linguistic and ethnic origins. The principal groups are the Ovambo, Kavango, Herero/Himba, Damara, mixed race ("Colored" and Rehoboth Baster), white (Afrikaner, German, and Portuguese), Nama, Caprivian (Lozi), Bushman, and Tswana. The minority white population is primarily of South African, British, and German descent. Approximately sixty percent of the white population speaks Afrikaans (a variation of Dutch), thirty percent German, and ten percent English.

**Niger**
Official name: Republic of Niger
Independence: August 3, 1960
Area: 490,000 sq. mi.
Population: (1991) 8.1 million
Ethnic divisions: Hausa 56%, Djerma 22%, Fulani 8.5% Tuareg 8%, Beri Beri (Kanouri) 4.3% Arab, Toubou, and Gourmantche 1.2%

Religious groups: Muslim, Traditional belief, and Christian
Languages spoken: French (official), Hausa, Djerma

Considerable evidence indicates that about 600,000 years ago, humans inhabited what has since become the desolate Sahara of northern Niger. Niger was an important economic crossroads, and the empires of Songhai, Mali, Gao, Kanem, and Bornu, as well as a number of Hausa states, claimed control over portions of the area.

During recent centuries, the nomadic Tuareg formed large confederations, pushed southward, and siding with various Hausa states, clashed with the Fulani empire of Sokoto, which had gained control of much of the Hausa territory in the late eighteenth century. In the nineteenth century, the first

A minaret in Agadez, Niger.

Hausa men on horseback.

European explorers reached the area searching for the mouth of the Niger River.

Although French efforts at colonization began before 1900, dissident ethnic groups, especially the desert Tuareg, were not defeated until 1922. On December 4, 1958, after the establishment of the Fifth French Republic, Niger became an autonomous state within the French Community. Following full independence on August 3, 1960, however, membership was allowed to lapse.

The two largest ethnic groups in Niger are the Hausa, who also constitute the major ethnic group in northern Nigeria, and the Djerma-Songhai. Both groups are farmers who live in the arable, southern tier. The rest of the population consists of nomadic or seminomadic livestock-raising peoples, which include the Fulani, Tuareg, Kanouri, and Toubou.

## Nigeria

Official name: Federal Republic of Nigeria
Independence: October 1, 1960
Area: 356,700 sq. mi.
Population: (1991) 88.5 million
Ethnic divisions: 250 tribal groups, the largest are Hausa-Fulani, Ibo, and Yoruba
Religious groups: Muslim, Christian, Traditional belief
Languages spoken: English (official), Hausa, Ibo, Yoruba

Evidence shows that more than 2,000 years ago, the Nok people who lived in what is now the Plateau state worked iron and produced sophisticated terra cotta sculpture. In the centuries that followed, the Hausa kingdom and the Bornu empire, near Lake Chad, prospered as important terminals of north-south trade between North African Berbers and forest people who exchanged slaves, ivory, and kola nuts for salt, glass beads, coral, cloth, weapons, brass rods, and cowrie shells used a currency. In the southwest, the Uoruba kingdom of Oyo, which was founded about 1400 and reached its height between the seventeenth and nineteenth centuries, attained a high level of political organization and extended as far as modern Togo. In the south-central part of present-day Nigeria, as early as the fifteenth century, the kingdom of Benin had developed an efficient army, an elaborate ceremonial court, and artisans whose works in ivory, wood, bronze, and brass are prized throughout the world today.

Between the seventeenth and nineteenth centuries, European traders established coastal ports for the increasing traffic in slaves destined for the Americas. In 1855, British claims to a sphere of influence in that area received international recognition, and, in the following year, the Royal Niger Company was chartered. In 1900, the company's territory came under the control of the British government. In 1914, the area was formally united as the "Colony and Protectorate of Nigeria." Nigeria was granted full independence on October 1, 1960, as a federation of three regions.

The most populous country in Africa, Nigeria accounts for one quarter of sub-Saharan Africa's people. The dominant ethnic group in the northern two-thirds of the country is the Hausa-Fulani, most of whom are Muslims. Other major ethnic groups of the north are the Nupe, Tiv, and Kanuri. The Yoruba people are predominant in the southwest. About half of the Yorubas are Christian and half Muslim. The predominately Catholic Ibos are the largest ethnic group in the southeast, with the Efik, Ibibio, and Ijaw comprising a substantial segment of the population in that area as well.

## Réunion

Independence: n/a (overseas department of France)

Area: 2,510 sq. km.

Population: (1992 estimate) 626,414

Ethnic divisions: Intermixed African, French, Malagasy, Chinese, Pakistani, and Indian ancestry

Religious groups: Roman Catholic 94%

Languages spoken: French (official), Creole

The island of Réunion, located in the Indian Ocean, remained uninhabited until 1654, when the French East India Company established bases and brought in slaves from Africa and Madagascar. France governed the island as a colony until 1946, when it was granted department status.

The population of Réunion is of mixed African, French, Indian, and Chinese origin.

Tomi of Ede, John Adetoyese, with a boy drummer.

## Rwanda

Official name: Republic of Rwanda
Independence: July 1, 1962
Area: 10,169 sq. mi.
Population: (1991 estimate) 7.9 million
Ethnic divisions: Hutu 85%, Tutsi 14%, Twa 1%
Religious groups: Christian 74%, Traditional belief 25%, Muslim 1%
Languages spoken: French, Kinyarwanda

For centuries Hutu farmers farmed the area that is now Rwanda; in the fifteenth century Tutsi herders settled in the area. In 1899, the court of Mwami submitted to a German protectorate with resistance. Belgian troops from Zaire occupied Rwanda in 1916; after World War I, the League of National mandated Rwanda and its southern neighbor, Burundi, to Belgium as the Territory of Ruanda-Urundi. Following World War II, Ruanda-Urundi became a United Nations trust territory with Belgium as the administering authority. The Party of the Hutu Emancipation Movement (PARMEHUTU) won an overwhelming victory in a United Nations-supervised referendum.

The PARMEHUTU government, formed as a result of the September 1961 election, was granted internal autonomony by Belgium on January 1, 1962. A June 1962 United Nations General Assembly resolution terminated the Belgian trusteeship and granted full independence to Rwanda (and Burundi) effective July 1, 1962. Gregiore Kayibanda, leader of the PARMEHUTU Party, became Rwanda's first elected president.

The indigenous population consists of three ethnic groups. The Tutsi (14 percent) are a pastoral people of Nilotic origin. The Hutus, who comprise the majority of the population (85 percent), are farmers of Bantu origin. The Twa pygmies (1 percent) are thought to be the remnants of the earliest settlers of the region.

## Saint Helena

Independence: n/a (dependent territory of the United Kingdom)
Area: 410 sq. km.
Population: (1992 estimate) 6,698
Religious groups: Anglican majority, Baptist, Seventh-Day Adventist, and Roman Catholic
Languages spoken: English

The islands of Saint Helena, Ascension, and Tristan da Cunha lie about one-thirds of the way between Africa and South America in the South Atlantic Ocean. The islands remained uninhabited, until they were visited by the Portuguese in 1502. In 1659, the British East India Company established a settlement on Saint Helena and in 1673 was granted a charter to govern the island.

## Sao Tome and Principe

Official name: Democratic Republic of Sao Tome and Principe
Independence: July 12, 1975
Area: 372 sq. mi.
Population: (1991 estimate) 128,000
Ethnic divisions: Mixed African, Portuguese-African
Religious groups: Christian 80%
Languages spoken: Portuguese

These uninhabited islands were first visited by Portuguese navigators between 1469 and 1472. The first successful settlement of Sao Tome was established in 1493. Principe was settled in 1500. By the mid-1500s, with the help of slave labor, the Portuguese settlers had turned the islands into Africa's foremost exporter of sugar. Sao Tome and Principe were taken over and administered by the Portuguese crown in 1522 and 1573 respectively. By 1908, Sao Tome had become the world's largest producer of cocoa, still the country's most important crop.

The rocas system, which gave the plantation managers a high degree of authority, led to abuses against the African farm workers. Although Portugal officially abolished slavery in 1876, the practice of forced paid labor continued. Sporadic labor unrest and dissatisfaction continued well into the twentieth century, culminating in an outbreak of riots in 1953 in which several hundred African laborers were killed.

By the late 1950s, a small group of Sao Tomeans had formed the Movement for the Liberation of Sao Tome and Principe (MLSTP). In 1974, Portuguese representatives met with the MLSTP in Algiers and worked out an agreement for the transfer of sovereignty. After a period of transition, Sao Tome and Principe achieved independence on July 12, 1975, choosing as its first president the MLSTP Secretary General Manuel Pinto da Costa.

Sao Tome and Principe's population consists of people descended from groups that have migrated to the islands since 1485. Six groups are identifiable: Mestizo, of mixed-blood, descendants of African slaves brought to the islands during the early years of settlement from Benin, Gabon, Congo, and Angola; Anglares, reputedly descendants of Angolan slaves who survived on a 1540 shipwreck and now earn their livelihood fishing; Forros, descendants of freed slaves; Servicais, contract laborers from Angola, Mozambique, and Cape Verde, living temporarily on the islands; Tongas, children of servicais born on the islands; and Europeans, primarily Portuguese.

**Senegal**

Official name: Republic of Senegal
Independence: April 4, 1960
Area: 76,000 sq. mi.
Population: (1991 estimate) 7.9 million
Ethnic divisions: Wolof 43%, Fulani (Peulh) and Toucouleur 23%, Serer 15%, Diola, Mandingo, others 22%

Religious groups: Muslim 94%, Christian 5%, Traditional belief 1%
Languages spoken: French (official), Solof, Pulaar, Diola, Mandingo

Archaeological findings throughout the area indicate that Senegal was inhabited in prehistoric times. Islam established itself in the Senegal River valley during the eleventh century. In the thirteenth and fourteenth centuries, the area came under the influence of the great Mandingo empires to the east, during which the Jolof empire of Senegal was founded. The empire comprised the states of Cayor, Baol, Oualo, Sine, and Soloum until the sixteenth century, when they revolted for independence.

The Portuguese were the first Europeans to trade in Senegal, arriving in the fifteenth century. They were soon followed by the Dutch and French. During the nineteenth century, the French gradually established control over the interior regions and administered them as a protectorate until 1920, and as a colony thereafter.

In January 1959, Senegal and the French Soudan merged to form the Mali Federation, which became fully independent on June 20, 1960. Due to internal political difficulties, the federation broke up on August 20, 1960; Senegal and Soudan (renamed the Republic of Mali) each proclaimed separate independence. Leopold Sedar Senghor, internationally renowned poet, politician, and statesman, was elected Senegal's first president in August 1960.

**Seychelles**

Official name: Republic of Seychelles
Independence: June 29, 1976
Area: 171 sq. mi.
Population: (1991 estimate) 68,000
Ethnic divisions: Creole (mixture of Asians, Africans, and Europeans)

Religious groups: Roman Catholic 90%,
    Anglican 8%, other 2%
Languages spoken: Creole, English, and
    French

In 1742, the French governor of Mauritius, sent an expedition to the islands. A second expedition in 1756 reasserted formal possession by France. The Seychelles islands were captured and freed several times during the French Revolution and the Napoleonic wars, then passed officially to the British under the Treaty of Paris in 1814. Negotiations with the British resulted in an agreement by which Seychelles became a sovereign republic on June 29, 1976.

Most Seychellois are descendants of early French settlers and the African slaves brought to the Seychelles in the nineteenth century by the British, who freed them from slave ships on the East African coast. Indians and Chinese (1.1 percent of the population) account for the other permanent inhabitants.

**Sierra Leone**
Official name: Republic of Sierra Leone
Independence: April 27, 1961
Area: 27,925 sq. mi.
Population: (1991 estimate) 4.2 million
Ethnic divisions: Temne 30%, Mende 29%,
    Creole 2%
Religious groups: Muslim 60%, Animist 30%,
    Christian 10%
Languages spoken: English (official), Krio
    (lingua franca), Temne, Mende, other
    tribal languages

Sierra Leone was one of the first West African British colonies. Foreign settlement did not occur for another two centuries, when the British laid plans for a refuge within the British Empire for freed slaves. In 1787, the site of Freetown received the first four-hundred freedmen from Great Britain. Disease and hostility from the indigenous

people almost eliminated this first group. Five years later, however, another group of settlers, 1,000 freed slaves who had fled from the United States to Nova Scotia during the American Revolution, arrived under the auspices of the newly formed British Sierra Leone Company. In 1800, about 550 blacks arrived from Jamaica via Nova Scotia; these were the Maroons, escaped slaves who maintained their independence in the mountains of Jamaica.

The 1951 constitution provided the framework for decolonization. Independence came in April 1961, and Sierra Leone became a parliamentary system within the British Commonwealth. In April 1971, it adopted a republican constitution, cutting the link to the British monarchy but remaining within the Commonwealth.

Eighteen ethnic groups make up the indigenous population of Sierra Leone. The Temne in the north and the Mende in the south are the largest. About 60,000 are Creoles, descendants of black settlers from Great Britain or North America.

**Somalia**
Official name: Somalia Democratic Republic
Independence: July 1, 1960
Area: 246,000 sq. mi.
Population: (1991 estimate) 6.7 million
Ethnic divisions: Somali 98.8%, Arab and
    Asian 1.2%
Religious groups: Muslim
Languages spoken: Somali

The British East India Company's desire for unrestricted harbor facilities led to the conclusion of treaties with the sultan of Tajura as early as 1840. It was not until 1886, however, that the British gained control over northern Somalia through treaties with various Somali chiefs. The boundary between Ethiopia and British Somaliland was established in 1897 through treaty negotiations between British negotiators and King Menellik.

In 1855, Italy obtained commercial advantages in the area from the sultan of Zanzibar and in 1889 concluded agreements with the sultans of Obbia and Caluula, who placed their territories under Italy's protection. Between 1897 and 1908, Italy made agreements with the Ethiopians and the British that marked out the boundaries of Italian Somaliland. In June 1940, Italian troops overran British Somaliland and drove out the British garrison. In 1941, British forces began operations against the Italian East African Empire and quickly brought the greater part of the Italian Somaliland under British control.

From 1941 to 1950, while Somalia was under British military administration, transition toward self-government had begun. Elections for the Legislative Assembly were held in February 1960. The protectorate became independent on June 26, 1960; five days later, on July 1, it joined Italian Somaliland to form the Somali Republic.

The Somali people are herders and farmers. The largest group in the country is the Somali, who are nomadic or seminomadic herders. The remaining population consists of Jiiddu, Tunni, and Maay.

**South Africa**
Official name: Republic of South Africa
Area: 472,359 sq. mi.
Population: (1991 estimate) 40.6 million
Ethnic divisions: Black 75%; white 14%;
    "colored" (mixed-race) 8%; Asian (Indian)
    3%.
Religious groups: Christian, Traditional
    belief, Hindu, Muslim, Jewish
Languages spoken: English and Afrikaans
    (official), Zulu, Xhosa, Luvenda, North and
    South SeSotho, SeTswana, other tribal
    languages.

Of the present inhabitants of South Africa, the earliest are Bushmen and Hottentots—members of the Khoisan language group, of whom only a few survive. The Portuguese were the first Europeans to reach the Cape of Good Hope, in 1488. Permanent white settlement began when the Dutch East India Company established a provisioning station there in 1652. In subsequent decades, French Huguenot refugees, Dutch, and Germans settled in the Cape area to form the Afrikaner segment of the modern population.

Britain seized the Cape of Good Hope at the end of the eighteenth century. Partly to escape British political rule and cultural hegemony, many Afrikaner farmers (Boers) undertook a northern migration (the "Great Trek") beginning in 1836. This movement brought them into contact with several African groups, the most formidable of which

Two black South African youth.

300

South African children behind a fence that separates them from a white community near Johannesburg.

were the Zulu. Under their powerful leader, Shaka (1787–1828), the Zulu conquered most of the territory between the Drakensberg Mountains and the sea (now Natal). The Zulu were defeated at the Battle of Blood River in 1838.

The independent Boer republics of the Transvaal (the South African Republic) and the Orange Free State were created in 1852 and 1854. Following the two Boer wars from 1880 to 1881 and 1899 to 1902, British forces conquered the Boer republics and incorporated them into the British Empire. A strong resurgence of Afrikaner nationalism in the 1940s and 1950s led to a decision, through a 1960 referendum among whites, to give up dominion status and establish a republic. The republic was established on May 31, 1961.

South African laws are based on the doctrine of apartheid, which prescribes basic rights and obligations according to racial or ethnic origin. The country's black majority continues to suffer from pervasive, legally sanctioned discrimination based on race in political, economic, and social aspects of life. The "colored" and Asian minorities also suffer from discrimination, although to a somewhat lesser degree than blacks. Political rights of the black majority are confined to participation in tightly controlled urban councils in the country's black residential areas (townships) and in the ten so-called homelands. The National Party extended racial segregation through passage of a number of legislative acts.

In 1950 the white parliament passed the Group Areas Act, which established residential and business sections in urban areas for each race and strengthened existing "pass laws," which require blacks to carry documents authorizing their presence in restricted areas. In the 1960s and the 1970s, other laws were passed to restrict every black African, irrespective of actual residence. Other laws were enacted to forbid most social contacts between the races, mandate segregated public facilities, establish separate educational standards, restrict each race to certain kinds of jobs, curtail black labor unions, and abolish nonwhite participation (through white representatives) in the national government.

The African National Congress (ANC), a predominantly black South African political and paramilitary organization founded in 1912, is the oldest organization opposing legalized racism and white rule in South Africa. It was banned by the South African government from 1960 to 1990, operating underground and in exile. The ANC was founded with the objectives of eliminating all restrictions based on color and obtaining black representation in Parliament. The long-term aims of the ANC were set forth in the "Freedom Charter," which was adopted in 1955. This document states that the ANC's ultimate goal is a liberated, nonracial South Africa in which individual rights would be guaranteed and nationalization of certain in-

The black South African village of Cross Roads.

dustries would occur within a basically mixed economy.

The government released two elderly long-term prisoners in 1988, Zeph Mothopeng, President of the Pan African Congress, and Henry Gwala, an ANC leader. In December 1988, under great international pressure, the government commuted the death sentences of the Sharpeville Six, who were convicted of murder for their presence in a crowd that killed a black township official. President F.W. DeKlerk took several steps in 1989 and 1990 to demonstrate his commitment to ending apartheid, including the release of ANC leader Nelson Mandela, imprisoned in 1962 and sentenced to life in 1964 for treason and sabotage, and other political prisoners and detainees; and unbanning the ANC and thirty-two other antiaparthied organizations.

South African law divides the population into four major racial categories—Africans (blacks), whites, "coloreds," and Asians. The Africans, who comprise seventy-five percent of the population, are mainly descendants of the Sotho and Nguni peoples, who migrated southward centuries ago. The largest African ethnic groups are the Zulu (nearly six million) and Xhosa (nearly 5.8 million). Africans are officially subdivided into ten groups corresponding to the ten ethnically based, government-created "homelands"—Bophuthatswana, Ciskei, Lebowa, Gazankulu, KaNgwane, KwaNdebele, KwaZaulu, Qwaqwa, Transkei, and Venda. The so-called homelands have been granted various degrees of automony (four have been granted independence) but none have been recognized by any other government. The four independent homelands are: Bophuthatswana, which is made-up of mostly SeTswana-speaking people; Ciskei and Transkei, which consist of mainly Xhosa; and Venda, which is composed largely of Luvenda-speaking peoples.

The white population consists primarily of descendants of Dutch, French, English, and German settlers, with smaller admixtures of other European peoples, and constitutes about fourteen percent of the total population. "Coloreds" are mostly descendants of indigenous peoples and the earliest European and Malay settlers in the area. "Coloreds" comprise nine percent of the population and live primarily in Cape Province. Asians, mainly descendants of the Indian workers brought to South Africa in the mid-nineteenth century to work as indentured laborers on sugar estates in Natal, constitute about three percent of the population.

## Sudan

Official name: Republic of the Sudan
Independence: January 1, 1956
Area: 967,500 sq. mi.
Population: (1991 estimate) 27.2 million
Ethnic divisions: Arab, black
Religious groups: Muslim, Traditional belief (southern Sudan), Christian
Languages spoken: Arabic (official), English, tribal languages

From the beginning of the Christian era until 1820, Sudan existed as a collection of small, independent states. In 1881, a religious leader named Mohammed Ahmed ibn Abdalla proclaimed himself the Mahdi, or "expected one," and began to unify tribes in western and central Sudan. The Mahdi led a nationalist revolt culminating in the fall of Khartoum in 1885. He died shortly thereafter, but his state survived until overwhelmed by Anglo-Egyptian forces in 1898; in 1899, Sudan was proclaimed a condominium under British-Egyptian administration. In February 1953, the United Kingdom and Egypt concluded an agreement providing for Sudanese self-government. Sudan achieved independence on January 1, 1956.

## Swaziland

Official name: Kingdom of Swaziland
Independence: September 6, 1968
Area: 6,704 sq. mi.
Population: (1991 estimate) 859,000
Ethnic divisions: Swazi, some Zulu
Religious groups: Christian and indigenous belief
Languages spoken: English, SiSwazi (both official)

The people of the present Swazi nation migrated south sometime before the sixteenth century to what is now Mozambique. After a series of conflicts with people living in the area that is now Maputo, the Swazi settled in northern Zululand in about 1750. Unable to match the growing Zulu strength there, the Swazis moved gradually northward in the early 1800s and established themselves in the area of modern Swaziland. The Swazi consolidated their hold in this area under several able leaders. The most

A Swazi woman.

important of these was Mswati, from whom the Swazi derive their name. Under his leadership in the 1840s, the Swazi expanded their territory to the northwest and stabilized the southern frontier with the Zulus.

The first Swazi contact with the British came early in Mswati's reign when he asked the British agent general in South Africa for assistance against Zulu raids into Swaziland. Agreements made between the British and the Transvaal (South Africa) governments in 1881 and 1884 provided that Swaziland should be independent. In 1903, Britain formally took over the administration of Swaziland.

Sobhuza II became head of the Swazi Nation in 1921. By the 1960s, political activity intensified, partly in response to events elsewhere in Africa. Several political parties were formed that agitated for independence. The traditional Swazi leaders, including King Sobhuza and his council, formed the Imbokodvo National Movement. In 1966, the British agreed to hold talks on a new constitution. The constitutional committee, consisting of representatives of the king and of the Swazi National Council, other political parties, and the British government agreed on a constitutional monarchy for Swaziland, with self-government to follow parliamentary elections in 1967. Swaziland became independent on September 6, 1968.

## Tanzania

Official name: United Republic of Tanzania
Independence: Tanganyika December 9, 1961
Area: 363,950 sq. mi.
Population: (1991 estimate) 26.8 million
Ethnic divisions: More than 130 groups
Religious groups: Muslim 35%, Traditional belief 35%, Christian 30%
Languages spoken: Swahili (official), English

The area that is now Tanzania is believed to have been inhabited originally by ethnic groups using a click-tongue language similar to that of southern Africa's Bushmen and Hottentots. Although remnants of these early tribes still exist, most were gradually displaced by Bantu farmers migrating from the west and south and by Nilotes and related northern peoples.

The coastal area first felt the impact of foreign influence as early as the eighth century. By the twelfth century, traders and immigrants came from as far away as Persia (now Iran) and India. The Portuguese navigator Vasco da Gama first visted the East African coast in 1498 on his voyage to India; by 1506, the Portuguese claimed control over the entire coast. This control was nominal, however, for the Portuguese did not attempt to colonize the area or explore the interior. By the early eighteenth century, Arabs from Oman had assisted the indigenous coastal dwellers in driving out the Portuguese from the area north of the Ruvuma River. They established their own garrisons at Zanzibar, Pemba, and Kilwa and carried on a lucrative trade in slaves and ivory.

German colonial interests were first advanced in 1884. Karl Peters, who formed the Society for German Colonization, concluded a series of treaties by which tribal chiefs in the interior accepted German protection. In 1886 and 1890, Anglo-German agreements were negotiated that delineated the British and German spheres of influence in the interior of East Africa. In 1891, the German government took over direct administration of the territory from the German East Africa Company and appointed a governor with headquarters at Dar es Salaam. German colonial administration spurred African resistance, culminating in the Maji Maji rebellion of 1905 to 1907. German colonial domination of Tanganyika ended with World War I. Control of most of the territory passed to the United Kingdom under a League of Nations mandate.

In the following years, Tanganyika moved gradually toward self-government and independence. In 1954, Julius K. Nyerere, a schoolteacher educated abroad, organized the Tanganyika African Union (UANU). In May 1961, Tanganyika became autonomous, and Nyerere became prime minister under a new constitution. Full independence was achieved on December 9, 1961. On April 26, 1964, Tanganyika united with Zanzibar to form the United Republic of Tanganyika and Zanzibar, renamed the United Republic of Tanzania on October 29.

Tanzania's population consists of more than one hundred thirty ethnic groups, of which only the Sukuma has more than one million members. The majority of Tanzanians, including such large tribes as the Sukuma and the Nyamwezi, are of Bantu stock. Groups of Nilotic or related origin include the nomadic Masai and the Luo, both of which are found in greater numbers in neighboring Kenya. Two small groups speak languages of the Khoisan family peculiar to the Bushman and Hottentot peoples. Cushitic-speaking peoples, originally from the Ethiopian highlands, reside in a few areas of Tanzania.

## Togo

Official name: Republic of Togo
Independence: April 27, 1960
Area: 21,853 sq. mi.
Population: (1991 estimate) 3.8 million
Ethnic divisions: Ewe, Mina, Kabye,
    Cotocoli, Moba
Religious groups: Animist 50%, Christian
    30%, Muslim 20%
Languages spoken: French (official), Ewe,
    Mina, Kabye

The Ewe people first moved into the area which is now Togo from the Niger River Valley, sometime between the twelfth and fourteenth centuries. During the fifteenth and

A Togolese woman making pottery.

sixteenth centuries, Portuguese explorers and traders visited the coast. For the next two hundred years, the coastal region was a major raiding center for Europeans in search of slaves, earning Togo and the surrounding region the name "the Slave Coast."

In a 1884 treaty signed at Togoville, Germany declared a protectorate over the area. In 1914, Togoland was invaded by French and British forces and fell after a brief resistance. Following the war, Togoland became a League of Nations mandate divided for administrative purposes between France and the United Kingdom. By statute in 1955, French Togo became an autonomous republic within the French Union. In 1957, the residents of British Togoland voted to join the Gold Coast as part of the new independent nation of Ghana. On April 27, 1960, Togo severed its juridical ties with France, shed its United Nations trusteeship status, and became fully independent.

Togo's population is composed of about twenty-one ethnic groups. The two major ones are the Ewe in the south and the Kabye in the north.

**Tunisia**

Official name: Republic of Tunisia

Area: 63,378 sq. mi.

Population: (1991 estimate) 8.2 million

Ethnic divisions: Arab 98%, Berber 1%, European 1%

Religious groups: Muslim 99%, Christian and Jewish less than 1%

Languages spoken: Arabic (official), French

Tunisians are descended mainly from indigenous Berber tribes and from Arab tribes which migrated to North Africa during the seventh century AD. Recorded history in Tunisia begins with the arrival of Phoenicians, who founded Carthage and other North African settlements. In the seventh century, the Muslim conquest transformed North Africa, and Tunisia became a center of Arab culture until its assimilation in the Turkish Ottoman Empire in the sixteenth century. In 1881, France established a protectorate there, only to see a rise of nationalism lead to Tunisia's independence in 1956.

## Uganda

Official name: Republic of Uganda
Independence: October 9, 1962
Area: 93,354 sq. mi.
Population: (1991 estimate) 18.6 million
Ethnic divisions: Baganda, Iteso, Basoga, Banyaruanda, Bakiga, Bagisu
Religious groups: Christian (majority), Muslim, Traditional belief
Languages spoken: English (official), Luganda, Swahili, other Bantu and Nilotic languages

Arab traders moving inland from Indian Ocean coastal enclaves reached the interior of Uganda in the 1830s and found several African kingdoms, one of which was the Buganda kingdom, that had well-developed political institutions dating back several centuries.

In 1888, control of the emerging British sphere of interest in East Africa was assigned by royal charter to the Imperial British East Africa Company, an arrangement strengthened in 1890 by an Anglo-German agreement confirming British dominance over Kenya and Uganda. In 1894, the Kingdom of Uganda was placed under a formal British protectorate. The British protectorate period began to change formally in 1955, when constitutional changes leading to Uganda's independence were adopted. The first general elections in Uganda were held in 1961, and the British government granted internal self-government to Uganda on March 1, 1962, with Benedicto Kiwanuka as the first prime minister.

In February 1966, Prime Minister Milton Obote suspended the constitution, assumed all government powers, and removed the president and vice president. On January 25, 1971, Obote's government was ousted in a military coup led by armed forces commander Idi Amin Dada. Amin declared himself president, dissolved the parliament, and amended the constitution to give himself absolute power. Idi Amin's eight-year rule produced economic decline, social disintegration, and massive human rights violations. In 1978, Tanzanian forces pushed back an incursion by Amin's troops. Backed by Ugandan exiles, Tanzanian forces waged a war of liberation against Amin. On April 11, 1979, the Ugandan capital was captured, and Amin and his remaining forces fled.

Bantu, Nilotic, and Nilo-Hamitic peoples constitute most of Uganda's population. The Bantu are the most numerous and include the Baganda, with more than one million members. The Nilo-Hamitic Iteso is the second largest group, followed by the Banyankole and Basoga, both of Bantu extraction.

## Zaire

Official name: Republic of Zaire
Independence: June 30, 1960
Area: 905,063 sq. mi.
Population: (1991 estimate) 37.8 million
Ethnic divisions: 250 tribal groups

Mbuti people of the Ituri forest in Zaire.

Tutsi dancers from Zaire.

Religious groups: Roman Catholic 50%, Protestant 20%, Muslim 10%, Kimbanguist 10%, other Syncretic sects and Traditional belief 10%

Languages spoken: French, Lingala, Swahili, Kingwana (a variant), Kikongo, Tshiluba

The area that is now Zaire is believed to have been populated as early as ten thousand years ago. An influx of peoples occurred in the seventh and eighth centuries AD, when Bantu people from present-day Nigeria settled, bringing with them knowledge of the manufacture and use of metals.

In 1482, the Portuguese arrived at the mouth of the Congo River. They found an organized society—the Bakongo Kingdom—which included parts of present-day Congo, Zaire, and Angola. The Portuguese named the area Congo.

At the Berlin Conference of 1885, King Leopold's claim to the greater part of the Zaire River basin was recognized. The Congo Free State remained his personal possession until he ceded it to the Belgian State in 1907, when it was renamed the Belgian Congo.

Following riots in Leopoldville in 1958, Belgian King Baudouin announced that the colony could look forward to independence. Roundtable conferences were convened at Brussels in January 1960, and Belgium granted independence on June 30, 1960. Parliamentary elections were held in April 1960. The Congolese National Movement (MNC) obtained a majority of the seats, and Patrice Lumumba was named prime minister. After much maneuvering, the leader of the Alliance of the Bakongo (ABAKO) Party, Joseph Kasavubu, was named president.

As many as two hundred fifty ethnic groups in Zaire have been distinguished and named. The largest group, the Kongo, may include as many as 2.5 million persons. Other socially and numerically important groups are the Luba, Lunda, Bashi, and Mongo. Some groups, including the aboriginal Pygmies, occupy isolated ecological niches and number only a few thousand.

Approximately seven hundred local languages and dialects are spoken; four serve as official languages. Lingala developed along the Congo River in the 1880s in response to the need for a common commercial language. Swahili, introduced into the country by Arabs and especially the Zanzibari Swahilis during the nineteenth century slaving operations, is spoken extensively in the eastern half of the country. Kikongo is used primarily in the area between Kinshasa and the Atlantic Ocean, as well as in parts of Congo and Angola. Tshiluba is spoken primarily by the tribal groups of south-central Zaire.

## Zambia

Official name: Republic of Zambia
Independence: October 24, 1964
Area: 290,585 sq. mi.
Population: (1991 estimate) 8.4 million
Ethnic divisions: More than 70 tribal groups
Religious groups: Christian, Traditional belief
Languages spoken: English (official), about 70 local languages and dialects, including Bemba, Tonga, Nyanja, Lozi, Luvale, Ndembu (Lundu), and Kaonde

About two thousand years ago, the indigenous hunter-gatherer occupants of Zambia began to be displaced or absorbed by more advanced migrating tribes. By the fifteenth century, the major waves of Bantu-speaking immigrants began, with the greatest influx occuring between the late seventeenth and early nineteenth centuries. These groups came primarily from the Luba and Lunda tribes of southern Zaire and northern Angola but were joined in the nineteenth century by Ngoni peoples from the south. By the latter part of that century, the various peoples of Zambia were largely established in the areas they currently occupy.

Except for an occasional Portuguese explorer, the area lay untouched by Europeans for centuries, until the mid-nineteenth century, when it was penetrated by European explorers, missionaries, and traders. In 1888, Northern and Southern Rhodesia (now Zambia and Zimbabwe) were proclaimed a British sphere of influence. In 1953, both Rhodesias were joined with Nyasaland (now Malawi) to form the Federation of Rhodesia and Nyasaland.

Northern Rhodesia was the center of much of the turmoil and crises that characterized the federation in its last years. At the core of the controversy were insistent African demands for greater participation in government and the Europeans' fear. A two-stage election held in October and December 1962 resulted in an African majority in the Legislative Council. The council passed resolutions calling for Northern Rhodesia's secession from the federation and demanding full internal self-government. On December 31, 1963, the federation was dissolved, and Northern Rhodesia became the Republic of Zambia on October 24, 1964.

Zambia's population comprises more than seventy Bantu-speaking tribes. Some tribes are small, and only two have enough people to constitute at least ten percent of the population.

## Zimbabwe

Independence: April 18, 1980
Area: 151,000 sq. mi.
Population: (1991 estimate) 10.7 million

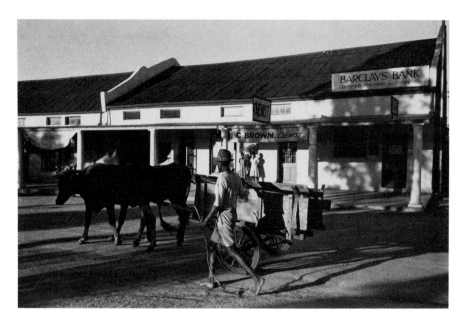

A Zimbabwean man with ox-drawn cart.

Ethnic divisions: Shona 80%, Ndebele 19%
Religious groups: 50% Syncretic (part
    Christian, part Traditional belief),
    Christian 25%, traditional belief 24%,
    Hindu and Muslim less than 1%
Languages spoken: English (official), Shona,
    SiNdebele

Archaeologists have found Stone Age implements and pebble tools in several areas of Zimbabwe, suggesting human habitation for many centuries, and the ruins of stone buildings provide evidence of early civilization.

In the sixteenth century, the Portuguese were the first Europeans to attempt colonization of south-central Africa, but the hinterland lay virtually untouched by Europeans until the arrival of explorers, missionaries, and traders some three hundred years later. In 1888, the area that became Southern and Northern Rhodesia was proclaimed a British sphere of influence. The British South Africa Company was chartered in 1889, and the settlement of Salisbury (now Harare, the capital) was established in 1890.

In 1895, the territory was formally named Rhodesia. In 1923, Southern Rhodesia's white settlers were given the choice of being incorporated into the Union of South Africa or becoming a separate entity within the British Empire. The settlers rejected incorporation, and Southern Rhodesia was formally annexed by the United Kingdom. In September 1953, Southern Rhodesia was joined with the British protectorates of Northern Rhodesia and Nyasaland. The federation was dissolved at the end of 1963 after much crisis and turmoil, and Northern Rhodesia and Nyasaland became the independent states of Zambia and Malawi in 1964.

Although prepared to grant independence to Rhodesia, the United Kingdom insisted that the authorities at Salisbury first demonstrate their intention to move toward eventual majority rule. Desiring to keep their dominant position, the white Rhodesians refused to give such assurance. On November 11, 1965, after lengthy and unsuccessful negotiations with the British government, Prime Minister Ian Smith issued a Unilateral

Declaration of Independence (UDI) from the United Kingdom. The British government considered the UDI unconstitutional and illegal but made clear that it would not use force to end the rebellion. The British government imposed unilateral economic sanctions on Rhodesia and requested other nations to do the same. On December 16, 1966, the United Nations Security Council, for the first time in its history, imposed mandatory economic sanctions on a state.

In the early 1970s, informal attempts at settlement were renewed between the United Kingdom and the Rhodesia administration. In 1974, the major African nationalist groups—the Zimbabwe African People's Union (ZAPU) and the Zimbabwe African National Union (ZANU), which split away from ZAPU in 1963—were united into the "Patriotic Front" and combined their military forces. In 1976, the Smith government agreed in principle to majority rule and to a meeting in Geneva with black nationalist leaders. Blacks represented at the Geneva meeting included ZAPU leader Joshua Nkomo, ZANU leader Robert Mugabe, UANC chairman Bishop Abel Muzorewa, and former ZANU leader, the Reverend Ndabaningi Sithole. The meeting failed.

On March 3, 1978, the Smith administration signed the "internal settlement" agreement in Salisbury with Bishop Muzorewa, Reverend Sithole, and Chief Jeremiah Chirau. The agreement provided for qualified majority rule and elections with universal suffrage. Following elections in April 1979, in which his UANC part won a majority, Bishop Muzorewa assumed office on June 1, becoming Zimbabwe's first black prime minister. However, the installation of the new black majority government did not end the guerrilla conflict that had claimed more than 20,000 lives.

The British and the African parties began deliberations on a Rhodesian settlement in London on September 10, 1979. On December 21, the parties signed an agreement calling for a cease-fire, new elections, a transition period under British rule, and a new constitution implementing majority rule while protecting minority rights. The elections were supervised by the British government and monitored. Robert Mugabe's ZANU Party won an absolute majority and was asked to form Zimbabwe's first government. The British government formally granted independence to Zimbabwe on April 18, 1980. Most nations recognized Zimbabwe following independence.

Zimbabwe's population is divided into two major language groups, which are subdivided into several tribal groups. The Mashona (Shona speakers), who constitute about eighty percent of the population, have lived in the area the longest and are the majority language groups. The Matabele (Sindebele speakers), representing about nineteen percent of the population and centered in the southwest near Bulawayo, arrived within the last 150 years. An offshoot of the South African Zulu group, they had maintained control over the Mashona until the white occupation of Rhodesia.

## Western Hemisphere (Excluding United States)

### Anguilla
Independence: n/a (dependent territory of the United Kingdom)
Area: 91 sq. km.
Population: (1992 estimate) 6,963
Ethnic divisions: Black Africans
Religious groups: Anglican 40%, Methodist 33%, Seventh-Day Adventist 7%, Baptist 5%, Roman Catholic 3%, other 12%
Languages spoken: English

Beginning in 1816, the islands of Anguilla, the (British) Virgin Islands, Saint Christopher (Saint Kitts), and Nevis were governed by the British as a single colony. However, when Saint Christopher was granted statehood in 1967, Anguilla unilaterally declared independence from Saint Christopher. Anguilla has remained a dependent territory of the United Kingdom.

## Antigua and Barbuda

Independence: November 1, 1981
Area: 108 sq. mi.
Population: (1991 estimate) 64,400
Ethnic divisions: Black Africans, some British and Portuguese
Religious groups: Principally Anglican, with evangelical Protestant and Roman Catholic minorities.
Languages spoken: English (official), regional dialects

Christopher Columbus first visited the islands of Antigua and Barbuda in 1493. Missionaries attempted to settle on the island but were hindered by the Carib Indians, who inhabited the islands, and the absence of natural freshwater springs. In 1632, the British successfully established a colony; Sir Christopher Codrington established the first large sugar estate in Antigua in 1674, bringing slaves from Africa's west coast to work the plantations. Although Antiguan slaves were emancipated in 1834, they remained bound to their plantation owners. Economic opportunities for the new freedmen were limited by a lack of surplus farming land, no access to credit, and an economy built on agriculture rather than manufacturing.

## Argentina

Official Name: Republic of Argentina

Blacks comprise a very small percentage of the population of Argentina.

## Aruba

Independence: n/a (autonomous part of the Kingdom of the Netherlands)
Population: 60,000
Ethnic divisions: Mixed European and Carib Indian 85%, black Africans
Religious groups: Roman Catholic, Protestant, Jewish
Languages spoken: Papiamento, English, Dutch, Spanish

The Spanish landed in Curacao (now the Netherlands Antilles) in 1499 and in 1527 took possession of Curacao, Bonaire, and Aruba. In 1634, the three islands passed to the Netherlands, where they have remained, except for two short periods of British rule during the Napoleonic Wars. Before the war, the Dutch Caribbean islands were administered as Dutch colonies; afterward, negotiations to confer a greater measure of self-government began. On December 15, 1954, the Netherlands Antilles became an autonomous part of the kingdom. In 1983, Aruba sought autonomy from the Netherlands Antilles; on January 1, 1986, it achieved separate status equal to that of the Antilles and is slated to become fully independent in 1996.

Some forty nationalities are represented in the Netherlands Antilles and Aruba; Arubans mostly are a mixture of European and Caribbean Indian.

## Bahamas

Official Name: Commonwealth of The Bahamas
Independence: July 10, 1973
Area: 5,380 sq. mi
Population: (1991 estimate) 251,000
Ethnic divisions: Black African 85%, European 15%
Religious groups: Baptist, Anglican, Roman Catholic, Methodist
Languages spoken: English, Creole

Christopher Columbus first visited the islands of the Bahamas in 1492, when he first

Nassau Police Band.

dos was divided into large plantation estates. Slaves were brought from Africa to work on these plantations until slavery was abolished throughout the British Empire in 1834. From 1958 to 1962, Barbados was one of ten members of the West Indies Federation. Barbados negotiated its own independence at a constitutional conference with the United Kingdom in June 1966. The country attained self-rule on November 30, 1966.

Ethnically, the population of Barbados is eighty percent African, sixteen percent mixed, and four percent European.

landed in the Western Hemisphere, either on Samana Cay or San Salvador Island. In 1647, the first permanent European settlement was founded. In 1717, the islands became a British crown colony. The Bahamas were granted self-government through a series of constitutional and political steps, culminating in independence on July 10, 1973.

Eighty-five percent of Bahamians are of African descent. Many of their ancestors arrived in the Bahamas when it was a staging area for the slave trade or were brought there by the thousands of British loyalists who fled the American colonies during the Revolutionary War.

## Barbados

Independence: November 30, 1966
Area: 166 sq. mi.
Population: (1991 estimate) 254,000
Ethnic divisions: African 80%, mixed 16%, European 4%
Religious groups: Anglican 70%, Roman Catholic, Methodist, Baptist and Moravian
Languages spoken: English

From the arrival of the first British settlers in 1627 until independence in 1966, Barbados had been under uninterrupted British control. As the sugar industry developed into the main commercial enterprise, Barba-

## Belize

Independence: September 21, 1981
Area: 8,866 sq. mi.
Population: (1991 estimate) 228,000
Ethnic divisions: Creole, African, mestizo, Amerindian
Religious groups: Roman Catholic, Anglican, Methodist, Muslim, Buddhist
Languages spoken: English (official), Spanish, Mayan

The Mayan civilization spread into the area of Belize between 1500 BC and AD 300 and flourished until about AD 1000. European contact began in 1502 when Columbus sailed along the coast; the first recorded European settlement was 1638. Over the next one hundred fifty years, more English settlements were established. Belize was named the Colony of British Honduras in 1840; it became a crown colony in 1862. Self-government was granted in January 1964. The official name of the territory was changed from British Honduras to Belize in June 1973, and full independence was granted on September 21, 1981.

Most Belizeans are of multiracial descent. About forty to forty-five percent of the population is of African ancestry; more than twenty-five percent is of mixed local Indian and European descent (mestizo). Another one-fifth of the population is composed of Carib, Mayan, or other Amerindian ethnic groups.

## Bermuda

Independence: n/a (parliamentary British colony with internal government since 1620)
Area: 20.6 sq. mi.
Population: (1987 estimate) 57,619
Ethnic divisions: Black Africans 61%, white and others 39%
Religious groups: Anglican 37%, Protestant 21%, Roman Catholic 14%, other 28%
Languages spoken: English

Located in the Atlantic Ocean about 650 miles east of North Carolina, Bermuda is relatively isolated.

The first Europeans to visit Bermuda were Spanish explorers in 1503. In 1609, a group of British explorers became stranded on the islands, and their reports aroused great interest about the islands in England. In 1612, British colonists arrived and founded the town of Saint George, the oldest, continuously inhabited English-speaking settlement in the Western Hemisphere.

Slaves from Africa were brought to Bermuda soon after the colony began. When the slave trade was outlawed in Bermuda in 1807, all slaves were freed in 1834. Although Bermuda is a British colony, it has a great degree of internal autonomy, based on the June 8, 1968 constitution.

Nearly two-thirds of the Bermudians are of African descent. An estimated seven thousand United States citizens live on the island, some 2,800 of them are military personnel and their dependents.

## Bolivia

Official Name: Republic of Bolivia

Blacks comprise a very small percentage of Bolivia's population.

## Brazil

Official Name: Federative Republic of Brazil
Independence: September 7, 1822
Area: 3,290,000 sq. mi.
Population: (1991 estimate) 150.1 million
Ethnic divisions: Portuguese, black Africans, Indians (principally Tupi and Guarani linguistic stock), Italian, German, Japanese
Religious groups: Roman Catholic 89%

Brazil was formally claimed in 1500 by the Portuguese and was ruled from Lisbon as a colony until 1808. Brazil successfully declared independence on September 7, 1922. Four major groups make up the Brazilian population: indigenous Indians of Tupi and Guarani language stock; the Portuguese; Africans brought to Brazil as slaves; and various European and Asian immigrant groups that have settled in Brazil since the mid-nineteenth century.

Slavery was introduced into Brazil in the 1530s, expanded greatly after 1540, when sugar became important, and grew most rapidly between 1580 and 1640, when Spain controlled the country. Estimates of the total number of slaves brought to Brazil varies from six to twenty million. Slavery did not finally end in Brazil until 1888. Though slavery in Brazil was often extremely brutal, and the death rate of blacks on sugar, coffee, and cotton plantations was enormous, large numbers of Africans achieved freedom. About twenty-five percent of Brazil's blacks were free during slavery.

During the nineteenth century, free blacks intermarried so rapidly their numbers fell from about 400,000 in 1800 to 20,000 by 1888 when slavery was finally abolished. Free blacks enjoyed full legal equality during both the period of slavery and after it was abolished.

In Brazil, slaves who served masters in cities were often allowed to seek part-time and temporary employment elsewhere.

They were able to read and write and develop employable skills. Blacks became important to the development and economy of the country and some became prominent in public life. Nilo Pecanha served as vice-president and briefly as president of Brazil in the first decade of this century. Blacks also achieved fame in Brazil's intellectual and artistic life.

## Canada

Blacks comprise a very small portion of Canada's population—less than 25,000, or 0.1 percent of the total population. Canada's major racial issue is its treatment of the Indians and Eskimos, who total about 200,000.

Blacks were prominent in the early seventeenth-century explorations and development of Canada by French explorers and Jesuit missionaries. The first black slave is believed to have been a native of Madagascar (Malagasy) and to have been sold to a French resident of Quebec in 1628. As French Canada expanded, slaves were purchased in the United States.

In 1749, the British brought slaves to Halifax, and slavery was legalized in British Canada in 1762. Slavery increased shortly thereafter, when the British took all of Canada in the French and Indian Wars. Many British fleeing from the revolutionary colonies to the south after 1775 brought slaves with them.

British slave codes were more severe than the French, under whom slaves could marry, own property, and maintain parental rights. However, the British were not to sustain slavery for long. London had divided Canada into two governments, Upper Canada and Lower Canada. The governor of Upper Canada, Colonel James Simcoe, an ardent abolitionist, induced the area's legislature to pass laws forbidding importation of slaves and freeing every slave born in the area by the

age of twenty-five. As a result, slavery in Upper Canada soon collapsed.

Similar legislation was not enacted in Lower Canada. However, by 1800 the courts, through complex legal decisions, established the principle that a slave could leave his master whenever he wished. In the Maritime Provinces, courts also acted so as to eliminate slavery in fact if not in theory. Slavery was formally abolished in Canada in 1833.

Meanwhile, starting slowly in the eighteenth century, Canada was becoming a haven for slaves fleeing across her southern borders. Slaves who had served with the British in the American War for Independence came to Halifax from New York in large numbers in 1782 and 1783. Though many were to migrate to Freetown on the West Coast of Africa, others stayed. In 1826, Canada defied the United States and formally refused to return fugitive slaves. In 1829, the legislature of Lower Canada announced that every slave that entered the Province was immediately free, a declaration that gave impetus to the underground railroad and stimulated moves for resettlement by blacks in Canada.

The passage of the Fugitive Slave Act in 1850 meant that any escaped slave who remained in the United States was to be returned to his owner. Within a year after passage of the law, some ten thousand slaves arrived in Canada, welcomed by a majority of Canadians who provided communities and services for them.

African-Americans were accepted into the mainstream of Canadian life, were allowed to choose separate or integrated schools, were elected to local office and served as officers in the Canadian Army. Black laborers contributed substantially to the expansion of the Canadian Pacific Railroad, as immigrants from Eastern and Southern Europe were to contribute to the development of railroads in the United States. Black skilled laborers were much in demand. By 1861, at the outbreak of the Civil War in the United States, there were 50,000 blacks in Canada. However, after the Civil War, feelings of fear among white Canadians led to discrimination in employment and schools. Many African-Americans re-emigrated to the United States, feeling that, with slavery outlawed there, a bright future awaited them. By 1871, the black population of Canada dipped to about 20,000.

Canada, the most sparsely populated country in the world with 1.5 persons per square mile, has become a haven for so many refugees that it has earned awards for outstanding achievement from human rights organizations. In fact, so many immigrants from Asia, Africa, the Caribbean and elsewhere have moved to Canada, that the established British-Caucasian population has expressed fears it will become extinct (assimilated) within one hundred years. Toronto alone has become one of the world's most cosmopolitan cities with more than one hundred cultural or ethnic groups.

## Cayman Islands

Independence: n/a (dependent territory of the United Kingdom)
Area: 260 sq. km.
Population: (1992 estimate) 29,139
Ethnic divisions: 40% mixed, 20% white, 20% black
Religious groups: United Church (Presbyterian and Congregational), Anglican, Baptist, Roman Catholic, Church of God, other Protestant denominations
Languages spoken: English

## Chile

Blacks comprise a very small percentage of Chile's population.

## Colombia

Official Name: Republic of Colombia
Independence: July 20, 1810
Area: 440,000 sq. mi.
Population: (1991 estimate) 33.7 million
Ethnic divisions: Mestizo 58%, white 20%, Mulatto 14%, black 4%, mixed black-Indian 3%, Indian 1%
Religious groups: Roman Catholic 95%
Languages spoken: Spanish

The diversity of ethnic origins results from the intermixture of indigenous Indians, Spanish colonists, and African slaves. In 1549, the area was established as a Spanish colony with the capital at Bogota. In 1717, Bogota became the capital of the viceroyalty of New Granada, which included what is now Venezuela, Ecuador, and Panama. On July 20, 1810, the citizens of Bogota created the first representative council to defy Spanish authority. Total independence was proclaimed in 1813, and in 1819 the Republic of Greater Colombia was formed.

## Costa Rica

Official Name: Republic of Costa Rica
Independence: September 15, 1821
Area: 51,032 sq. km.
Population: (1991 estimate) 3.1 million
Ethnic divisions: European (including a few mestizos), 96%, black 3%, indigenous 1%
Religious groups: Roman Catholic 95%
Languages spoken: Spanish, Jamaican dialect of English spoken around Puerto Limon

In 1502, on his fourth and last voyage to the New World, Christopher Columbus made the first European landfall in the area. Settlement of Costa Rica began in 1522. In 1821, Costa Rica joined other Central American provinces in a joint declaration of independence from Spain. Unlike most of their Central American neighbors, Costa Ricans are largely of European rather than mestizo

Stevedores transfering bananas in the Caribbean.

descent, and Spain is the primary country of origin. The indigenous population today numbers no more than 25,000. Blacks, descendants of nineteenth-century Jamaican immigrant workers, constitute a significant English-speaking minority of about 30,000, concentrated around the Caribbean port city of Puerto Limon.

**Cuba**

Official name: Republic of Cuba
Independence: May 20, 1902
Area: 44,200 sq. mi.
Population: (1991 estimate) 10.7 million
Ethnic divisions: Spanish-African mixture
Languages spoken: Spanish

Cuba is a multi-racial society with a population of mainly Spanish and African origins.

317

Before the arrival of Columbus in 1492, Cuba was inhabited by three groups— Cyboneys, Guanahabibes, and Tainos. As Spain developed its colonial empire in the Western Hemisphere, Havana became an important commercial seaport. Settlers eventually moved inland, devoting themselves mainly to sugarcane and tobacco farming. As the native Indian population died out, African slaves were imported to work on the plantations. A 1774 census counted 96,000 whites, 31,000 free blacks, and 44,000 slaves in Cuba. Slavery was abolished in 1886.

## Dominica

Official name: Commonwealth of Dominica
Independence: November 3, 1978
Area: 290 sq. mi.
Population: (1991 estimate) 86,000
Ethnic divisions: Black African, Carib
   Indians
Religious groups: Roman Catholic 80%,
   Church of England, other Protestant
   denominations
Languages spoken: English (official), a
   French patois is widely spoken

Dominica was first visited by Europeans on Columbus's second voyage in 1493. Spanish ships frequently landed on Dominica during the sixteenth century, but toiled at establishing settlements. In 1635, France claimed Dominica. As part of the 1763 Treaty of Paris that ended the Seven Years' War being fought in Europe, North America, and India, the island became a British possession.

In 1763, the British established a legislative assembly, representing only the white population. In 1831, reflecting a liberalization of official British racial attitudes, the "Brown Privilege Bill" conferred political and social rights on nonwhites. Three blacks were elected to the Legislative Assembly the

following year, and by 1838 the recently enfranchised blacks dominated that body. Most black legislators were smallholders or merchants, who held economic and social views diametrically opposed to the interests of the small, wealthy English planter class. Reacting to a perceived threat, the planters lobbied for more direct British rule. In 1865, after much agitation and tension, the colonial office replaced the elective assembly with one of half of the members appointed.

The power of the black population progressively eroded until all political rights for the vast majority of the population were effectively curtailed. On November 3, 1978, the Commonwealth of Dominica was granted independence by the United Kingdom. Almost all 81,000 Dominicans are descendants of African slaves imported by planters in the eighteenth century.

## Dominican Republic

Independence: February 27, 1844
Area: 18,704 sq. mi.
Population: (1991 estimate) 7.3 million
Ethnic divisions: Mixed 73%, black African
   11%
Religious groups: Roman Catholic 95%
Languages spoken: Spanish

The island of Hispaniola, of which the Dominican Republic forms the eastern two-thirds and Haiti the remainder, was originally occupied by members of the Taino tribe when Columbus and his companions landed there in 1492. Brutal colonial conditions reduced the Taino population from an estimated one million to about five hundred in only fifty years. To assure adequate labor for plantations, the Spanish began bringing African slaves to the island in 1503.

In the next century, French settlers occupied the western end of the island, which Spain ceded to France in 1697. In 1804, this became the Republic of Haiti. The Haitians

Improvised housing in Santo Domingo, Dominican Republic.

conquered the whole island in 1822 and held it until 1844, when forces led by Juan Pablo Duarte, the hero of Dominican independence, drove the Haitians out and established the Dominican Republic as an independent state. In 1861, the Dominicans voluntarily returned to the Spanish Empire; in 1865, independence was restored.

## Ecuador

Official name: Republic of Ecuador

Blacks comprise a very small percentage of Ecuador's population.

## El Salvador

Official name: Republic of El Salvador

Blacks comprise a very small percentage of El Salvador's population.

## French Guiana

Area: 43,740 sq. mi.

Population: (1988 estimate) 90,240

Ethnic divisions: African and Afro-European 66%, European 18%, East Asian, Chinese, Amerindian, Brazilian 16%

Religious groups: Roman Catholic, Protestant sects, Hindu, traditional African belief

Languages spoken: French

The first French settlement in French Guiana was established in 1604. The first permanent settlement began in 1634, and in 1664, the town of Cayenne was established. Following the abolition of slavery in 1848, the fragile plantation economy declined precipitously. French Guiana as an overseas department of France since 1946 is an integral part of the French Republic. About two-thirds of the population of French Guiana are Afro-European Creoles or Guianese. The

319

remainder include French serving in military or administrative positions.

### Grenada

Independence: February 7, 1974
Area: 133 sq. mi.
Population: (1991 estimate) 84,000
Ethnic divisions: Black African descent, some East Indian, European, Arawak/ Carib Indian
Religious groups: Roman Catholic 63%, Church of England, other Protestant denominations
Languages spoken: English (official), some vestigial French patois

Like the rest of the West Indies, Grenada was originally settled to cultivate sugar, which was grown on estates using slave labor. Most of Grenada's population is of African descent; there is little trace of the early Arawak and Carib Indians.

Columbus first visited Grenada in 1498. Grenada remained uncolonized for more than one hundred years after the first visit by Europeans; British efforts to settle the island were unsuccessful. In 1650, a French company purchased Grenada from the British and established a small settlement. The island remained under French control until captured by the British a century later during the Seven Year's War. Slavery was outlawed in 1833. In 1833, Grenada was made part of the British Windward Islands Administration. In 1958, the Windward Islands Administration dissolved. Grenada became an associated state on March 3, 1967, but sought full independence, which the British government granted on February 7, 1974.

### Guadeloupe

Independence: n/a (overseas department of France)
Area: 660 sq. mi.
Population: (1988 estimate) 337,524

An open-air market in Guadeloupe.

Ethnic divisions: Afro-European, European, Afro-East Asian, East Asian
Religious groups: Roman Catholic, Hindu, and traditional African belief
Languages spoken: French, Creole

Columbus sighted Guadeloupe in 1493. The area was permanently settled by the French in the seventeenth century. The first slaves were brought from Africa to work the plantations around 1650, and the first slave rebellion occurred in 1656. Guadeloupe was poorly administered in its early days and was a dependency of Martinique until 1775.

Most Guadeloupeans are of mixed Afro-European and Afro-East Asian ancestry (descendants of laborers brought over from India during the nineteenth century). Several thousand metropolitan French reside there; most are civil servants, business people, and their dependents.

### Guatemala

Blacks comprise a very small precentage of Guatemala's population.

## Guyana

Official name: Co-operative Republic of
Guyana
Independence: May 26, 1966
Area: 83,000 sq. mi.
Population: (1991 estimate) 748,000
Ethnic divisions: East Indian 49.6%, African
30.4%, mixed 14.1%, European and
Chinese 0.5%
Religious groups: Christian 46%, Hindu 37%,
Muslim 9%, other 8%
Languages spoken: English, Guyanese
Creole, Amerindian dialects

Guiana was the name given the area
sighted by Columbus in 1498, comprising
modern Guyana, Suriname, French Guiana,
and parts of Brazil and Venezuela. The
Dutch settled in Guyana in the late sixteenth
century. Dutch control ended when the British became the de facto rulers in 1796. In
1815, the colonies of Essequibo, Demerara,
and Berbice were officially ceded to the British by the Congress of Vienna and, in 1831,
were consolidated as British Guiana.

Slave revolts, such as the one in 1763 led by
Guyana's national hero, Cuffy, stressed the desire to obtain basic rights and were underscored by a willingness to compromise. Following the abolition of slavery in 1834,
indentured workers were brought primarily
from India but also from Portugal and China. A
scheme in 1862 to bring black workers from
the United States was unsuccessful.

Independence was achieved in 1966, and
Guyana became a republic on February 23,
1970, the anniversary of the Cuffy slave rebellion.

## Haiti

Official name: Republic of Haiti
Independence: 1804
Area: 10,714 sq. mi.

Workers on a banana plantation in Central America.

Population: (1991 estimate) 6.2 million
Ethnic Group: Black African 95%, mulatto and European 5%
Religious groups: Roman Catholic 80%, Protestant 10%, traditional (voodoo) practices 10%
Languages spoken: French (official), Creole

Columbus first visited the Island of Hispaniola in 1492. In 1697, Spain ceded the western third of Hispaniola to France. During this period, slaves were brought from Africa to work the sugarcane and coffee plantations. In 1791, the slave population, led by Toussaint L'Ouverture, Jean Jacques Dessalines, and Henri Christophe, revolted and gained control of the northern part of Saint-Domingue. The French were unable to regain control. In 1804, the slaves established an independent nation, renaming the area Haiti.

Haiti is the world's oldest black republic and the second oldest republic in the Western Hemisphere, after the United States. In September 1991, the newly elected President Jean-Bertrand Aristide was ousted in a coup leading by Brigadier General Raoul Cedras. Since Aristide's ouster, thousands of Haitians have attempted to immigrate to the United States, with no success. The United States government has forcibly returned Haitian refugees, maintaining that the majority have been economic, and not political, refugees.

Almost ninety-five percent of the Haitians are of black African descent; the rest of the population are mostly of mixed African-Caucasian ancestry (mulattoes).

## Honduras
Official name: Republic of Honduras

Blacks comprise a very small percentage of Honduras' population.

## Jamaica
Independence: August 6, 1962
Area: 4,244 sq. mi.
Population: (1991 estimate) 2.4 million.
Ethnic divisions: African 76.3%, Afro-European 15.1%, Chinese and Afro-Chinese 1.2%, East Indian and Afro-East Indian 3.4%, European 3.2%
Religious groups: Anglican, Baptist and other Protestant denominations, Roman Catholic
Languages spoken: English, Creole

Jamaica was first visited in 1494 by Christopher Columbus and settled by the Spanish during the early sixteenth century. In 1655, British forces seized the island, and in 1670 gained formal possession through the Treaty of Madrid.

In 1958, Jamaica joined nine other British territories in the West Indies Federation but withdrew when, in a 1961 referendum, Ja-

Linstead market, Jamaica.

Two Jamaican children.

maican voters rejected membership. Jamaica gained independence from the United Kingdom in 1962 but has remained a member of the Commonwealth.

Sugar and slavery were important elements in Jamaica's history and development. With the abolition of slavery in 1834, the settlers were forced to recruit other sources of cheap labor, resorting to the importation of East Indian and Chinese farm hands. As a result, Jamaica is a multi-racial society.

## Martinique

Independence: n/a (overseas region of France)

Area: 425 sq. mi.

Population: (1988 estimate) 351,105

Ethnic divisions: Afro-European, Afro-Indian, European

Religious groups: Roman Catholic 95%, Baptist, Seventh-day Adventist, Jehovah's Witness, Pentecostal, Hindu, traditional African belief 5%

Languages spoken: French

Columbus sighted Martinique in 1493 or 1502. The area was permanently settled by the French in the seventeenth century. Except for three short periods of British occupation, Martinique has been a French possession since 1635.

About ninety-five percent of the people of Martinique are of Afro-European or Afro-European-Indian descent. The rest are traditional white planter families, commonly referred to as bekes or creoles, and a sizable number of metropolitan French who work in administration and business.

## Mexico

Official name: The United Mexican States

Blacks accompanied the Spanish as conquerors to Mexico in the sixteenth century, and later were brought in large numbers as slaves. It is estimated that there were 150,000 black slaves in Mexico in the sixteenth century. One of the earlier slaves, Estevanico, is credited with opening up the northern interior lands of what is now New Mexico and Arizona to Spanish conquest.

The use of slavery dropped sharply in the eighteenth and early nineteenth centuries. In 1829, Mexico abolished slavery in all its states except Texas, allowing it to remain there to pacify the United States. As slavery in the United States moved westward into Texas, Mexico became a haven for escaped slaves who slipped into the heart of the country and blended with the population.

Since the sixteenth century, Mexico's blacks have intermarried with Indians and whites so that their African heritage is no longer clearly identifiable. Some 100,000 blacks, about 0.5 percent of the population, do live in Mexico, mostly in the port cities of Vera Cruz and Acapulco. Blacks in lesser density live in Mexico City and in border cities across the Rio Grande River from Texas.

## Montserrat

Independence: n/a (dependent territory of the United Kingdom)
Population: (1992 estimate) 12,617
Ethnic divisions: Black African, European
Religious groups: Anglican, Methodist, Roman Catholic, Pentecostal, Seventh-Day Adventist, other Christian denominations
Languages spoken: English

When the Leeward Islands (Antigua, Anguilla, Barbuda, Montserrat, Nevis, and Saint Kitts) were first visited by Christopher Columbus in 1493, they were inhabited by Carib Indians. Montserrat was first colonized in 1632. The French captured some of the islands in 1666 and again in 1782, but the islands were returned to the British under the Treaty of Versailles in 1783.

Most of the population is an intermixture of European settlers and the descendants of West African slaves.

## Netherlands Antilles

Independence: n/a (autonomous part of the Kingdom of the Netherlands)
Area: 324 sq. mi.
Population: 187,500
Ethnic divisions: Black African 85%, European, Carib Indian
Religious groups: Roman Catholic, Protestant
Languages spoken: Papiamento, English, Dutch, Spanish

The Spanish first landed in Curacao in 1499, and in 1527 they took possession of Curacao, Bonaire, and Aruba. In 1634, the three islands were passed to the Netherlands, where they have remained except for two short periods of British rule during the Napoleonic Wars.

Curacao was the center of the Caribbean slave trade until emancipation in 1863. Before the war, the Dutch Caribbean islands were administered as Dutch colonies; afterward, negotiations to confer a greater measure of self-government began. On December 15, 1954, the Netherlands Antilles became an autonomous part of the kingdom.

Some forty nationalities are represented in the Netherlands Antilles and Aruba. The people of the Netherlands Antilles primarily are of African or mixed African and European descent.

## Nicaragua

Official name: Republic of Nicaragua
Independence: 1838
Area: 57,000 sq. mi.
Population: 3.3 million
Ethnic divisions: Mestizo 69%, white 17%, black African 9%, Indian 5%
Religious groups: Roman Catholic 85%

A market at Managua, Nicaragua.

Languages spoken: Spanish

Columbus sailed along the Nicaraguan coast on his last voyage in 1502. Wars between the Spanish on the Pacific and Indians and British on the Caribbean (the British presence did not end until 1905) marked the colonial period. Guatemala declared its independence from Spain in 1821, but Nicaragua did not become an independent republic until 1838.

Most Nicaraguans are a mix of European and Indian. Only the Indians of the Caribbean coast remain ethnically distinct and retain tribal customs and dialects. A large black minority (of Jamaican origin) is concentrated on the Caribbean coast.

A Panamanian craftsman.

### Panama
Official name: Republic of Panama
Independence: November 3, 1903
Area: 29,762 sq. mi.
Population: (1991 estimate) 2.4 million
Ethnic divisions: Mestizo 70%, West Indian
    14%, white 10%, Indian 6%
Religious groups: Roman Catholic 93%,
    Protestant (Evangelical) 6%
Languages spoken: Spanish (official),
    English, Indian languages

Prior to the arrival of Europeans, Panama was inhabited by Amerindian groups. By 1519 the Spanish had established settlements, killing or enslaving much of the indigenous Indian population. Africans were brought in to replace the Indian slave population. Today, most Panamanians are of mixed ancestry—Spanish, Indian, or black.

### Paraguay
Official name: Republic of Paraguay

Blacks comprise a very small percentage of Paraguay's population.

### Peru
Official name: Republic of Peru

Blacks comprise a small percentage of Peru's population.

### Puerto Rico
Independence: n/a (commonwealth
    associated with the United States)
Area: 9,104 sq. km.
Population: (1992 estimate) 3,776,654
Ethnic division: Mixed, black, Indian, whites
Religious groups: Roman Catholic 85%,
    Protestant denominations and other 15%
Languages spoken: Spanish (official), English

First visited by Columbus in 1493 on his second voyage to the New World, Puerto Rico was soon conquered by the Spaniard Ponce de Leon, who was appointed governor of the island in 1509. The indigenous Carib Indians, almost all of whom were utilized by the Spaniards as plantation laborers, were eventually wiped out—to be replaced beginning in 1513 by African slaves. Puerto Rico was held by the English in 1598 and San Juan was besieged by the Dutch in 1625. Otherwise, Spanish control remained unchallenged until the Spanish-American War.

The island was captured by United States forces during this conflict and ceded outright to the United States under the Treaty of Paris (1898). In 1900, Congress established a local administration, with a governor appointed by the American president, an executive council, and an elected house of delegates. Puerto Ricans were granted United States citizenship in 1917. After World War II, Congress provided that the governor of the island be an elected official. In 1950, a further act of Congress enabled Puerto Rico to draft its own constitution and, in three years, it became a United States Commonwealth.

Many Puerto Ricans today are of mixed black and Spanish ancestry. For the most part, the original Indian inhabitants of the island were exterminated in the sixteenth century.

## Saint Kitts and Nevis

Official name: Federation of Saint Kitts and
  Nevis
Independence: September 19, 1983
Area: Saint Kitts, (68 sq. mi.); Nevis, (36 sq.
  mi.)
Population: (1991 estimate) 40,293
Ethnic divisions: Black Africans, some
  British
Religious groups: Principally Anglican, with
  evangelical Protestant and Roman
  Catholic minorities
Languages spoken: English

Christopher Columbus first visited the islands in 1493 on his second voyage to the area, naming the larger Saint Christopher, after his patron saint. In 1624, Saint Christopher became the first English settlement in the West Indies, and it was from here that colonists spread to other islands in the region. In 1624, the French colonized part of the island. However, it was ceded entirely to Britain by the Treaty of Utrecht in 1713. The Federation of Saint Kitts and Nevis attained full independence on September 19, 1983.

## Saint Lucia

Independence: February 22, 1979
Area: 238 sq. mi.
Population: (1991 estimate) 163,075.
Ethnic divisions: Black African 90.3%, mixed
  5.5%, East Indian 3.2%, Caucasian 0.8%
Religious groups: Roman Catholic 90%,
  Church of England 3%
Languages spoken: English (official), French
  patois

Europeans first visited the island in either 1492 or 1502. In the seventeenth century, the Dutch, English, and French all tried to establish trading outposts on Saint Lucia but faced opposition from Carib Indians, who inhabited the island. The French, who had claimed the island, established a successful settlement in 1651 as an offshoot of the colony in neighboring Martinique; for the next century and a half, ownership was disputed hotly between France and England.

The English, with their headquarters in Barbados, and the French, centered on Martinique, found Saint Lucia even more attractive when the sugar industry developed in 1765. By 1780, almost fifty sugarcane estates had been established on the island; heavy labor needs of the estates led to large scale importation of slaves from West Africa.

A 1924 constitution gave the island its first form of representative government. As an associated state of the United Kingdom from 1967 to 1979, Saint Lucia had full responsibility for internal self-government, but left its external affairs and defense responsibilities to Great Britain. This interim arrangement ended on February 22, 1979, when Saint Lucia achieved full independence.

Saint Lucia is now inhabited mainly by people of African and mixed African-European descent, with small Caucasian and East Indian minorities.

### Saint Vincent and the Grenadines

Independence: October 27, 1979
Population: (1992 estimate) 115,339
Ethnic division: Black African, white, East
    Indian, Carib Indian
Religious groups: Anglican, Methodist,
    Roman Catholic, Seventh-Day Adventist
Languages spoken: English, French patois

Saint Vincent and the Grenadine islands began as a British territory during the eighteenth century. The islands were granted full autonomy in 1969 and attained full independence in 1979.

### Suriname

Official name: Republic of Suriname
Independence: November 25, 1975
Area: 63,037 sq. mi.
Population: (1991 estimate) 402,000
Ethnic divisions: Hindustani (East Indian)
    37%, Creole 31%, Javanese 15%, Bush
    Negro 10%, Amerindians 3%, Chinese 1.7%
Religious groups: Hindu, Muslim, Roman
    Catholic, Dutch Reformed, Moravian and
    several other Christian groups
Languages spoken: Dutch (official) English,
    Sranang Tongo (a Creole language),
    Hindustani, Javanese

Columbus first sighted the Suriname coast in 1498; Spain claimed the area in 1593.

Suriname became a Dutch colony in 1667. However, the new colony, Dutch Guiana did not thrive. The colony experienced frequent uprisings by the slave population, which was often treated with extraordinary cruelty. Many of the slaves fled to the interior, where they resumed a West African culture and established the five major Bush Negro tribes in existence today: the Djuka, Saramaccaner, Matuwari, Paramaccaner, and Quinti.

Beginning in 1951, Suriname began to acquire an increasing measure of autonomy

A statue of former Surinamese President John Adolf Pengel.

from the Netherlands. On December 15, 1954, Suriname became an autonomous part of the Kingdom of the Netherlands and gained independence on November 25, 1975.

### Trinidad and Tobago

Official name: Republic of Trinidad and
    Tobago
Independence: August 31, 1962
Area: 1,980 sq. mi.
Population: (1988) 1,279,920
Ethnic divisions: (1988): African 43%, East
    Indian 40%, mixed 14%
Religious groups: Roman Catholic 32,9%,
    Hindu 25.0%, Anglican 14.7%, other
    Christian denominations 14.3%, Muslim
    5.9%
Languages spoken: English

The island of Trinidad was first visited by Columbus in 1498 on his third voyage to the Western Hemisphere. The Spanish made the first successful attempt to colonize Trinidad in 1592. Trinidad continued under Spanish rule until it was captured by the British in 1797.

Africans were brought to the islands during the eighteenth century to provide labor on the sugar cane plantations. Following the abolition of slavery, Indian and Chinese labor was brought in.

Trinidad was ceded formally to the United Kingdom in 1802; the island of Tobago was ceded to the United Kingdom in 1814. In 1888, Trinidad and Tobago merged to form a single colony. In 1958, the United Kingdom established the autonomous Federation of the West Indies. Jamaica withdrew in 1961, and when Trinidad and Tobago followed, the federation collapsed. Trinidad and Tobago obtained full independence and joined the Commonwealth in 1962.

## Turks and Caicos Islands
Independence: n/a (dependent territory of the United Kingdom)
Area: 430 sq. km.
Population: (1992 estimate) 12,697
Ethnic divisions: Black African
Religious groups: Baptist 41.2%, Methodist 18.9%, Anglican 18.3%, Seventh-Day Adventist 1.7%
Languages spoken: English (official)

Between 1874 and 1959, the Turks and Caicos islands were administered as a dependency of Jamaica. In 1962, the islands became a separate colony.

## Uruguay
Official name: Oriental Republic of Uruguay

Blacks comprise a very small percentage of Uruguay's population.

## Venezuela
Official name: Republic of Venezuela
Independence: July 5, 1821
Area: 352,143 sq. mi.
Population: (1991 estimate) 20.1 million.
Ethnic divisions: Spanish, Italian, Portuguese, Amerindian, black African
Religious groups: Roman Catholic 96%
Languages spoken: Spanish (official), Indian dialects

About 900,000 of Venezuela's seventeen million people are black and another 500,000 are Zambos. In the sixteenth and seventeenth centuries, Caracas was a major center for the import of slaves. In the early nineteenth century, blacks and mulattoes comprised more than half of the population of The Captaincy General of Caracas, as Venezuela was then known. Blacks remain a significant part of the country because of its proximity to the Caribbean and employment opportunities that have been available in this oil-rich nation.

## Virgin Islands, British
Independence: n/a (dependent territory of the United Kingdom)
Area: 150 sq. km.
Population: (1992 estimate) 12,555
Ethnic divisions: Black African 90%, remainder white and Asian
Religious groups: Protestant 86%, 21%, Roman Catholic 6%, Seventh-Day Adventist 5%, Jehovah's Witness 2%
Languages spoken: English (official)

First visited by Christopher Columbus in 1493, the Virgin Islands (an archipelago of seventy-four islands) is now divided into two distinct clusters—the British Virgin Islands (six main islands, nearly forty islets) and the United States Virgin Islands (three main islands, sixty-five islets). Great Britain obtained title to the islands and islets in 1666 and, until 1960, administered them as part of the Leeward Islands. At present, the government is headed by a Crown-appointed administrator who is assisted by both executive and legislative councils. Almost the entire population is of African descent.

## Virgin Islands, United States

Independence: n/a (territory of the United
   States)
Area: 352 sq. km.
Population: (1992 estimate) 98,942
Ethnic divisions: Black African
Religious groups: Baptist, 42%, Roman
   Catholic 34%, Episcopalian 17%, other 7%
Languages spoken: English (official),
   Spanish, Creole

The United States Virgin Islands—the largest of which are the islands of Saint Croix, Saint John, and Saint Thomas—were originally settled by the Danish West India Company. Saint Thomas was the first to be colonized in 1672; in 1683 Saint John was colonized; and by 1733, Saint Croix had been acquired from France. Some twenty years later, the holdings of this company were taken over by the Danish crown, which then reconstituted them as the Danish West Indies.

The United States bought the territory from Denmark in 1917 for some $25 million and granted citizenship to its inhabitants ten years later. In 1931, its administration was transferred from the United States Navy to the Department of the Interior. The first black governor, William H. Hastie, was appointed in 1946.

Under the terms of the constitution, the United States retains the authority to introduce and enact legislation to govern the territory. The courts are also controlled by the United States, with an American district judge serving as the territory's highest judicial officer. Pursuant to a bill passed by Congress in 1968, the governor of the island is elected, rather than appointed. In 1972, the Virgin Islands were granted the right to send one nonvoting delegate to the House of Representatives. Island residents enjoy the same rights as mainlanders with the exception that they may not vote in a presidential election.

# 6

# *Africans in America: 1600 to 1900*

# 6

# Africans in America: 1600 to 1900

Exploration and the First Settlements in the Americas ■ Slavery in Colonial America: 1619–1787 ■ African-American Status in the New Republic ■ Expansion of Slavery ■ Anti-Slavery Movements ■ The Compromise of 1850 ■ Civil War ■ Reconstruction ■ African-American Status after Reconstruction

## ■ EXPLORATION AND THE FIRST SETTLEMENTS IN THE AMERICAS

The presence of the first African Americans in the Americas is a point of contention among historians. Some scholars assert that Africans established contact with the Americas prior to the Europeans, arguing from archeological, anthropological, botanical, and linguistic evidence that Africans were present in pre-Columbian America; the work of Ivan Van Sertima is notable in this regard. Others mark the advent of the African presence as coinciding with the presence of the Europeans. Pedro Alonzo Niño, an explorer and companion to Christopher Columbus on his exploratory journey of 1492, appears to have been of African extraction; and it is known that an African named Estevanico accompanied the Spanish explorers Panfilo de Narvaez and Alvar Nuñez Cabeza de Vaca on trips throughout the American southwest during the 1500s. Several other European explorers, including Vasco Nuñez de Balboa

and Hernán Cortés, also had African members in their parties.

In 1496 Santo Domingo was established as the first permanent European settlement in the Americas. Indigenous Carib Indians were at first used as laborers; however, they were ill suited to the rigors of the European system of slavery and died in large numbers from either disease or the constant pressure of forced labor. Portuguese explorers first visited the west coast of Africa in the fifteenth century and found that slave trading was an established institution. West Africans had for some time sold each other to Arabic traders from North Africa. By the early sixteenth century the Portuguese and Spanish were supplying newly established colonies in the Americas with African slave labor, and by the seventeenth century several other European nations had entered the trade. African slaves proved to be a relatively cheap and inexhaustible source of labor, and from about 1501 they were increasingly used as slaves, replacing the dwindling Indian labor pool.

## ■ SLAVERY IN COLONIAL AMERICA: 1619–1787

### The Emergence of Slave Status

Twenty Africans accompanied the Europeans who landed at Jamestown, Virginia, in 1619. These people were not slaves but indentured servants, and upon completing their contracts they were free to enjoy the liberties and privileges of the "free laboring class." By 1650 there were about three hundred Africans in the American colonies, most of whom were indentured servants and some of whom eventually became property holders and active citizens. The first African American born in the colonies, William Tucker, shared with the other settlers the common birthright of freedom. The slave Anthony Johnson apparently became free about 1622 and had by 1651 amassed enough wealth to import five servants of his own, for which he obtained two hundred and fifty acres from the colonial government; the African American carpenter Richard Johnson imported two white servants in 1654 and received one hundred acres.

It is unclear when the first African slaves arrived in the North American colonies. From the 1640s Africans were increasingly regarded as chattel (or persons regarded as fixed items of personal property). In 1641 Massachusetts became the first state to make perpetual bondage legal, and the institution gradually spread among the original thirteen colonies. Rhode Island had an anti-slavery ordinance, but this was openly violated, and only Pennsylvania maintained a sustained opposition to slavery. By the 1650s Africans were commonly sold for life, and in 1661 the Virginia House of Burgesses formally recognized the institution of black slavery. The erosion of African indentured servitude in Maryland was finalized with the slave law of 1663, which stated specifically that "All negroes or other slaves within the

Early map of Virginia.

province, [and] all negroes to be hereafter imported, shall serve *durante vita.*"

As white indentured servitude gradually disappeared from the colonial labor market, the flow of African labor into the colonies was accelerated, and planters rigidly institutionalized the perpetual servitude of Africans. One practical reason for this system was that slaves of African origin could be more easily detected than whites should they escape. And among the common rationalizations for the enslavement of Africans was reference to their non-Christian status; it was asserted that Africans were primitive and savage, and fit for nothing better than a life of unbroken labor. Even after African Americans became Christianized, their slave status was not altered; in 1667 the Virginia legislature enacted a statute which proclaimed that "baptism doth not alter the con-

dition of the person as to his bondage or freedom."

### The Trans-Atlantic Slave Trade

The Dutch West India Company began to provide slave labor to the American colonies in 1621. By the late seventeenth century the Royal African Company, an English company whose most profitable commodity was slaves, began to exert powerful influence within the English court and parliament. The British government in turn exerted great pressure upon the American colonies to develop attitudes and laws which would support a slave economy. The influence of the Royal African Company contributed to William Penn's decision to overrule the objections of fellow Quakers and permit slavery in Pennsylvania. The company also drew the shipping industry of New England into the slave trade. By the time the Royal African Company lost its monopoly on the West African slave trade in 1696, the sea captains of New England were participating in the massive slave incursions into Africa.

The majority of Africans who were transported to the Americas as slaves came from the area comprising the modern nations of Senegal, Gambia, Guinea, Sierra Leone, Liberia, Upper Volta, Ivory Coast, Ghana, Togo, Benin, Nigeria, Cameroon, Gabon, the Congo Republic, and the Republic of the Congo. The number of Africans who reached the Americas is estimated at between ten and twenty million. About six hundred thousand Africans were brought during the sixteenth century, two million in the seventeenth century, five million in the eighteenth century; and three million in the nineteenth century. In addition to those who reached the Americas must be added the enormous number who died in passage. It is estimated that 15 percent of those who were shipped to the Americas died of disease on

A group of African slaves disembark in America.

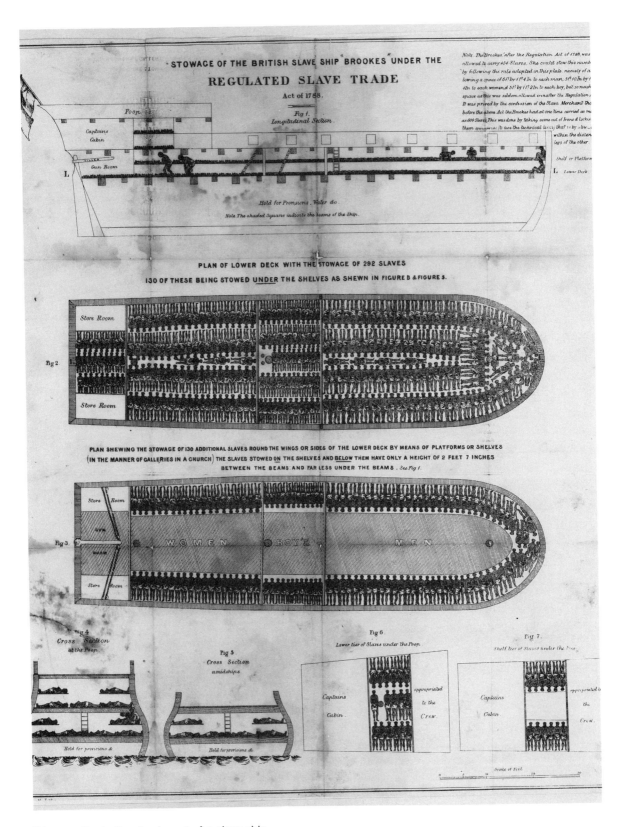

Diagram illustrating the layout of a slave ship.

the overcrowded boats of the "Middle Passage," and that another 30 percent died during the brutal training period faced in the West Indies before shipment to the American mainland.

## The Growth of Slavery in Colonial America

The colonies of New England played a principal role in the slave trade, despite their having little local need for slave labor. By 1700 African Americans of New England numbered only one thousand among a population of ninety thousand. In the mid-Atlantic colonies the population comprised a larger percentage, as small slaveholdings employed slaves as farm laborers, domestics, and craftsmen. In New York slaves comprised 12 percent of the population during the mid eighteenth century. The Quakers

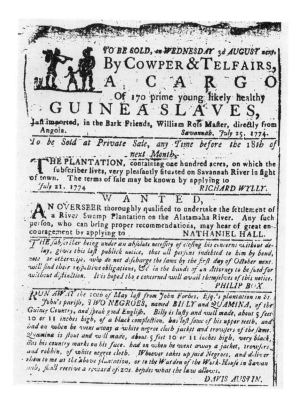

Poster advertising a slave sale.

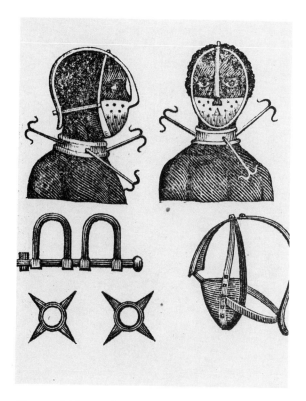

Slave catching and trading apparatuses.

of Pennsylvania protested that slavery violated the principles of Christianity and the rights of man, and passed laws prohibiting the slave trade in 1688, 1693, and 1696, but the British parliament overruled these statutes in 1712. Most slaves lived in the South. The southern colonies were divided between the tobacco producing provinces of Virginia, Maryland, and North Carolina, and the huge rice and indigo plantations now comprising Carolina and Georgia. Tobacco tended to be grown on family farms around the Chesapeake Bay area, and because of this the slave population was not as concentrated as it was on the plantations further to the south.

The growth of a plantation economy and the concentration of a large number of African Americans in the southern states led first Virginia (1636) and then the other states to form all white militias. The terror of slave uprisings led the slaveholders to institute ever harsher slave codes. Ultimately, a slave could not own anything, carry a weapon, or even leave his plantation without a written pass. Murder, rape, arson, and even lesser offenses were punishable by death; small offenses were commonly punished by whipping, maiming, and branding. In the area where 90 percent of colonial African Americans lived, a slave had no rights to defend himself against a white, and as far north as Virginia it was impossible for a white to be convicted for the murder of a slave.

The large slave revolt in New York City in 1712 and the public paranoia over the alleged slave conspiracy of 1741 led to the development of slave codes which were in some cases as severe as those in the South, but in general the North was a relatively less oppressive environment. In Pennsylvania the Quakers allowed African Americans a relative degree of freedom, and in New England the slave codes tended to reflect Old Testament law, maintaining the legal status of slaves as persons with certain limited rights.

### African-American Military Service before and during the Revolutionary War

Records of King William's War (1689–1697) relate that the first to fall in Massachusetts was "an Naygro of Colo. Tyng," slain at Falmouth. During Queen Anne's War (1702–1713), African Americans were drafted and sent to fight the French and the Indians when white colonists failed to provide the number of requisitioned men. Many armed African Americans fought at Fort William Henry in New York. Slaves sought freedom as their payment for fighting, and those who were already free sought the wider benefits of land and cash payments. The colony of Virginia ended its policy of excluding African Americans from the militia by 1723, and

in 1747 the South Carolina Company made slaves eligible for enlistment in the territorial militia according to a quota system in which a 3:1 ratio was maintained between whites and blacks, thus abating the white's fears of insurrection. African Americans also fought for the British in the French and Indian War.

### African-American Patriots

In the years leading up to the Revolutionary War it became apparent that, despite the growth of slavery, at least some African Americans were willing to fight alongside white Americans. On 5 March 1770 an African American named Crispus Attucks was one of the first men killed in the Revolutionary War, when British troops fired on a crowd of protesters in the Boston Massacre.

Crispus Attucks

Many African-American Minutemen fought at the defense of Concord Bridge: among them were Lemuel Haynes, a gifted speaker and later a prominent Congregationalist minister, and Peter Salem, who had received his freedom to enlist. Other figures of the Revolutionary War include Pomp Blackman, Caesar Ferrit and his son John, Prince Estabrook (who was wounded at Lexington), Samuel Craft, and Primas Black and Epheram Blackman (who were members of Ethan Allen's Green Mountain Boys).

### The Move to Disarm African Americans

A major issue during the Revolutionary War was whether African-American slaves, and even freemen, should be permitted to bear arms. On 29 May 1775 the Massachusetts Committee of Safety, in a move which reflected their desire to strengthen ties with southern states, proclaimed that the enlistment of slaves "was inconsistent with the principles that are to be supported, and reflect[ed] dishonor on the colony." On 9 July 1775 Horatio Gates, the adjutant general of the Continental Army, issued from General Washington's headquarters the order that recruiting officers should not accept "any stroller, Negro, or vagabond."

The enormous slave populations of certain southern states meant that many whites lived in perpetual fear of slave uprisings. In South Carolina slaves outnumbered whites, and in Georgia the population was above 40 percent slaves. To minimize the risk of slaves arming themselves, Edward Rutledge of South Carolina introduced a measure in Congress to discharge all African Americans (whether free or enslaved) from the Continental Army. Although the proposal was rejected, General George Washington's own council of war decided to terminate all African-American enlistment two weeks later, and on 13 October 1775 Congress passed the

law. Colonial generals like John Thomas argued that African Americans soldiered as well as whites and had already "proved themselves brave" in action, but their protests went unheeded. At the close of 1775 it was extremely difficult for African Americans to join the revolutionary forces at any level.

As the leaders of the Revolution realized that there were inadequate numbers of white troops, they brought an end to their racially exclusionary policy. Local militias which were unable to fill their muster rolls won the quiet agreement of recruiting boards and the reluctant acceptance of slave owners as slaves were substituted for those white men who bought their way out of service. As the war progressed slaveowners were compensated for the enlistment of slaves who were then made free. During the course of the Revolution many colonies granted freedom to slaves in return for military service. Rhode Island passed the first slave enlistment act on 2 February 1778, raising a regiment that participated gallantly in many important battles. In 1780 Maryland became the only southern state to enroll slave troops, while South Carolina and Georgia refused altogether to even arm their slaves. While slave conscripts were at first assigned to combat support, in the heat of battle they were often armed. African Americans were often enlisted for longer terms than whites, and by the latter years of the war many of the most seasoned veterans were African American troops.

### ■ AFRICAN-AMERICAN STATUS IN THE NEW REPUBLIC

#### Slaves and Freemen After the Revolution

At the end of the war about five thousand African Americans had been emancipated through military service. In the following

| Year | Total | North | South |
|------|-------|-------|-------|
| 1630 | 60 | 10 | 50 |
| 1640 | 597 | 427 | 170 |
| 1650 | 1,600 | 880 | 720 |
| 1660 | 2,920 | 1,162 | 1,758 |
| 1670 | 4,535 | 1,125 | 3,410 |
| 1680 | 6,971 | 1,895 | 5,076 |
| 1690 | 16,729 | 3,340 | 13,389 |
| 1700 | 27,817 | 5,206 | 22,611 |
| 1710 | 44,866 | 8,303 | 36,563 |
| 1720 | 68,839 | 14,091 | 54,748 |
| 1730 | 91,021 | 17,323 | 73,698 |
| 1740 | 150,024 | 23,958 | 126,066 |
| 1750 | 236,420 | 30,222 | 206,198 |
| 1760 | 325,806 | 40,033 | 285,773 |
| 1770 | 459,822 | 48,460 | 411,362 |
| 1780 | 575,420 | 56,796 | 518,624 |

The Slave Population: 1630 to 1780.

years the northern states abolished slavery: Vermont in 1777, Massachusetts in 1783, Connecticut and Rhode Island in 1784, New York in 1785, New Jersey in 1786, and Pennsylvania in 1789. In the mid-Atlantic state of Virginia, Thomas Jefferson convinced the state legislature to allow slaveowners to manumit their slaves in 1783. In 1790 there were 757,208 African Americans comprising 19 percent of the population of the United States: 697,681 were slave, and 59,527 were free. During this time the free population faced many of the same restrictions as the slave population: they could not walk on the streets after dark, travel between towns without a pass, or own weapons. There was also the danger of being captured and enslaved, whether one was free or not.

## The United States Constitution

The United States Constitution, drafted in 1787 and ratified in 1788, provided fundamental political principles for the nation. Key among these principles were the belief that all people share a fundamental equality, that they possess certain unalienable rights, and that government derives its power from the people. But African Americans were not afforded the rights and privileges of the Constitution. At the time, it was generally believed by whites that people of African descent were racially inferior and incapable of being assimilated into society. It was also widely believed that they were not citizens of the new republic. Article I, section 2 of the Constitution specifies that all persons who are not free shall be counted as three-fifths a person for the sake of tax purposes, and article I, section 9 authorizes the continued importation of slaves until 1808.

## Slavery in the New Nation

In 1793 Eli Whitney invented the cotton gin, which separated cotton from cotton fiber, led to a subsequent increase in the consumption of cotton, and heightened the demand for slaves in the cotton producing states. In 1800 there were more than 893,600 African slaves in the United States; by 1810 there were 1,191,300. Although the slave trade was technically discontinued in 1808, it is estimated that from that date until 1860 more than 250,000 slaves were illegally imported; furthermore, nothing prohibited slaves from being bartered, and the breeding of slaves for sale became a specialized business. Some of the largest slave trading firms in the nation were located in Maryland, Virginia, and the District of Columbia. Such was the expansion of slavery that, between 1800 and 1859, the population of Mississippi

Engraving depicting slaves cultivating cotton.

grew from 3489 slaves and 5179 whites to 309,878 slaves and 295,718 whites.

By the mid-eighteenth century, three-fourths of the cotton produced in the world came from the United States, and profits from cotton were so great that vast plantations were hacked from the wilderness, allowing armies of slaves to work the fields. By mid-century the states of Georgia, Alabama, Mississippi, and Louisiana annually produced 1,726,349 bales of cotton, forty-eight million pounds of rice, and 226,098,000 pounds of sugar. With the outbreak of the Civil War there were nearly four million slaves in the United States, and nearly three-fourths of them worked in cotton agriculture.

## Slave Life

Slavery was by its very nature a brutal and exploitative business, and the average slave lived a terribly grim life. The more fortunate slaves tended to work on family sized farms or had positions as house servants. Whatever one's surroundings, much of one's fortune depended on the kindness of the master. On the larger plantations slaves were divided between house and field hands. The former group was charged with such

Slaves outside their quarters.

assorted tasks as caring for the grounds and garden of the house, maintenance of the rigs and appliances, house cleaning, and caring for the master's children. House servants were frequently allowed to practice trades such as smithery, masonry, and tailoring, some becoming skilled musicians, and some even becoming doctors. Body slaves served their masters as valets and personal messengers, and from this intimacy real friendships sometimes developed.

But house servants were in a sense aristocrats among slaves. Their daily lives had little in common with those of the faceless masses of field hands who confronted the brutal monotony of sowing and reaping without respite or prospect of change. On larger plantations with twenty-five or more slaves, the only contact between field hands and whites occurred through the overseer, who often employed cruel and vicious brutality to maintain control. Many planters felt that the largest profits were made by working a slave to death in eight or ten years and then buying a new one. Even tenderhearted masters often had little contact with their field workers, and so long as the overseer returned a profit no questions were asked. In many places slaves were given no free time at all, but were forced to work fourteen or fifteen hours a day. Louisiana was the only state with a law regarding the amount of work that could be demanded of a slave; the law permitted a slave to be worked twenty-one hours every day.

Most slaves could only expect to live with the bare necessities of shelter, clothing, and food. Shelter often consisted of a cramped, windowless, mud-floored shack in which a large family was expected to live; clothing was basic in design and made of course materials; and food was often limited to a bucket of rice or corn per week with no meat. The only break in the routine occurred on holidays such as Christmas, though in some cases slaves were able to hunt, fish, or garden in the hours after work.

Slaves working on a cotton plantation.

### The Denmark Vesey Conspiracy

The mistreatment of slaves in the years after the Revolution led to an atmosphere of suspicion and terror. Masters lived in constant fear of uprisings, and much time was given over to surveillance. Although organized rebellions were rare, there were many instances of angry slaves burning dwellings and murdering their masters. Slave codes became increasingly strict, but no amount of regulation could dissipate the anger of the slaves, nor the guilt and unease which many slave owners experienced.

In 1800 an African American named Denmark Vesey purchased his freedom and from about 1817 planned a slave revolt in Charleston, South Carolina. The revolt was scheduled to begin on 14 July 1822. With the help of five other African Americans as many as nine thousand slaves were re-

Fieldworkers returning from the fields.

cruited before their plans were uncovered. As word of the revolt began to leak out, Vesey was forced to move the date forward to 16 June; again word was leaked. The state militia was mustered, and an intense investigation of the plot was begun. One hundred and thirty-five slaves were arrested during the course of the investigation; ninety-seven were bound over for trial; forty-five were transported out of the country; and Vesey and thirty-four others were hanged. As news of the conspiracy spread, southern states further tightened their slave codes.

## ■ EXPANSION OF SLAVERY

### Slavery in the Northwest Territory

In the early seventeenth century the French began to settle in what comprises present-day Illinois, Indiana, Michigan, Ohio, and Wisconsin, and part of Minnesota. The British began to settle in the area during the mid-eighteenth century; and in July 1787 Congress passed the Northwest Ordinance, which established a government for the Northwest Territory and provided terms under which states could be formed for entrance into the Union. The ordinance also contained controversial provisions: one prohibited slavery and involuntary servitude in the territory, and the other provided for the return of fugitive slaves to the states from which they had escaped. The European farmers who had brought slaves into the territory were angered by the clause prohibiting slavery and Congress was petitioned for its repeal. The prohibition against slavery was practically circumvented when the Illinois and Indiana territories established a system of indentured servitude under which any person owning slaves could bring them into the region and place them under lifetime indenture. The restrictions placed on these servants were much like the slave codes of the southern colonies—indentured servants could not travel alone without a pass or attend public gatherings independently.

### The Missouri Compromise

In April 1803 the United States paid $15 million for the Louisiana Territory, an area comprising the entire Mississippi drainage basin, which had been settled by the French in the late seventeenth century. Many southerners hoped to extend slavery into the vast new territory, and it was widely expected that Missouri would be admitted to the Union as a slave state. A series of heated debates erupted over the extension of slavery in the region, and in 1819 the House of Representatives introduced legislation authorizing statehood for Missouri while prohibiting the further introduction of slavery into the new state. This drew angry protest from proslavery supporters. The controversy was further escalated by two events: Alabama was admitted to the Union as a slave state in 1819, making the total number of slave and free states equal, and Maine applied for statehood in 1820. In 1820–1821 the Missouri Compromise was reached, admitting Missouri to the Union as a slave state with a slave population of almost 10,000, and Maine as a free state, with the understanding that the future expansion of slavery would be prohibited above the latitude of 36°33′N.

### Texas and the Mexican-American War

The territory comprising Texas was part of the Louisiana Territory when the United States purchased it in 1803, but by 1819 it had become part of Mexico. Mexico provided land grants to American settlers (many of whom brought their slaves with them), and soon Americans outnumbered

The United States c. 1821.

the Mexicans of the region. In 1836 Texas declared its independence from Mexico and requested annexation to the United States. The possibility of another slave state entering the Union stirred fresh debate. On 1 March 1845 President John Tyler signed the joint resolution of Congress to admit Texas as a slave state; the voters of Texas supported the action, and Texas became a slave state on 29 December 1845. In 1846 Mexican and American troops clashed in Texas, and the United States declared war on the Republic of Mexico. The war ended in 1848, with Mexico relinquishing its claims to Texas, and with the United States having acquired all of the region extending to the Pacific Ocean.

### The Wilmot Proviso

In 1846 David Wilmot, a Democrat from Pennsylvania, introduced an amendment to a bill appropriating $2 million for President James Polk to use in negotiating a territorial settlement with Mexico; the amendment stipulated that none of the newly acquired land would be open to slavery. Although the amendment received strong support from northern Democrats and was passed by the House of Representatives, the Senate adjourned without voting on it. During the next session of Congress a new bill providing $3 million for territorial settlement was introduced. Wilmot again proposed an amendment prohibiting the expansion of slavery into the newly acquired territory. The bill was passed by the House of Representatives, but the Senate drew up a new bill excluding the Wilmot proviso.

### Fugitive Slave Laws

Tensions between northern and southern politicians continued to mount over the issue of fugitive slaves. Article IV, Section 2 of the Constitution authorized the return of fugitive slaves and provided procedures for recovery, and in 1793 the Fugitive Slave Act was passed. In northern states that strongly opposed slavery, "personal liberty" laws were passed in order to undermine federal law; liberty laws placed the burden of proof on masters in cases concerning alleged fugitive slaves. Such a law was enacted in Pennsylvania in 1826, requiring state certification before alleged fugitives could be returned. When Edward Prigg, a professional slave catcher, attempted to capture a fugitive slave residing in the state, he was arrested on kidnapping charges for failing to acquire necessary certification. The Supreme Court ruled in *Prigg v. Pennsylvania* (1842) that the state's law could not interfere with federal action regarding fugitives and the right of slaveholders to recover property; it also found that states would not be obligated to enforce federal fugitive slave statutes. This

Poster warning blacks of the ever present danger of slave catchers.

led abolitionists to seize upon the idea of not enforcing federal statutes. Following the court's decision several northern states enacted even more radical personal liberty laws prohibiting the enforcement of the Fugitive Slave Act.

## ■ ANTI-SLAVERY MOVEMENTS

### Quakers and Mennonites

The early opposition to slavery was generally based on religious beliefs; Christian ethics were seen as incompatible with slavery. Quakers (or the Society of Friends) and Mennonites were two of first groups to oppose the practice in the United States. Quakers and Mennonites settled mainly in Pennsylvania, though also in the South, and advocated simple living, modest dress, and nonviolence. In 1652 the Quakers passed a resolution against lifetime indenture, and in 1688 the Mennonites did the same. With the continued rise of slavery in the South, many Quakers protested and moved north into Indiana and Ohio.

### The Free African Society

In 1787 the Free African Society was organized in Philadelphia by two African Americans, the Reverends Richard Allen and Absalom Jones; Adams later founded the Bethel African Methodist Church, and Jones became the rector of a Protestant Episcopal Church. The society was an important model for political consciousness and economic organization for African Americans throughout the country. It provided economic and medical aid, advocated abolition, and maintained channels of communication with African Americans in the South. Like the many other African-American organizations that followed, the society was rooted in religious principles. Throughout the nineteenth century a number of mutual aid societies also sprung up in African-American communities of the eastern seaboard, providing loans, insurance, and various other economic and social services to their members and the larger community.

### The American Colonization Society

In 1816 the American Colonization Society was organized in Washington, DC, with the objective of encouraging the repatriation of African Americans to Africa. While the idea of returning free African Americans was motivated in part by humanitarian intent, the society was rather moderate in its

A photograph of the Pennsylvania Abolition Society.

A page from the *American Anti-Slavery Almanac*, 1840.

opposition to slavery. Support for the society came in part from those who feared the possibility of a large free African-American population in the United States.

Congress issued a charter to the society for the transportation of freed slaves to the west coast of Africa, provided funds, and assisted in negotiations with African chiefs who ceded the land that comprised what became Liberia. While northerners contributed support and donations to the society, southern patrols threatened freedmen into emigrating. In 1822 the first settlers landed at the site on the western coast of Africa which was later named Monrovia after President James Monroe. In 1838 the Commonwealth of Liberia was formed and placed under the administration of a governor appointed by the society.

## The Abolition Movement

The earliest abolition societies were the Pennsylvania Society for Promoting the Abolition of Slavery, formed in Philadelphia in 1775, and the New York Manumission Society, formed in the city in 1785. Prior to the 1830s a number of anti-slavery societies arose in both the North and the South, and during the 1830s and 1840s numerous abolitionist organizations arose alongside the women's rights organizations as part of the general social reform movement. The American Anti-Slavery Society was formed in Philadelphia in 1833, and after attending one of its meetings, the Quaker abolitionist Lucretia Coffin Mott formed the Philadelphia Female Anti-Slavery Society with the assistance of Elizabeth Cady Stanton. Mott and her husband, James, were active in the underground railroad and various other anti-slavery activities, and James served as a delegate to the World Anti-Slavery Convention.

The primary tool of the anti-slavery movement was the press. In 1827 the journalists Samuel Cornish and John Russwurm launched *Freedom's Journal*, the first African American owned and edited newspaper; in 1831 William Lloyd Garrison published the first issue of the *Liberator*; and other anti-slavery papers followed, including *Anti-Slavery Record*, the *Emancipator*, *Human Rights*, and the *North Star*, launched by Frederick Douglass.

While many of the anti-slavery organizations were dominated by whites, African-American leaders played an important role in the abolition movement. Some of the most notable leaders were Alexander Crummell, Frederick Douglass, Sarah Mapp Douglass, Charlotte Forten, Henry Highland Garnet, Sojourner Truth, and David Walker. Most of these leaders were committed to cooperative relations with whites and op-

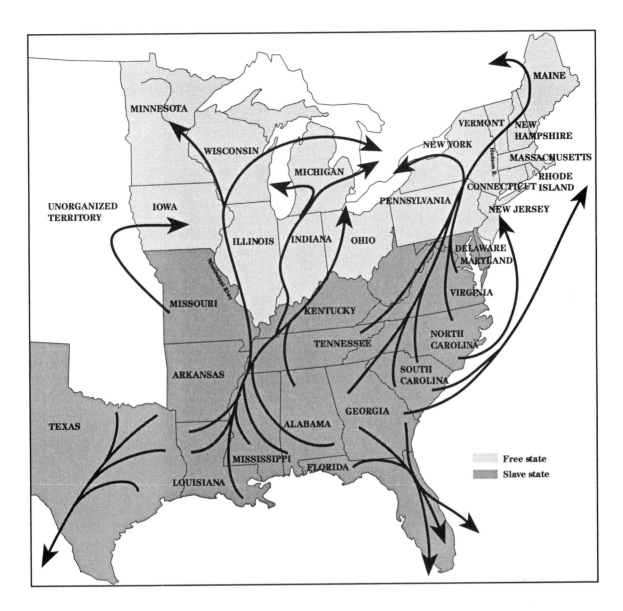

Underground Railroad Routes.

posed separatist doctrines, while some of the more militant abolitionists (like Garnet and Walker) stressed the conditional necessity of violence in the struggle against slavery.

In the South the activities of the abolition movement only hardened the resolve of the slaveholding class to maintain the system of slavery. Depending on the circumstances, southern justification of slavery continued along several lines: it was an economic necessity, a means of converting African pagans to Christianity, and a means of controlling an inferior race.

### The Underground Railroad

A vast network of individuals and groups developed throughout the country to assist African Americans in escaping from slavery.

Abolitionists provided "stations," food, shelter, and financial assistance, while experienced "conductors," who were often themselves runaway slaves, led thousands of "passengers" to freedom in the North, Canada, and the Caribbean. Most of the movement occurred at night, with passengers hiding in the barns and homes of sympathetic whites and African Americans during the day. Two of the most famous conductors were Josiah Henson and Harriet Tubman.

### Nat Turner

In February 1831 Nat Turner, a slave in Southampton County, Virginia, began to plan a slave revolt, and on 22 August Turner and his co-conspirators killed Turner's master and family. Within twenty-four hours about sixty whites in the county had been killed. Turner was captured on 30 October and hanged on 11 November. The incident contributed to the increasing paranoia of southern society.

### The Free Labor and Free Soil Movements

Radical Democrats and members of the Whig party who opposed slavery united to form a new political party in Buffalo, New York, in 1848. The party adopted a platform supporting free labor and free soil in response to feelings among northerners that slavery restricted the freedom of northern workers to contract for work and should therefore be excluded from the developing

Slaves believed to have used the Underground Railroad to escape the South.

The United States c. 1850.

regions of the West. Southerners wanted the freedom to expand westward and take their slaves with them. Senator John C. Calhoun of South Carolina and other southern delegates maintained that both Congress and the territorial legislatures lacked the authority to restrict the expansion of slavery into the territories. The control of northern states over the national government led these men to consider secession from the Union.

## ■ THE COMPROMISE OF 1850

As the debate over the admission of new western states continued, southerners argued that the South should be given guarantees of equal positioning in the territories. In 1850 Senator Henry Clay proposed a compromise in which California would be admitted as a free state, the new territories of New Mexico and Utah would be organized, slavery would be abolished in the District of

351

Columbia, more forceful fugitive slave legislation would be enacted, and the Texas war debt would be resolved. At the time the compromise was hailed by many as the solution to the debate over slavery.

### Dred Scott v. Sandford

The slavery debate presented supporters and opponents of the institution with two very important questions: how should fugitives from slavery be treated in jurisdictions where slavery was illegal, and should a slave brought into a free state by his master be viewed as free? The first question was partially addressed by Article IV, Section 2 of the Constitution and by the Fugitive Slave Acts of 1793 and 1850; however the second question had not as yet been addressed. During the 1830s and 1840s a slave by the name of Dred Scott accompanied his master, a surgeon in the U.S. Army on numerous trips to military posts around the country, including the free states of Illinois and the territory of Wisconsin. In 1846 Scott sued his master for his freedom, asserting that his sojourns in free jurisdictions made him free. After numerous delays, trials, and retrials, the case reached the Supreme Court in 1856. The court responded with nine separate opinions, and Chief Justice Roger Brook Taney delivered the deciding opinion. The ruling was both complex and controversial: the Missouri Compromise of 1820 was ruled unconstitutional on the grounds that Congress did not have authority to limit the expansion of slavery; slavery was found to be legal in the territories until the citizens voted for or against it; and Africans and their descendants were found to be ineligible for citizenship in the United States as the framers of the Constitution had not viewed Africans as citizens. Since African Americans were not viewed by the court as citizens, they could not file suit. Despite the finality of the court's

decision, the issue of slavery remained unresolved.

### John Brown and Harpers Ferry

On 16 October 1859 a white, visionary abolitionist named John Brown led a band of twenty-one men (five of whom were African Americans) in the seizure of the federal arsenal at Harpers Ferry. After holding the site for several hours, Brown and his followers were captured by federal troops under the command of Robert E. Lee. Southerners were outraged by Brown's actions, interpreting them as symptomatic of a willingness among northerners to attempt the forcible overthrow of slavery. In December 1859 Brown was hanged alongside Dangerfield Newby, a runaway slave; John A. Copeland of Carolina; Sheridan Leary, a harness maker and freedman; and Shields Gree, a sailor from South Carolina.

### ■ CIVIL WAR

In 1860 Abraham Lincoln, a northern Republican, was elected president amid continuing polarization over the issue of slavery. Lincoln had voiced opposition to the expansion of slavery in the past, and with his election southerners became even more fearful of an ideological assault on state's rights and the abolition of slavery nationwide. In 1860 a delegation from South Carolina voted unanimously for the repeal of the state's 1788 ratification of the Constitution and the severing of all relations with the Union; Georgia, Florida, Alabama, Mississippi, Louisiana, and Texas soon followed. In February 1861 the seven states drew up a constitution and elected Jefferson Davis as president of the Confederate States of America. As northern leaders sought a means of preserving the nation, southern troops

Abraham Lincoln

seized federal installations, post offices, and customs houses, and in April 1861 Confederate forces took one of the last Union holds in the south, Fort Sumter in Charleston Harbor, South Carolina. Lincoln was forced to retaliate.

### African-American Soldiers in the Civil War

From the beginning of the war African Americans engaged in the fighting, although Lincoln at first refused to officially employ them in the Union army. By 1862 Lincoln concluded that the use of African-American soldiers was a necessity. An estimated 180,000 black soldiers served in the Union army and another 20,000 served in its navy. But not all of those African Americans who participated in the war fought on the Union side; although there are no accurate records

of how many fought for the south, the numbers grew as white southerners became more desperate.

Lincoln faced a dilemma in that if he issued an order of universal emancipation, as the abolitionists encouraged him to do, he risked alienating the border states that remained supportive of the Union: these were Delaware, Maryland, Kentucky, and Missouri. In a letter to Horace Greely, Lincoln stated:

> If I could save the Union without freeing any slave, I would do it; if I could save it by freeing all the slaves, I would do it; and if I could save it by freeing some and leaving others alone, I would also do that. What I do about slavery and the colored race, I do because I believe it helps save the Union. . . .

During the summer of 1862 Lincoln began to feel that the emancipation of the slaves would be necessary to realizing victory over the South, and on 1 January 1863 he issued the Emancipation Proclamation, freeing slaves in those states that had seceded from the Union. Because the proclamation did not apply to the areas under occupation by Union forces, 800,000 slaves remained unaffected by its provisions. He dared not alienate the slave owning states on the Union side, especially in light of the growing antipathy toward African Americans in many northern cities. In the Draft Riots of 13–16 July 1863 huge mobs of whites in New York City (angry over the provisions of the Conscription Act) attacked blacks and abolitionists, destroying property and viciously beating many to death.

The Civil War lasted from April 1861 to April 1865, and at the end more than 360,000 Union soldiers and 258,000 Confederate soldiers were dead. By the end of the war twenty-one African Americans had received the Medal of Honor, and indeterminate numbers of others had made sacrifices for the cause. On 18 December 1865 the Thirteenth Amendment of the Constitution was ratified, formally abolishing slavery in the United States.

## ■ RECONSTRUCTION

### Civil Rights and Reconstruction Acts

On 3 March 1865 Congress enacted the first of several acts, which set up and empowered the Bureau of Refugees, Freedmen and Abandoned Lands (or the Freedmen's Bureau). The organization provided former slaves with basic health and educational services, and administered land which had been abandoned during the war. In 1866 Congress passed the Civil Rights Act, in which a number of personal liberties were outlined, including the right to make contracts, sue or be sued, own and sell property, and receive the equal benefit of the law. The Reconstruction Act of 2 March 1867 outlined

Freed black migrants leaving the South.

the terms under which the southern states might re-enter the Union; one of these terms required the drafting of a new state constitution with the guarantee of voting rights for all races. President Andrew Johnson vetoed this bill, but radical Republicans in Congress

Engraving depicting freed blacks in North Carolina.

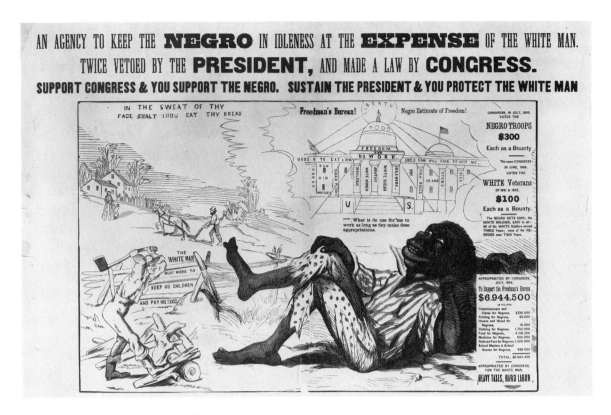

Poster mocking the Freedman's Bureau.

were able to muster the necessary two-thirds majority needed to override the veto.

## ■ AFRICAN-AMERICAN STATUS AFTER RECONSTRUCTION

### The Fourteenth and Fifteenth Amendments

On 23 July 1868 the Fourteenth Amendment was ratified, providing definitions of national and state citizenship, effectively overriding the Supreme Court's decision in *Dred Scott v. Sandford*, and providing for equal privileges of citizenship and protection of the law. On 30 March 1870 the Fifteenth Amendment was ratified to ensure the right to vote. But the amendment proved unsuccessful in its aims, as many state and local governments created voting regulations that ensured African Americans would

not vote: these included grandfather clauses, requiring that one's grandfather had voted; literacy tests; poll taxes; and "white primaries," which were held prior to general elections and permitted only whites to vote. In addition, southern states enacted many laws (known as black codes) which curbed the new rights of the freed slaves: South Carolina made it illegal for African Americans to possess firearms, and other states restricted their right to make and enforce contracts; to marry and intermarry; and even to assemble, "wander," or be "idle."

### The Civil Rights Act of 1875

In 1875 Congress attempted to establish a semblance of racial equality by enacting a law which made it illegal to deprive another person of the "full and equal enjoyment of the accommodations, advantages, facilities, and privileges of inns, public conveyance, . . . and other places of public amusement" on account of race. In a number of cases (known as the *Civil Rights Cases*) the Supreme Court ruled that the Fourteenth Amendment did not authorize Congress to legislate against discriminatory state action, while disregarding discrimination by private individuals, including the owners of hotels, theaters, and restaurants. This point led to an end of federal efforts to protect the civil rights of African Americans until the mid-twentieth century.

### Plessy v. Ferguson

In *Hall v. DeCuir* (1878) the Supreme Court decided that states could not outlaw segregation on common carriers such as streetcars and railroads, and in 1896 the Court again faced the issue of segregation on public transportation in the case of *Plessy v. Ferguson*. The case concerned Homer Adolph Plessy, an African American who was arrested for refusing to ride in the "colored" railway coach while traveling by train from New Orleans to Covington, Louisiana. The law in Louisiana required that "equal but separate" accommodations for blacks and whites be maintained in public facilities, but Plessy challenged this. Justice Billings Brown delivered the majority opinion that separate but equal accommodations constituted a reasonable use of state police power and that the Fourteenth Amendment could not have been an effort to abolish social or racial distinctions or to force a comingling of the races. In his dissenting opinion, Justice John Marshall Harlen remarked that,

A typical rural residence.

The judgement this day rendered will, in time, prove to be quite as pernicious as the decision made by this tribunal in the *Dred Scott* case. The thin disguise of equal accommodation for passengers in railroad coaches will not mislead anyone nor atone for the wrong this day done.

The ruling paved the way for the doctrine of separate but equal in all walks of life, and not until the case of *Brown v. Board of Education of Topeka* (1954) would the constitutionality of segregation be seriously challenged.

## ■ FIGURES OF THE PAST

### Crispus Attucks (c. 1723–1770)
*Revolutionary Patriot*

A runaway slave who lived in Boston, he was the first of five men killed on 5 March 1770 when British troops fired on a crowd of colonial protesters in the Boston Massacre. The most widely accepted account of the incident is that of John Adams, who said at the subsequent trial of the British soldiers that Attucks undertook "to be the hero of the night; and to lead this army with banners, to form them in the first place in Dock Square, and march them up to King Street with their clubs." When the crowd reached the soldiers it was Attucks who "had hardiness enough to fall in upon them, and with one hand took hold of a bayonet, and with the other knocked the man down." At that point the panicked soldiers fired, and in the echoes of their volley, five men lay dying; the seeds of the Revolution were sown. Attucks is remembered as "the first to defy, the first to die."

### Edward Wilmot Blyden (1832–1912)
*Black Nationalist, Repatriationist*

*See* Black Nationalism.

### Joseph Cinque (1811–1852)
*Leader of the* Amistad *Mutiny*

Purchased by Spaniards in Havana, Cuba, in 1839, he was placed aboard the *Amistad* bound for Puerto Principe. When the crew became exhausted from battling a storm, Cinque led the slaves in seizing the ship and killing all but two of the crew, who were kept alive to navigate a course back to Africa. The captive pilots headed north, against the slaves' knowledge, and when the ship was sighted off the coast of Long Island the slaves were taken to Connecticut and placed in prison. Abolitionists took up the cause of the men and enabled Cinque to raise funds for judicial appeals by speaking on their lecture circuit; his words were translated from Mendi, and he became known as an excellent speaker. In 1841 John Quincy Adams won the slaves' case, and they were released.

Joseph Cinque

### Alexander Crummell (1819–1898)
*Black Nationalist, Repatriationist, Minister*

*See* Black Nationalism.

### Paul Cuffe (1759–1817)
*Black Nationalist, Repatriationist,*
*Entrepreneur*

*See* Black Nationalism.

### Martin Robins Delany (1812–1885)
*Black Nationalist, Repatriationist*

*See* Black Nationalism.

### Frederick Douglass (c. 1817–1875)
*Abolitionist*

Born in Talbot County, Maryland, he was sent to Baltimore as a house servant at the age of eight, where his mistress taught him to read and write. Upon the death of his master he was sent to the country to work as a field hand. During his time in the South he was severely flogged for his resistance to slavery. In his early teens he began to teach in a Sunday school which was later forcibly shut down by hostile whites. After an unsuccessful attempt to escape from slavery, he succeeded in making his way to New York disguised as a sailor in 1838. He found work as a day laborer in New Bedford, Massachusetts, and after an extemporaneous speech before the Massachusetts Anti-Slavery Society became one of its agents.

Douglass quickly became a nationally recognized figure among abolitionists. In 1845 he bravely published his *Narrative of the Life of Frederick Douglass*, which related his experiences as a slave, revealed his fugitive status, and further exposed him to the danger of reenslavement. In the same year he went to England and Ireland, where he

Frederick Douglass

remained until 1847, speaking on slavery and women's rights, and ultimately raising sufficient funds to purchase his freedom. Upon returning to the United States he founded the *North Star*. In the tense years before the Civil War he was forced to flee to Canada when the governor of Virginia swore out a warrant for his arrest.

Douglass returned to the United States before the beginning of the Civil War, and after meeting with President Abraham Lincoln he assisted in the formation of the 54th and 55th Negro regiments of Massachusetts. During Reconstruction he became deeply involved in the civil rights movement, and in 1871 he was appointed to the territorial legislature of the District of Columbia. He served as one of the presidential electors-at-large for New York in 1872 and shortly thereafter became the secretary of the Santo Domingo Commission. After serving for a short time as the police commissioner of the District of Columbia, he was appointed marshall in 1871 and held the post until he was appointed the recorder of deeds in 1881. In 1890 his support of the presidential campaign of Benjamin Harrison won him his most important federal posts: he became minister resident and consul general to the Republic of Haiti and, later, the charge d'affaires of Santo Domingo. In 1891 he resigned the position in protest of the unscrupulous business practices of American businessmen. Douglass died at home in Washington, DC.

### James Forten (1766–1842)
*Black Nationalist, Entrepreneur*

*See* Black Nationalism.

### Lemuel Haynes (1753–1833)
*Revolutionary Soldier, Minister*

The son of a black father and white mother, he was deserted and brought up by Deacon David Rose of Granville, Massachusetts. He was a precocious child and began writing mature sermons while still a boy. His preparation for the ministry was interrupted by the American Revolution. On 19 April 1775 he fought in the first battle of the war at Lexington, Massachusetts; he then joined the regular forces and served with Ethan Allen's Green Mountain Boys at the capture of Fort Ticonderoga.

### Josiah Henson (1789–1883)
*Abolitionist*

Born a slave in Charles County, Maryland, he grew up with the experience of his family being cruelly treated by his master. By the time he was eighteen he was supervising the master's farm. In 1825 he and his wife and children were moved to Kentucky, where conditions were greatly improved, and in 1828 he became a preacher in a Methodist Episcopal Church. Under the threat of being sold, he and his family escaped to Ohio in 1830, and in the following year entered Canada by way of Buffalo, New York. In Canada he learned to read and write from one of his sons, and he soon began preaching in Dresden, Ontario.

While in Canada he became active in the underground railroad, helping nearly two hundred slaves to escape to freedom. In 1842 he and several others attempted to start the British-American Manual Labor Institute, but the industrial school proved unsuccessful. Henson related his story to Harriet Beecher Stowe (the author of *Uncle Tom's Cabin*), and it has been disputed whether or not her story is based in part on aspects of his life. He traveled to England three times, where he met distinguished people, was honored for his abolitionist ac-

Lemuel Haynes

tivities and personal escape from slavery, and was offered a number of positions which he turned down in order to return to Canada. He published his autobiography in 1849 and rewrote and reissued it in 1858 and 1879. Henson died in Ontario.

### James Armistead Lafayette (17?–?)
*Revolutionary Spy*

Born a slave, he risked his life behind enemy lines collecting information for the Continental Army. He furnished valuable information to the Marquis de Lafayette and enabled the French commander to check the troop advances of British General Cornwallis; this set the stage for General George Washington's victory at Yorktown in 1781 and for the end of the Revolutionary War. In recognition of his services, he was granted his freedom by the Virginia legislature in 1786, although it was not until 1819 that Virginia awarded him a pension of $40 a year and a grant of $100. He adopted the surname "Lafayette" in honor of his former commander, who visited him during a trip to the United States in 1824.

### Toussaint L'Ouverture (1743–1803)
*Haitian Revolutionary*

Born Francois Dominique Toussaint L'Ouverture, a slave on the island of Hispaniola (now Haiti and the Dominican Republic), he learned to read and write under a benevolent master. When he was fifty a violent revolt erupted on the island. White French planters, African slaves, and free mulattoes (some of whom owned slaves) clashed over issues of rights, land, and labor, as the forces of France, Britain, and Spain manipulated the conflict. At first the slaves and mulattoes shared the goals of the French revolution in opposition to the Royalist French planters, but with time a coali-

James Armistead Lafayette

tion of planters and mulattoes arose in opposition to the slaves.

Toussaint became the leader of the revolutionary slave forces, which by 1794 consisted of a disciplined group of four thousand mostly ex-slaves. He successfully waged various campaigns first against the French and then against the British, and was at the height of his power and influence when in 1796 General Rigaud (who led the mulatto forces) sought to re-impose slavery on the black islanders. He quickly achieved victory, captured Santo Domingo, and by 1801 had virtual control of the Spanish part of the island. In 1802 a French expeditionary force was sent to re-establish French control of the island. Toussaint was tricked, captured, and sent to France where he died on 7 April 1803 under inhumane conditions.

## Gabriel Prosser (c. 1775–1800)
*Leader of Slave Insurrection*

The coachman of Thomas Prosser of Henrico County, Virginia, he planned a large, highly organized revolt to take place on the last night of August 1800 around Richmond, Virginia. There were about 32,000 slaves and only eight thousand whites in the area, and it was his intention to kill all of the whites except for the French, Quakers, elderly women, and children. The ultimate goal was that the remaining 300,000 slaves in the state would follow his lead and seize the entire state. The revolt was set to coincide with the harvest so that his followers would be spared any shortage of food, and it was decided that the conspirators would meet at the Old Brook Swamp outside of Richmond and marshal forces to attack the city.

The insurrection fell apart when a severe rainstorm made it impossible for many of the slaves to assemble and a pair of house slaves who did not wish their master killed revealed the plot. Panic swept through the city, martial law was declared, and those suspected of involvement were rounded up and hanged; when it became clear that the slave population would be decimated if all of those implicated were dealt with in like fashion, the courts began to mete out less severe sentences. Prosser was apprehended in the hold of a schooner that docked in Norfolk, Virginia, and was brought back in chains, interrogated by the governor (though he refused to divulge details of the conspiracy), and hanged.

## Dred Scott (1795–1858)
*Litigator*

Born in Southhampton, Virginia, his first name was simply "Sam." He worked as a farmhand, handyman, and stevedore, and moved with his master to Huntsville, Alabama, and later to St. Louis, Missouri. In 1831 his owner, Peter Blow, died, and he was bought by John Emerson, a surgeon in the U.S. Army. Sam accompanied his new master to Illinois (a free state) and Wisconsin (a territory). Sometime after 1836 he received permission to marry, and by 1848 he had changed his name to Dred Scott. At various times he attempted to buy his freedom or escape but was unsuccessful. In 1843 Emerson died and left his estate to his widow Irene Emerson, who also refused Scott his freedom. He then obtained the assistance of two attorneys who helped him to sue for his freedom in county court.

Scott lost this case, but the verdict was set aside, and in 1847 he won a second trial on the grounds that his slave status had been nullified upon entering into a free state. Scott received financial backing and legal representation through the sons of Peter Blow, Irene Emerson's brother John Sanford, and her second husband Dr. C.C. Chaffee, all of whom apparently saw the case as an important challenge to slavery. In 1857 the United States Supreme Court ruled against Scott, stating that slaves were not legally citizens of the United States and therefore had no standing in the courts. Shortly after the decision was handed down Mrs. Emerson freed Scott. The case led to the nullification of the Missouri Compromise of 1820, allowing the expansion of slavery into formerly free territories, and strengthening the abolition movement.

## Sojourner Truth (c. 1797–1883)
*Abolitionist, Women's Rights Advocate*

Born Isabella Baumfree in Ulster County, New York, she was freed by the New York State Emancipation Act of 1827 and lived in New York City for a time. After taking the

Sojourner Truth

## Harriet (Ross) Tubman (1820–1913)
### *Underground Railroad Conductor and Rights Activist*

Born about 1820 in Dorchester County, Maryland, she had the hard childhood of a slave: much work, little schooling, and severe punishment. In 1848 she escaped, leaving behind her husband John Tubman, who threatened to report her to their master. As a free woman, she began to devise practical ways of helping other slaves escape. Over the following ten years she made about twenty trips from the North into the South and rescued more than three hundred slaves. Her reputation spread rapidly, and she won the admiration of leading abolitionists (some of whom sheltered her passengers). Eventually a reward of $40,000 was posted for her capture.

name Sojourner Truth, which she felt God had given her, she assumed the "mission" of spreading "the Truth" across the country. She became famous as an itinerant preacher, drawing huge crowds with her oratory (and some said "mystical gifts") wherever she appeared. She became one of an active group of black women abolitionists, lectured before numerous abolitionist audiences, and was friends with such leading white abolitionists as James and Lucretia Mott and Harriet Beecher Stowe. With the outbreak of the Civil War she raised money to purchase gifts for the soldiers, distributing them herself in the camps. She also helped African Americans who had escaped to the North to find habitation and shelter. Age and ill health caused her to retire from the lecture circuit, and she spent her last days in a sanatorium in Battle Creek, Michigan.

Harriet Tubman

Tubman met and aided John Brown in recruiting soldiers for his raid on Harpers Ferry—Brown referred to her as "General Tubman." One of her major disappointments was the failure of the raid, and she is said to have regarded Brown as the true emancipator of her people, not Lincoln. In 1860 she began to canvass the nation, appearing at anti-slavery meetings and speaking on women's rights. Shortly before the outbreak of the Civil War she was forced to leave for Canada, but she returned to the United States and served the Union as a nurse, soldier, and spy; she was particularly valuable to the army as a scout because of the knowledge of the terrain she had gained as a conductor on the underground railroad.

Tubman's biography (from which she received the proceeds) was written by Sarah Bradford in 1868. Tubman's husband, John, died two years after the end of the war, and in 1869 she married the war veteran Nelson Davis. Despite receiving many honors and tributes (including a medal from Queen Victoria), she spent her last days in poverty, not receiving a pension until thirty years after the Civil War. With the $20 dollars a month that she finally received, she helped to found a home for the aged and needy, which was later renamed the Harriet Tubman Home. She died in Auburn, New York.

## Henry McNeal Turner (1834–1915)
*Black Nationalist, Repatriationist, Minister*

*See* Black Nationalism.

## Nat Turner (1800–1831)
*Leader of Slave Insurrection*

A slave in Southampton County, Virginia, he was an avid reader of the Bible who prayed, fasted, and experienced "voices," ultimately becoming a visionary mystic with a belief that God had given him the special destiny of conquering Southampton County. After recruiting a handful of conspirators, he struck at isolated homes in his immediate area, and within forty-eight hours the band of insurrectionists had reached sixty armed men. They killed fifty-five whites before deciding to attack the county seat in Jerusalem, but while en route they were overtaken by a posse and dispersed. Turner took refuge in the Dismal Swamp and remained there for six weeks before he was captured, brought to trial, and hanged along with sixteen other African Americans.

## Denmark Vesey (1767–1822)
*Leader of Slave Insurrection*

Sold by his master at an early age and later bought back because of epilepsy, he sailed with his master, Captain Vesey, to the Virgin Islands and Haiti for twenty years. He enjoyed a considerable degree of mobility in his home port of Charleston, South Carolina, and eventually purchased his freedom from his master for $600—he had won $1500 in a lottery. He became a Methodist minister and used his church as a base to recruit supporters to take over Charleston. The revolt was planned for the second Sunday in July 1822.

Vesey's plans were betrayed when a slave alerted the white authorities of the city. Hundreds of African Americans were rounded up, though some of Vesey's collaborators most likely escaped to the Carolinas where they fought as maroons. After a twenty-two day search, Vesey was apprehended and stood trial. During the trial he adeptly cross examined witnesses, but ultimately could not deny his intention to overthrow the city, and he was hanged along with several collaborators.

## Prince Whipple (17?–1797)
*Revolutionary Soldier*

Born in Amabon, Africa, it has been claimed that he was sent to the United States to obtain an education and sold into slavery upon arriving in Baltimore. He succeeded in joining the Continental Army as a body guard to General Whipple of New Hampshire and served in many of General George Washington's campaigns. After enduring the hardship of the Long Island retreat, he crossed the Delaware with Washington on Christmas night, an event commemorated in the painting by Emanuel Gottlieb Leutze. Whipple is buried at North Cemetery in Portsmouth, New Hampshire.

# 7

# *Civil Rights*

# Civil Rights

Early Rights Movements ■ Civil Rights at the End of the Civil War ■ Civil Rights in the Twentieth Century ■ Civil Rights Activists ■ Federal and State Civil Rights Agencies

*Throughout the history of this country, African Americans have struggled to obtain basic civil rights. It is a stuggle that has spanned several centuries—from the mutinies by Africans during the Atlantic crossing, to the insurrections organized by slaves in the New World, to the founding of such organizations as the Free African Society, the abolition movement, and to the civil rights marches and demonstrations of the twentieth century.*

## ■ EARLY RIGHTS MOVEMENTS

### The Free African Society

As a result of segregation and discrimatory practices within the Methodist church, the Free African Society was organized in 1787 in Philadelphia by the Reverends Richard Allen and Absalom Jones. As the Philadelphia organization grew, other Free African societies formed in such places as Boston, New York, and Newport. Like many black movements to follow, the Free African Society provided spiritual guidance and religious instruction, while providing economic aid, burial assistance, and relief to widows and orphans. The society also helped to faciliate communications between free blacks throughout the country.

Richard Allen

367

### The Abolition Movement

The press and the pulpit served as important tools in the anti-slavery movement. In 1827 in New York, Samuel Cornish and John Russwurm founded *Freedom's Journal*, the first black owned and operated newspaper in the United States. *Freedom's Journal*, which ceased publication after only three years, was concerned not only with eradicating slavery but also with the growing discrimination and cruelty against free blacks in both the South and North.

In 1847 abolitionist Frederick Douglass published the first edition of *The North Star*, which eventually became one of most successful black newspapers in America prior to the outbreak of the Civil War. Douglass, an escaped slave from Maryland, became one of the best known black abolitionists

Frederick Douglass

in the country. He lectured extensively throughout the United States and England. In 1845 he published his autobiography, *Narrative of Frederick Douglass*.

Although the abolition movement was dominated by whites, numerous black leaders played a major role in the movement, including such figures as Henry Highland Garnet, Harriet Tubman, and Sojourner Truth.

## ■ CIVIL RIGHTS AT THE END OF THE CIVIL WAR

Following the war Republicans, who controlled the United States Congress, took up the cause of the newly freed African Americans. Between 1865 and 1875, three amendments to the Constitution and a string of civil rights and Reconstruction legislation was passed by Congress. The Thirteenth Amendment, ratified December 18, 1865, abolished slavery and involuntary servitude. The Fourteenth Amendment, ratified July 28, 1868, guaranteed citizenship and provided equal protection under the laws. Ratified March 30, 1870, the Fifteenth Amendment was designed to protect the right of all citizens to vote. In 1866, 1870, 1871, and 1875 Congress passed civil rights legislation outlining and protecting basic rights, including the right to purchase and sell property and access to public accommodations. The Reconstruction acts, passed between 1867 and 1869, called for new state constitutional conventions in those states which had seceded from the Union prior to the Civil War.

Reconstruction eventually produced a wave of anti-African sentiment. White organizations, like the Ku Klux Klan, aimed at intimidating blacks and preventing them from taking their place in society, sprang up throughout the North and the South. In 1871

Congress enacted the Ku Klux Klan Act as an effort to end intimidation and violence directed at blacks. However the act failed to exterminate the Klan and other terrorist organizations.

The civil rights and Reconstruction legislation were difficult for many whites to accept and did little to change their attitudes. The last of the civil rights acts, passed by Congress in 1875, prohibited discrimination in public accommodations. However, by the 1880s the debate as to the constitutionality of such legislation had reached the United States Supreme Court. Ruling in a group of five cases in 1883, which became known as the *Civil Rights Cases*, the United States Supreme Court concluded that the 1875 Civil Rights Act was unconstitutional on the grounds that the Fourteenth Amendment authorized Congress to legislate only against discriminatory state action, and not discrimination by private individuals. The Court's ruling brought about an end to federal efforts to protect the civil rights of African Americans until the mid-twentieth century.

### Anti-lynching Efforts

By the late nineteenth and early twentieth century, lynching had become a weapon used by whites against blacks throughout the country. Between 1882 and 1990, approximately 1,750 African Americans were lynched in the United States. Victims, who included women, had been accused of a variety of "offenses" ranging from testifying in court against a white man to failing to use the word "mister" when addressing a white person. Ida B. Wells Barnett, a journalist and social activist, became one of the leading voices in the anti-lynching crusade by writing and lecturing throughout the United States against the practice of lynching.

Ida B. Wells Barnett

### Institutionalized Segregation

In 1896 the United States Supreme Court was faced with the issue of segregation on public transportation. At the time, as was the case in many parts of the South, a Louisiana state law was enacted requiring that "equal but separate" accommodations for blacks and whites be maintained in all public facilities. When Homer Adolph Plessy, a black man traveling by train from New Orleans to Covington, Louisiana, refused to ride in the "colored" railway coach, he was arrested.

Prior to the case of *Plessy v. Ferguson*, the Court had started to build a platform upon which the doctrine of separate but equal would be based. In 1878, ruling in the case *Hall v. DeCuir* the Court declared that states could not outlaw segregation on common carriers, such as streetcars and rail-

369

A Colored drinking fountain in North Carolina.

roads. Segregation laws sprung up throughout the South.

With Justice Billings Brown delivering the majority opinion in the *Plessy* case, the Court declared that "separate but equal" accommodations constituted a reasonable use of state police power and that the Fourteenth Amendment of the Constitution could not be used to abolish social or racial distinctions or to force a co-mingling of the two races.

The Supreme Court had effectively reduced the significance of the Fourteenth Amendment, which was designed to give blacks specific rights and protections. The ruling, in the *Plessy* case, which was termed the "separate but equal" doctrine, paved the way for the segregation of African Americans in all walks of life.

## ■ CIVIL RIGHTS IN THE TWENTIETH CENTURY

### Booker T. Washington and W.E.B. DuBois

During the late nineteenth and early twentieth centuries, two figures—Booker T. Washington and William Edward Burghardt DuBois—emerged as leaders in the struggle for black political and civil rights.

Washington, an educator and founder of the Tuskegee Normal and Industrial Institute, was a strong advocate of practical, utilitarian education and manual training as a means for developing African Americans. Tuskegee Normal and Industrial Institute, which was founded in 1881 and based on a program at Hampton Institute, provided vocational training and prepared its students to survive economically in a segregated society. In Washington's opinion, education was to provide African Americans with the means to become economically self-supporting. Speaking at the Cotton States International Exposition in Atlanta in 1895, Washington outlined his philosophy of self-help and cooperation between blacks and whites.

To those of my race who depend on bettering their condition in a foreign land, or

W.E.B. Dubois

who underestimate the importance of cultivating friendly relations with the Southern white man, who is their next door neighbor, I would say: "Cast down your bucket where you are"—cast it down in making friends in every manly way of the people of all races by whom we are surrounded.

W.E.B. DuBois, a young historian and Harvard graduate, challenged Washington's passive policies in a series of stinging essays and speeches. DuBois advocated the uplifting of African Americans through an educated black elite, which he referred to as the "talented tenth," or roughly a tenth of the African American population. He beleived that these African Americans must become proficient in education and culture, which would eventually benefit all.

Booker T. Washington

In 1905 DuBois, along with a group of other black intellectuals, formed the Niagara Movement. The group drew up a platform which called for full citizenship rights for blacks and public recognition of their contributions to America's stability and progress. The movement eventually evolved into what became known as the National Association for the Advancement of Colored People.

## Civil Rights in the Mid- to Late-Twentieth Century

The civil rights movement suffered many defeats in the first half of the twentieth century. Repeated efforts to obtain passage of federal anti-lynching bills failed. The all-white primary system, which effectively disenfranchised southern blacks, resisted numerous court challenges. The Depression worsened conditions on farms and in ghettos. On the positive side, the growing political power of blacks in northern cities and an increasing liberal trend in the Supreme Court portended the legal and legislative victories of the 1950s and 1960s.

### Brown v. Board of Education of Topeka

A great deal of the civil rights struggle throughout this period was carried on by the National Association for the Advancement of Colored People, which had begun chipping away at the roots of legalized segregation in a series of successful lawsuits. A major breakthrough for the NAACP came in 1954 when the United States Supreme Court ruled in *Brown v. Board of Education of Topeka* that discrimination in education was unconstitutional. This decision was as momentous as the Supreme Court's ruling in *Plessy v. Ferguson* in 1896, which legalized the doctrine of "separate but equal" treatment for blacks.

The *Brown* case involved the practice of denying black children equal access to state public schools due to state laws requiring or permitting racial segregation. The United States Supreme Court unanimously held that segregation deprived the children of equal protection under the Fourteenth Amendment to the United States Constitution, overturning the "separate but equal" doctrine established in *Plessy*.

### A. Philip Randolph

In 1941 A. Philip Randolph, organizer of an employment bureau for untrained blacks and founder the Brotherhood of Sleeping Car Porters, came up with the idea of lead-

Police officers using police dogs to break-up a demonstration in Birmingham, Alabama, 1963.

Bayard Rustin (left) and A. Philip Randolph at a news conference, 1963.

ing a protest march of blacks in Washington, DC to protest discrimination. On July 25, less than a week before the scheduled demonstration, President Franklin D. Roosevelt issued Executive Order No. 8802, which banned discrimination in the defense industry and led to the creation of the Fair Employment Practices Committee.

### Civil Rights in the 1960s

Rosa Parks was one of the major catalysts of the 1960s civil rights movement. When on December 1, 1955, Parks refused to give up her seat on a Montgomery bus to a white man, as the law required, she was arrested and sent to jail. As a result of Parks' arrest, blacks throughout Montgomery refused to ride city buses. The Montgomery Bus Boycott led by Martin Luther King, Jr. was highly

successful and ultimately led to the integration of all Montgomery city buses.

The eventual success of the Montgomery Bus Boycott encouraged a wave of massive demonstrations that swept across the South. In 1960 a group of students denied service at a Greensboro, North Carolina lunch counter started the "sit-in" movement. That same year, the Student Non-Violent Coordinating Committee was created and would include among its members Julian Bond, H. Rap Brown, Stokely Carmichael, and John Lewis.

The civil rights movement of the 1960s galvinized blacks and sympathetic whites as nothing had ever done before, but was not without cost. Thousands of people were jailed because they defied Jim Crow laws. Others were murdered and homes and churches were bombed. People lost their jobs and their homes because they supported the movement.

On August 28, 1963, nearly 250,000 blacks and whites marched in Washington, DC to awaken the nation's consciousness regarding civil rights and to encourage the passage of civil rights legislation pending in Congress. The march was a cooperative effort of several civil rights organizations, including the Southern Christian Leadership Conference, the Congress of Racial Equality, the National Association for the Advancement of Colored People, the Negro American Labor Council, and the National Urban League. It was during this demonstration that Dr. Martin Luther King, Jr., in the shadow of the Lincoln Memorial, gave his "I Have a Dream" speech.

At its zenith, the civil rights movement was the most important event taking place in America. Through demonstrations, "sit-ins," marches, and soaring rhetoric, the movement aroused widespread public indignation, thus creating an atmosphere in which it was possible to make positive changes in American society.

## Civil Rights Legislation in the 1990s

Although the civil rights movement of the 1950s and 1960s produced significant gains for African Americans, progress continues today. This progress is evident in the passage of the most recent civil rights legislation. In June 1989, the United States Supreme Court delivered opinions in several cases dealing with seniority systems and racial discrimination in employment. Ruling in the cases *Lorance v. AT&T Technologies Inc.*, *Martin v. Wilks*, *Patterson v. McLean*

High pressure hoses are turned on demonstrators in Birmingham, Alabama, 1963.

Nearly 250,000 gather in Washington, DC, August 1963.

*Credit Union*, and *Wards Cove Packing Co. v. Antonio*, the Court appeared to reverse earlier civil rights rulings.

Prior to the Court's ruling in *Wards Cove*, the burden of proof in job discrimination suits had been placed on employers, requiring businesses to prove that there was a legitimate business reason for alleged discriminatory practices. With the *Wards Cove* decision, the Court made it more difficult for groups to win such suits by requiring workers to prove that there was no clear business reason for an employer's use of practices that result in discrimination.

Civil rights organizations were quick to protest the rulings; opponents of the ruling, including the NAACP Legal Defense and Educational Fund and the Leadership Conference on Civil Rights argued that the Court had undermined the protection granted by federal civil rights and equal employment legislation.

On October 16 and 17, 1990 both houses of Congress approved a bill designed to reverse the Court's ruling. The proposed legislation, not only reversed the Court's ruling in *Wards Cove*, but strengthened provisions of the 1964 Civil Rights Act. On October 22, President George Bush vetoed the bill, claiming that the bill's provisions would encourage employers to establish hiring quotas.

This was not the first time that Congress moved to reverse a Court action in the area of civil rights—in 1987 Congress passed the Civil Rights Restoration Act of 1988 which reversed the Court's ruling in *Grove City College v. Bell* (1984). In the *Grove City College* case, the United States Supreme Court ruled that not all programs and activities of an institution were covered by Title IX of the Education Amendments of 1972 (Public Law 89–10, 79 Stat. 27), which prohibits discrimination in educational programs receiving federal financial assistance.

After vetoing Congress' 1990 civil rights legislation, the Bush administration joined both houses of Congress in working on alternative bills. On October 30, following months of negotiation, the Senate passed a bill designed to provide additional remedies to deter harassment and intentional discrimination in the workplace, provide guidelines for the adjudication of cases arising under Title VII of the Civil Rights Act of 1964, and expand the scope of civil rights legislation weakened by Supreme Court decisions 1745. The House of Representatives passed the bill on November 7, and on November 21, President George Bush signed the Civil Rights Act of 1991.

## ■ CIVIL RIGHTS ACTIVISTS

### Ralph D. Abernathy (1926–1990)
*Former President, Southern Christian Leadership Conference*

Born March 11, 1926, in Linden, Alabama, the Reverend Ralph David Abernathy was ordained a minister in 1948. He received his bachelor's degree from Alabama State College (now Alabama State University) in 1950 and his master's degree from Atlanta University in 1951.

The alliance between Abernathy and Martin Luther King, Jr. stretched back to the mid-1950s. While attending Atlanta University, Abernathy had the opportunity to hear King preach at Ebenezer Baptist Church. After obtaining his master's degree, Abernathy returned to Alabama to serve as a part-time minister at the Eastern Star Baptist Church

Ralph Abernathy

Ralph Abernathy (left) and Martin Luther King, Jr. (rear) were active in the boycott of segregated buses in Montgomery, Alabama.

in Demoplis. In 1951 Abernathy moved to First Baptist Church in Montgomery. Around this time King accepted a position at Montgomery's Dexter Avenue Baptist Church; Abernathy and King became close friends.

In 1955 Abernathy and King organized the Montgomery Improvement Association to coordinate a citywide bus boycott. The suc-cess of the boycott led to the creation of the Southern Negro Leaders Conference; the or-ganization's name was later changed to the Southern Leadership Conference and finally the Southern Christian Leadership Confer-ence. In January 1957 Dr. King was elected the organization's first president.

From the time of Martin Luther King's death in 1968 until 1977, Abernathy served as president of the Southern Christian Leadership Conference. Abernathy continued as a leading figure in the movement until his resignation in 1977.

In 1977 Abernathy made an unsuccessful bid for a United States Congressional seat. In 1989 he published his autobiography, *And The Walls Came Tumbling Down*, which was criticized by some black leaders for Abernathy's inclusion of details regarding King's extramarital affairs. Abernathy died of cardiac arrest on April 17, 1990.

### Ella Josephine Baker (1903–1986)
*Civil Rights Activist*

Ella Baker was born in Norfolk, Virginia to Blake and Georgiana Ross Baker, both educated people who worked hard to educate their children. The family and community in which she grew up instilled in her a sense of sharing and community cooperation; neighbors shared food from their gardens and gave a helping hand when needed. Her family instilled in her a sense of racial pride and resistance to any form of oppression. Her grandfather, a minister and community leader, was an ardent proponent of civil rights and universal suffrage, and passed his beliefs on to her.

When she was fifteen, Baker was sent to the Shaw Boarding School in Raleigh. The Shaw school was both a high school and college, and she graduated with a bachelor's degree as valedictorian in 1927. After graduation, she moved to New York City. She quickly became involved in progressive politics and attended as many meetings and discussions as she could find. During the depression, she was outraged at the poverty she saw in the black areas of the city. Believing in the power of community and group action, in 1930 she became involved with the Young Negroes Cooperative League, a buying cooperative that bought food in bulk to distribute at low prices to members; in 1931, she became the national director of the League. When President Franklin Roosevelt's Works Progress Administration started, she became involved with their literacy program. Throughout these years she worked closely with other politically aware and motivated people, discussing and evolving a political philosophy of cooperation, equality, and justice.

In the 1940s, Baker began to work for the NAACP. Between 1940 and 1943, she was a field secretary, traveling all over the country setting up branch offices and teaching people to fight for their own rights; her traveling gave her the opportunity to develop a vast network of contacts in the south that she later relied on when working for the Student Non-Violent Coordinating Committee and Southern Christian Leadership Conference. In 1943, she became the director of branches for the NAACP. During the 1950s, she started fund raising activities in New York for the civil-rights struggles in the south, and in 1958, moved to Atlanta to work with the SCLC.

Working for the Southern Christian Leadership Conference, Baker became disillusioned with the top-heavy, male-dominated organizational structure of the group. In 1960 she quit the SCLC and took a job with the Young Women's Christian Association instead. When students began leading sit-ins, she shifted her focus to the development of the Student Non-Violent Coordinating Committee. She acted as an unofficial advisor for the group, counseling them to set up their own student-run organization rather than be subsumed under the SCLC or the NAACP. She helped launch the Mississippi Freedom Democratic Party that challenged the all-white Democratic delegation at the 1964 presidential convention. She also acted as staff consultant for the interracial SCLC educational fund.

Baker returned to New York City in 1965, but kept working with national and international civil rights organizations. Among her other activities, she raised money to send to the freedom fighters in Rhodesia and South Africa. She remained an active organizer and speaker as long as her health allowed.

Baker's belief in the power of communal action and reliance on the workers rather than the leaders had an enormous impact. She worked for all of the major civil-rights organizations at their time of greatest need. By the time the SCLC and the SNCC were formed, she had almost thirty years of civil-rights and community organizing experience to offer. She continually strove to keep the movement people oriented, and she succeeded in helping the SNCC remain a student group. Through her philosophy and actions, she motivated hundreds to act, to help themselves, and their neighbors as she had learned to do as a child.

### Daisy Lee Gatson Bates (1920–    )
*Civil Rights Activist*

After attending segregated schools where all of the new equipment and up-to-date texts were reserved for whites only, Daisy Bates spent much of her energy as an adult successfully integrating the schools of Little Rock, Arkansas.

Shortly after their marriage in 1941, Daisy and her husband Lucius Christopher Bates, a journalist, started to publish a newspaper, the Arkansas *State Press*. They made it a point in their paper to keep track and report incidents of police brutality and other racially-motivated violence; their paper became known throughout the state for its campaign to improve the social and economic circumstances of African Americans. Because of their work, the city of Little Rock began to hire black police officers, and the number of racial incidents lessened.

Daisy Bates leaving Little Rock Police headquarters, 1957.

In 1952, Daisy Bates became the Arkansas president of the NAACP; after the 1954 court decision in the *Brown v. Board of Education* case, she became very active in school desegregation. She began taking black children to white schools to be registered. If the school refused to register the children, she would report it in her paper. In 1957, the superintendent of schools in Little Rock decided to try to integrate the schools and chose nine students, now called the Little Rock Nine, to be the first black children to attend Central High, a white school. Most white citizens of Little Rock objected. Bates organized the Little Rock Nine, accompanied them to Central High, and stood with them against the state troopers that Governor Orval Faubus had sent in to prevent the integration. For days she escorted the children to school, only to be turned away by an angry mob. On September 25, 1957, Daisy Bates entered Central High in Little Rock with the nine children, escorted by 1000 paratroopers President Dwight Eisenhower had sent in; the first steps towards integration were successful. For the rest of their years at Central High, Bates kept track of the students and acted as their advocate when problems arose, frequently accompanying them and their parents to meetings with school officials.

In October of 1957, one month after she marched into Central High, Daisy Bates was arrested on charges of failing to provide membership information on the NAACP to city officials. The charges were later overturned. Two years later, the Arkansas *State Press* folded, but Bates kept active in the civil-rights fight, touring and speaking, and working with the Student Non-Violent Coordinating Committee to register voters. In 1985, the *State Press* began to publish again, and it has continued to serve the needs of the African-American community in Little Rock.

Stokely Carmichael

### Stokely Carmichael (Kwame Toure) (1941– )

*Political Activist, Student Non-Violent Coordinating Committee Former President*

If there was one individual during the 1960s who stood at the forefront of the Black Power movement, it was Stokely Carmichael. He soared to fame as popularizer of the dynamic phrase "black power" and as one of the most powerful and influential leader of the Student Non-Violent Coordinating Committee (SNCC).

He was born in Trinidad and moved to the United States with his family when he was eleven. As a teenager, Carmichael was jolted by ghetto life in which "black" and "impo-

tent" seemed to be synonymous terms. He was not reassured later when he was admitted to the Bronx High School of Science, encountered white liberals, and felt he had been adopted by them as a mascot. Although he was offered good scholarships to white universities, Carmichael opted to attend Howard University. During his first year there, 1960, he joined the Congress of Racial Equality in its efforts to integrate public accommodations in the South. After graduation in 1964, he rejected scholarship opportunities for graduate school, and went south to join the SNCC. As one of their finest organizers, he worked ceaselessly registering and educating voters in the south. In 1966, he was elected chairman of the SNCC, but as the youngest chair the group had, his views were considered too radical by some members.

Carmichael's cry for "black power" thrilled many disenfranchised young African-Americans, but troubled others, who thought it sounded too violent. He was labeled as potentially violent by the media and the legal authorities. Disagreement with SNCC members arose over the issues of self-defense versus non-violence, and the participation of whites in black grass-roots organizations. In 1967, he resigned as chairman, and was later expelled from the SNCC.

Carmichael spent much of 1968 traveling around the world, speaking to many organizations, including some in communist countries. His travels included Ghana, where he joined the Pan-African movement. After returning to the United States, he went to work for the Black Panther party. In this country, however, he was subject to almost constant harassment from the FBI because of his connection with the Panthers, and because he had visited communist countries while traveling. In 1969, he resigned from the Black Panthers, and moved to Guinea, where he had been offered political asylum.

In Guinea, Carmichael turned his efforts to supporting Pan-Africanism; he has organized many local chapters through the world of the All African Peoples Revolutionary Party. In 1978, to honor the two men who most influenced his Pan-African philosophical education, SeKou Toure and Kwame Nkrumah, he changed his name to Kwame Toure. Toure continues to live in Guinea and travel throughout the world, working toward a united African people.

**Benjamin Franklin Chavis, Jr. (1948– )**
*National Association for the Advancement of Colored People Executive Director*

*See* Organizations.

**Angela Davis (1944– )**
*Political Activist*

Angela Davis was born in Alabama to middle class parents who stressed both academic excellence and political awareness and activism. He mother, Sallye E. Davis, had been politically active since her college days, and Angela participated in demonstrations with her mother from the time she was in elementary school. To insure her a better education than she would be able to receive in the segregated schools of the south, her parents sent her to Elizabeth Irwin High School, a private progressive school in New York. The school had many radical teachers and students, and Angela soon joined a Marxist study group.

After graduation, she continued to seek high-quality education. She majored in French at Brandeis College, studying at the

Angela Davis

Sorbonne in Paris her junior year. She then pursued graduate studies in philosophy at the Goethe University in Frankfurt, and in 1967 she returned to the United States to study with the well-known philosopher, Herbert Marcuse, at the University of California at San Diego. When she was almost done with her degree, she took a teaching job at the University of California at Los Angeles.

In 1969, she joined the communist party; the regents of UCLA tried to fire her, but she fought them in court. The following year she became involved with the Black Panther Party. Guns she had bought for self defense were used by a member of the Black Panthers in a courtroom shooting. Believing she was involved, the FBI sought her arrest, so she went underground to avoid them. She was put on the FBI's most wanted list, and later arrested. In 1972, she was acquitted of all charges, but was not hired back by the university. California Governor Ronald Reagan and the Regents of the University decreed that she would never teach in California again.

Since her trial, Davis has served as co-chair of the National Alliance against Racism and Political Repression, a legal group providing defense of minority prisoners. A writer and philosopher, she has written several books, including *If They Come in the Morning* (1971), *Women, Race and Class* (1983), *Angela Davis: An Autobiography* (1988), and *Women, Culture and Politics* (1989). She continues to write and lecture and remains politically active.

## William Edward Burghardt DuBois (1868-1963)

*Civil Rights Activist, National Association for the Advancement of Colored People Founding Member*

An outstanding critic, editor, scholar, author, and civil rights leader, W.E.B. DuBois

W.E.B. DuBois

is certainly among the most influential blacks of the twentieth century.

Born in Great Barrington, Massachusetts on February 23, 1868, DuBois received a bachelors degree from Fisk University and went on to win a second bachelors, as well as a Ph.D., from Harvard. He was for a time professor of Latin and Greek at Wilberforce and the University of Pennsylvania, and also served as a professor of economics and history at Atlanta University.

One of the founders of the National Association for the Advancement of Colored People (NAACP) in 1909, DuBois served as that organization's director of publications and editor of *Crisis* magazine until 1934. In 1944 he returned from Atlanta University to become head of the NAACP's special research department, a post he held until 1948. Dr. DuBois emigrated to Africa in 1961 and became editor-in-chief of the *Encyclopedia Africana*, an enormous publishing venture which had been planned by Kwame Nkrumah, since then deposed as president of Ghana. DuBois died in Ghana in 1963 at the age of ninety-five.

His numerous books include *The Suppression of the Slave Trade* (1896), *The Philadelphia Negro* (1899), *The Souls of Black Folk* (1903), *John Brown* (1909), *Quest of the Silver Fleece* (1911), *The Negro* (1915), *Darkwater* (1920), *The Gift of Black Folk* (1924), *Dark Princess* (1928), *Black Folk: Then and Now* (1939), *Dusk of Dawn* (1940), *Color and Democracy* (1945), *The World and Africa* (1947), *In Battle for Peace* (1952), and a trilogy, *Black Flame* (1957–1961).

It is this enormous literary output on such a wide variety of themes which offers the most convincing testimony to DuBois' lifetime position that it was vital for blacks to cultivate their own aesthetic and cultural values even as they made valuable strides toward social emancipation. In this he was opposed by Booker T. Washington, who felt that the black should concentrate on developing technical and mechanical skills before all else.

DuBois was one of the first male civil rights leaders to recognize the problems of gender discrimination. He was among the first men to understand the unique problems of black women, and to value their contributions. He supported the women's suffrage movement and strove to integrate this mostly white struggle. He encouraged many black female writers, artists, poets, and novelists, featuring their works in *Crisis* and sometimes providing personal financial assistance to them. Several of his novels feature women as prominently as men, an unusual approach for any author of his day. DuBois spent his life working not just for the equality of all men, but for the equality of all people.

## Medgar Evers (1925–1963)
*Civil Rights Activist*

Medgar Evers, field secretary for the NAACP, was one of the first martyrs of the civil-rights movement. On June 13, 1963, he drove home from a meeting, stepped out of his car, and was shot in the back.

Evers was born in 1925 in Decatur, Mississippi to James and Jessie Evers. After a short stint in the army, he enrolled in Alcorn A&M College, graduating in 1952. His first job out of college was traveling around rural Mississippi selling insurance. He soon grew enraged at the despicable conditions of poor black families in his state, and joined the

Medgar Evers

NAACP. In 1954, he was appointed Mississippi's first field secretary.

Evers was outspoken, and his demands were radical for his rigidly segregated state. He fought for the enforcement of the 1954 court decision of *Brown v. Board of Education of Topeka* which outlawed school segregation; he fought for the right to vote, and he advocated boycotting merchants who discriminated. He worked unceasingly despite the threats of violence that his speeches engendered. He gave much of himself to this struggle, and in 1963, he gave his life.

Immediately after his death, the shotgun that was used to kill him was found in bushes nearby, with the owner's fingerprints still fresh. Byron de la Beckwithde la Beckwith, Byronde la beckwith byron], a vocal member of a local white-supremacist group, was arrested. Despite the evidence against him, which included an earlier statement that he wanted to kill Evers, two trials with all-white juries ended in deadlock decisions, and Beckwith walked free.

Twenty years later, in 1989, information surfaced that suggested the jury in both trials had been tampered with. The assistant District Attorney, with the help of Evers' widow, began putting together a new case. In 1990, Beckwith was arrested one more time; the case is still pending.

While knowing that Evers did not die in vain is small comfort, it is nevertheless true. His death changed the tenor of the civil-rights struggle. Anger replaced fear in the south, as hundreds of demonstrators marched in protect. His death prompted President John Kennedy to ask Congress for a comprehensive civil-rights bill, which President Lyndon Johnson signed into law the following year. Evers death, as his life had, contributed much to the struggle for equality.

### James Farmer (1920–    )
*Congress of Racial Equality Founder and Former National Director*

*See* Organizations.

### Fannie Lou Hamer (1917–1977)
*Civil Rights Activists*

As a poor sharecropper she had only an elementary education, yet Fannie Lou Hamer was one of the most eloquent speakers for the civil rights movement in the south. She worked for political, social and economic equality for herself and all African Americans; she fought to integrate the national Democratic party, and became one of its first black delegates to a presidential convention.

Hamer, the youngest of twenty siblings born to Jim and Ella Townsend in Montgomery County, Mississippi, began picking cotton when she was six; she attended school until she had to drop out in the sixth grade to

Fannie Lou Hamer

work full time. She worked first as a share cropper, and then as a time keeper on the same plantation in Mississippi for almost forty years. In 1962, because she tried to exercise her right to vote, she lost her job and, frightened by threats of violent reprisals, was forced to move away from her home and her family. Angered into action, she went to work for the Student Non-Violent Coordinating Committee, helping many blacks register to vote.

Because the Democratic party refused to send blacks as delegates to the national presidential convention, in 1964, Hamer and others formed the Mississippi Freedom Democratic party to send black delegates to the convention. They challenged the Democratic delegates from Mississippi for their seats at the convention, arguing that the all-white delegation could not adequately represent their state which had a large black population. Hamer's own speech on their behalf frightened the incumbent President Lyndon Johnson so much so that he tried to block the televised coverage of her. The MFDP lost its bid that year, but their actions did result in a pledge from the national party not to seat delegations excluding blacks in the 1968 convention. In 1968, Fannie Lou Hamer was among the first black delegates to the Democratic National Convention.

For the next decade, Hamer remained active in the struggle for civil and economic rights. In 1969, she founded the Freedom Farms Corporation to help needy families raise food and livestock. They also provided basic social services, scholarships and grants for education, and helped fund minority business opportunities. She became a sought-after speaker, and in the 1970s, even as her health was failing from cancer, she still toured the country speaking about civil rights for all.

## Benjamin L. Hooks (1925– )

*National Association for the Advancement of Colored People Former Executive Director*

See Organizations.

## Roy Innis (1934– )

*Congress of Racial Equality National Chairman*

See Organizations.

## Jesse Jackson (1941– )

*President, People United to Save Humanity*

Jesse Louis Jackson was born October 8, 1941, in Greenville, South Carolina. In 1959 Jackson left South Carolina to attend the University of Illinois. However, he became dissatisfied with his treatment on campus and decided to transfer to North Carolina Agricultural and Technical College. After receiving his B.A. in sociology he went on to attend the Chicago Theological Seminary. He was ordained a Baptist minister in 1968.

Jackson joined the Southern Christian Leadership Conference (SCLC) in 1965. In 1966 Jackson became involved with the SCLC's Operation Breadbasket, and from 1967 to 1971 he served as the program's executive director. Jackson resigned from the SCLC in 1971 to found his own organization, Operation PUSH (People United to Save Humanity). Through PUSH Jackson continued to pursue the economic objectives of Operation Breadbasket and expanded into areas of social and political development.

From that point on, Jackson was on his way to becoming the most visible and sought-after civil rights leader in the country. His magnetic personality came across as appealing on television, and while he described himself as "a country preacher," his command of issues and his ability to reach the heart of matters marked him as an individual of intellectual depth. Of all the civil rights leaders, Jackson was the one who could relate best to the young. He was possessed with a gift of being able to summon out the best in them, in a phrase that became his trademark, "I am somebody."

Out of this came Jackson's program, PUSH-EXCEL, which sought to motivate young school children to do better academically. In 1981 *Newsweek* magazine credited Jackson with building a struggling community improvement organization into a nationwide campaign to revive pride, discipline, and the work ethic in inner-city schools. With funding from the Carter administration, the PUSH-EXCEL program was placed in five other cities.

The Jesse Jackson of the 1980s will be best remembered for his two runs for the Democratic nomination for President of the United States. In 1983, many, but not all, black political leaders endorsed the idea of a black presidential candidate to create a "people's" platform, increase voter registration and have a power base from which there could be greater input into the political process. His 1984 campaign was launched under the aegis of the National Rainbow Coalition, Inc., an umbrella organization of minority groups. Black support was divided, however, between Jackson and former Vice President Walter Mondale. During this campaign, Jackson attracted considerable media coverage with controversial remarks and actions, demonstrating a lack of familiarity with national politics.

The 1988 campaign of Jackson showed enormous personal and political growth, his candidacy was no longer a symbolic gesture but was a real and compelling demonstration of his effectiveness as a candidate. By the time the Democratic convention rolled around, media pundits were seriously discussing the likelihood of Jackson's nomination as the Democratic presidential candidate, and "what to do about Jesse" became the focus of the entire Democratic leadership. At the end of the primary campaign, Jackson had finished a strong second to Massachusetts Governor Michael Dukakis, and changed forever the notion that a black President in America was inconceivable. Jackson took his defeat in stride and continued to campaign for the Democratic ticket until the November election.

Since the 1988 election, Jackson has worked less publicly, but no less energetically. In 1989 he moved with his Rainbow Coalition from Chicago to Washington, DC; he believed that the coalition could be more effective working in the nation's capital. Still fighting hard for social change, his concerns include child care, health care, housing, as well as discrimination and a newer issue, statehood for Washington, DC. While he has concentrated his efforts on national issues, he keeps active in foreign affairs as well. He has traveled all over the world to meet with leaders of other nations. He has used his fame and influence to help Americans in trouble abroad. In 1991, he traveled to Iraq, and convinced Saddam Hussein to begin releasing Americans held hostage after Hussein's invasion of Kuwait.

Although many expected him to run for president again in 1992, Jackson decided against it, saying that he was too tired, and the strain on his family too severe. He did not, however, rule out 1996.

**John E. Jacob (1934–   )**
*National Urban League President*

*See* Organizations.

## Coretta Scott King (1927–   )
*Civil Rights Activist*

As the wife of civil-rights leader Martin Luther King, Jr., Coretta Scott King was ready to continue his work and perpetuate his ideals after his 1968 assassination. While her primary role in the early years of marriage was to raise her four children, she became increasingly involved in the struggle for civil rights through her husband's activities. After his death, she quickly became a dynamic activist and peace crusader.

Born one of three children on April 27, 1927, Mrs. King is a native of Heilberger, Alabama. During the Depression she was forced to contribute to the family income by hoeing and picking cotton, but she resolved early to overcome adversity, seek treatment as an equal, and struggle to achieve a sound education. After graduating from the private Lincoln High School in 1945, she entered Antioch College in Yellow Springs, Ohio, on a scholarship, majoring in education and music. A teaching career appealed to her, but she became badly disillusioned when she was not allowed to do her practice teaching in the public schools of the town. No black had ever taught there, and she was not destined to be the first to break the tradition.

Musical training in voice and piano absorbed much of her time, with the result that, upon graduation, she decided to continue her studies at the New England Conservatory of Music in Boston, attending on a modest fellowship which covered tuition but made part-time work a necessity. Her meeting with Martin Luther King thrust her into a whirlwind romance, and also presented her with the opportunity to marry an exceptional young minister whose intense convictions and concern for humanity brought her a measure of rare self-realization early in life. Sensing his incredible dynamism, she suffered no regrets at the pros-

Coretta Scott King

pect of relinquishing her own possible career.

Completing her studies in 1954, Mrs. King moved back south with her husband, who became pastor of Drexel Avenue Baptist Church in Montgomery, Alabama. Within a year, King had led the Montgomery bus boycott, and given birth to a new era of civil rights agitation. Two years later, he was the head of the Southern Christian Leadership Conference (SCLC).

Over the years she became gradually more involved in her husband's work. She would occasionally perform at his lectures, raising her voice in song as he did in speech. She became involved in separate activities as well. In 1962, she served as a Woman's Strike for Peace delegate to the seventeen-nation Disarmament Conference in Geneva, Switzerland. In the mid 1960s, she sang in the multi-arts Freedom Concerts that raised money for the SCLC. As demands on Martin became too much, she began to fill the speaking engagements he could not. After his assassination, she filled many of the commitments his death left empty, but soon became sought-after in her own right.

Her speech on Solidarity Day, June 19, 1968, is often identified as a prime example of her emergence from the shadow of her husband's memory. In it, she called upon American women to "unite and form a solid block of women power" to fight the three great evils of racism, poverty, and war. Much of her subsequent activity revolved around building plans for the creation of a Martin Luther King, Jr. Memorial in Atlanta, which she began to work on in 1969, and which was established under the care of the National Park Service in 1980. She also published a book of reminiscences, *My Life with Martin Luther King, Jr.*

Today, Mrs. King still remains an eloquent and respected spokesperson on behalf of black causes and nonviolent philosophy. As its president, she devotes most of her time to the Martin Luther King Jr. Center for Non-Violent Social Change in Atlanta, which has grown into a well-respected institution visited by persons from across the world. Mrs. King has also championed the cause against apartheid in South Africa. In 1985, she and two of her children were arrested for demonstrating outside the South African embassy in Washington, DC. In 1986, she visited South Africa for eight days, meeting with businessmen and anti-apartheid leaders.

### Martin Luther King, Jr. (1929–1968)
*Civil Rights Activist*

Any number of historic moments in the civil rights struggle have been used to identify Martin Luther King Jr.—prime mover of the Montgomery bus boycott

Coretta Scott King (left), Dr. Martin Luther King, Jr., and Floyd McKissick attend a rally in Chicago, 1966.

Dr. King joins other civil rights leaders at a rally in Selma, Alabama, 1965.

(1956), keynote speaker at the March on Washington (1963), youngest Nobel Peace Prize laureate (1964). But in retrospect, single events are less important than the fact that King, and his policy of nonviolent protest, was the dominant force in the civil rights movement during its decade of greatest achievement, from 1957 to 1968.

King was born Michael Luther King in Atlanta on January 15, 1929—one of the three children of Martin Luther King, Sr., pastor of Ebenezer Baptist Church, and Alberta (Williams) King, a former schoolteacher. (He did not receive the name of "Martin" until he was about six years of age.)

After attending grammar and high schools locally, King enrolled in Morehouse College (also in Atlanta) in 1944. At this time he was not inclined to enter the ministry, but while there he came under the influence of Dr.

Benjamin Mays, a scholar whose manner and bearing convinced him that a religious career could have its intellectual satisfactions as well. After receiving his B.A. in 1948, King attended Crozer Theological Seminary in Chester, Pennsylvania, winning the Plafker Award as the outstanding student of the graduating class, and the J. Lewis Crozer Fellowship as well. King completed the course work for his doctorate in 1953, and was granted the degree two years later upon completion of his dissertation.

Married by then, King returned South, accepting the pastorate of the Dexter Avenue Baptist Church in Montgomery, Alabama. It was here that he made his first mark on the civil rights movement, by mobilizing the black community during a 382-day boycott of the city's bus lines. Working through the Montgomery Improvement Association,

King overcame arrest and other violent harassment, including the bombing of his home. Ultimately, the U.S. Supreme Court declared the Alabama laws requiring bus segregation unconstitutional, with the result that blacks were allowed to ride Montgomery buses on equal footing with whites.

A national hero and a civil rights figure of growing importance, King summoned together a number of black leaders in 1957 and laid the groundwork for the organization now known as the Southern Christian Leadership Conference (SCLC). Elected its president, he soon sought to assist other communities in the organization of protest campaigns against discrimination, and in voter-registration activities as well.

After completing his first book and making a trip to India, King returned to the United States in 1960 to become co-pastor,

Dr. Martin Luther King, Jr.

with his father, of Ebenezer Baptist Church. Three years later, in 1963, King's nonviolent tactics were put to their most severe test in Birmingham, Alabama during a mass protest for fair hiring practices, the establishment of a biracial committee, and the desegregation of department-store facilities. Police brutality used against the marchers dramatized the plight of blacks to the nation at large with enormous impact. King was arrested, but his voice was not silenced as he issued his classic "Letter from a Birmingham Jail" to refute his critics.

Later that year King was a principal speaker at the historic March on Washington, where he delivered one of the most passionate addresses of his career. At the beginning of the next year *Time* magazine designated him as its Man of the Year for 1963. A few months later he was named recipient of the 1964 Nobel Peace Prize.

Upon his return from Oslo, where he had gone to accept the award, King entered a new battle, in Selma, Alabama, where he led a voter-registration campaign which culminated in the Selma-to-Montgomery Freedom March. King next brought his crusade to Chicago where he launched a slum-rehabilitation and open-housing program.

In the North, however, King soon discovered that young and angry blacks cared little for his pulpit oratory and even less for his solemn pleas for peaceful protest. Their disenchantment was clearly one of the factors influencing his decision to rally behind a new cause and stake out a fresh battleground: the war in Vietnam. Although his aim was to fuse a new coalition of dissent based on equal support for the peace crusade and the civil rights movement, King antagonized many civil rights leaders by declaring the United States to be "the greatest purveyor of violence in the world."

The rift was immediate. The NAACP saw King's shift of emphasis as "a serious tactical mistake"; the Urban League warned that the "limited resources" of the civil rights movement would be spread too thin; Bayard Rustin claimed black support of the peace movement would be negligible; Ralph Bunche felt King was undertaking an impossible mission in trying to bring the campaign for peace in step with the goals of the civil rights movement.

From the vantage point of history, King's timing could only be regarded as superb. In announcing his opposition to the war, and in characterizing it as a "tragic adventure" which was playing "havoc with the destiny of the entire world," King again forced the white middle class to concede that no movement could dramatically affect the course of government in the United States unless it involved deliberate and restrained aggressiveness, persistent dissent, and even militant confrontation. These were precisely the in-

gredients of the civil rights struggle in the South in the early 1960s.

As students, professors, intellectuals, clergymen and reformers of every stripe rushed into the movement (in a sense forcing fiery black militants like Stokely Carmichael and Floyd McKissick to surrender their control over antiwar polemics), King turned his attention to the domestic issue which, in his view, was directly related to the Vietnam struggle: the War on Poverty.

At one point, he called for a guaranteed family income, he threatened national boycotts, and spoke of disrupting entire cities by nonviolent "camp-ins." With this in mind, he began to draw up plans for a massive march of the poor on Washington, DC itself, envisioning a popular demonstration of unsurpassed intensity and magnitude designed to force Congress and the political parties to recognize and deal with the unseen and ig-

Dr. Martin Luther King, Jr. addressing a crowd of protestors.

Outside of Ebenezer Baptist Church in Atlanta, while King's body had been lying in state.

nored masses of desperate and downtrodden Americans.

King's decision to interrupt these plans to lend his support to the Memphis sanitation men's strike was based in part on his desire to discourage violence, as well as to focus national attention on the plight of the poor, unorganized workers of the city. The men were bargaining for little else beyond basic union representation and long-overdue salary considerations. Though he was unable to eliminate the violence which had resulted in the summoning and subsequent departure of the National Guard, King stayed on in Memphis and was in the process of planning for a march which he vowed to carry out in defiance of a federal court injunction if necessary.

On the night of April 3, 1968, he told a church congregation: "Well I don't know what will happen now . . . But it really doesn't matter. . . . (At other times, musing over the possibility he might be killed, King had assured his colleagues that he had "the advantage over most people" because he had "conquered the fear of death.")

Death came for King on the balcony of the black-owned Lorraine Motel just off Beale Street on the evening of April 4. While standing outside with Jesse Jackson and Ralph Abernathy, a shot rang out. King fell over, struck in the neck by a rifle bullet which left him moribund. At 7:05 P.M. he was pronounced dead at St. Joseph's Hospital.

King's death caused a wave of violence in major cities across the country. However, King's legacy has lasted much longer than the memories of those post-assassination riots. In 1969, his widow, Coretta Scott King, organized the Martin Luther King, Jr. Center for Nonviolent Social Change, Inc. Today it stands next to his beloved Ebenezer Baptist

Church in Atlanta, and with the surrounding buildings is a national historic landmark under the administration of the National Park Service. His birthday, January 15, is a national holiday, celebrated each year with educational programs, artistic displays, and concerts throughout the United States. The Lorraine Motel where he was shot is now the National Civil Rights Museum.

## Joseph E. Lowery (1924–   )

*Southern Christian Leadership Conference President*

*See* Organizations.

## Floyd B. McKissick (1922–1981)

*Congress of Racial Equality Former National Director*

*See* Organizations.

## Rosa Louise McCauley Parks (1913–   )

*Civil Rights Activist*

Rosa Parks has been called the spark that lit the fire, and the mother of the movement. Her courage to defy custom and law to uphold her personal rights and dignity inspired the African Americans in Montgomery, Alabama to fight for their rights by staging one of the longest boycotts in history.

Born Rosa Louise McCauley, she was raised by her mother and grandparents in Tuskegee and Montgomery, Alabama. After attending segregated schools, she went to the all-black Alabama State College. In 1932, she married Raymond Parks, a barber. Both of them worked for the local NAACP chapter, and Rosa became local NAACP secretary in the 1950s.

On December 1, 1955, as she was riding home from work, she was ordered by the bus driver to give up her seat so that a white man might sit. She refused. She was arrested and fined $14. Her case was the last straw for the blacks of Montgomery, as tired of being underclass citizens as Parks was. A city-wide boycott was organized to force the city to desegregate public transportation. A young, unknown minister by the name of Martin Luther King, Jr. became involved, and lectured the nation on the injustice of it all. Blacks, and a few whites, organized peacefully together to transport boycotters to and from work, and they continued, despite opposition from the city and state governments, for 382 days.

When the boycott ended on December 21, 1956, both Parks and King were national heroes, and the Supreme Court had ruled that segregation on city buses was unconstitutional. The mass movement of non-violent social change that was started would last over a decade, and would culminate in the Civil Rights Act of 1964 and the Voter's Rights Act of 1965.

Because of the harassment Rosa Parks and her family received during and after the boycott, they moved to Detroit, Michigan in 1957. She found a job with Congressman John Conyers, but continued to be involved in the civil rights struggle. She gave speeches and attended marches and demonstrations. She marched on Washington in 1963, and into Montgomery in 1965. Even as her life has quieted down, she has received tributes for her dedication and inspiration; in 1980, she received the Martin Luther King, Jr. Nonviolent Peace Prize. As she headed towards retirement from John Conyers office in 1988, she became involved in other activities, like the Rosa and Raymond Parks Institute of Self Development in Detroit, founded in 1987.

**Asa Philip Randolph (1889–1979)**

*Brotherhood of Sleeping Car Porters and A.
Philip Randolph Institute Founder*

*See* Organizations.

**Bayard Rustin (1910–1987)**

*A. Philip Randolph Institute Former
Executive Director*

*See* Organizations.

**Al Sharpton (1954–   )**

*Social Activist*

Sharpton was born in 1954 in Brooklyn,
New York. He went to public schools, graduated from Tilden High School and briefly
attended Brooklyn College.

At the early age of four, Sharpton began
delivering sermons and at the age of thirteen
he was ordained a Pentecostal minister.
During and after high school Sharpton
preached in neighborhood churches and
went on national religious tours, often with
prominent entertainers.

Sharpton was soon befriended by a number of well known and influential African-
Americans including Congressman Adam
Clayton Powell, Jr., Jesse Jackson, and
singer James Brown. In 1969 Jackson
appointed Sharpton youth director of
Operation Breadbasket.

Around this same time James Brown
made Sharpton one of his bodyguards and
soon he was doing promotions for the
singer. In 1983 Sharpton married singer
Kathy Jordan and soon became involved
with fight promoter Don King.

Al Sharpton (center) leads a demonstration in New York City, 1992.

Even though Sharpton was promoting boxers and entertainers he had long before put himself in the public spotlight in the role of social activist. In 1971 he founded the National Youth Movement (later called the United African Movement) ostensibly to combat drug use. The movement however soon became a vehicle for Sharpton to draw attention to himself. He urged children to forsake Christmas in favor of a Kwanza celebration and the elderly to protest New York City police tactics.

Sharpton made himself part of the publicity surrounding the Bernard Goetz murder trial (1984), the Howard Beach racial killing (1986), the Twana Brawley debacle (1987) and the Yusef Hawkins-Bensonhurst killing (1989). In 1988 Sharpton was accused of being an FBI informant and passing on information about Don King, reputed organized crime figures and various African-American leaders. In 1989 and 1990 he was acquitted on charges of income tax evasion and embezzling National Youth Movement funds. In 1991 Sharpton was briefly hospitalized after being stabbed by a man wielding a pocket knife.

While being shunned by many middle class African-Americans, Sharpton draws support from the ranks of the youth and the disenfranchised. Does Sharpton embrace social causes in order to promote himself or does he employ outrageous tactics to better fight for racial justice? That is a difficult question to answer and the answer goes to the heart of the man.

### Leon Howard Sullivan (1922–   )
*Civil Rights Activist*

Sullivan was born October 16, 1922 in Charlestown, West Virginia. After being ordained a Baptist minister at the age of seventeen, Sullivan earned a B.A. from West Virginia State College (1943) and an M.A. from Columbia University (1947). Sullivan also attended the Union Theological Seminary (1945) and earned a D.D. from Virginia Union University.

From 1950 to 1988 Sullivan was the pastor of the Zion Baptist Church in Philadelphia. While there he entered into a lifelong crusade to provide better and expanding job opportunities for African-Americans.

Sullivan fought racist hiring practices by protest and economic boycott. He provided job training through the Opportunities Industrialization Center. Opening in 1964 with money from a Ford Foundation grant, the Center offered training in electronics, cooking, power-sewing and drafting. Sullivan also founded Zion Investment Associates which makes available seed money for new African-American business ventures.

Sullivan has also been associated with Progress Aerospace Inc., General Motors, Mellon Bank and he is a co-founder of Self-Help.

Sullivan is a recipient of the Russwurm Award (National Publisher's Association, 1963), American Exemplar Medal (1969), Philadelphia Book Award (1966), Philadelphia Fellowship Community Award (1964) and the Franklin D. Roosevelt Four Freedoms Medal (1987). Upon retiring from the Zion Baptist Church in 1988 Sullivan was made Pastor Emeritus.

### William Monroe Trotter (1872–1934)
*Civil Rights Activist*

An honor student and Phi Beta Kappa at Harvard, Trotter founded the militant newspaper, *Boston Guardian*, in 1901, for the purpose of "propaganda against discrimination."

In 1905 Trotter joined W.E.B. DuBois in founding the Niagara Movement but refused to move with him into the NAACP because he felt it would be too moderate. Instead, Trotter formed the National Equal Rights League. In 1919 Trotter appeared at the Paris Peace Conference in an unsuccessful effort to have it outlaw racial discrimination. The State Department had denied him a passport to attend, but he had reached Paris nonetheless, by having himself hired as a cook on a ship.

Because of his strident unwillingness to work with established groups, the civil rights movement has been slow to recognize Trotter. But many of his methods were to be adopted in the 1950s, notably his use of non-violent protest. In 1903 Trotter deliberately disrupted a meeting in Boston at which Booker T. Washington was preaching support of segregation; Trotter's purpose was to be arrested to gain publicity for his militant position. Trotter also led demonstrations against plays and films which glorified the Ku Klux Klan.

### Booker Taliaferro Washington (1856–1915)
*Political Activist, Educator*

Booker T. Washington was born a slave in Hale's Ford, Virginia, reportedly in April 1856. After emancipation, his family was so poverty stricken that he worked in salt furnaces and coal mines from age nine. Always an intelligent and curious child, he yearned for an education and was frustrated when he could not receive good schooling locally. When he was sixteen his parents allowed him to quit work to go to school. They had no money to help him, so he walked 200 miles to attend the Hampton Institute in Virginia and paid his tuition and board there by working as the janitor.

Dedicating himself to the idea that education would raise his people to equality in this country, Washington became a teacher. He first taught in his home town, then at the

Booker T. Washington

Hampton Institute, and then in 1881, he founded the Tuskegee Normal and Industrial Institute in Tuskegee, Alabama. As head of the Institute, he traveled the country unceasingly to raise funds from blacks and whites both; soon he became a well-known speaker.

In 1895 he was asked to speak at the opening of the Cotton States Exposition, an unprecedented honor for a black man. His speech explained his major thesis, that blacks could secure their constitutional rights through their own economic and moral advancement rather than through legal and political changes. Although his conciliatory stand angered some blacks who feared it would encourage the foes of equal rights, whites approved of his views. Thus his major achievement was to win over diverse elements among southern whites, without whose support the programs he envisioned and brought into being would have been impossible.

In addition to Tuskegee Institute, which still educates many today, he instituted a variety of programs for rural extension work, and helped to establish the National Negro Business League. Shortly after the election of President William McKinley in 1896, a movement was set in motion that Washington be named to a cabinet post, but he withdrew his name from consideration, preferring to work outside the political arena.

## Roy Wilkins (1901–1981)
*National Association for the Advancement of Colored People Former Executive Director*

*See* Organizations.

## Whitney M. Young, Jr. (1922–1971)
*National Urban League Former Executive Director*

*See* Organizations.

## ■ FEDERAL AND STATE CIVIL RIGHTS AGENCIES

### Equal Employment Opportunity Commission
1801 L St., NW
Washington, DC 20507
(202)663-4900

### United States Commission on Civil Rights
1121 Vermont Ave. NW
Washington, DC 20425
(800)552-6843

### Alabama Attorney General's Office
State House
Montgomery, AL 36130
(205)242-7300

### Alaska Human Rights Commission
800 A St., Ste. 202
Anchorage, AK 99501-3669
(907)276-7474

### Arizona Attorney General's Office
1275 W. Washington
Phoenix, AZ 85007
(602)542-5025

### Arkansas Attorney General's Office
200 Tower Bldg.
323 Center St.
Little Rock, AR 72201-2610
(501)682-2007

### California Attorney General
Public Rights Div.
1515 K. Street Suite 511
PO Box 944255
Sacramento, CA 94244-2550
(916)445-9555

### California Fair Employment and Housing Department
2014 T. St., Ste. 210
Sacramento, CA 95814-6835
(916)739-4600

### Colorado Attorney General's Office
1525 Sherman St., 5th Fl.
Denver, CO 80203
(303)866-3611

### Connecticut Attorney General's Office
55 Elm St.
Hartford, CT 06106
(203)566-2026

**Delaware Attorney General's Office**
Carvel State Office Bldg.
820 N. French St.
Wilmington, DE 19801
(302)577-3047


**Florida Attorney General's Office, Legal
  Affairs Dept.**
The Capitol
Tallahassee, FL 32399-1050
(904)488-2526


**Georgia Equal Opportunity Commission**
710 Cain Tower, Peachtree Ctr.
229 Peachtree St. NE
Atlanta, GA 30303
(404)656-1736


**Hawaii Attorney General's Office**
425 Queen St.
Honolulu, HI 96813
(808)586-1500


**Idaho Human Rights Commission**
450 W. State St.
1st Fl. West
Boise, ID 83720
(208)334-2873


**Illinois Human Rights Department**
100 W. Randolph St.
Ste. 10-100
Chicago, IL 60601
(312)814-6200


**Indiana Civil Rights Commission**
Indiana Government Ctr. North
100 N. Senate Ave., Rm. N-103
Indianapolis, IN 46204
(317)232-2600


**Iowa Human Rights Department**
Lucas Bldg
Des Moines, IA 50319
(515)281-5960


**Kansas Human Rights Commission**
851-S. Landon State Office Bldg.
900 SW Jackson St.
Topeka, KS 66612-1252
(913)296-3206


**Kentucky Human Rights Commission**
The Heyburn Bldg., 7th Fl.
PO Box 69
Louisville, KY 40202-0069
(502)588-4024


**Louisiana Attorney General's Office**
Justice Dept.
PO Box 94005
Baton Rouge, LA 70804-9005
(504)342-7013


**Maine Human Rights Commission**
State House Sta. 51
Augusta, ME 04333-0051
(207)624-6050


**Maryland Human Relations Commission**
20 E. Franklin St.
Baltimore, MD 21202-2274
(410)333-1700


**Massachusetts Attorney General's Office**
1 Ashburton Pl., Rm. 2010
Boston, MA 02108
(617)727-2200

**Michigan Attorney General's Office**
Law Bldg.
PO Box 30212
Lansing, MI 48909
(517)373-1100

**Michigan Civil Rights Department**
303 W. Kalamazoo, 4th Fl.
Lansing, MI 48913
(517)335-3165

**Minnesota Human Rights Department**
500 Bremer Tower K
St. Paul, MN 55101
(612)296-5663

**Missouri Human Rights Commission**
3315 W. Truman Blvd.
PO Box 504
Jefferson City, MO 65102
(314)751-3325

**Montana Attorney General's Office**
Justice Bldg.
215 N. Sanders
Helena, MT 59620
(406)444-2026

**Nebraska Equal Opportunity Commission**
PO Box 94934
Lincoln, NE 68509-4934
(402)471-2024

**Nevada Equal Rights Commission**
1515 E. Tropicana Ave., Ste. 590
Las Vegas, NV 89158
(702)486-7161

**New Hampshire Human Rights Commission**
163 Loudon Rd.
Concord, NH 03301
(603)271-2767

**New Jersey Attorney General's Office**
Civil Rights Division
383 W. State St.
CN 089
Trenton, NJ 08625
(609)984-3100

**New Mexico Labor Department**
Human Rights Division
Aspen Plaza
1596 Pacheco St.
Santa Fe, NM 87502
(505)827-6838

**New York Human Rights Division**
55 W. 125th St.
New York, NY 10027
(212)870-8400

**North Carolina Human Relations Commission**
Elks Bldg.
121 W. Jones St.
Raleigh, NC 27603-1368
(919)733-7996

**North Dakota Attorney General's Office**
State Capitol, 1st Fl.
600 E. Boulevard Ave.
Bismarck, ND 58505
(701)224-2210

**Ohio Civil Rights Commission**
220 Parsons Ave.
Columbus, OH 43266-0543
(614)466-2785

**Oklahoma Human Rights Commission**
2101 N. Lincoln Blvd., Rm. 480
Oklahoma City, OK 73105
(405)521-3441

**Oregon Attorney General's Office**
Justice Department
100 Justice Bldg.
Salem, OR 97310
(503)378-4400

**Pennsylvania Human Relations
Commission**
101 2nd St., Ste. 300
Box 3145
Harrisburg, PA 17015-3145
(717)787-4410

**Rhode Island Human Rights Commission**
10 Abbott Park Pl.
Providence, RI 02903-3768
(401)277-2661

**South Carolina Human Affairs
Commission**
PO Box 4490
Columbia, SC 29240
(803)253-6336

**South Dakota Attorney General's Office**
State Capitol
500 E. Capitol Ave.
Pierre, SD 57501-5070
(605)773-3215

**Tennessee Human Rights Commission**
400 Cornerstone Square Bldg.
530 Church St.
Nashville, TN 37243-0745
(615)741-5825

**Texas Attorney General's Office**
Price Daniel, Sr. Bldg.
PO Box 12548
Austin, TX 78711-2548
(512)463-2100

**Utah Attorney General's Office**
236 State Capitol
Salt Lake City, UT 84114
(801)538-1015

**Vermont Attorney General's Office**
Pavilion Office Bldg.
109 State St.
Montpelier, VT 05609-1001
(802)828-3171

**Virginia Human Rights Council**
PO Box 717
Richmond, VA 23206
(804)225-2292

**Washington Human Rights Commission**
711 S. Capitol Way, Ste. 402
PO Box 42490
Olympia, WA 98504-2490
(206)753-4840

**West Virginia Human Rights Commission**
1321 Plaza East
Charleston, WV 25301
(304)558-2616

**Wisconsin Attorney General's Office**
PO Box 7857
Madison, WI 53707-7857
(608)266-1221

**Wyoming Attorney General's Office**
123 State Capitol
Cheyenne, WY 82002
(307)777-7841

# ⑧
# *Black Nationalism*

# 8

# *Black Nationalism*

The Ideology of Black Nationalism ■ Early Black Nationalism in the United States
■ Black Nationalism in the Twentieth Century

**Essay by Wilson Jeremiah Moses**

*Black nationalism, in its classic nineteenth-century form, consisted of efforts by African-American groups and individuals to create a sovereign nation-state. The quest for a national homeland expressed a perceived need to demonstrate the capacity of black people for self-government. In its more inclusive form, black nationalism has been indistinguishable from such movements as African Civilizationism, Pan-Negro Nationalism, and Pan-Africanism. Sometimes it has advocated a "back-to-Africa movement," but often it has simply implied moral support for decolonizing Africa and advancing the material and spiritual interests of African peoples everywhere.*

## ■ THE IDEOLOGY OF BLACK NATIONALISM

The back-to-Africa movement went through several phases of rise and decline, from its resurgence in the 1850s to its apex in the Garvey movement, to its denouement thereafter. The major proponents of classical black nationalism invariably placed religious historicism and teleology at the center

of their ideological conceptions or utopian visions. While their goals were political and economic, they usually included a cultural agenda as well—though the cultural concerns of nineteenth-century nationalists were often Eurocentric and are not to be confused with the Negritude movement or the cultural nationalism of the late twentieth century. Black nationalism met the psychological need for a response to the slavery, colonialism, and racism imposed by Europeans and white Americans. In the minds of its adherents, it was the only sensible reaction to the almost universal military, technological, and economic domination of blacks by whites.

Documents expressing the ideology of black nationalism began to appear during the late eighteenth century. As Elie Kedourie has argued, nationalism, the idea that peoples are naturally divided into nations, is European in its origins. The American and French revolutions, and conceptions of the nation-state arising with them, came to dominate political thought, not only in the North Atlantic but also among African and Asian peoples. The 1804 slave revolt and seizure of the state in Haiti, as W.E.B. DuBois and Eugene Genovese have argued, was both a cause and an effect of rising conceptions of nationalism and manifest destiny in the United States. It was also an inspiration to black nationalism among both the slaves and the free African-Americans of the black population in the United States. Literary documents of black nationalism in England and the United States coincided with the revolutions in France or Haiti. Immanuel Geiss has referred to these expressions, typified by *The Interesting Narrative of the Life of Olaudah Equiano or Gustavus Vassa, the African, Written by Himself* (1787), as "proto-Pan-Africanism." (For a time, Vassa believed that the African condition could be improved by repatriating Afro-Europeans in Africa. Although he was to abandon that plan, he remained committed to the destruction of African slavery through the agencies of Christian missionary activity and free trade.)

Early black nationalism in the United States has been associated with Paul Cuffe.

## ■ EARLY BLACK NATIONALISM IN THE UNITED STATES

Early black nationalism in the United States is associated with the activities of two enterprising capitalists in the maritime industries, Paul Cuffe, a New Bedford sea captain, and James Forten, a Philadelphia sailmaker. These two figures combined a bourgeois economic nationalism with a Christian thrust, and hoped to develop Christianity, commerce, and civilization in Africa while providing a homeland for African Americans. Their repatriationist activities were brought to a halt in 1817, when Henry Clay, Andrew Jackson, and other white Americans formed the American Society for Colonizing the Free People of Color in the United States, usually called the American Colonization Society. The American Colonization Society had other prominent slave holders

among its leadership, and expressly denied any sympathy for abolition; large numbers of blacks reacted by demonstrating a marked hostility to the society and its aims. Cuffe died shortly after the society's founding, and Forten felt constrained to silence, although he continued to believe that black Americans would "never become a people until they come out from amongst the white people." Those who continued to support repatriation, or who migrated under the auspices of the American Colonization Society, became the objects of extreme vituperation.

Black nationalism and repatriationism were not the same thing, however, and hostility to the American Colonization Society did not always lead to the abandonment of nationalist rhetoric. Maria Stewart referred to herself as an African, but was hostile to the colonization movement. She insisted on her rights as an American, but at the same time denounced the United States with strident jeremiadic rhetoric. Stewart clearly viewed black America as a captive nation, existing in a type of Babylonian captivity, and conceived of African Americans as a people with a national destiny without advocating political separatism or the desire to form a nation-state. In a similar vein, David Walker denounced colonization and emigration with the religious fervor of an Old Testament prophet. Curiously, he insisted on the separate mission and destiny of African Americans as colored citizens of the world, while simultaneously maintaining that black and white Americans could be "a united and happy people."

Black nationalist motivations have been attributed to the major slave conspiracies of Gabriel Prosser and Denmark Vesey, who were inspired by the Haitian revolt, and both seem to have had as their goal the creation of a black nation with ties to the Caribbean. For the most part, however, evidence of black nationalism in the United States is found among the free black population of the North. It was in the so-called Free African Societies, which sprang up in the black communities of New York, Boston, and Philadelphia, that a conception of black historical identity and destiny was strongest. During the 1830s and 1840s, black nationalist thinking was associated with religious leadership such as that provided by the bishop of the African Methodist Episcopal Church, Richard Allen, who believed in a special God-given mission for black Americans as a people, but steadfastly opposed the American Colonization Society. Peter Williams, leader of the Afro-American Group of the Episcopal Church in New York, took a more tolerant view of colonization. He eulogized Paul Cuffe and remained friendly with John Russwurm, even after the latter emi-

grated to Liberia and was burned in effigy by anti-colonization activists.

The flourishing of black nationalism occurred during the 1850s and 1860s. To some degree, the movement owed its rebirth to the passage of the Fugitive Slave Act (1850) and the *Dred Scott v. Sandford* decision (1858). Emigration sentiment, which had been quiescent since the death of Cuffe, experienced a resurgence marked by the calling of several colonization conventions. The leaders of the movement were Henry Highland Garnet and Martin R. Delany, who founded the African Civilization Society in 1858. Edward Wilmot Blyden, the principal nineteenth century Pan-African theorist, migrated to Liberia in 1850. Alexander Crummell emigrated to Liberia under the auspices of the Domestic and Foreign Missionary Society of the Protestant Episcopal Church in

Martin R. Delany

1853, but eventually became involved with the American Colonization Society. During the early years of the Civil War, *The Weekly Anglo-African* became the principal journal of the emigration movement.

Emigrationism died out during the peak years of Reconstruction that followed the Civil War, as the black American population strove to take advantage of opportunities presented by emancipation. During the years from 1876 to 1914, a number of back-to-Africa movements were organized. Most prominent among these were the movements under the leadership of Rev. Henry McNeal Turner, an AME Bishop, Rev. Orishatukeh Faduma, a Yoruba man from Barbados, and Chief Alfred C. Sam, a Twi speaker from the Gold Coast. Some scholars

Although Garvey was less successful as a repatriationist than some of his predecessors, he enjoyed tremendous success as a journalist and community organizer.

In the twentieth century, the search for a black nationality was kept alive by such religious groups as the Nation of Islam.

have detected black nationalist elements in the Kansas Exodus of the 1870s and the Oklahoma movement that established all-black towns during the 1890s. Fadumah had been a missionary in Oklahoma, which proved an important recruiting ground for Alfred C. Sam.

## ■ BLACK NATIONALISM IN THE TWENTIETH CENTURY

Marcus Garvey's revitalization of the emigration movement came at an opportune moment. He arrived in the United States in 1916, shortly after Alfred C. Sam's voyage to the Gold Coast and a few months after the death of Bishop Turner. His Universal Negro Improvement Association was, according to some speculations, the largest mass movement ever to occur among black Americans. Although Garvey was less successful as a repatriationist than some of his predecessors, he enjoyed tremendous success as a journalist and community organizer. His reputation became a source of great inspiration to many black leaders, and spread among the masses of people in Africa and the Americas.

Cultural nationalism, the exaltation of the "African personality" and the celebration of the contributions of black people to world history, made its appearance in the mid-nineteenth century. Cultural nationalist rhetoric occasionally has been adopted even by persons who have strongly opposed political nationalism. Frederick Douglass shared with Edward Wilmot Blyden an admiration for the ancient Egyptians, whom he believed to be of exactly the same racial type as African Americans. Towards the end of the century, younger scholars, such as W.E.B. DuBois, were to make much of Egypt, Ethiopia, and Meroe as black contributors to world civilization. Writers such as William H. Ferris and John E. Bruce, who, like DuBois, were protégés of Alexander Crummell, sought to vindicate the black race and to popularize the notion that black peoples of the upper Nile were the progenitors of civilization. The height of the vindicationist school was reached in the writings of Joel Augustus Rogers, sometime contributor to Marcus Garvey's paper, the *Negro World*.

During the 1930s, new versions of cultural nationalism began to focus on the importance of West Africa, in addition to that of ancient Egypt. This development was par-

tially due to the Negritude movement among Francophone intellectuals, but also due to the "Jazz Age" interest in Africa among white artists and social scientists. The researches of Leo Frobenius, the German scholar, kindled the interest of DuBois, Aime Cesaire, and Leopold Senghor in the cultures of "tribal" Africa. The growing interest of European artists such as Picasso and Modigliani in primitivism and African cultural expression led black Americans to a revaluation of their folk heritage and its African roots. The new-found respectability of jazz after its acceptance in continental Europe was another factor in the rise of black cultural nationalism. The ideology of scientific relativism in the writings of Franz Boas and Melville Herskovits, which stressed cultural relativism and a respect for "primitive" cultures also helped to make an interest in sub-Saharan Africa fashionable.

Elijah Muhammad being interviewed by Buzz Anderson.

Black Muslim rally, 1961.

After the deportation of Marcus Garvey in 1925, black nationalism went into decline, as John Henrik Clarke and other scholars have noted. The search for a black nationality was kept alive by such religious groups as the Black Jews of Harlem, the Moorish Science Temple, and the Nation of Islam, which was under the leadership of the Honorable Elijah Muhammad. The rise of Malcolm X, a follower of Elijah Muhammad did much to popularize black nationalism with young radical intellectuals during the early 1960s. After his split with Elijah Muhammad, Malcolm X seemed to abandon traditional black nationalist separatism as well, embracing socialism and, at the same time, his white Muslim brethren. Black nationalist attitudes persisted in some radical groups during the late 1960s, but seldom showed any relationship to or awareness of the black nationalist traditions of the nineteenth cen-

tury. In recent years, cultural black nationalists such as Molefi K. Asante have shown a renewed interest in black nationalist intellectual history, especially as it relates to figures like Edward Wilmot Blyden and Marcus Garvey.

## ■ BLACK NATIONALIST AND PAN-AFRICAN THEORISTS

**Molefi Kete Asante (1942– )**
*Black Nationalist, Educator, Author*

See Education.

**Edward Wilmot Blyden (1832–1912)**
*Black Nationalist, Repatriationist*

Although he was not an American, Edward Blyden had a great influence on American Pan-African philosophy. As a scholar he wrote at great length about blacks in Africa and America, and about Christianity and Islam. He also held many different political and diplomatic offices in Liberia where he tried to put his beliefs into action.

Blyden was born in St. Thomas in the West Indies. When he was twelve, a white pastor undertook his education, encouraging him to become a minister. When he was eighteen he went to America, but was unable to find a seminary that would accept a black student. Instead, under the sponsorship of the New York Colonization Society, he went to Liberia to study at the new Alexander High School in Monrovia. Seven years later, he was the principal of the school.

Throughout his adult life, Blyden had two concurrent careers. He was a teacher and scholar. As a writer and editor he constantly defended his race, championed the achievements of other blacks, attacked slavery, and advocated the repatriation of blacks in Af-

Edward Wilmont Blyden

Because of his own religious training, Blyden was interested in Islam as a religion for Africans. Between 1901 and 1906, he was director of education in Sierra Leone. He studied both Christianity and Islam extensively, and summed up his views in an influential book, *Christianity, Islam and the Negro Race*. After his death in 1912, his funeral was attended by large numbers of both Christians and Muslims.

## Alexander Crummell (1819–1898)
*Black Nationalist, Repatriationist, Minister*

Crummell was born in New York City on March 3, 1819. He was descended from African royalty, as his paternal grandfather was the son of a West African ruler. Crummell began his schooling at the Mulberry Street School in New York City. In 1831 he began attending high school but in 1835 transferred to a school founded by abolitionists in Canaan, New Hampshire. The school however was destroyed by a mob of angry townspeople and Crummell began attending the Oneida Institute in Whitesboro, New York where he stayed for three years. He later studied in Boston and was ordained into the Episcopal Church in 1844. In 1847 he went to England and studied at Queens College, Cambridge from 1851 to 1853 where he was awarded an A.B. degree.

Crummell then spent twenty years in Liberia and Sierra Leone where he served as professor of Mental and Moral Science at the College of Liberia. In 1873 he returned to St. Mary's Mission in Washington DC and soon founded St. Luke's Protestant Episcopal Church where he spent his last twenty-two years. In 1897 he was instrumental in the founding of the American Negro Academy.

Crummell published many collections of his essays and sermons including *Future of Africa* (1862), *Greatness of Christ* (1882), and *Africa and America* (1892). Crummell

rica. As a teacher, he held many prominent posts, including professor of classics (1862–1871) and president of Liberia College (1880–1884). At the same time, Blyden was also a politician and diplomat in Liberia, holding many different offices. He was secretary of state from 1864 to 1866, minister of the interior from 1880 to 1882, minister to Britain from 1877 to 1878 and again in 1892, and minister plenipotentiary to London and Paris in 1905.

Blyden traveled to America eight times. In 1861, he was commissioned by the Liberian government to interest Americans in a Liberian education. He returned again the following year to recruit African-American emigrants to Africa. His last visit in 1895 was in hopes of furthering racial accommodation in the south so that racial problems in America would not travel to Africa with new emigrants.

died September 10, 1898 at Point Pleasant, New York.

## Paul Cuffe (1759–1817)
*Black Nationalist, Repatriationist, Entrepreneur*

Cuffe was born January 17, 1759 on Cuttyhunk Island near New Bedford, Massachusetts. He was the son of Cuffe Slocum, a freed slave and Ruth Moses, a Wampanoag Indian.

By the time Cuffe was sixteen he was earning a living as a sailor on a whaling vessel. After making numerous voyages he was captured by the British but later released. He studied arithmetic and navigation but soon returned to the sea. In 1795 he had his own ship, *Ranger*, and in eleven years he had become a landholder and owner of numerous other sailing vessels.

Besides being a merchant seaman Cuffe was also a civil rights activist. He discarded his father's slave surname and took his father's Christian first name in its place. He filed suffrage complaints in the Massachusetts' court and although unsuccessful, his court actions laid the groundwork for later civil rights legislation.

Cuffe was also a believer in free blacks voluntarily returning to Africa. In 1811 aboard his ship *Traveller* he sailed to Sierra Leone where he founded the Friendly Society which helped blacks return to Africa. In 1815 he sailed with thirty-eight colonists for Africa. It was to be his last voyage however, for he died September 9, 1817.

## Martin Robins Delany (1812–1885)
*Black Nationalist, Repatriationist*

Born in Charles Town, West Virginia, editor, author, physician, abolitionist and black nationalist Martin Delany received his first education from a book peddler who also served as an itinerant teacher. Since blacks in the south were forbidden to learn to read, when others found out he could read, the family was forced to flee north to Pennsylvania so that their children could continue to study. At the age of nineteen, he left home to seek further education. He studied with a young divinity student and a white doctor for a time.

As an adult, he became involved in anti-slavery reform, and the literacy movement. He began to publish *The Mystery*, a weekly newspaper devoted to news of the anti-slavery movement. When it folded after only a year of publication, Delany became co-editor of the *North Star*, a newspaper started by Frederick Douglass.

In 1848, Delany quit the *North Star* to pursue his medical studies. After being rejected on account of his race from several prominent Pennsylvania medical schools, he was able to attend the Harvard Medical School for a year before he was expelled from there due to his race. While he did not receive his degree, he did learn enough to practice medicine the rest of his life. In the 1850s, he became something of a local legend when he saved many lives during a fierce cholera epidemic in Pittsburgh.

The years following medical school were a grave disappointment to Delany, for blacks in America continued to be treated inhumanely no matter how hard he worked against slavery. He became an ardent black nationalist and recommended emigration to establish an independent colony for African Americans in South America or Africa. He wrote prolifically on the subject, held several national conventions, and set out on an exploratory expedition to Africa.

After the Emancipation Proclamation of 1863, Delany met with President Abraham Lincoln to discuss the establishment of black regiments in the army. Lincoln commissioned him as the first black major in the United States Army.

After the Civil War, Delany continued to work with reconstructionists trying to get fair treatment for newly freed slaves, still advocating emigration. He continued to pursue his scholarship, and in 1879 published his *Principal of Ethnology: The Origin of Races and Color* in which he discussed the role of black people in the world's civilization. He died in 1885, before he was able to actually move to Africa himself.

## Louis Farrakhan (1933–  )
*Black Nationalist, Nation of Islam National Minister*

Born in New York City, Louis Farrakhan (then known as Louis Eugene Walcott) was an outstanding student at Boston English High School and then attended (but did not earn a degree at) Winston-Salem Teacher's College. Farrakhan was an excellent musician; he played the violin and was a calypso singer. It was as a singer that he earned his livelihood prior to converting to Elijah Muhammad's Nation of Islam in the 1950s. He quickly worked his way up to a leadership position, becoming the minister of the Boston mosque. He loudly denounced Malcolm X after the latter split with Elijah Muhammad in 1963. He soon assumed leadership of the Harlem mosque which Malcolm had previously led. After Elijah Muhammad's death in 1975, he briefly supported Muhammad's son and designated successor, Warith Muhammad, as leader of the Nation of Islam. Shortly after Warith Muhammad began accepting whites as members within the Na-

Louis Farrakhan

tion of Islam, now renamed the World Community of Al-Islam in the West, Farrakhan split from him and established a rival organization with about 10,000 members.

Farrakhan's vigorous support for Jesse Jackson's presidential candidacy in 1984 quickly became an issue after Farrakhan made several controversial statements, most notably calling Judaism a "gutter religion." Overshadowed in the controversy was the involvement of Nation of Islam leaders in American electoral politics for the first time. Previously, Black Muslims had generally followed Elijah Muhammad's counsel not to vote or to take part in political campaigns.

## James Forten (1766–1842)
*Black Nationalist, Entrepreneur*

Forten was born of free African-American parents in Philadelphia in 1766. He studied at a Quaker school but at the age of fifteen he quit to serve as a powder boy aboard the privateer *Royal Louis* during the American Revolution. He was captured by the British and held prisoner for seven months. He eventually spent a year in England where he was introduced to abolitionist philosophy.

Upon returning to America he was apprenticed to a sailmaker, but by 1786 he was foreman and in 1798 he became owner of the company. The business prospered and in 1832 employed forty white and African-American workers.

By the 1830s Forten had become active in the abolitionist movement and was a strong opponent of African colonization. He became a noted pamphleteer, a nineteenth century form of social activism and was an early fund-raiser for William Lloyd Garrison's *The Liberator*.

Forten was president and founder of the American Moral Reform Society and was active in the American Anti-Slavery Society. He was a vigorous opponent of northern implementation of the 1793 Fugitive Slave Act. Forten died in Philadelphia in 1842.

## Marcus Garvey (1887–1940)
*Black Nationalist, Pan-African Theorist*

Born in St. Ann's Bay, Jamaica, Garvey was the youngest of eleven children. Garvey moved to Kingston at the age of fourteen, found work in a printshop, and became acquainted with the abysmal living conditions of the laboring class. He quickly involved himself in social reform, participating in the first Printers' Union strike in Jamaica in 1907 and in setting up the newspaper *The Watchman*. Leaving the island to earn money to finance his projects, he visited Central and South America, amassing evidence that black people everywhere were victims of discrimination.

Garvey returned to Jamaica in 1911 and began to lay the groundwork of the Universal Negro Improvement Association, to which he was to devote his life. Undaunted by lack of enthusiasm for his plans, Garvey left for England in 1912 in search of additional financial backing. While there, he met a Sudanese-Egyptian journalist, Duse Mohammed Ali. While working for Ali's publication *African Times and Oriental Review*, Garvey began to study the history of Africa—particularly, the exploitation of black peoples by colonial powers. He read Booker T. Washington's *Up From Slavery*, which advocated black self-help.

In 1914 Garvey organized the Universal Negro Improvement Association and its coordinating body, the African Communities League. In 1920 the organization held its first convention in New York. The convention opened with a parade down Harlem's Lenox Avenue. That evening, before a crowd of

25,000, Garvey outlined his plan to built an African nation-state. In New York City his ideas attracted popular support, and thousands enrolled in the UNIA. He began publishing the newspaper *The Negro World* and toured the United States preaching black nationalism to popular audiences. In a matter of months, he had founded over thirty UNIA branches and launched some ambitious business ventures, notably the Black Star Shipping Line.

In the years following the organization's first convention, the UNIA began to decline in popularity. With the Black Star Line in serious financial difficulties, Garvey promoted two new business organizations—the African Communities League and the Negro Factories Corporation. He also tried to salvage his colonization scheme by sending a delegation to appeal to the League of Nations for transfer to the UNIA of the African colonies taken from Germany during World War I.

Financial betrayal by trusted aides and a host of legal entanglements (based on charges that he had used the U.S. mails to defraud prospective investors) eventually led to Garvey's imprisonment in Atlanta Federal Penitentiary for a five-year term. In 1927 his half-served sentence was commuted, and he was deported to Jamaica by order of President Calvin Coolidge.

Garvey then turned his energies to Jamaican politics, campaigning on a platform of self-government, minimum wage laws, and land and judicial reform. He was soundly defeated at the polls, however, because most of his followers did not have the necessary voting qualifications.

In 1935 Garvey left for England where, in near obscurity, he died five years later in a cottage in West Kensington.

## Malcolm X (El-Hajj Malik El-Shabazz) (1925–1965)
*Black Nationalist*

Malcolm X was one of the most fiery and controversial blacks of the twentieth century.

Born Malcolm Little in Omaha, Nebraska on May 19, 1925, Malcolm was the son of a Baptist minister, who was an avid supporter of Marcus Garvey's United Negro Improvement Association. While living in Omaha, the family was often harassed—at one point the family's house was set afire. In 1929 the family moved to Lansing, Michigan. While in Michigan, Malcolm's father was killed; his body severed in two by a streetcar and his head smashed. In his autobiography, written with Alex Haley, Malcolm asserted that his father may have been killed by members of the Ku Klux Klan. His mother, stricken by the death of her husband and the demands of providing for the family, was committed to a mental institution.

Leaving school after the eighth grade, Malcolm made his way to New York, working for a time as a waiter at Smalls Paradise in Harlem. Malcolm began selling and using drugs, turned to burglary, and, in 1946, was sentenced to a ten-year prison term on burglary charges.

While in prison Malcolm became acquainted with the Black Muslim sect, headed by Elijah Muhammad, and was quickly converted. Following his parole in 1952, he soon became an outspoken defender of Muslim doctrines, accepting the basic argument that evil was an inherent characteristic of the "white man's Christian world."

Unlike Muhammad, Malcolm sought publicity, making provocative and inflammatory statements to predominantly white civic groups and college campus audiences. Branding white people "devils," he spoke bitterly of a philosophy of vengeance and

Malcolm X

week later, Malcolm was shot and killed at the Audubon Ballroom in Harlem, while preparing to speak. Three of the men arrested were later identified as members of the Nation of Islam.

Malcolm X had a profound influence on both blacks and whites. Many blacks responded to a feeling that he was a man of the people, experienced in the ways of the street rather than the pulpit or the college campus, which traditionally had provided the preponderance of black leaders. Many young whites responded to Malcolm's blunt, colorful language and unwillingness to retreat in the face of hostility.

The memory and image of Malcolm X has changed as much after his death as his own philosophies changed during his life. At first thought to be a violent fanatic, he is now understood as an advocate of self-help, self-defense, and education; as a philosopher and pedagogue, he succeeded in integrating history, religion, and mythology to establish a framework for his ultimate belief in world brotherhood and in human justice. Faith, in his view, was a prelude to action; ideas were feckless without policy. At least three books published since his death effectively present his most enduring thoughts. In 1992, a monumental film by Spike Lee based on his autobiography, renewed interest and understanding in the meaning of the life and death of Malcolm X.

## Elijah Muhammad (1897–1975)
*Black Nationalist, Nation of Islam Spiritual Leader*

Elijah Muhammad was born Elijah Poole in Sandersville, Georgia. His father, a Baptist preacher, had been a slave.

As a boy, Elijah worked at various jobs involving manual labor. At the age of twenty-six, he moved with his wife and two children

"an eye for an eye." When, in 1963, he characterized the Kennedy assassination as a case of "chickens coming home to roost," he was suspended from the Black Muslim movement by Elijah Muhammad.

Disillusioned with Elijah Muhammad's teachings, Malcolm formed his own organizations, the Organization of Afro-American Unity and the Muslim Mosque Inc. In 1964 he made a pilgrimage to Islam's holy city, Mecca, and adopted the name El-Hajj Malik El Shabazz. He also adopted views that were not popular with other black nationalists, including the idea that not all whites were evil and that blacks could make gains by working through established channels.

As a result of Malcolm's new views, he became the victim of death threats. On February 14, 1965, his home was firebombed; his wife and children escaped unharmed. A

Elijah Muhammad

prison was probably significant in his later, successful attempts to convert large numbers of black prison inmates, including Malcolm X, to the Nation of Islam. During the 1950s and 1960s, the Nation grew under Muhammad's leadership. Internal differences between Muhammad and Malcolm X, followed by the break between the two men and Malcolm's assassination, for which three Black Muslim gunmen were convicted, provided a great deal of unfavorable media coverage, but this did not slow the growth of the movement. In the late 1960s and early 1970s, Elijah Muhammad moderated the Nation's criticism of whites without compromising its message of black integrity. When Muhammad died in 1975, the Nation was an important religious, political, and economic force among America's blacks, especially in this country's major cities.

Elijah Muhammad was not original in his rejection of Christianity as the religion of the oppressor. Noble Drew Ali and the Black Jews had arrived at this conclusion well before him. But Muhammad was the most suc-

(he was to have eight children in all) to Detroit. There in 1930, Poole met Fard Muhammad, also known as W.D. Fard, who had founded the Lost-Found Nation of Islam. Poole soon became Fard's chief assistant and in 1932 went to Chicago where he established the Nation of Islam's Temple, Number Two, which soon became the largest. In 1934, he returned to Detroit. When Fard disappeared in that year, political and theological rivals accused Poole of foul play. He returned to Chicago where he organized his own movement, in which Fard was deified as Allah and Elijah (Poole) Muhammad became known as Allah's Messenger. This movement soon became known as the Black Muslims.

During World War II, Elijah Muhammad expressed support for Japan, on the basis of its being a nonwhite country, and was jailed for sedition. The time Muhammad served in

Henry McNeal Turner

cessful salesman for this brand of African-American religion. Thus he was able to build the first strong, black religious group in the United States that appealed primarily to the unemployed and underemployed city dweller, and ultimately to some in the black middle class. In addition, his message on the virtues of being black was explicit and uncompromising, and he sought with at least a little success to bolster the economic independence of African Americans by establishing schools and businesses under the auspices of the Nation of Islam.

## Henry McNeal Turner (1834–1915)

*Black Nationalist, Repatriationist, Minister*

Henry McNeal Turner was born near Abbeville, South Carolina of free parents. He was ordained a minister in the African Meth-odist Episcopal Church in 1853 and bishop in 1880. In 1863 Turner became the first African-American Army chaplain. He was also president of Morris Brown College for twelve years.

Turner was a leading advocate of repatriation. In 1876 he was elected vice president of the American Colonization Society. He made several trips to Africa and lectured throughout world.

Turner was convinced that blacks had no future in America. Instead, he felt that God had brought blacks to the New World as a means of spreading Christianity and preparing them to redeem Africa. Turner edited and published several papers, including *Voice of Missions* and *Voice of the People*, in which he advocated black colonization of Africa.

# 9

# *National Organizations*

# 9

# *National Organizations*

A Brief History ■ Organization Leaders ■ National Organizations

*In a dispute between the National Association for the Advancement of Colored People and the state of Alabama, Justice Harlen of the United States Supreme Court, pointed out the significance of association membership, claiming that it is through associations that individuals have sought "to make more effective the expression of their own views." Associations are one of the largest and most influential forces in the United States and have played an important part in the economic, social, and educational development of African Americans; organizations have been crucial in developing and disseminating information, ensuring representation for private interests, and promoting social and policy objectives.*

## ■ A BRIEF HISTORY

### Early Black Organizations

Due to restrictive ordinances and limited tolerance by whites, prior to the eighteenth century only the most informal and limited assembling of blacks was permitted. Most often meeting as religious assemblies, African Americans were forced to meet secretly, in small numbers. Thus the very first black

organizations to exist in the United States cannot definitively be identified.

The Free African Society, organized in Philadelphia in 1787, has been generally accepted as the first African-American organization in the United States. Founded by Methodist ministers Richard Allen and Absalom Jones, the Free African Society served as an important source of political consciousness and welfare for blacks throughout the country, combining economic and medical aid for poor blacks with support of abolition and sub rosa communication with blacks in the South.

The abolitionist movement of the nineteenth century, produced numerous organizations concerned with issues of importance to African Americans, including the American Colonization Society (founded in 1816), the New England Anti-Slavery Society (founded in 1832), and the American Anti-Slavery Society (founded in 1833). Although most of these organizations were dominated by whites, black leaders, including Paul Cuffe and Frederick Douglass played an active role in the movement and in anti-slavery organizations of the time.

During the late nineteenth and early twentieth centuries a great many black organiza-

W.E.B. DuBois

tions came into existence; the thrust of most of these groups was toward education, betterment, and religious training. In 1895 the National Medical Association was founded to further the interests of black physicians, pharmacists, and nurses; Mary McLeod Bethune organized the National Association of Colored Women in 1896; and in 1900 the National Negro Business League was formed to promote commercial development.

### The Niagara Movement

The Niagara Movement of 1905, marked a turning point in African-American history. This new organization, founded by a group of black intellectuals—headed by W.E.B. DuBois, a professor at Atlanta University— met July 11–13, 1905 in Buffalo, New York. The organization represented a formal re-

nunciation of Booker T. Washington's program of manual and industrial training for the black, as a means of gaining economic security, and conciliation, as a means of gaining social equality.

The Niagara Movement, however, suffered from weak finances and a policy which restricted membership to black intellectuals. In 1909 the Niagara Movement was succeeded by a new organization—one which would later become the National Association for the Advancement of Colored People.

### National Association for the Advancement of Colored People

The new organization was largely the brainchild of three people: William English Walling, a white Southerner who feared that racists would soon carry "the race war to the North"; Mary White Ovington, a wealthy young white woman who had attended the 1905 meeting of the Niagara group as a reporter for the *New York Evening Post* and had experience with conditions in the black ghettos of New York City; and Dr. Henry Moskowitz, a New York social worker. The trio proposed that a conference be called "for the discussion of present evils, the voicing of protests, and the renewal of the struggle for civil and political liberty." The three-day conference, held May 30 through June 1, was followed by four meetings, the results of which were an increase in membership and the selection of an official name—the National Negro Committee. In 1910 the organization adopted its present name and was incorporated in New York state; by 1914 the association had established some fifty branches throughout the country.

Over the years, the organization has attempted to better the condition of African Americans through litigation, legislation,

An early NAACP office.

and education; *Crisis* magazine, edited by W.E.B. DuBois, became its chief vehicle for the dissemination of information. Perhaps its most significant victory was won in 1954 when the historic *Brown v. Board of Education of Topeka* case threw out the "separate but equal" doctrine established by the Supreme Court in *Plessy v. Ferguson* in 1896 and eliminated segregation in public education.

### NAACP Legal Defense and Educational Fund, Inc.

Established in 1939 by the National Association for the Advancement of Colored People, the NAACP Legal Defense and Educational Fund maintained its own board, program, staff, office, and budget for some twenty years. It has served in the forefront of legal assaults against discrimination and segregation and has an outstanding record of victories. In addition to its litigation, the Legal Defense Fund provides scholarships and training for young lawyers, advises lawyers on legal trends and decisions, and monitors federal programs.

Originally for tax purposes, the NAACP Legal Defense Fund had been maintained as a separate arm of the NAACP, until it officially was divorced from its parent organization in 1959. Following the separation of the organizations, a dispute over identity and the use of the parent organization's name erupted. The National Association for the Advancement of Colored People sued the NAACP Legal Defense Fund for name infringement. However, after several months of legal wrangling, a federal court ruled that the LDF could keep NAACP in its name, since the NAACP was its parent organization.

## Organizations Concerned with Urban Problems

During the early part of the twentieth century several organizations concerned with the plight of urban blacks emerged. In 1906, at the urging of William H. Baldwin, president of the Long Island Railroad, a group of blacks and whites met for the purpose of studying the employment needs of African Americans. This group, known as the Committee for the Improvement of Industrial Conditions Among Negroes in New York, studied the racial aspects of the labor market (particularly the attitudes and policies of employers and unions) and sought to find openings for qualified African Americans.

At the same time, the League for the Protection of Colored Women was established to provide similar services for black women in New York and Philadelphia arriving from various parts of the South. These women, who often had no friends or relatives in the North, often fell prey to unscrupulous employment agencies which led them into low wage jobs.

A third organization, the Committee on Urban Conditions Among Negroes, appeared in 1910. It was organized by Ruth Standish Baldwin, widow of the former Long Island Railroad president, and Dr. George Edmond Haynes, one of only three trained black social workers in the country and the first black person to receive a doctorate

Black women looking for work in Northern cities often fell prey to unscrupulous employment practices and to low wage jobs.

426

from Columbia University. Haynes was named as the first executive secretary of the new agency. A year later the organization merged with the Committee for the Improvement of Industrial Conditions Among Negroes in New York and the National League for the Protection of Colored Women to form the National League on Urban Conditions Among Negroes. That name was later shortened to the now-familiar National Urban League.

From the outset, the organization focused on the social and economic needs of blacks, seeking training, improved housing, health, recreation, and job assistance for blacks. The organizational model that the League had established in New York City attracted attention and soon affiliates were formed in various cities across the country.

A major goal of the National Urban League and its affiliates was to broaden economic opportunities for African Americans. It was not until the 1960s when Whitney M. Young, Jr. became its new leader that the League began to emerge as a force in the civil rights struggle.

A. Philip Randolph

### Leadership Conference on Civil Rights

The Leadership Conference on Civil Rights was organized in 1950 by A. Philip Randolph, Roy Wilkins, and Arnold Aronson to implement the historic report of President Harry S. Truman's Committee on Civil Rights, *To Secure These Rights.* Beginning with only thirty organizations, the conference has grown in numbers, scope, and effectiveness, and has been responsible for coordinating the campaigns that have resulted in the passage of the civil rights legislation of the 1950s and 1960s, including the Civil Rights Acts of 1957, 1960, and 1964, the Voting Rights Act of 1965, and the Fair Housing Act of 1968.

The Leadership Conference on Civil Rights currently consists of approximately 157 national organizations representing minorities, women, major religious groups, the handicapped, the aged, labor, and minority businesses and professions. These organizations speak for a substantial portion of the population and together comprise one of the most broad based coalition in the nation.

### Southern Christian Leadership Conference

Following the arrest of Rosa Parks, who had refused to give up her seat on a public bus, the Reverends Dr. Martin Luther King, Jr. and Ralph Abernathy organized the Montgomery Improvement Association in 1955 to coordinate a citywide bus boycott. The success of the boycott led to the creation of a new organization.

Dr. Martin Luther King, Jr.

doms of speech and press, has from time to time been questioned and challenged.

Since the founding of the National Association for the Advancement of Colored People and similar organizations, state and local governments have attempted to prevent the operation of such groups. During the late 1950s the state of Alabama set out to ban the NAACP from conducting activities with the state, claiming that the association had failed to comply with statutes governing corporations operating within the state. The dispute, *NAACP v. Alabama*, was finally resolved by the United States Supreme Court in 1958 in favor of the association. However, the association was met with other interferences—some of the most notable disputes include, *Bates v. Little Rock* (1960), *Louisiana ex rel. Gremillion v. NAACP* (1961), and *Gibson v. Florida Legislative Investigating Committee* (1963).

This new organization, consisting mainly of black ministers, met at the Ebenezer Baptist Church in January 1957 and elected Dr. King as its first president. Initially called the Southern Negro Leaders Conference, and later the Southern Leadership Conference, the Southern Christian Leadership Conference grew to become one of the most influential and effective of all the civil rights organizations.

## Organizations and the Court

Although public and private associations of all kinds have traditionally flourished in this country, it has not always been an easy road for organizations for blacks and other minorities. The freedom of association—the freedom to assemble, immunity from state scrutiny—like the First Amendment free-

## Congress of Racial Equality

The Congress of Racial Equality (CORE), an interracial organization organized to confront racism and discrimination, was founded in 1942 by James Farmer, as the result of a campaign protesting discrimination at a Chicago restaurant. From Chicago, the organization spread to other cities and other causes, organizing sit-ins and Freedom Rides throughout the South.

By the mid-1960s, CORE had changed directions, and Farmer turned leadership of the organization over to Floyd McKissick, a North Carolina lawyer. With McKissick as national director, the organization moved toward an all-black membership and staff. (In 1967 CORE, at its convention, eliminated the word "multiracial" from its constitution). McKissick left the organization in 1968 and was replaced by the present national director, Roy Innis, former chairman of the Harlem chapter.

### Student Non-Violent Coordinating Committee

In 1960 a group of black college students founded the Student Non-Violent Coordinating Committee (SNCC) to coordinate the activities of students engaged in direct action protest. SNCC achieved enormous results in the desegregation of public facilities and earned respect from the country for its determination to act peacefully, no matter how violent or demeaning the provocation.

However, by 1964 the organization's leader, Stokely Carmichael, had become convinced that the American system could not be turned around without the threat of wholesale violence. In 1967 Carmichael left the organization to join the more militant Black Panther Party. H. Rap Brown, the former minister of justice in the old organization, took over leadership, renaming the organization the Student National Coordinating Committee and promoting violent retaliation when situations so demanded. The organization gradually declined in membership and is now essentially defunct.

### Black Panther Party

From its founding by Huey P. Newton and Bobby Seale in 1966, the Black Panther Party departed from the platform and tactics of other civil rights organizations. It rejected the institutional structure which, in its view, made American society corrupt; it rejected established channels of authority which oppressed the black community; it rejected middle-class values, which it felt contributed to indifference toward, and contempt for, the disinherited black urban youth.

The party imposed strict discipline on its members, denouncing the use of intoxicants, drugs, and artificial stimulants "while doing party work." The intellectual fare of every party member is the ten-point pro-

Floyd McKissick (at microphone) speaks at a demonstration, 1967.

Stokely Carmichael at a rally at the University of California, 1966.

gram (supplemented by daily reading of political developments), which every member is obliged to know and understand, presumably even to commit to memory.

However, by 1970 most of the organization's leadership was either jailed, in exile, or dead—Newton was jailed in 1968 on manslaughter changes; Seale had been jailed on charges steming from the 1968 Chicago convention riot; minister of information, Eldridge Cleaver, in 1969 fled to Algeria to avoid a prison sentence; in 1970 Mark Clark and Fred Hampton were killed during a police raid.

## Organizations Providing Community Support

In 1967 the National Urban Coalition was founded to improve the quality of life for the disadvantaged in urban areas through the combined efforts of business, labor, government, and community leaders. Another organization, the National Black United Fund, which provides financial and technical support to projects serving the critical needs of black communities nationwide, was founded in 1972.

The Reverend Jesse Jackson, in 1971, organized Operation PUSH (People United to Save Humanity). The organization has pursued its economic objectives through its Operation Breadbasket program. It also has worked to motivate young people through its PUSH-EXCEL program, which is designed to instill pride and build confidence in young people. Jackson left Operation PUSH to organize another group, the National Rainbow Coalition, Inc., in 1984.

## Organizations Responding to Africa and the Caribbean

During the nineteenth and early part of the twentieth century, a number of individuals and organizations arose to unite Africans throughout the world. Most notable was Marcus Garvey, black nationalist and advocate of repatriation of blacks to Africa, who founded the Universal Negro Improvement

Bobby Seale (left) and Huey Newton, 1969.

Randall Robinson meets with African National Congress President, Nelson Mandela, 1991.

Association in 1914. Garvey's organization, whose goal was to instill pride, gain economic and political power for blacks in the United States, and to establish an independent black colony in Africa, and to promote unity between African throughout the world, attracted millions worldwide. On February 19 1918, under the leadership of W.E.B. DuBois, the first Pan-African Congress was held in Paris. The meeting was attending by blacks from around the world and focused on the problems facing Africans worldwide.

More recently new organizations have formed to address the concerns of Africans around the world. Founded in 1977 by Randall Robinson, TransAfrica has worked to influence American foreign policy regarding political and human rights in African and the Caribbean by informing the public of violations of social, political, and civil rights. Responding to the continued policy of apartheid in South Africa, TransAfrica has supported sanctions against South Africa and has organized demonstrations in front of the South African embassy in Washington, DC. During one such demonstration, Robinson and numerous others were arrested. Other organizations have also taken a stand on policies affecting Africans around the world. In 1986 leaders representing major black organizations united to press for passage of the more stringent legislation regarding sanctions against South Africa.

# ■ ORGANIZATION LEADERS

## H. Rap Brown (Jamil Abdullah Al-Amin) (1943– )

*Student National Coordinating Committee Chairman*

In 1967 H. Rap Brown took over leadership of the Student Non-Violent Coordinating Committee renaming the organization the Student National Coordinating Committee. Since the late 1960s the organization has gradually declined in membership and is now essentially defunct.

In 1968 Brown was charged with inciting a riot in Cambridge, Maryland and was convicted in New Orleans on a federal charge of carrying a gun between states. In 1969 Brown published the book *Die Nigger Die*. Brown disappeared in 1970, after being slated for trial in Maryland, and in 1972 he was shot, arrested, and eventually convicted for a bar holdup in New York City.

While in prison, Brown converted to the Islamic faith and took the name of Jamil Abdullah Al-Amin. On his release, he founded a community grocery store in Atlanta. He is currently leader of the Community Mosque in Atlanta.

## Stokely Charmichael (Kwame Toure) (1941– )

*Student Non-Violent Coordinating Committee Founder*

*See* Civil Rights.

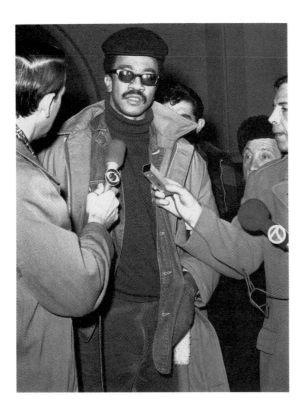

H. Rap Brown

## Benjamin Franklin Chavis, Jr. (1948– )

*National Association for the Advancement of Colored People Executive Director*

Benjamin Chavis was born on January 22, 1948 in Oxford, North Carolina. He received a B.A. from the University of North Carolina in 1969. Chavis went on to earn an M.A. from the Duke University Divinity School and a Ph.D. in theology from Howard University in Washington DC.

He came to national attention in 1971, when as a civil rights organizer for the United Church of Christ he was indicted along with nine other people for the firebombing of a grocery store in Wilmington, Delaware during a period of racial unrest. In the controversial trial that followed all of the "Wilmington 10" were found guilty. Chavis was sentenced to a prison term of twenty-nine to thirty-four years. Chavis was granted parole and in 1980 his conviction was re-

Benjamin Chavis

versed amidst conflicting testimony by various witnesses.

Prior to becoming active in the civil rights movement, Chavis taught chemistry at the high school level. He also worked as an AFSCME labor organizer (1969), a civil rights organizer for the Southern Christian Leadership Council (1967–1969), as a minister for the United Church of Christ, and as director of their Commission for Racial Justice in Washington, DC (1972). In 1985 he was appointed executive director of the Commission for Racial Justice. Chavis has also served as co-chairman of the National Alliance Against Racism and Political Repression (1977) and as co-chairman of the Organizing Committee for Economic and Social Justice.

In 1977 Chavis wrote *Let My People Go: Psalms From Prison*. He also received the George Collins Service Award (1977), given by the Congressional Black Caucus, the William L. Patterson award given by the Patterson Foundation, and the Shalom

award presented by the Eden Theological Seminary.

Chavis has since become active in the South African civil rights struggle and continues his position with the United Church of Christ.

On April 9, 1993, the NAACP board elected Chavis to succeed retiring executive director, Benjamin Hooks.

## Ramona Hoage Edelin (1945– )
*National Urban Coalition President and Chief Executive*

Born in Los Angeles, California, Ramona Hoage Edelin received her B.A. (magna cum laude) from Fisk University, her M.A. from the University of East Anglia, in Norwich, England, and her Ph.D from Boston University. She has been a lecturer at the University of Maryland and a visiting professor at Brandeis University; she has also served as chair of Afro-American studies at Emerson College.

In 1977 Edelin joined the National Urban Coalition as an executive assistant to the president. The National Urban Coalition, an organization to improve the quality of life for the disadvantaged in urban areas, has been active in advocating initiatives designed to encourage youth and promote leadership. Between 1979 and 1982 she moved from director of operations, to vice president of operations, then to senior vice president of program and policy, during which time she directed programs in housing, health, education, and advocacy. In 1982 Edelin became the organization's chief executive.

## Marian Wright Edelman (1939–   )
*Children's Defense Fund President*

A native of Bennettsville, South Carolina, Marian Wright Edelman received her undergraduate degree from Spelman College and her law degree from Yale. In 1963 she joined the NAACP Legal Defense and Education Fund as staff attorney. A year later she organized the Jackson, Mississippi branch of the NAACP Legal Defense and Education Fund, serving as its director until 1968. In 1968 she founded the Washington Research Project of the Southern Center for Public Policy which later developed into the Children's Defense Fund.

Wright has served as director of the Harvard University Center for Law and Education, chairman of the Spelman College board of trustees, a member of the Yale University Corporation, the National Commission on Children, and on the boards of the Center on Budget and Policy Priorities, the US Committee for UNICEF, and the Joint Center for Political and Economic Studies.

As Children's Defense Fund president, Edelman has become the nation's most effective lobbyist on behalf of children. Even while social spending was being cut, she has managed to score some victories. In 1986, nine federal programs known as "the Children's Initiative" received a $500 million increase in their $36 billion budget for families and children's health care, nutrition, and early education.

The most visible focus of CDF is its teen pregnancy prevention program. Through Edelman's efforts, Medicaid coverage for expectant mothers and children was boosted in 1984. In 1985, Edelman began holding an annual Pregnancy Prevention Conference, bringing thousands of religious leaders, social and health workers and community organizations to Washington to discuss ways of dealing with the problem.

In her 1987 book, *Families in Peril: An Agenda for Social Change*, Edelman wrote, "As adults, we are responsible for meeting the needs of children. It is our moral obligation. We brought about their births and their lives, and they cannot fend for themselves." Her other books include, *Children Out of School in America, School Suspensions: Are They Helping Children?, Portrait of Inequality: Black and White Children in America, Families in Peril: An Agenda for Social Change*, and *The Measure of Our Success: A Letter to My Children*.

## James Farmer (1920–   )
*Congress of Racial Equality Founder and
    Former National Director*

Born in Marshall, Texas on January 12, 1920, Farmer attended public schools throughout the South. He earned his B.S. degree in chemistry from Wiley College in 1938 and his B.D. degree from Howard University in 1941. Active in the Christian Youth Movement, and once vice-chairman of the

James Farmer, 1965.

National Council of Methodist Youth and the Christian Youth Council of America, Farmer refused ordination when confronted with the realization that he would have to practice in a segregated ministry.

In 1941 Farmer accepted a post as race relations secretary for the Fellowship of Reconciliation. The following year he and a group of University of Chicago students organized the Congress of Racial Equality (CORE), the first protest organization in the United States to utilize the techniques of nonviolence and passive resistance advocated by the Indian nationalist Mohandas Karamchand Gandhi.

In June 1943 CORE staged the first successful sit-in demonstration at a restaurant in the Chicago Loop. The organization soon supplemented this maneuver with what came to be known as the standing-line, which involved the persistent waiting in line by CORE members at places of public accommodation where blacks had been denied admission.

In 1961 CORE introduced the Freedom Ride into the vocabulary and methodology of civil rights protest, dispatching bus riders throughout the South for the purpose of testing the desegregation of terminal facilities. Attacked in Alabama and later arrested in Mississippi, the Freedom Riders eventually succeeded in securing the court ordered desegregation of bus terminals, with the United States Supreme Court decision of 1960 which outlawed segregated in interstate transportation.

Farmer left the organization in 1966. In 1969, President Richard Nixon appointed Farmer to the post of assistant secretary of Health, Education and Welfare. The appointment created a furor in some black circles, where it was felt that it was inappropriate for a former civil rights leader to serve in such an administration; in other circles, the appointment was praised by those who

thought it necessary for African Americans to be represented in all areas. However, Farmer found that there was little of substance in the position and resigned.

Farmer began to give lectures, and for a while headed a think tank at Howard University. In 1976 he broke all ties with CORE, criticizing its leader, Roy Innis, for such things as attempting to recruit black Vietnam veterans as mercenaries in Angola's civil war. Disturbed over the course that the organization had taken, Farmer and a score of former CORE members attempted to create a new racially mixed civil rights organization in 1980. Farmer, along with Floyd McKissick, attempted to meet with Innis to reach an agreement on the future of the organization, but nothing developed.

Farmer has written several books, including *Freedom When?* and *Lay Bare the Heart*.

### Prince Hall (1735?–1807)
*Founder of Black Freemasonry in the United States*

Prince Hall, is believed to have been born in Bridge Town, Barbados and have migrated to the United States in 1765; other records claim that during the late 1740s he had been a slave to William Hall of Boston, Massachusetts, and freed by William Hall on April 9, 1770.

In March 1775 Hall along with fifteen other blacks were initiated into a lodge of British army Freemasons stationed in Boston. The group of black masons was issued a permit to meet at a lodge on March 17, 1775, and on July 3, 1775, they organized the African Lodge No. 1, with Hall as master of the lodge. The lodge received official recognition from England as a regular Lodge of Free and Accepted Masons in 1784 and was designated the African Lodge No. 459.

Grand Lodge No. 1, Greensville, Mississippi, 1887.

Hall, in addition to leading the organization of black Freemasonry, was active as an abolitionist. In January 1777, he was the prime force behind a black petition sent to the Massachusetts state legislature requesting the abolition of slavery in the state. Another important petition, drawn up under his leadership in 1788, called for an end to the kidnapping and sale of free blacks into slavery. He also actively lobbied for the organization of schools for black children in Boston. Prince Hall died on December 4, 1807 in Boston.

### Dorothy I. Height (1912–   )
*National Council of Negro Women President*

A native of Richmond, Virginia, Dorothy Height holds a masters degree from New York University and has studied at the New York School of Social Work. In the fall of 1952, she served as a visiting professor at the Delhi School of Social Work in New Delhi, India. Six years later, she was appointed to the Social Welfare Board of New York by Governor Averell Harriman, and was reappointed by Governor Nelson Rockefeller in 1961. Since 1957 she has been president of the National Council of Negro Women, an organization founded by Mary McLeod Bethune in 1935.

Before becoming the fourth president of the National Council of Negro Women, Height had served on the organization's board of directors. She has also served as associate director for leadership training services for the Young Women's Christian Association, as a member of the Defense Advisory Committee on Women in the Services, as president of Delta Sigma Theta sorority, as vice president of the National Council of Women, as president of Women

Dorothy Height

Memphis and the Greater New Mount Moriah Baptist Church in Detroit. As a prominent local businessman, he was the co-founder and vice president of the Mutual Federal Savings and Loan Association in Memphis.

On January 10, 1977, Hooks was unanimously elected executive director of the National Association for the Advancement of Colored People by the NAACP board of directors, succeeding the retiring Roy Wilkins.

Under his progressive leadership, the association took an aggressive posture on United States policy toward African nations. Among his many battles on Capitol Hill, Hooks led the historical prayer vigil in Washington, DC in 1979 against the Mott anti-busing amendment, which was eventually defeated in Congress; led in the fight for passage of the District of Columbia Home

in Community Services, Inc., as well as in numerous other organizations.

### Benjamin L. Hooks (1925–   )
*National Association for the Advancement of Colored People Former Executive Director*

Hooks was born in Memphis, Tennessee and attended LeMoyne College and Howard University. He received his J.D. degree from DePaul University College of Law in 1948. During World War II he served in the 92nd Infantry Division in Italy.

From 1949 to 1965, and again from 1968 to 1972, Hooks worked as a lawyer in Memphis. In 1966 Hooks became the first black judge to serve in the Shelby County (Tennessee) criminal court. As an ordained minister, he preached at Middle Baptist Church in

Benjamin Hooks

Roy Innis, 1976.

Rule bill; and was instrumental in gathering important Senate and House votes on the Humphrey-Hawkins Full Employment Bill.

At the NAACP's national convention in 1986, Hooks was awarded the association's highest honor, the Spingarn Medal. In February 1992 Hooks announced his retirement.

### Roy Innis (1934–    )
*Congress of Racial Equality National Chairman*

Born June 6, 1934 in St. Croix, Virgin Islands, Roy Emile Alfredo Innis has lived in the United States since the age of twelve. He attended Stuyvesant High School in New York City and majored in chemistry at City College of New York.

In 1963 Innis joined the Congress of Racial Equality (CORE). In 1965 Innis was elected chairman of the Harlem branch and went on to become associate national director three years later. In 1968 Innis became national director of the organization. Innis founded the Harlem Commonwealth Council, an agency designed to promote the development of black-owned businesses and economic institutions in Harlem. He also took a plunge into journalism, serving with William Haddad as co-editor of the *Manhattan Tribune*, a weekly featuring news from Harlem and the upper West Side.

Innis' leadership of CORE, however, has been marked with controversy. Numerous members have left the organization, charging that Innis has run the organization as a one-man show. CORE was also the target of a three-year investigation by the New York state attorney general's office into allegations that it had misused charitable contributions. (An agreement was reached in 1981 that did not require CORE to admit to any wrong doing in its handling of funds, but stipulated that Innis would have to contribute $35,000 to the organization over the next three years.) Innis was challenged by a group of former CORE members, headed by James Farmer, the founder and former chairman of organization; the effort was unsuccessful and Innis continued as head of the organization.

While remaining president of the largely inactive CORE, Innis has sought to build a political base in Brooklyn. He has run for public office twice, most recently as a Republican candidate in the 1986 elections for Brooklyn's 12th congressional district, but has lost both times. In 1981 Innis became national chairman of the organization.

### Jesse Jackson (1941–    )
*National Rainbow Coalition Founder and President, Operation PUSH Founder*

*See* Civil Rights.

John Jacob

## John E. Jacob (1934–  )
*National Urban League President*

Born in Trout, Louisiana on December 16, 1934, John Edward Jacob grew up in Houston, Texas. He received his bachelor and master degrees in social work from Howard University. During the early 1960s Jacob worked for the Baltimore Department of Public Welfare, first as a caseworker, then later as a child welfare supervisor. In 1965 he joined the Washington Urban League as director of education and youth incentives.

During his early career with the organization he held a number of increasingly important positions, serving as director of its Northern Virginia Branch in 1966, associate director for administration of the affiliate in 1967, and as its acting executive director from 1968 until 1970. He also spent several months as director of community organization training in the Eastern Regional Office of the NUL.

Jacob left the Washington Urban League in 1970 to serve as executive director for the San Diego Urban League, a post he held until his return to the Washington Urban League in 1975. In 1982 Jacob replaced Vernon E. Jordan, Jr. as the organization's president, when Jordan retired after ten years as Urban League president.

Jacob has also served on the Howard University board of trustees, the Board of the Local Initiatives Support Corporation, the board of A Better Chance, Inc., the community Advisory Board of New York Hospital, and the National Advertising Review Board, among others.

## Vernon E. Jordan, Jr. (1935–  )
*National Urban League Former President*

Vernon Eulion Jordan, Jr. was born in Atlanta in 1935. After graduating from DePauw University in 1957 and from Howard Law School in 1960, he returned to Georgia.

From 1962 to 1964 Jordan served as field secretary for the Georgia branch of the

NAACP. Between 1964 and 1968 Jordan served as director of the Voter Education Project of the Southern Regional Council and led its successful drives that registered nearly two million blacks in the South. In 1970 Jordan moved to New York to become executive director of the United Negro College Fund, helping to raise record sums for its member colleges, until he was tapped by the Urban League to become the successor to the late Whitney Young.

Taking over as National Urban League executive director in January 1972, Jordan moved the organization into new areas, including voter registration in northern and western cities, while continuing and strengthening the League's traditional social service programs. An outspoken advocate of the cause of the black and the poor, Jordan has taken strong stands in favor of busing, an income maintenance system that ends poverty, scatter-site housing, and a federally financed and administered national health system. Maintaining that the "issues have changed," since the 1960s, Jordan has called for "equal access and employment up to and including top policy-making jobs."

The nation was stunned on May 29, 1980 when Jordan, who had just delivered an address to the Fort Wayne Urban League, was shot by a sniper as he returned to his motel; Jordan was confined to the hospital, first in Fort Wayne and later in New York City, for ninety days.

On September 9, 1981, Jordan announced his retirement, after ten years as head of the National Urban League. During Jordan's tenure, the League increased its number of affiliates from 99 to 118, its staff from 2,100 to 4,200, and its overall budget, from $40 million annually to $150 million.

## Joseph E. Lowery (1924– )
*Southern Christian Leadership Conference President*

The Reverend Joseph E. Lowery was born in Huntsville, Alabama. He holds a doctor of divinity degree, among others, and has attended numerous educational institutions, including Clark College, the Chicago Ecumenical Institute, Garrett Theological Seminary, Payne College and Theological Seminary, and Morehouse University. Reverend Lowery's ministry began in 1952 at the Warren Street Church in Birmingham, where he served until 1961. From there he moved on to become pastor of St. Paul Church from 1964 to 1968. Since 1986, Lowery has served as pastor of the Cascade United Methodist Church in Atlanta, Georgia.

Lowery was one of the co-founders of the Southern Negro Leaders Conference (which later became the Southern Christian Leadership Conference); the Reverend Dr. Martin Luther King, Jr. served as the organizations' first president, with Lowery serving as vice-president.

Vernon Jordan

Reverend Joseph Lowery, 1988.

In 1977, Lowery succeeded Reverend Ralph David Abernathy, as president of the SCLC. Under his leadership, SCLC has broadened its activities to include the reinstitution of its Operation Breadbasket to encourage businesses that earn substantial profits in the black community to reinvest equitably and employ blacks in equitable numbers; involvement in the plight of Haitian refugees jailed by the American government; and a march from Selma to Washington, DC in connection with the renewal of the Voting Rights Act of 1982.

### Floyd B. McKissick (1922–1981)
*Congress of Racial Equality Former
    National Director*

Born in Asheville, North Carolina on March 9, 1922, Floyd Bixler McKissick did

his undergraduate work at Morehouse and North Carolina colleges. Having determined that he wanted to become a lawyer, McKissick applied to the University of North Carolina at Chapel Hill Law School. Since the school was not integrated at that time, he was denied admission. With the help of NAACP lawyer Thurgood Marshall, McKissick sued the university and became the first African American to earn an LL.B degree there.

While still in school, McKissick had become an active member of the Congress of Racial Equality (CORE). When McKissick replaced James Farmer as head of CORE on January 3, 1966, he quickly made a name for himself. Under McKissick's direction, the organization moved more firmly into the Black Power movement, refusing to support Martin Luther King's call for massive nonviolent civil disobedience in northern cities, concentrating instead on programs aimed at increasing the political power and improving the economic position of African Americans. In 1967 the organization moved to eliminate the word "multiracial" from its constitution.

McKissick resigned as national director of CORE in 1968. After leaving CORE, he launched a plan to establish a new community, Soul City, in Warren County, North Carolina. McKissick saw Soul City as community with sufficient industry to support a population of 50,000. For his venture, he received a $14 million bond issue guarantee from the Department of Housing and Urban Development and a loan of $500,000 from the First Pennsylvania Bank.

Soul City, however, ran into difficulties and despite the best efforts of McKissick, the project never developed as planned. In June 1980 the Soul City Corporation and the federal government reached an agreement that would allow the government to assume control project. Under the agreement, the company retained 88 acres of the project, including the site of a mobile home park and a 60,000 square foot building that had served as the project's headquarters.

McKissick died on April 28, 1991 of lung cancer and was buried at Soul City.

### Huey P. Newton (1942–1989)
*Black Panther Party Co-Founder*

The youngest of seven children, Huey Newton was born in Monroe, Louisiana on February 17, 1942. He attended Oakland City College, where he founded the Afro-American Society, and later studied at San Francisco Law School. In 1966, Newton joined forces with Bobby Seale and established the Black Panther Party for Self-Defense.

Huey Newton

Newton and his partner almost immediately became targets of sharp police resentment and uneasiness. The hostility came to a climax in 1967, when Newton allegedly killed an Oakland police officer. His eight-week trial was a cause celebre in which more than 2,500 demonstrators surrounded the courthouse chanting Panther slogans and demanding his release. Newton was convicted of voluntary manslaughter and sent to the California Men's Colony. His conviction was later overturned by the California court of appeals.

By the 1970s the Black Panther Party became a potent political force in California. Co-leader Bobby Seale made an almost-successful bid for the mayorship of Oakland in 1973. In 1977, the Panthers helped to elect the city's first black mayor, Lionel Wilson. Meanwhile, Newton continued to have problems with the law. He was charged with shooting a prostitute, but after two hung juries, the charges were dropped. He was retried and convicted for the 1969 death of the police officer; however, the conviction was reversed.

443

A. Philip Randolph Institute, Cincinnati, Ohio.

In 1980, he earned his Ph.D. in philosophy from the University of California; his doctoral thesis was "War Against the Panthers: Study of Repression in America." However, this achievement was followed by further problems. He was charged with embezzling state and federal funds from an educational and nutritional program he headed in 1985 and in 1987, he was convicted of illegal possession of guns. In 1989, he was fatally shot by a small-time drug dealer.

### Asa Philip Randolph (1889–1979)

*Brotherhood of Sleeping Car Porters and A. Philip Randolph Institute Founder*

Asa Philip Randolph was born in Crescent City, Florida on April 15, 1889. He attended Cookman Institute in Jacksonville, Florida, before moving to New York City.

In New York Randolph worked as a porter, railroad waiter, and an elevator operator. While attending the College of the City of New York, he was exposed to the socialist movement, and in 1917 he organized *The Messenger*, a socialist newspaper. In 1925 Randolph founded the Brotherhood of Sleeping Car Porters to help black railway car attendants working for the Pullman Palace Car Company. After a ten year struggle, in 1935, Randolph and the union negotiated a contract with Pullman.

Randolph served as a member of New York City's Commission on Race and as president of the National Negro Congress. In 1941 Randolph organized a march on Washington, DC to bring attention to discrimination in employment. In 1942 he was appointed to the New York Housing Authority and in 1955 was appointed to the AFL-CIO executive council.

In 1960 Randolph organized the Negro American Labor Council. He was also one of the organizers of the 1963 march on Washington. In 1964 he founded the A. Philip Randolph Institute in New York City to eradicate discrimination and to defend human and civil rights.

### Randall S. Robinson (1942?– )
*TransAfrica Founder and Director*

Randall Robinson, brother to the late news anchor Max Robinson, was born in Richmond, Virginia is a graduate of Virginia Union University and Harvard Law School. In 1977 Robinson founded TransAfrica to lobby Congress and the White House on foreign policy matters involving Africa and the Caribbean. Since its creation, the organization has grown from two to over 15,000 members.

Randall Robinson

In 1984 and 1985, in protest to the policy of apartheid in South Africa, TransAfrica organized demonstrations in front of the South African embassy in Washington, DC; Robinson along with other protesters, including singer Stevie Wonder, were arrested. In addition to its opposition to apartheid, the organization has been active in the Free South Africa Movement and is an advocate for the cessation of aid to countries with human rights problems. In 1981 TransAfrica Forum, an educational and research arm of TransAfrica, was organized to collect and disseminate information on foreign policy affecting Africa and the Caribbean and to encourage public participation in policy debates.

### Bayard Rustin (1910–1987)
*A. Philip Randolph Institute Former
   Executive Director*

Bayard Rustin was born in West Chester, Pennsylvania. While in school, he was an honor student and star athlete, experiencing his first act of discrimination when he was refused restaurant service in Pennsylvania while on tour with the football team. He attended Wilberforce University, Cheyney State Normal School (now Cheyney State College) and the City College of New York.

Rustin was active in various peace organizations, efforts to restrict nuclear armaments, and movements toward African independence. Between 1936 and 1941, Rustin worked as an organizer of the Young Communist League. In 1941 he joined the Fellowship of Reconciliation, a nonviolent antiwar group, and later served as its director of race relations. In 1942 Rustin, along with James Farmer, became active in the Chicago Committee of Racial Equality, out of which the Congress of Racial Equality grew.

Rustin was one of the founding members of the Southern Christian Leadership Conference (SCLC). In 1963 he was named chief logistics expert and organizational coordinator of the March on Washington. From 1964 to 1979, Rustin served as executive director of the A. Philip Randolph Institute in New York City. In 1975 he founded the Organization for Black Americans to Support Israel.

Throughout the 1960s Rustin was hard pressed to maintain support for the nonviolent philosophy to which he had dedicated his life. Nonviolence, he argued, was not outdated; it was a necessary and inexorable plan called for by the black's condition in the United States. Guerrilla warfare and armed insurrection, Rustin explained, required friendly border sanctuaries, a steady source of arms and equipment, and the support of the majority of a country's inhabitants. Rustin continued to be active in the civil rights movement until his death in August 1987 at the age of seventy-seven.

## Bobby Seale (1936– )
*Black Panther Party Co-founder*

Born Robert George Seale in Dallas, Texas, Bobby Seale, along with Huey P. Newton and Bobby Hutton, was one of the founding members of the Black Panther Party for Self-Defense. His family, poverty-stricken, moved from Dallas to Port Arthur, Texas, before settling in Oakland, California.

Seale joined the United States Air Force and trained as a sheet-metal mechanic, after leaving high school. However, he was discharged for disobeying an officer. Returning home, he found sporadic work as a sheet-metal mechanic. In 1959 Seale enrolled at Merritt College in engineering drafting. While attending Merritt, Seale joined the Afro-American Association, a campus organization that stressed black separatism and self-improvement. It was through this orga-

nization that Seale met Panther co-founder Huey Newton.

Seal and Newton soon became disenchanted with the association. In 1966 Seale and Newton formed the Black Panther Party for Self-Defense. One of their objectives was to form armed patrols to protect citizens from what they considered racist police abuse.

In March of 1971, Seale was charged with kidnapping and killing Panther Alex Rackley, a suspected police informant. However, a mistrial was declared, and the charges dismissed. Seale began to steer the Panthers away from its revolutionary agenda and toward one of creating community action programs. In 1974 Seale left the party to form Advocates Scene, an organization aimed at helping the underprivileged from grass-root political coalitions.

Bobby Seale

More recently Seale has served as a community liaison for Temple University's African-American Studies department. He has lectured throughout the country and has written several books—*Seize the Time: The Story of the Black Panther Party* (1970), *A Lonely Rage: The Autobiography of Bobby Seale* (1978), and *Barbeque'n with Bobby Seale* (1987).

## Roy Wilkins (1901–1981)

*National Association for the Advancement of Colored People Former Executive Director*

Born in St. Louis, Missouri on August 30, 1901, Wilkins was reared in St. Paul, Minnesota. He attended the University of Minnesota, where he majored in sociology and minored in journalism. He served as night editor of the *Minnesota Daily* (the school paper) and edited a black weekly, the St. Paul *Appeal*. After receiving his B.A. in 1923, he joined the staff of the Kansas City *Call*, a leading black weekly.

In 1931 Wilkins left the *Call* to serve under Walter White as assistant executive secretary of the NAACP. In 1934 he succeed W.E.B. DuBois as editor of *Crisis* magazine. Wilkins was named acting executive secretary of the NAACP in 1949, when White took a year's leave of absence from the organization. Wilkins assumed the position as executive secretary of the NAACP in 1955. He quickly established himself as one of the most articulate spokesmen in the civil rights movement. He testified before innumerable Congressional hearings, conferred with United States Presidents, and wrote extensively.

For several years, Wilkins served as chairman of the Leadership Conference on Civil Rights, an organization of more than 100 national civic, labor, fraternal, and religious organizations. He was a trustee of the Elea-

Roy Wilkins

nor Roosevelt Foundation, the Kennedy Memorial Library Foundation, and the Estes Kefauver Memorial Foundation. He was also a member of the Board of Directors of the Riverdale Children's Association, the John LaFarge Institute, and the Stockbridge School, as well as the international organization Peace with Freedom.

## Whitney M. Young, Jr. (1922–1971)

*National Urban League Former Executive Director*

Whitney Moore Young Jr., was born in Lincoln Ridge, Kentucky. He received his B.A. degree from Kentucky State College in 1941. He went on to attend the Massachusetts Institute of Technology, and in 1947 he earned an M.A. degree in social work from the University of Minnesota.

Whitney Young, Jr.

In 1947 Young was made director of industrial relations and vocational guidance for the St. Paul, Minnesota Urban League. In 1950 he moved on to become executive secretary at the St. Paul chapter. Between 1954 and 1961 Young served as dean of the Atlanta University School of Social Work. He also served as a visiting scholar at Harvard University under a Rockefeller Foundation grant.

In 1961 the National Urban League's board of directors elected Young as president of the organization. Young instituted new programs like the National Skills Bank, the Broadcast Skills Bank, the Secretarial Training Project and an on-the-job training program with the United States Department of Labor. Between 1961 and 1971, the organization grew from sixty-three to ninety-eight affiliates.

In addition to his work with the National Urban League, Young served as president of the National Association of Social Workers and the National Conference on Social Welfare, and on the boards and advisory committees of the Rockefeller Foundation, Urban Coalition, and Urban Institute, and on seven presidential commissions. In 1969 Young was selected by President Johnson to receive the Medal of Freedom, the nation's highest civilian award. Young authored two books, *To Be Equal* (1964) and *Beyond Racism: Building an Open Society* (1969), and coauthored *A Second Look* (1958).

Young died in 1971, while attending a conference in Africa.

## ■ NATIONAL ORGANIZATIONS

### A. Philip Randolph Educational Fund
1444 I St. NW, No. 300
Washington, DC 20005
(202)289-2774

Founded in 1964. Seeks to: eliminate prejudice and discrimination from all areas of life; educate individuals and groups on their rights and responsibilities; defend human and civil rights; assist in the employment and education of the underprivileged; combat community deterioration, delinquency, and crime.

### Africa Faith and Justice Network
3700 Oakview Terr. NE
PO Box 29378
Washington, DC 20017
(202)832-3412

Founded in 1983. Purpose is to examine the role the network believes Europe, America, and other northern countries play in causing injustices in Africa. Challenges national policies found to be detrimental to the interest of African peoples. Gathers information on issues and policies that adversely affect Africa, analyzes the data, and makes recommendations for advocacy or action. Consults with churches of Africa, field missionaries, and other African individuals and groups.

## The Africa Fund
198 Broadway
New York, NY 10038
(212)962-1210

Founded in 1966. Established by the American Committee on Africa. Works to: defend human and civil rights of needy Africans by providing or financing legal assistance; provide medical relief to Africans, particularly refugees; render aid to indigent Africans in the U.S., Africa, or elsewhere who are suffering economic, legal, or social injustices; provide educational aid or grants to Africans, particularly refugees; inform the American public about the needs of Africans; engage in study, research, and analysis of questions relating to Africa. Encourages divestment by U.S. corporations in South Africa; seeks to increase public support for U.S. economic sanctions against South Africa; has supported legislation which prevents U.S. corporations operating in South Africa from claiming U.S. tax credits for taxes paid to the South African government. Operates Unlock Apartheid's Jails Project, which seeks to inform the U.S. public about the plight of political prisoners in South Africa; disseminates information on the activities of South African puppet forces, including those in other areas of southern Africa.

## Africa Guild
518 Fifth Ave., 2nd Fl.
New York, NY 10036
(212)944-2440

Founded in 1981. Seeks to educate the consumer on the size, capital currency, language, geographical description, and main exports of countries in Africa. Maintains the Africa Guild Readers' Service, which provides general information on Africa, including references and resources. Bestows awards. Presently inactive.

## Africa News Service
PO Box 3851
Durham, NC 27702
(919)286-0747

Founded in 1973. News agency whose purpose is to supply material on Africa for broadcast and print media. Covers African politics, economy and culture, and U.S. policy and international issues affecting Africa. Obtains news by monitoring African radio stations on short-wave equipment, by subscribing to African publications, and through a network of reporters based in Africa. Also produces investigative stories on U.S. policy and its implications. Provides audio news and programming for radio, articles and graphics for newspapers and magazines, and prints for libraries and institutions. Carries out research for feature articles, news programs, and individuals.

## Africa Travel Association
347 5th Ave., Ste. 610
New York, NY 10016
(212)447-1926

Founded in 1975. Conducts regional seminars and trade show exhibitions. Sponsors Africa Guild (see separate entry) to help develop a general interest in Africa.

## Africa Watch
485 5th Ave.
New York, NY 10017
(212)972-8400

Founded in 1988. Monitors and promotes internationally recognized human rights in Africa.

**Africa World Press**
PO Box 1892
Trenton, NJ 08607
(609)771-1666

Founded in 1979. Scholar activists and members of the African intellectual community. Promotes and maintains the development of an independent, democratic, and critical thinking African intellectual community. Utilizes the scientific knowledge and skills of the community to give service to African peoples and social movements. Conducts seminars on subjects such as the energy crisis, human rights, political repression, and food.

**African-American Institute**
833 United Nations Plaza
New York, NY 10017
(212)949-5666

Founded in 1953. Works to further development in Africa, improve African-American understanding, and inform Americans about Africa. Engages in training, development assistance, and informational activities. Sponsors African-American conferences, media and congressional workshops, and regional seminars.

**African-American Labor Center**
1400 K St. NW, Ste. 700
Washington, DC 20005
(202)789-1020

Founded in 1964. Assists, strengthens, and encourages free and democratic trade unions in Africa. Has undertaken projects in forty-three countries in partnership with African trade unions. Programs are developed upon request and advice of African unions with knowledge of host government. Projects are geared to eventual assumption of complete managerial and financial responsibility by African labor movements. Objective is to help build sound national labor organizations that will be of lasting value to workers and the community, institutions that contribute to the economic and social development of their countries and to Africa's total political and economic independence. Major areas of activity are workers' education and leadership training, vocational training, cooperatives and credit unions, union medical and social service programs, administrative support for unions, and communication and information. Sponsors study tours and visitor programs to permit African and American trade unionists to become familiar with each other's politics, economies, and trade union movements; Africans are exposed to technical training not available in their homeland.

**Africare**
440 R St. NW
Washington, DC 20001
(202)462-3614

Founded in 1971. Seeks to improve the quality of life in rural Africa. Provides health and environmental protection services in rural areas of Africa; works to improve African water and agricultural resources; conducts public education programs in the U.S. on African development.

**Alcoholism in the Black Community**
ABC Addiction Services
East Orange General Hospital
East Orange, NJ 07019

**Alliance of Minority Women for Business and Political Development**
c/o Brenda Alford
Brassman Research
PO Box 13933
Silver Spring, MD
(301)565-0258

Founded in 1982. Objectives are to unite Minority women entrepreneurs and to encourage joint ventures and information exchange.

## Alpha Kappa Alpha

5656 S. Stony Island Ave.
Chicago, IL 60637
(317)684-1282

Founded in 1908. Social and service sorority.

## Alpha Phi Alpha

4432 Martin Luther King Dr.
PO Box 53147
Chicago, IL 60653
(312)373-1819

Founded in 1906. Service fraternity.

## Alpha Pi Chi

PO Box 255
Kensington, MD 20895

Founded in 1963. Service sorority.

## All-African People's Revolutionary Party

1738 A St. SE
Washington, DC 20003

Founded in 1971. Africans and persons of African descent who support Pan-Africanism, "the total liberation and unification of Africa under an all-African socialist government."

## Alliance to End Repression

523 S. Plymouth Ct., Ste. 800
Chicago, IL 60605
(312)427-4064

Founded in 1970. Religious, community, and human relations organizations united to safeguard the Bill of Rights and constitu-tional freedoms and to ensure the just application of state and local laws. Has initiated and developed three organizations: Citizens Alert (deals with police and community problems); Illinois Gay and Lesbian Task Force; and Illinois Prisons and Jails Project (monitoring county and state prisons). Other areas of activity include media accountability, cable television license ordinances, rights of minors, juvenile justice, national and state legislation, and rights of immigrants.

## American Association of Blacks in Energy

801 Pennsylvania Ave., SE, Ste. 250
Washington, DC 20003
(202)547-9378

Founded in 1977. Blacks in energy-related professions, including engineers, scientists, consultants, academicians, and entrepreneurs; government officials and public policymakers; interested students. Represents blacks and other minorities in matters involving energy use and research, the formulation of energy policy, the ownership of energy resources, and the development of energy technologies. Seeks to increase the knowledge, understanding, and awareness of the minority community in energy issues by serving as an energy information source for policymakers, recommending blacks and other minorities to appropriate energy officials and executives, encouraging students to pursue professional careers in the energy industry, and advocating the participation of blacks and other minorities in energy programs and policymaking activities. Updates members on key legislation and regulations being developed by the Department of Energy, the Department of Interior, the Department of Commerce, the Small Business Administration, and other federal and state agencies.

## American Baptist Black Caucus

c/o Dr. Jacob L. Chatman
St. John Missionary Baptist Church
34 W. Pleasant St.
Springfield, OH 45506
(513)323-4401

Founded in 1968. Concerned with reforming the American Baptist Convention in terms of bridging the gap between whites and minority members. Seeks to develop convention support for: scholarship aid for disadvantaged students; resources for business and religious projects in the inner city; adequate representation of minorities in the convention structure; support for black colleges and universities; open hiring policies on local, state, and national levels.

## American Black Book Writers Association

PO Box 10548
Marina Del Rey, CA 90295
(213)822-5195

Founded in 1980. Represents African Americans in the U.S. publishing industry. Encourages development of black authors; works to preserve and advance black literature. Promotes and gives market support to members' works; holds mutual promotions and tours; sponsors cooperative advertising in black-oriented media. Conducts research on problems affecting black authors and their works in the U.S.

## American Black Chiropractors Association

1918 E. Grand Blvd.
St. Louis, MO 63107
(314)531-0615

Founded in 1980. Objectives are to: educate the public, health care institutions, and health care providers about chiropractic and promote black chiropractic in the community; develop career orientation programs for high school and college students and sponsor scholarship funds; study history of chiropractic; sponsor publicity programs, public forums, counseling services, research, and establishment of free chiropractic clinics; provide for exchange of information, techniques, and reports of researchers and clinicians.

## American Committee on Africa

198 Broadway
New York, NY 10038
(212)962-1210

Founded in 1953. Devoted to supporting African people in their struggle for freedom and independence. Focuses on southern Africa and the Western Sahara and support for African liberation movements. Works with legislators, churches, trade unions, and interested students to help stop what the group feels is U.S. collaboration with racism in South Africa. Arranges speaking tours for African leaders; publicizes conditions and developments in Africa; sponsors research, rallies, and demonstrations.

## American Constitutional and Civil Rights Union

18055 SW Jay St.
Aloha, OR 97006
(503)649-9310

Founded in 1979. Provides consulting services to trustees of established trusts who believe their constitutional and/or civil rights are being violated.

## American-African Affairs Association

1001 Connecticut Ave. NW, Ste. 1135
Washington, DC 20036
(202)223-5110

Founded in 1965. Educational organization designed to circulate information about African countries to the people of the U.S., especially with respect to "the cause of freedom in its struggle against world Communism and the best interests of the United States of America." Distributes literature to opinion molders, political leaders, university personnel, and business leaders, both here and in other countries.

## Anti-Repression Resource Team
PO Box 122
Jackson, MS 39205
(601)969-2269

Founded in 1979. Combats all forms of political repression including: police violence and misconduct; Ku Klux Klan and Nazi terrorism; spying and covert action by secret police and intelligence agencies. Focuses on research, writing, lecturing, organizing, and publishing. Conducts training workshops for church, labor, and community organizations.

## Association of African American People's Legal Council
c/o William Bert Johnson
13902 Robson St.
Detroit, MI 48227
(313)837-0627

Founded in 1959. Seeks to achieve equal justice under the law for African-Americans and to provide free legal counsel to people of African-American descent. Compiles statistics and reports on cases of international inequality. Obtains research from public systems on education and its effect on discrimination.

## Association of Black Admissions and Financial Aid Officers of the Ivy League and Sister Schools
c/o Lloyd Peterson
Yale University
149 Elm St.
New Haven, CT 06520
(203)432-1916

Founded in 1970. Present and former minority admissions and financial aid officers employed at Ivy League or sister schools. These schools include: Brown, Columbia, Cornell, Dartmouth, Harvard/Radcliffe, Massachusetts Institute of Technology, University of Pennsylvania, Princeton, Yale, Barnard, Bryn Mawr, Mount Holyoke, Smith, and Wellesley. Aids minority students who wish to pursue a college education. Seeks to improve methods of recruitment, admittance, and financial services that support the growth and maintenance of the minority student population at these institutions. Encourages Ivy League and sister schools to respond to the needs of minority students and admissions and financial aid officers.

## Association of Black Anthropologists
c/o American Anthropological Association
1703 New Hampshire Ave. NW
Washington, DC 20009
(202)232-8800

Founded in 1970. Works to: formulate conceptual and methodological frameworks to advance understanding of all forms of human diversity and commonality; advance theoretical efforts to explain the conditions that produce social inequalities based on race, ethnicity, class, or gender; develop research methods that involve the peoples studied and local scholars in all stages of investigation and dissemination of findings.

## Association of Black Cardiologists

3201 Del Paso Blvd., Ste. 100
Sacramento, CA 95815
(916)641-2224

Founded in 1974. Seeks to improve prevention and treatment of cardiovascular diseases.

## Association of Black CPA Firms

1101 Connecticut Ave., NW, Ste. 700
Washington, DC 20036
(202)857-1100

Founded in 1984. Black and minority certified public accounting (CPA) firms united to represent their common interests.

## Association of Black Foundation Executives

1828 L St. NW
Washington, DC 20036
(202)466-6512

Founded in 1971. Encourages increased recognition of economic, educational, and social issues facing blacks in the grantmaking field. Promotes support of blacks and their status as grantmaking professionals. Seeks an increase in the number of blacks entering the grantmaking field; helps members improve their job effectiveness. Though involved with grantmaking organizations, the ABFE itself does not award grants.

## Association of Black Nursing Faculty

5823 Queens Cove
Lisle, IL 60532
(708)969-3809

Founded in 1987. Works to promote health-related issues and educational concerns of interest to the black community and ABNF. Serves as a forum for communication and the exchange of information among members; develops strategies for expressing concerns to other individuals, institutions, and communities. Assists members in professional development; develops and sponsors continuing education activities; fosters networking and guidance in employment and recruitment activities. Promotes health-related issues of legislation, government programs, and community activities.

## Association of Black Psychologists

PO Box 55999
Washington, DC 20040-5999
(202)722-0808

Founded in 1968. Aims to: enhance the psychological well-being of black people in America; define mental health in consonance with newly established psychological concepts and standards; develop policies for local, state, and national decision-making which have impact on the mental health of the black community; support established black sister organizations and aid in the development of new, independent black institutions to enhance the psychological, educational, cultural, and economic situation.

## Association of Black Sociologists

Howard University
PO Box 302
Washington, DC 20059
(202)806-6856

Founded in 1968. Purposes are to: promote the professional interests of black sociologists; promote an increase in the number of professionally trained sociologists; help stimulate and improve the quality of research and the teaching of sociology; provide perspectives regarding black experiences as well as expertise for understanding and dealing with problems confronting black people; protect professional rights and safeguard the civil rights stemming from executing the above objectives.

## Association of Black Storytellers

PO Box 27456
Philadelphia, PA 19118

Founded in 1984. Seeks to establish a forum to promote the black oral tradition and to attract an audience. Works for the reissue of out-of-print story collections.

## Association of Black Women in Higher Education

c/o Lenore R. Gall
Fashion Institute of Technology
Office of V.Pres. of Academic Affairs
227 W. 27th St. C-913
New York, NY 10001
(212)760-7911

Founded in 1979. Objectives are to nurture the role of black women in higher education, and to provide support for the professional development goals of black women.

## Association of Concerned African Scholars

PO Box 11694
Berkeley, CA 94701-2694

Founded in 1977. Facilitates scholarly analysis and opinion in order to impact U.S. policy toward Africa; formulates alternative government policy toward Africa and disseminates it to the public; works to develop a communication and action network among African scholars. Mobilizes support on current issues; participates in local public education programs; stimulates research on policy-oriented issues and disseminates findings; informs and updates members on international policy developments.

## A Better Chance

419 Boylston St.
Boston, MA 02116
(617)421-0950

Founded in 1963. Identifies, recruits, and places academically talented and motivated minority students into leading independent and selected public secondary schools. Prepares students to attend selective colleges and universities and encourages their aspirations to assume positions of responsibility and leadership in American society.

## Big Eight Council on Black Student Government

Minority Student Services
Hester Hall, Rm. 213
731 Elm Ave.
University of Oklahoma
Norman, OK 73019

Founded in 1978. Black student unions and other groups at Big Eight Athletic Conference universities. Seeks to represent the concerns of black collegians at universities where the majority of students are white. Encourages the genesis of all black student organizations and lends support to them. Seeks to effect changes in curricula and to help legitimize and develop black studies departments as accredited degree programs. Functions as a communications medium among member schools and assists in efforts to reduce the attrition rate of black students. Promotes the placement of students and the hiring of black faculty and staff.

## Black Affairs Center for Training and Organizational Development

c/o Margaret V. Wright
10918 Jarboe Ct.
Silver Spring, MD 20901
(301)681-9822

Founded in 1970. Multidisciplinary management research organization which promotes social change, educational improvement, organization renewal and goal achievement, systematic problem solving and multicultural skills development through custom-designed training programs and consultation services. Individuals, groups, educational systems, and governmental and community agencies use programs such as Equal Employment Opportunity Training; Employee Motivation, Productivity and Improvement Training; Career Education and Development Training. Programs are continually being developed in areas including women's concerns, single parents, youth and sex, drugs and alcoholism, the aging, daycare, sexual harassment, and stress management.

## Black American Cinema Society

3617 Monclair St.
Los Angeles, CA 90018
(213)737-3292

Founded in 1975. Works to bring about an awareness of the contributions made by blacks to the motion picture industry in silent films, early talkies, and short and feature films. Feels that by viewing these films black children can see the sacrifice and humiliation endured by black actors and actresses, directors, film writers, and producers while making films. Maintains collection of early black films owned by the Western States Black Research Center. Conducts research projects, film shows, and Black History Month seminars. Provides financial support to independent black filmmakers.

## Black American Response to the African Community

127 N. Madison Ave., Ste. 400
Pasadena, CA 91101
(818)584-0303

Founded in 1984. A grass roots organization of entertainers, journalists, clergy, and business, health, and community leaders working to assist the victims of drought and famine in Africa. Focuses on emergency efforts involving medical needs, water irrigation, housing, and food supplies. Provides relief for orphans through its Family Network Program. Disseminates current information on drought-stricken areas in Africa; assists in the development of regeneration projects in affected areas. Maintains the National Education Task Force to educate Americans on the African crisis; sponsors media updates.

## Black Americans for Life

419 7th St. NW, Ste. 500
Washington, DC 20004
(202)626-8833

Promotes alternatives to abortion for women with crisis pregnancies; strives to be a visible presence defending the rights of the unborn in the black community. Asserts that black women are twice as likely as white women to have abortions; believes that abortions are counterproductive to advances made through civil rights efforts.

## Black and Indian Catholic Indian Commission

2021 H St. NW
Washington, DC 20006
(202)331-8542

Founded in 1884. Coordinates the distribution of funds from the annual Black and Indian Mission Collection in Catholic churches across the U.S.; these funds go to support priests, nuns, and other religious workers at black and Indian missions and schools.

## Black Awareness in Television
13217 Livernois
Detroit, MI 48238-3162
(313)931-3427

Founded in 1970. Produces black media programs for television, video, radio, film, and theatre. Trains individuals in the media and conducts research projects including surveys. Produces public affairs, cultural arts, soap opera, and exercise programs; sponsors theatre companies. Seeks television exposure for black-produced products and black performing artists. Promotes September is Black Reading Month program.

## Black Business Alliance
PO Box 26443
Baltimore, MD 21207
(410)467-7427

Founded in 1979. Act as a national and international support system for black businesses, providing assistance in organizational management and resource development. Provides children's services; sponsors fundraising events; offers placement services.

## Black Caucus of Health Workers
353 Lewis
Carbondale, IL 62901

## Black Caucus of the American Library Association
c/o Dr. Alex Boyd
Newark Public Library
5 Washington St.
Newark, NJ 07101
(201)733-7780

Founded in 1970. Promotes librarianship; encourages active participation of blacks in library associations and boards and all levels of the profession. Monitors activities of the American Library Association with regard to its policies and programs and how they affect black librarians and library users. Reviews, analyzes, evaluates, and recommends to the ALA actions that influence the recruitment, development, advancement, and general working conditions of black librarians. Facilitates library services that meet the informational needs of black people including increased availability of materials related to social and economic concerns. Encourages development of authoritative information resources concerning black people and dissemination of this information to the public.

## Black Citizens for a Fair Media
156-20 Riverside Dr., No. 13L
New York, NY 10032
(212)568-3168

Founded in 1971. Community organizations concerned with employment practices in the television industry, images of black people projected by television, and how those images affect viewers. Works to improve programming, employment practices, and training of blacks; evaluates compliance with the Federal Communication Commission's equal opportunity rules for the electronic media. Believes that the airways belong to the people and seeks to prevent any change in that ownership.

## Black Coaches Association
PO Box J
Des Moines, IA 50311
(515)271-3010

Founded in 1986. Promotes the creation of a positive environment in which issues such as stereotyping, lack of significant media coverage, and discrimination can be exposed, discussed, and resolved. Provides member services. Petitions the NCAA legislative bodies to design, enact, and enforce diligent guidelines and policies to improve professional mobility for minorities.

## Black Data Processing Associates
PO Box 7466
Philadelphia, PA 19101
(215)843-9120

Founded in 1975. Seeks to accumulate and share information processing knowledge and business expertise in order to increase the career and business potential of minorities in the information processing field.

## Black Entertainment and Sports Lawyers Association
PO Box 508067
Chicago, IL 60650
(708)386-8338

Founded in 1979. Purpose is to provide more efficient and effective legal representation to African-American entertainers and athletes. Offers referral system for legal representation and a resource bank for providing information to students, groups, and nonprofit and civic organizations involved in the entertainment industry; and serves as an industry watchdog in protecting the rights of blacks within the entertainment community.

## Black Filmmaker Foundation
Tribeca Film Center
375 Greenwich, Ste. 600
New York, NY 10013
(212)941-3944

Founded in 1978. Fosters audience development by programming local, national, and international film festivals. Maintains video library. Conducts seminars and workshops.

## Black Filmmakers Hall of Fame, Inc.
405 14th St., Ste. 515
Oakland, CA 94612
(510)465-0804

Founded in 1973. Seeks to study, teach, and preserve the contributions of black filmmakers to American cinema. Fosters cultural awareness through educational, research, and public service programs in the film arts. Holds film-lecture series, Black Filmworks Festival, and annual International Film Competition.

## Black Gay Archives
PO Box 30024
Philadelphia, PA 19103

## Black Health Research Foundation
14 E. 60th St., Ste. 307
New York, NY 10022
(212)408-3485

Founded in 1988. Voluntary health agency devoted to reducing preventable causes of premature death among African Americans. Funds scientific research in areas including AIDS, alcoholism, infant mortality, sickle cell disease, substance abuse, and other diseases that have a disproportionate impact on African Americans. Seeks recognition as the foremost authority on health and science regarding African Americans. Promotes professional and community education; recruits and trains volunteers. Seeks to influence public policy on crucial issues.

**Black Methodists for Church Renewal**
601 W. Riverview Ave.
Dayton, OH 45406
(513)227-9460

Founded in 1968. Serves as platform from which blacks can express concerns to the general church on issues such as: revival and survival of the black church; involvement of blacks within the structure of the church; the conduct of the church as it relates to investment policies and social issues; economic support in the black community; the support of the 12 black colleges. Encourages black Methodists to work for economic and social justice. Works to expose racism in agencies and institutions of the United Methodist church. Seeks improvement of educational opportunities for blacks, the strengthening of black churches, and an increase in the number of black persons in Christian-related vocations. Advocates liberation, peace, justice, and freedom for all people. Supports programs that alleviate suffering in third world countries.

**Black Military History Institute of America**
c/o Col. William A. De Shields
404 Golf Course Ct.
Arnold, MD 21012
(301)757-4250

Founded in 1987. Seeks to: provide archival facilities to collect, preserve, and exhibit materials pertaining to military history; motivate and support underprivileged youths by using military role models as a source of inspiration; foster a spirit of camaraderie and goodwill among all persons sharing an interest in community involvement programs for the underprivileged.

**Black Music Association**
c/o Louise West
1775 Broadway, 7th Fl.
New York, NY 10019
(212)307-1459

Founded in 1978. Goal is to preserve, protect, and perpetuate black music on an international level and to work with schools and universities to bring blacks into music not only as performers, but as businesspersons. Sponsors seminars. Plans to sponsor annual Black Music Awards Show for television, and other educational and research projects; also plans to open a museum and institute for black music studies.

**Black PAC**
PO Drawer 6865
McLean, VA 22106
(703)442-7510

Founded in 1984. Represents political interests of working-class and middle-class African-Americans. Does not lobby, but assists in the election of favorable candidates to Congress. Supports economic growth, traditional family values, and a strong national defense.

**Black Psychiatrists of America**
c/o Dr. Isaac Slaughter
2730 Adeline St.
Oakland, CA 94607
(415)465-1800

Founded in 1968. Black psychiatrists, either in practice or training, united to promote black behavioral science and foster high quality psychiatric care for blacks and minority group members. Sponsors public information service.

**Black Resources Information
    Coordinating Services**
614 Howard Ave.
Tallahassee, FL 32304
(904)576-7522

Founded in 1972. Designed to solidify the various sources of information and research by and about minority groups in America and convert them into a coordinated information system by using bibliographic control, storage, retrieval, transfer, and dissemination. Focuses on information by and about Afro-Americans, but also includes other minorities. Acts as referral and consulting service; aids in genealogical research and archival management and organization. Offers bibliographic services and lecture demonstrations on Afro-American culture. Sponsors seminars, workshops, and institutes.

**Black Revolutionary War Patriots
    Foundation**
1612 K St. NW, Ste. 1104
Washington, DC 20006
(202)452-1776

Founded in 1985. Raises private funds for the establishment of a memorial, in Washington, DC, to black patriots of the American Revolutionary War.

**Black Rock Coalition**
PO Box 1054, Cooper Station
New York, NY 10276
(212)713-5097

Founded in 1985. Promotes, produces, and distributes alternative/black music and provides information, technical expertise, and performance and recording opportunities for "musically and politically progressive musicians." Also works to increase the visibility of black rock artists in music media and on college radio stations.

**Black Silent Majority Committee of the
    U.S.A.**
Box 5519
San Antonio, TX 78201
(512)340-2424

Founded in 1970. Seeks to show the people of America and the world that there is a black majority in the U.S. which is patriotic and believes in saluting the flag, going to church, and paying taxes. Organizes Americans who do not want to be identified with black "radicals" and emphasizes the positive gains that blacks have made. Works throughout the U.S. and the world for better race relations. Opposes forced busing and supports prayer in public schools.

**Black Stuntmen's Association**
8949 W. 24th St.
Beverly Woods, CA 90034
(213)870-9020

Founded in 1966. Serves as an agency for stuntpeople in motion pictures and television. Plans to operate school for black stuntpeople.

**Black Tennis and Sports Foundation**
1893 Amsterdam Ave.
New York, NY 10032

Founded in 1977. Participants include members of the business community involved in sports who are dedicated to helping black and minority inner-city youths and developing athletes interested in tennis or other individual sports such as skating and gymnastics. Acts as a source of support and resources for black and minority youth. Organizes tennis teams and sponsors these teams and their coaches on trips and games overseas. Sponsors the Annual Arthur Ashe/Althea Gibson Tennis Classic in New York City.

**Black Veterans**
686 Fulton St.
Brooklyn, NY 11217
(718)935-1116

Founded in 1979. Seeks to aid black veterans in obtaining information concerning their rights, ways to upgrade a less-than-honorable discharge, and Veterans Administration benefits due them and their families. Seeks to prohibit discrimination against black veterans. Provides educational programs; facilitates veterans' sharing of skills acquired while in service. Services include counseling and community workshops on veteran issues and a program to provide services to veterans in local prisons. Assists veterans who have suffered from the effects of Agent Orange, an herbicide containing dioxin, used as a defoliant in Vietnam until 1969.

**Black Women's Agenda**
208 Auburn Ave. NE
Atlanta, GA 30303
(404)524-8279

Founded in 1977. Works to educate the public about the economic, social, and political issues relevant to African-American women. Recommends public policy that will benefit women and their families. Conducts workshops.

**Black Women in Church and Society**
c/o Interdenominational Theological Center
671 Beckwith St. SW
Atlanta, GA 30314
(404)527-7740

Founded in 1982. Seeks to provide: structured activities and support systems for black women whose goals include participating in leadership roles in church and society; a platform for communication between laywomen and clergywomen. Conducts research into questions and issues pivotal to black women in church and society. Maintains a research/resource center and a library with subject matter pertaining to liberation and black theology, feminism, and womanist movements.

**Black Women in Publishing**
PO Box 6275, F.D.R. Sta.
New York, NY 10150
(212)772-5951

Founded in 1979. A networking and support group whose purpose is to encourage minorities interested in all sectors of the print industry, including book, newspaper, and magazine publishing. Promotes the image of minorities working in all phases of the book, newspaper, and magazine industries; recognizes achievements of minorities in the media. Works for a free and responsible press. Facilitates the exchange of ideas and information among members, especially regarding career planning and job security. Keeps members informed about the publishing industry and their impact on it. Encourages and works to maintain high professional standards in publishing. Collaborates with other organizations in striving to improve the status of women and minorities.

**Black Women Organized for Educational Development**
518 17th St., Ste. 202
Oakland, CA 94612
(510)763-9501

Founded in 1984. Fosters self-sufficiency in and encourages empowerment of low-income and socially disadvantaged women by establishing and maintaining programs that improve their social and economic well-being. Sponsors mentor program for junior high-age young women in low-income urban areas; offers support groups, workshops, and seminars. Maintains Black Women's Resource Center, an information and referral service for African American women and youth.

## Black Women's Educational Alliance

6625 Greene St.
Philadelphia, PA 19119

Founded in 1976. Active and retired women in the field of education. Seeks a strong union among members in order to foster their intellectual and professional growth. Conducts public awareness programs to improve educational standards and delivery of educational services; works for equal opportunities for women.

## Black Women's Network

PO Box 12072
Milwaukee, WI 53212
(414)562-4500

Founded in 1979. Black professional women organized to improve the political, economic, and educational conditions of minority women. Offers support services and networking opportunities to address issues affecting African-American women.

## Black Women's Roundtable on Voter Participation

1430 K St. NW, Ste. 401
Washington, DC 20011
(202)898-2220

Founded in 1983. A program of the National Coalition on Black Voter Participation (see separate entry). Black women's organizations committed to social justice and economic equity through increased participation in the political process. Organizes voter registration, education, and empowerment programs in the black community; emphasizes the importance of the women's vote.

Seeks to: develop women's leadership skills through nonpartisan political participation; encourage black women's involvement in discussions concerning the influence of the women's vote in elections. Supports volunteer coalitions that work on voter registration, voter education, and get-out-the vote efforts.

## Black World Foundation

PO Box 2869
Oakland, CA 94609
(415)547-6633

Founded in 1969. Black persons united to develop and distribute black educational materials and to develop black cultural and political thought. Offers books in the areas of black literature, history, fiction, essays, political analysis, social science, poetry, and art. Maintains library.

## Black-Jewish Information Center

15 E. 84th St.
New York, NY 10028
(212)879-4577

Founded in 1975. Purpose is to disseminate information that reinforces understanding and cooperation among the black and Jewish communities in the United States. Conducts seminars on advertising strategies for black-Jewish newspapers.

## Blacks in Government

5015 11th St. NW
Washington, DC 20001
(202)667-3280

Founded in 1975. Federal, state, or local government employees or retirees concerned with the present and future status of blacks in government. Develops training and other programs to enhance the liberty and sense of well-being of blacks in government.

## Blacks in Law Enforcement

256 E. McLemore Ave.
Memphis, TN 38106
(901)774-1118

Founded in 1986. Seeks to educate the public concerning the contributions made by blacks in the field of law enforcement. Documents the lives and achievements of the first blacks to participate in law enforcement in the U.S. Develops programs to improve the public image of law enforcement officers; has established a short-term training program for law enforcement officers.

## Catholic Interracial Council of New York

899 10th Ave.
New York, NY 10019
(212)237-8255

Founded in 1934. Works in cooperation with local parishes and governmental and voluntary groups to combat bigotry and discrimination and to promote social justice for all racial, religious, and ethnic groups. Sponsors research, educational forums, workshops, and community action programs. Presents annual John LaFarge Memorial Award for Interracial Justice to community leaders and annual Hoey Award to community leaders who have worked to promote objectives of the council.

## Center for Constitutional Rights

666 Broadway, 7th Fl.
New York, NY 10012
(212)614-6464

Founded in 1966. "Works in areas such as abuse of the grand jury process, women's rights, civil rights, freedom of the press, racism, electronic surveillance, criminal trials, and affirmative action. Conducts the Ella Baker Student Program, the Movement Support Network, and in Mississippi, The Voting Rights Project.

## Center for Third World Organizing

3861 Martin Luther King Jr. Way
Oakland, CA 94609
(415)654-9601

Founded in 1980. Provides training, issue analyses, and research to low-income minority organizations including welfare, immigrant, and Native American rights groups. Monitors and reports on incidents of discrimination against people of color. Sponsors Minority Activist Apprenticeship Program, which works to develop minority organizers and leaders for minority communities.

## Center for Urban Black Studies

Graduate Theological Union
2465 LeConte Ave.
Berkeley, CA 94709
(415)841-8401

Founded in 1969. Provides seminarians and laypersons with resources "to respond to life in the urban community and to represent its oppressed minority people." Develops and offers courses, seminars, and other training programs dealing with issues of race, social justice, urban life, and the black religious experience. Initiates new ministries; develops and implements community service programs; counsels and assists black seminarians in placement and in obtaining and developing employment. Conducts workshops and seminars addressing racial justice, church and race, and urban ministry.

## Chi Eta Phi

3029 13th St. NW
Washington, DC 20009
(202)232-3858

Founded in 1932. Registered and student nurses. Objectives are to: encourage continuing education; stimulate friendship among members; develop working relationships with other professional groups for the improvement and delivery of health care services. Sponsors leadership training seminars. Offers educational programs for entrance into nursing and allied health fields. Presents scholarships and other financial awards to assist students. Sponsors recruitment and retention programs for minority students. Operates speakers' bureau on health education and biographical archives on African-American nurses.

## Christians Concerned for Racial Equality

PO Box 1643
Oroville, WA 98844
(604)498-3895

## Citizens for a Better America

PO Box 356
Halifax, VA 24558
(804)476-7757

Founded in 1975. Churches and individuals united to create a better America by strengthening individual rights in the U.S. Serves as a public advocacy organization that lobbies for civil rights and environmental legislation. Conducts legal research in civil rights cases; provides research services to communities investigating issues such as fair housing and toxic waste disposal.

## Coalition of Black Trade Unionists

PO Box 73120
Washington, DC 20056-3120
(202)429-1203

Founded in 1972. Members of seventy-six labor unions united to maximize the strength and influence of black and minority workers in organized labor. Activities include voter registration and education, improvement of economic development, and employment opportunities for minority and poor workers. Sponsors regional seminars.

## Co-ette Club

2020 W. Chicago Blvd.
Detroit, MI 48206

Founded in 1941. Teenage high school girls "outstanding in one or all of the following categories—Academic Scholarship, School and Community, Extra-Curricular, Community Volunteer Service, and Leadership." Helps members channel interests and become leaders in educational, cultural, and artistic activities on local and national levels. Raises funds for the United Negro College Fund and contributes to local charity and social service groups in each community.

## Commission for Racial Justice

475 Riverside Dr., Rm. 1948
New York, NY 10115
(212)870-2077

Founded in 1963. A racial justice agency representing the 1.7 million members of the United Church of Christ. Promotes human rights programs and strategies to foster racial justice in black, Third World, and other minority communities.

## Commission on U.S.-African Relations

c/o International Center for Development Policy
731 8th St. SE
Washington, DC 20003
(202)547-3800

Founded in 1983. Primarily a research and educational commission of the International Center for Development Policy. Provides resources and information to the president, congressional representatives, and other officials on U.S.-African issues.

**Committee of Concerned Africans**
PO Box 1892
Trenton, NJ 08608
(609)771-1666

Founded in 1980. Monitors violations of human rights in Africa. Publicizes issues and developments regarding such violations; petitions states and organizations regarding the conditions of peoples or individuals whose human rights are being violated.

**Conference of Minority Public Administrators**
1120 G St. NW, Ste. 700
Washington, DC 20005
(202)393-7878

Founded in 1971. Members of the American Society of Public Administration who belong to a minority group or are intersted in the promotion of minorities within public administration.

**Conference of Prince Hall Grand Masters**
4311 Portland Ave. S.
Minneapolis, MN 55407
(612)825-2474

**Congress of National Black Churches**
1225 I St. NW, Ste. 750
Washington, DC 20005-3914
(202)371-1091

Founded in 1978. Seeks to find answers to problems that confront blacks in the U.S. and Africa, including economic development, family and social support, housing, unemployment, education, and foreign relations. Focus is on religious education and evangelism.

**Congressional Black Associates**
1504 Longworth
Washington, DC 20515
(202)225-5865

Founded in 1979. Provides information on the operations of the federal government to members and the black community; fosters contacts among members and the community. Works to enhance the social, political, and economic status of all people, but concentrates on the black experience in America.

**Congressional Black Caucus**
House Annex 2, Rm. 344
Washington, DC 20515
(202)226-7790

Founded in 1971. Black members of the U.S. House of Representatives. Seeks to address the legislative concerns of black and other underrepresented citizens and to formalize and strengthen the efforts of its members. Establishes a yearly legislative agenda setting forth the key issues which it supports: full employment, national health care, education, minority business assistance, urban revitalization, rural development, welfare reform, and international affairs. Works to implement these objectives through personal contact with other House members, through the dissemination of information to individual black constituents, and by working closely with black elected officials in other levels of government. Operates the Congressional Black Caucus Foundation.

**Council for a Black Economic Agenda**
1367 Connecticut Ave. NW
Washington, DC 20036
(202)331-1103

Founded in 1984. Dedicated to advancing the economic self-sufficiency of black Americans. Works to reverse the dependence of many blacks on government programs; advocates strategies based on a spirit of free enterprise and individual initiative. Encourages full use of the black community's own resources for selfhelp and development. Goals include: financial incentives for development of areas with vacant or underused property; legislation allowing tax write-offs for investments in small businesses that are in distressed areas; a program of underwriting rehabilitation, ownership, and management of public housing by residents' organizations; authorization for black churches and other neighborhood institutions to arrange adoptions of those children presently within the government's foster care system; expanded educational choice for low-income persons; an increase in work incentives for poor families. The latter goal, in the council's view, would be achieved by: providing affordable day-care for children of working parents; boosting the earned income tax credit and the income tax exemption for dependents; allowing unemployment compensation and other government payments to be used for education, job training, or self-employment.

### Council of Black Architectural Schools
Dept. of Architecture
Tuskegee Institute
Tuskegee, AL 36088
(205)727-8330

Founded in 1969. One faculty member and one student from each of seven schools of architecture united for collective effort in advancing architectural programs and funding for predominantly black schools of architecture.

### Delta Sigma Theta
1707 New Hampshire Ave. NW
Washington, DC 20009
(202)986-0000

Founded in 1913. Service sorority.

### Educational Equity Concepts
114 E. 32nd St., Ste. 306
New York, NY 10016
(212)725-1803

Founded in 1982. Organized to create educational programs and materials that are free of sex, race, and disability bias. Offers training programs for parents, teachers, and students; conducts seminars, symposia, and workshops. Provides conference planning, consulting, and materials development services. Conducts Women and Disability Awareness Project, which discusses and writes on matters concerning disabled women, feminism, and the links between the disability rights and women's movements.

### Episcopal Commission for Black Ministries
c/o Episcopal Church
815 2nd Ave.
New York, NY 10017
(212)867-8400

Founded in 1973. Works to strengthen the witness of black Episcopalians in the church through programs that include parish and clergy development, scholarships and grants, and international relations. Provides financial assistance and consultations to parishes and church organizations.

### Eta Phi Beta
c/o Elizabeth Anderson
1724 Mohawk Blvd.
Tusla, OK 74110
(918)425-7717

Founded in 1942. Professional business sorority.

## Freedom Information Service

PO Box 3568
Jackson, MS 39207
(601)352-3398

Founded in 1965. Researches activities of workers, blacks, and grass roots organizations through the FIS Deep South People's History Project. Maintains extensive Mississippi-centered library and archives. Distributes press releases on current southern news; reprints items on women's liberation and political education.

## Institute for the Advanced Study of Black Family Life and Culture

175 Filbert St., Ste. 202
Oakland, CA 94607
(415)836-3245

Seeks to reunify African American families and to revitalize the black community. Advocates the reclamation of what the group considers traditional African-American culture. Conducts research on issues impacting the black community such as teenage pregnancy, child-rearing practices, mental health support systems, and the effects of alcohol and drugs. Maintains HAWK Federation (High Achievement, Wisdom, and Knowledge Federation), a training program employed in school systems to aid in the character development of young black males. Sponsors in-service training for agencies, school systems, and the juvenile justice system. Develops training curricula for teen parents.

## Institute of Black Studies

6376 Delmar Blvd.
St. Louis, MO 63130
(314)889-5690

Founded in 1970. Functions as a clearinghouse and serves as a base for action research, program evaluation, development of innovative cultural programs, educational, and training models and other activities appropriate to needs of the black community that are not normally provided by traditional institutions. Goals include: to bridge the gap between the community and educational institutions; to discover and develop new models for the solution of the many issues facing the black community. Supports development of psychological tests for minority groups. Conducts research and activities in areas of children, family, intelligence, language, parenting, personality, psychological testing, and juvenile deliquency. Has designed several training modules including the Black Family Cultural Heritage Project from which developed a training model, materials, and techniques for use in teaching trainers of black parenting.

## Institute of the Black World

87 Chestnut St., SW
Atlanta, GA 30314
(404)523-7805

Founded in 1969. An independent institution of research and political analysis and advocacy, placing special emphasis on the need to shape all elements of black education into effective instruments which may be used to advance the black movement for equality and social change. Specific tasks have been: definition and refining of the field loosely called black studies; encouragement of basic academic research in the experiences of the peoples of African descent; encouragement of black artists; development of new materials and methods for the teaching of black children; development of a Black Policy Studies Center to create tools for social analysis of the black community; establishment of creative links with counterparts in other areas of the black world; preparation of a "new cadre" of men and women precisely trained in the scholarship of the black experience and fully committed to the struggles of the black world. Sponsors conferences, seminars, lectures, workshops, and symposia. Conducts research. The Institute is located in a house where the late Dr. W.E.B. DuBois, American editor, educator, writer, and black rights activist is said to have lived.

## International Association of African and American Black Business People

13902 Robson St.
Detroit, MI 48227

Founded in 1965. Establishes, operates, and fosters business education and related activities among African-American and African members of the business community worldwide.

## International Association of Black Business Educators

3810 Palmira Ln.
Silver Spring, MD 20906

Founded in 1978. Institutions of higher education and individuals interested in promoting development of business related academic programs and educational activities designed to enhance participation of minorities in business. Purposes are to: develop channels of communication and opportunities for interfacing with constituencies; generate constructive relationships between the U.S. and other nations concerning development of business education and related fields; study and propose minority business programs; promote cooperation within and between institutions and individuals in the business community; identify and evaluate business opportunities; promote the IABBE's involvement in academic affairs. Operates Strategic Business Development Network, which designs and produces a

business development educational video series.

## International Association of Black Professional Fire Fighters

1025 Connecticut Ave. NW, Ste. 610
Washington, DC 20036
(202)296-0157

Founded in 1970. Strives to: promote interracial communication and understanding; recruit blacks for the fire services; improve working conditions for blacks in the fire services; assist blacks in career advancement; promote professionalism; represent black fire fighters before the community.

## International Black Peoples' Foundation

158 Clairmount
Detroit, MI 48202
(313)871-0597

Founded in 1981. Works to: eradicate world hunger, especially in Africa and among persons of African descent; promote black humanitarianism. Conducts fundraising programs that supply money, food, or services to afflicted populations; works with United Nations agencies.

## International Black Toy Manufacturers Association

PO Box 348
Springfield Gardens, NY 11413

Founded in 1987. Works to provide shelf space and distribution opportunities commensurate with the spending power of the black community. Promotes black toy manufacturers.

## International Black Women's Congress
1081 Bergen St.
Newark, NJ 07112
(201)926-0570

Founded in 1983. Objective is to unite members for mutual support and socioeconomic development through: annual networking tours to Africa; establishing support groups; assisting women in starting their own businesses; assisting members in developing resumes and other educational needs; offering to answer or discuss individual questions and concerns.

## International Black Writers
PO Box 1030
Chicago, IL 60690
(312)924-3818

Founded in 1970. Seeks to discover and support new black writers. Conducts research and monthly seminars in poetry, fiction, nonfiction, music, and jazz. Operates library of 500 volumes on black history. Provides writing services and children's services. Plans to establish hall of fame, biographical archives, and museum.

## International Black Writers and Artists
PO Box 43576
Los Angeles, CA 90043
(213)964-3721

Founded in 1974. Black writers and artists in the United States and West Indies. Provides encouragement and support to members.

## International Committee Against Racism
PO Box 904
Brooklyn, NY 11202
(212)629-0003

Founded in 1973. Is dedicated to fighting all forms of racism and to building a multi-racial society. Opposes racism in all its economic, social, institutional, and cultural forms. Believes racism destroys not only those minorities that are its victims, but all people.

## International Council of African Women
PO Box 91812
Washington, DC 20090
(202)546-8459

Founded in 1982. Promotes worldwide networking between African-American women. Addresses such issues as: employment, poverty and welfare, health, child care, housing. Disseminates information to disadvantaged women on developments and events of interest to women. Conducts self-help programs.

## Iota Phi Lamba
503 Patterson St.
Tuskegee, AL 36088
(205)727-5201

Founded in 1929. Business and professional civic sorority. Seeks to develop leadership expertise among business and professional women. Promotes increased interest in business education among high school and college women through planned programs and scholarships.

## John Brown Anti-Klan Committee
220 9th St., No. 443
San Francisco, CA 94103
(415)330-5363

Activists fighting racism and sexism; advocates of freedom for political prisoners. (Abolitionist John Brown is best known for his command of the "raiders", a group of men who burned a U.S. armory at Harpers Ferry in 1859 in order to further the fight against slavery.) Offers educational programs. Disseminates information.

**Kappa Apha Psi**
2322-24 N. Broad St.
Philadelphia, PA 19132
(215)228-7184

Founded in 1911. Social fraternity.

**Leadership Conference on Civil Rights**
2027 Massachusetts Ave., NW
Washington, DC 20036
(202)667-1780

Founded in 1950. Coalition of national organizations working to promote passage of civil rights, social and economic legislation, and enforcement of laws already on the books. Has released studies examining former President Ronald Reagan's tax and budget programs in areas including housing, elementary and secondary education, social welfare, Indian affairs, and tax cuts. Has evaluated the enforcement of activities in civil rights by the U.S. Department of Justice; has also reviewed civil rights activities of the U.S. Department of Education.

**Minorities in Media**
c/o Barbara Noble
Parkway School District
455 N. Woods Mill Rd.
Chesterfield, MO 63017
(314)469-8538

Founded in 1975. Works to facilitate communication and convey ideas in the area of educational communications and technology.

**Minority Business Enterprise Legal Defense and Education Fund**
220 I St. NE, Ste. 280
Washington, DC 20002
(202)543-0040

Founded in 1980. Serves as an advocate and legal representative for the minority business community.

**Minority Business Information Institute**
130 5th Ave., 10th Fl.
New York, NY 10011
(212)543-0040

Founded in 1970. Maintains library focusing on minority businesses.

**Most Worshipful National Grand Lodge Free and Accepted Ancient York Masons**
26070 Tryon Rd.
Oakwood Village, OH 44146
(216)232-9495

Founded in 1847. Also known as the Most Worshipful National Grand Lodge Free and Accepted Ancient York Masons Prince Hall Origin National Compact U.S.A.

**NAACP Legal Defense and Educational Fund, Inc.**
99 Hudson St., 16th Fl.
New York, NY 10013
(212)219-1900

Founded in 1940. Legal arm of the civil rights movement, functioning independently of the National Association for the Advancement of Colored People since the mid-1950s. Works to provide and support litigation in behalf of blacks, other racial minorities, and women defending their legal and constitutional rights against discrimination in employment, education, housing, and other areas. Represents civil rights groups as well as individual citizens who have bona fide civil rights claims. Contributed funds are used to finance court actions for equality in schools, jobs, voting, housing, municipal services, land use, and delivery of health care services. Has organized litigation campaign for prison reform and the abolition of capital punishment. Hosts annual institute to develop public awareness of new problems being faced by minorities. Maintains Herbert Lehman Education Fund, through which scholarships are awarded to black students attending state universities; sponsors Earl Warren Legal Training Program, which provides scholarships to black law students.

### National Action Council for Minorities in Engineering

3 W. 35th St.
New York, NY 10001
(212)279-2626

Founded in 1980. Seeks to increase the number of minority students enrolled in and graduating from engineering schools. Works with support organizations to motivate and encourage precollege students to engage in engineering careers. Operates project to assist engineering schools in improving the retention and graduation rates of minority students.

### National Alliance Against Racist and Political Repression

11 John St., Rm. 702
New York, NY 10038
(212)406-3330

Founded in 1973. Coalition of political, labor, church, civic, student, and community organizations; individuals dedicated to protecting people's right to organize. Seeks to mobilize millions of people to unite in word and action against many forms of repression of human rights in the U.S. including: persecution and jailing of political activists; attempts to suppress prisoners' rights movements and use of behavior control against prisoners and the poor; assaults on labor's right to organize, strike, and act effectively; police crimes against the people, especially nonwhites; legislation and court decisions repressing basic rights; the death penalty.

### National Alliance of Black Organizations

3724 Airport Blvd.
Austin, TX 78722
(512)478-9802

Founded in 1976. Presidents of black organizations and associations. Coordinates and encourages voter registration efforts among member organizations. Serves as a forum for the exchange of ideas and experiences.

### National Alliance of Black School Educators

2816 Georgia Ave. NW
Washington, DC 20001
(202)483-1549

Founded in 1970. Purpose is to promote awareness, professional expertise, and commitment among black educators. Goals are to: eliminate and rectify the results of racism in education; work with state, local, and national leaders to raise the academic achievement level of all black students; increase members' involvement in legislative activities; facilitate the introduction of a curriculum that more completely embraces black America; improve the ability of black educators to promote problem resolution; create a meaningful and effective network of strength, talent, and professional support. Plans to establish a National Black Educators Data Bank and offer placement service.

**National Alumni Council of the United
Negro College Fund**
c/o United Negro College Fund
500 E. 62nd St.
New York, NY 10021
(212)326-1203

Founded in 1946. Provides a structure for cooperation among black college alumni groups and friends of black colleges. Works to acquaint the public with the value of black colleges and black higher education. Informs students and the public about contributions of black college alumni to civic betterment and community progress. Recruits students for United Negro College Fund member colleges.

**National Association for Black Veterans**
PO Box 11432
Milwaukee, WI 53211
(414)265-8940

Founded in 1970. Represents the interests of minority veterans before the Veterans Administration. Operates Metropolitan Veterans Service to obtain honorable discharges for minority and low-income veterans who in the organization's opinion unjustly received a less than honorable discharge. Defends incarcerated veterans through its Readjustment Counseling Program; operates job creation program; offers services to geriatric and homeless veterans.

**National Association for the
Advancement of Black Americans in
Vocational Education**
c/o Dr. Ethel O. Washington
5057 Woodward, Rm. 976
Detroit, MI 48202
(313)494-1660

Founded in 1977. Goal is to generate national leadership and increase the impact of blacks in the field of vocational/technical ed-

ucation by: assuring opportunities and promoting recruitment and the retention of black Americans in all areas and levels; utilizing research discoveries as a basis for influencing key funding sources at the national, state, and local levels; providing a career information exchange system. Develops training models for marketable skills; links black talent with vocational/technical employment opportunities in the public and private sectors at the federal, state, and local levels; identifies, assesses, and evaluates critical issues that affect the extent of participation of blacks and offers recommendations for improvement.

**National Association for the
Advancement of Colored People**
4805 Mt. Hope Dr.
Baltimore, MD 21215
(212)481-4100

Founded in 1909. Persons "of all races and religions" who believe in the objectives and methods of the NAACP. To achieve equal rights through the democratic process and eliminate racial prejudice by removing racial discrimination in housing, employment, voting, schools, the courts, transportation, recreation, prisons, and business enterprises. Offers referral services, tutorials, job referrals, and day care. Sponsors seminars; maintains law library. Awards Spingarn Medal annually to a black American for distinguished achievement. Sponsors the NAACP National Housing Corporation to assist in the development of low and moderate income housing for families.

**National Association for Equal
Educational Opportunities**
2181 Brigden Rd.
Pasadena, CA 91104
(714)625-6607

Founded in 1975. College and university professionals concerned with the development and operation of secondary school and collegiate programs to serve the needs of low-income and disadvantaged students.

## National Association of Black Accountants

220 I St. NE, Ste. 150
Washington, DC 20002
(202)546-6222

Founded in 1969. Works to unite accountants and accounting students who have similar interests and ideals, who are committed to professional and academic excellence, who possess a sense of professional and civic responsibility, and who are concerned with enhancing opportunities for minorities in the accounting profession.

## National Association of Black Catholic Administrators

c/o Ministry for Black Catholics
50 N. Park Ave.
Rockville Centre, NY 11570
(516)678-5800

Founded in 1976. Assists the church in its role of evangelization and in defining its mission to the black community. Seeks to provide an inner resource for the social and spiritual needs and concerns of Catholics of African ancestry.

## National Association of Black Consulting Engineers

6406 Georgia Ave. NW
Washington, DC 20012
(202)291-3550

Founded in 1975. Purpose is to gain recognition and increase professional opportunities for black consulting engineers. Lobbies the federal government.

## National Association of Black Geologists and Geophysicists

PO Box 720157
Houston, TX 77272

Founded in 1981. Assists minority geologists and geophysicists in establishing professional and business relationships. Informs minority students of career opportunities in geology and geophysics. Seeks to motivate minority students to utilize existing programs, grants, and loans. Provides scholarships and oversees the educational careers of scholarship recipients.

## National Association of Black Hospitality Professionals

PO Box 5443
Plainfield, NJ 07060-5443
(908)354-5117

Founded in 1985. Works to develop global educational and economic opportunities for the hospitality industry through the expansion and diversification of minority involvement in the industry. Encourages professional development and opportunity in the industry through the design and implementation of workshops and seminars. Seeks to increase the number, size, and capability of minority-owned businesses within the hospitality and tourism industries.

## National Association of Black Journalists

PO Box 17212
Washington, DC 20041
(703)648-1270

Founded in 1975. Aims are to: strengthen the ties between blacks in the black media and blacks in the white media; sensitize the white media to the "institutional racism in its coverage"; expand the white media's coverage and "balanced reporting" of the black community; become an exemplary group of professionals that honors excellence and outstanding achievement among black journalists. Works with high schools to identify potential journalists; awards scholarships to journalism programs that especially support minorities.

### National Association of Black Owned Broadcasters

1730 M St. NW, Rm. 412
Washington, DC 20036
(202)463-8970

Founded in 1976. Represents the interests of existing and potential black radio and television stations. Is currently working with the Office of Federal Procurement Policy to determine which government contracting major advertisers and advertising agencies are complying with government initiatives to increase the amount of advertising dollars received by minority-owned firms. Conducts lobbying activities; provides legal representation for the protection of minority ownership policies.

### National Association of Black Professors

PO Box 526
Chrisfield, MD 21817
(301)968-2393

Founded in 1974. Goals are to: provide a forum for the exchange of information among college professors; enhance education for black people and enrich the educational process in general; support and promote intellectual interests of black students.

### National Association of Black Real Estate Professionals

PO Box 21421
Alexandria, VA 22320
(703)920-7661

Founded in 1984. Provides a forum for the discussion of information related to the industry. Offers career development and networking opportunities.

### National Association of Black Social Workers

271 W. 125th, Rm. 317
New York, NY 10027
(212)348-0035

Founded in 1968. Seeks to support, develop, and sponsor community welfare projects and programs which will serve the interest of the black community and aid it in controlling its social institutions. Assists with adoption referrals.

### National Association of Black Women Attorneys

3711 Macomb St., NW, 2nd Fl.
Washington, DC 20016
(202)966-9693

Founded in 1972. Seeks to: advance jurisprudence and the administration of justice by increasing the opportunities of black and non-black women at all levels; aid in protecting the civil and human rights of all citizens and residents of the U.S.; expand opportunities for women lawyers through education; promote fellowship among women lawyers.

### National Association of Black Women Entrepreneurs

PO Box 1375
Detroit, MI 48231
(313)341-7400

Founded in 1979. Black women who own and operate their own businesses; black women interested in starting businesses; organizations and companies desiring mailing lists. Acts as a national support system for black businesswomen in the U.S. and focuses on the unique problems they face. Objective is to enhance business, professional, and technical development of both present and future black businesswomen.

## National Association of Blacks in Criminal Justice

PO Box 9499
Washington, DC 20016
(301)681-2365

Founded in 1972. Criminal justice professionals concerned with the impact of criminal justice policies and practices on the minority community. Advocates with local, state, and federal criminal justice agencies for the improvement of minority recruitment practices and for the advancement of minority career mobility within those agencies. Sponsors regional conferences, career development seminars, and annual training institutes; maintains speakers' bureau. Provides financial and in-kind services to community groups.

## National Association of Blacks Within Government

1820 11th St., NW
Washington, DC 20001-5015
(202)667-3280

Founded in 1982. Purpose is to enhance and increase the employability of black officials within government and to prepare black youths for government and private sector careers. Sponsors yearly seminar to help young people develop management, learning, interpersonal, and specialized skills.

## National Association of Colored Women's Clubs

5808 16th St. NW
Washington, DC 20011
(202)726-2044

Founded in 1896. Federation of black women's clubs. Carries on civic service, education, social service, and philanthropy programs.

## National Association of Investment Companies

1111 14th St. NW, Ste. 700
Washington, DC 20005
(202)289-4336

Founded in 1971. Represents the minority small business investment company industry. Monitors regulatory action. Collects and disseminates trade and business information.

## National Association of Minority Automobile Dealers

23300 Greenfield, Ste. 220
Oak Park, MI 48237
(313)967-1900

Founded in 1980. Serves as a liaison between automobile dealers, the government, the community, and industry representatives.

## National Association of Minority Contractors

1333 F St. NW, Ste. 500
Washington, DC 20004
(202)347-8259

Founded in 1969. Minority construction contractors and companies interested in doing business with minority contractors. Identifies procurement opportunities. Provides specialized training. Serves as a national advocate for minority construction contractors.

## National Association of Minority Political Women

6120 Oregon Ave. NW
Washington, DC 20005
(202)686-1216

Founded in 1983. Professional women interested in the American political process. Conducts research and educational programs.

## National Association of Minority Women in Business

906 Grand Ave., Ste. 200
Kansas City, MO 64106
(816)421-3335

Founded in 1972. Serves as a network for the exchange of ideas and information on business opportunities for minority women.

## National Association of Negro Business and Professional Women's Clubs

1806 New Hampshire Ave. NW
Washington, DC 20009
(202)483-4206

Founded in 1935. Women actively engaged in a business or a profession and who are committed to rendering service through club programs and activities.

## National Association of Negro Musicians

PO Box S-011
237 E. 115th St.
Chicago, IL 60628
(312)779-1325

Founded in 1919. Promotes the advancement of all types of music, especially among young black musicians. Sponsors annual competitions in which winners compete for scholarships.

## National Association of Urban Bankers

122 C. St., Ste. 580
Washington, DC 20001
(202)783-4743

Founded in 1975. Minority professionals in the financial services industry.

## National Bankers Association

122 C. St., Ste. 580
Washington, DC 20001
(202)783-3200

Founded in 1927. Minority banking institutions. Serves as an advocate for the minority banking industry.

## National Bar Association

1225 11th St. NW
Washington, DC 20001
(202)842-3900

Founded in 1925. Minority attorneys, members of the judiciary, law students, and law faculty. Sponsors educational and research programs.

## National Black Alcoholism Council

1629 K St. NW, Ste. 802
Washington, DC 20006
(202)296-2696

Founded in 1978. Works to support and initiate activities that will improve alcoholism treatment services and lead to the prevention of alcoholism in the black community. Provides training on how to treat black alcoholics from a cultural perspective. Compiles statistics concerning alcoholism among blacks.

## National Black Alliance for Graduate Level Education

c/o Dr. John W. Wilson
University College
Spicer Hall
University of Akron
Akron, OH 44325
(216)972-7066

Founded in 1970. Black educators, administrators, students, and individuals interested in the recruitment, financial assistance, retention, and placement of black graduate students. Advocates on behalf of black students, faculty, and administrators. Provides the opportunity to discuss and resolve problems and issues affecting blacks in graduate and professional schools. Seeks to increase educational opportunities for black students.

## National Black Catholic Clergy Caucus

343 N. Walnut St.
PO Box 1088
Opelousas, LA 70571
(318)942-2392

Founded in 1968. Black priests, brothers, seminarians, and deacons. Purpose is to support the spiritual, theological, educational, and ministerial growth of the black Catholic community within the church. Serves as a vehicle to bring contributions of the black community to the church. Advances the fight against racism within the Catholic church and society.

## National Black Catholic Seminarians Association

780 Porter St.
Beaumont, TX 77701

Founded in 1969. Black Catholic seminarians united for the growth and development of each member as a person, Christian, and potential priest or religious brother. "At-tempts to reflect both the heritage of the church and black people in terms of the richness of their spirituality." Stresses the importance of individual contribution and total involvement of each black seminarian to the organization.

## National Black Caucus of Local Elected Officials

1301 Pennsylvania Ave. NW, Ste. 400
Washington, DC 20004
(202)626-3597

Founded in 1970. Elected black municipal and county officials united to recognize and deal with problems of members. Attempts to provide the organizational structure required to better present and respond to issues affecting constituents. Seeks to influence the National League of Cities in the development of policies affecting black Americans; promotes legislative and economic development initiatives directed toward the needs of the black community.

## National Black Caucus of State Legislators

Hall of States
444 N. Capitol St. NW, Ste. 206
Washington, DC 20001
(202)624-5457

Founded in 1977. Organized to provide more political networking to black legislators from the federal and state levels. Goals are to: provide a network through which state legislators can exchange information and ideas on state and national legislation; provide a unified front or platform; serve as a focal point for involvement of black legislators in the "new federalism." Activities include arranging meetings between all governmental groups representing black elected officials and analyzing and forming a position on the "new federalism." Conducts seminars. Maintains speakers' bureau and biographical archives; compiles statistics.

## National Black Chamber of Commerce

5741 Telegraph Ave.
Oakland, CA 94609-1709
(415)601-5741

Founded in 1983. Black chambers of commerce organized to create a strategy for members of local chambers to share in the collective buying power of black minority communities. Primary focus is on the tourism industry, because, according to the association, blacks spend approximately $25 billion in the tourism market each year, but black-owned businesses net very little from this industry. Conducts training sessions to acquaint black businesspeople with the tourism market and marketing strategies.

## National Black Child Development Institute

1023 15th St. NW, Ste. 600
Washington, DC 20005
(202)387-1281

Founded in 1970. Conducts direct services and advocacy campaigns aimed at both national and local public policies focusing on issues of health, child welfare, education, and child care. Organizes and trains network of members in a volunteer grassroots affiliate system to voice concerns regarding policies that affect black children and their families. Stimulates communication between black community groups, through conferences and seminars, to discuss and make recommendations that will be advantageous to the development of black children. Analyzes selected policy decisions and legislative and administrative regulations to determine their impact on black children and youth. Informs national

policymakers of issues critical to black children.

## National Black Coalition of Federal Aviation Employees

Washington Headquarters
PO Box 44392
Washington, DC 20026-4392
(202)267-9941

Founded in 1976. Purposes are to: promote professionalism and equal opportunity in the workplace; locate and train qualified minorities for FAA positions; help the FAA meet its affirmative action goals; monitor black, female, and minority trainees; educate members and the public about their rights and FAA personnel and promotion qualifications; develop a voice for black, female, and minority FAA employees.

## National Black Evangelical Association

5736 N. Albina Ave.
Portland, OR 97217
(503)289-5754

Founded in 1963. Conducts seminars; sponsors educational programs on drug abuse, church education, evangelism, black theology mission, and social action.

## National/Black Law Student Association

1225 11th St. NW
Washington, DC 20001

Founded in 1967. Black law students united to meet the needs of black people within the legal profession and to work for the benefit of the black community. Objectives are to: articulate and promote professional competence, needs, and goals of black law students; focus on the relationship between black students and attorneys and the American legal system; instill in black law students and attorneys a greater commitment to the black community; encourage the legal community to bring about change to meet the needs of the black community.

## National Black Leadership Roundtable
2135 Rayburn House Bldg.
Washington, DC 20515

Founded in 1983. Goals are to: provide a forum for leaders of national black organizations to discuss and exchange ideas on issues critical to black Americans; aid in the development of political, economic, and networking strategies that are advantageous to the needs of the black community; ensure that elected and appointed officials represent and are accountable to the black community.

## National Black MBA Association
180 N. Michigan Ave., Ste. 1820
Chicago, IL 60601
(312)236-2622

Founded in 1971. Business professionals, lawyers, accountants, and engineers concerned with the role of blacks who hold Master of Business Administration degrees. Encourages blacks to pursue continuing business education; assists students preparing to enter the business world. Provides programs for minority youths, students, and professionals, including workshops, panel discussions, and Destination MBA seminar. Works with graduate schools; grants scholarships to graduate business students.

## National Black McDonald's Operators Association
c/o Mrs. Fran Jones
6363 W. Sunset Blvd., Ste. 809
Los Angeles, CA 90028-7330
(213)962-2806

Founded in 1972. Provides a forum for the exchange of ideas on the improvement of community relations and on the operation and management of restaurants. Seeks to build and improve the McDonald's restaurant image throughout the community. Sponsors training seminars on marketing, better sales practices, labor relations, and profit sharing.

## National Black Media Coalition
38 New York Ave. NE
Washington, DC 20002
(202)387-8155

Founded in 1973. Black media advocacy group seeking to maximize media access for blacks and other minorities in the communications industry through employment, ownership, and programming. Has been recognized by the FCC, Congress, and trade organizations concerned with blacks and other minorities in the media. Past activities include participating in FCC rulemaking proceedings, speaking before university and professional audiences, conducting classes, and negotiating affirmative action plans with large media corporations.

## National Black Music Caucus of the Music Educators National Conference
c/o Dr. Willis Patterson
University of Michigan
Ann Arbor, MI 48109
(313)764-0586

Founded in 1972. Purpose is to foster the creation, study, and promotion of black-derived music in education. Seeks to heighten public awareness of the problems faced by black music educators and students and to increase public understanding of those problems. Provides a forum for the discussion of concerns. Coordinates and disseminates materials concerning black-derived music in order to assist music teachers in teaching black music and students. Encourages blacks to aspire to leadership positions and to demand inclusion in the development and presentation of Music Educators National Conference activities, including participation in MENC's regional conferences.

## National Black Nurses Association
PO Box 1823
Washington, DC 20013-1823
(202)393-6870

Founded in 1971. Functions as a professional support group and as an advocacy group for the black community and their health care. Recruits and assists blacks interested in pursuing nursing as a career.

## National Black on Black Love Campaign
401 N Michigan Ave., 24th fl.
Chicago, IL 60611-4267
(312)644-6610

Founded in 1983. Individuals and businesses united to promote the motto, "Replace Black on Black crime with Black on Black love" and foster love and respect in all communities where people are, the group believes, inordinately affected by crime. Organizes No Crime Day in various communities and Adopt A Building Program for businesses. Sponsors youth organizations and seminars in schools and communities to educate the public in ways of dealing with crime.

## National Black Police Association
3251 Mt. Pleasant St. NW
Washington, DC 20010-2103
(202)986-2070

Founded in 1972. Seeks to: improve relationships between police departments and the black community; recruit minority police officers on a national scale; eliminate police corruption, brutality, and racial discrimination.

## National Black Programming Consortium
929 Harrison Ave., Ste. 104
Columbus, OH 43215
(614)299-5355

Founded in 1979. Objectives are to: assist the public broadcasting system in supplying programming that serves the needs of all population segments of the U.S.; serve as a collection, distribution, and archival center for black-oriented television programming; coproduce black programming; serve as a liaison between the black community and telecommunications systems with regard to black programming; provide funds for and encourage more and better black productions. Participates in the acquisition and distribution of programs for the cable and international markets.

## National Black Republican Council
375 South End Ave., Plaza 400-84
New York, NY 10280
(202)662-1335

Founded in 1972. Black Republicans in the U.S. Works to elect more black Republicans to national, state, and local offices. Maintains speakers' bureau.

## National Black Sisters' Conference
1001 Lawrence St. NE, Ste. 102
Washington, DC 20017
(202)529-9250

Founded in 1968. Seeks to develop the personal resources of black women; challenges society, especially the church, to address issues of racism in the U.S. Activities include: retreats; consulting, leadership, and cultural understanding; formation workshops for personnel. Maintains educational programs for facilitating change and community involvement in inner-city parochial schools and parishes. Operates Sojourner House to provide spiritual affirmation for black religious and laywomen.

## National Black Survival Fund

PO Box 3005
Lafayette, LA 70502
(318)232-7672

Founded in 1982. A project of the Southern Development Foundation. Objective is to improve the ability of black and other minority poor to achieve economic progress through their own effort and initiative. Believes that the economic, cultural, and physical survival of the nation's black community is endangered due to the recession, discrimination, and the Reagan administration's cutbacks in social assistance programs. Seeks to maintain and increase support for programs that can avert the economic and human catastrophe the fund says will result if the opportunities offered to blacks are undermined by current assistance cutbacks. Maintains: Food for Survival Program in which landowners and sharecroppers in Mississippi volunteer land, equipment, and labor to provide food and employment for needy families; Health Care for Survival Program, a cooperative low-cost health center in Mississippi; Jobs for Survival Program, which has assisted in providing jobs for black workers in Alabama in construction, farming, and community service.

## National Black United Front

PO Box 470665
Brooklyn, NY 11247

Founded in 1980. Purpose is to unite black people of diverse political ideologies, age groups, socioeconomic backgrounds, and religious beliefs in order to build "a viable force for social transformation."

Goals are: the elimination of racism, sexism, bigotry, and racial violence; redistribution of the resources and wealth of the nation to provide abundantly for all citizens; elimination of the "genocidal mis-education system," police brutality, and denial of human rights nationally and internationally. Believes that current conditions in the U.S. threaten the survival of black people as a whole, and urges blacks to overlook individual differences by working together for common goals. Addresses such issues as unemployment, police brutality, budget cuts harmful to black communities, and the resurgence of the Ku Klux Klan. Conducts seminars and forums; maintains speakers' bureau; offers charitable program; sponsors competitions. Plans to organize boycotts, hold demonstrations, engage in electoral politics, and seek new vehicles for change.

## National Black United Fund

50 Park Pl., Ste. 1538
Newark, NJ 07102
(201)643-5122

Founded in 1972. Provides financial and technical support to projects serving the critical needs of black communities nationwide. Local affiliates solicit funds through payroll deduction to support projects in the areas of education, health and human services, economic development, social justice, arts and culture, and emergency needs. Programs supported by NBUF emphasize self-help, volunteerism, and mutual aid. Maintains Walter Bremond Memorial Fund campaign.

## National Black Women's Consciousness Raising Association

1906 N. Charles St.
Baltimore, MD 21218
(301)727-8900

Founded in 1975. Acts as a support group for women. Provides educational and informational workshops and seminars on subjects of concern to black women and women in general.

## National Black Women's Health Project
175 Trinity Ave. SW, 2nd Fl.
Atlanta, GA 30306
(404)681-4554

Founded in 1981. Encourages mutual and selfhelp advocacy among women to bring about a reduction in health care problems prevalent among black women. Urges women to communicate with health care providers, seek out available health care resources, become aware of selfhelp approaches, and communicate with other black women to minimize feelings of powerlessness and isolation, and thus realize they have some control over their physical and mental health. Points out the higher incidence of high blood pressure, obesity, breast and cervical cancers, diabetes, kidney disease, arteriosclerosis, and teenage pregnancy among black women than among other racial or socioeconomic groups. Also notes that black infant mortality is twice that of whites and that black women are often victims of family violence. Offers seminars outlining demographic information, chronic conditions, the need for health information and access to services, and possible methods of improving the health status of black women. Sponsors Center for Black Women's Wellness.

## National Black Women's Political Leadership Caucus
3005 Bladensburg Rd., NE, No. 217
Washington, DC 20018
(202)529-2806

Founded in 1971. Women interested in understanding their political role and the need for females to work toward equality; auxiliary membership includes men, senior citizens, and youths. Works to educate and incorporate all black women and youth in the political and economic process through participation. Encourages women to familiarize themselves with the role of city, state, and federal governments. Presents awards for humanitarianism; trains speakers and conducts research on the black family and on topics concerning politics and economics; compiles statistics.

## National Black Youth Leadership Council
250 W. 54th St., Ste. 800
New York, NY 10019
(212)541-7600

Founded in 1983. Conducts workshops for groups involved with black youth and minority student academic and leadership development; works to reduce the number of minority students that do not finish high school. Provides resources, information, skills, and strategies for fostering such development. Advises educators and parents on their role and responsibility to display leadership and success skills to youths they come in contact with; makes available to educational institutions training and expertise on cultural diversity, multiculturalism, and problems of bigotry and racism. Sponsors drug abuse awareness programs.

## National Business League
1629 K. St. NW, Ste. 695
Washington, DC 20006
(202)466-5483

Founded in 1900. Encourages minority ownership and management of small businesses and supports full minority participation in the free enterprise system.

## National Minority Business Council
National Catholic Conference for Interracial Justice
3033 4th St. NE
Washington, DC 20017-1102
(202)529-6480

Founded in 1959. Catholic organization working for interracial justice and social concerns in America. Initiates programs within and outside the Catholic church to end discrimination in community development, education, and employment.

## National Caucus and Center on Black Aged
1424 K St. NW, Ste. 500
Washington, DC 20005
(202)637-8400

Founded in 1970. Seeks to improve living conditions for low-income elderly Americans, particularly blacks. Advocates changes in federal and state laws in improving the economic, health, and social status of low-income senior citizens. Promotes community awareness of problems and issues effecting low-income aging population. Operates an employment program involving 2000 older persons in fourteen states. Sponsors, owns, and manages rental housing for the elderly. Conducts training and intern programs in nursing home administration, long-term care, housing management, and commercial property maintenance.

## National Center for the Advancement of Blacks in the Health Professions
PO Box 21121
Detroit, MI 48221
(313)345-4480

Founded in 1988. Participants belong to organizations including the American Public Health Association, National Urban League, National Black Nurses Association, and the American Hospital Association. Promotes the advancement of blacks in the health professions. Publicizes the disparity between the health of black and white Americans and its relationship to the underrepresentation of blacks in the health professions. (According to the National Center for Health Statistics, blacks have a higher death rate from cancer, heart disease, stroke, and diabetes than whites; blacks also have a higher infant mortality rate.) Acts as clearinghouse.

## National Coalition for Quality Integrated Education
1201 16th St. NW
Washington, DC 20036
(202)822-7708

Founded in 1975. National organizations committed to desegregating and improving the quality of elementary and secondary schools in the U.S. Serves as a forum for issues and developments pertaining to quality integrated education; encourages and coordinates citizen involvement in legislative developments.

## National Coalition of 100 Black Women
300 Park Ave., 2nd Fl.
New York, NY 10022
(212)974-6140

Founded in 1981. African-American women actively involved with issues such as economic development, health, employment, education, voting, housing, criminal justice, the status of black families, and the arts. Seeks to provide networking and career opportunities for African-American women in the process of establishing links between the organization and the corporate and political arenas. Encourages leadership development; sponsors role-model and mentor programs to provide guidance to teenage mothers and young women in high school or who have graduated from college and are striving for career advancement.

## National Coalition of Black Meeting Planners

50 F St. NW, Ste. 1040
Washington, DC 20001
(202)628-3952

Founded in 1983. Purposes are to: act as liaison with hotels, airlines, convention centers, and bureaus in an effort to assess the impact of minorities in these fields; assess the needs of the convention industry and how best to meet these needs; enhance members' sophistication in planning meetings; maximize employment of minorities in the convention industry.

## National Coalition on Black Voter Participation

1430 K St. NW, Ste. 401
Washington, DC 20005
(202)898-2220

Founded in 1976. Seeks to: increase black voter registration and participation in electoral voting; develop and fund local independent coalitions that will conduct campaigns to increase nonpartisan voter participation and citizenship empowerment programs. Conducts training programs. Collects and analyzes data; disseminates information on voter education including data on the black voting age population. Sponsors Operation Big Vote and Black Women's Roundtable on Voter Participation.

## National Committee on Concerns of Hispanics and Blacks

c/o Natl. Council of La Raza
20 F St., NW
Washington, DC 20001

Founded in 1979. Seeks to increase understanding among blacks and Hispanics. Participates in government projects concerning health and the media. Encourages dialogue and joint action on policy and advocacy issues by major black and Hispanic organizations.

## National Conference of Black Lawyers

2 W. 125th St.
New York, NY 10027
(212)864-4000

Founded in 1968. Maintains projects in legal services to community organizations, voting rights, and international affairs; provides public education on legal issues affecting blacks and poor people. Researches racism in law schools and bar admissions. Conducts programs of continuing legal education for member attorneys. Maintains general law library. Compiles statistics; maintains lawyer referral and placement services.

## National Conference of Black Mayors

1430 W. Peachtree St. NW, Ste. 700
Atlanta, GA 30309
(404)892-0127

Founded in 1974. Objectives are to: improve the executive management capacity and efficiency of member municipalities in the delivery of municipal services; create viable communities within which normal government functions can be performed efficiently; provide the basis upon which new social overhead investments in the infrastructure of municipalities can utilize federal, state, local, and private resources to encourage new industry and increase employment; assist municipalities in stabilizing their population through improvements of the quality of life for residents and, concurrently, create alternatives to outward migration. Facilitates small town growth and development through energy conservation.

## National Conference of Black Political Scientists

c/o Franklin D. Jones
Dept. of Public Affairs
Texas Southern University
Houston, TX 77045
(404)656-0763

Founded in 1969. Political and social science faculty, lawyers, and related professionals interested in black politics and related fields. Seeks to encourage research, publication, and scholarship by black Americans in political science; and to improve the political life of black Americans.

## National Conference of Black Student Retention

PO Box 10121
Tallahassee, FL 32302-2121
(904)599-3466

Founded in 1985. Members share programs, research, and strategies to reduce the dropout rate of minority students in colleges and universities.

## National Consortium for Black Professional Development

PO Box 18308
Louisville, KY 40218-0308
(502)896-2838

Founded in 1974. Goal is to increase substantially, by the year 2000, the number of black professionals in business administration, communications, applied and natural sciences, engineering, and law. Sponsors a science and engineering competition for black students and Ph.D. programs in the agricultural sciences and business administration. Maintains clearinghouse and placement bureau for black professionals seeking employment. Provides recruitment service for universities seeking qualified black faculty and students.

## National Consortium of Arts and Letters for Historically Black Colleges and Universities

PO Box 19033
Washington, DC 20036
(202)833-1327

Founded in 1984. Encourages academic excellence with an emphasis on cultural growth. Promotes study of African-American history and culture in the context of the scholarly study of world cultures. Offers no grants, but helps sponsor programs through fundraising efforts.

## National Council for Black Studies

Ohio State University
1030 Lincoln Tower
1800 Cannon Dr.
Columbus, OH 43210
(614)292-1035

Founded in 1975. Faculty members, students, and institutions united to promote and strengthen academic and community programs in black and/or African-American studies. Bestows awards for scholarly contributions; sponsors undergraduate and graduate student essay contests. Offers professional opportunities referral service; compiles statistics on black studies activities including information on students, faculty, research, and curricula.

## National Council on Black Aging

Box 51275
Durham, NC 27717
(919)493-4858

Founded in 1975. Persons interested in research and policies affecting older blacks and other minorities and in the dissemination of research findings. Maintains speakers' bureau. Conducts lectures on minority aging.

## National Council of Negro Women

1211 Connecticut Ave. NW, Ste. 702
Washington, DC 20036
(202)659-0006

Founded in 1935, by Mary McLeod Bethune. Assists in the development and utilization of the leadership of women in community, national, and international life. Maintains the Women's Center for Education and Career Advancement, which offers programs designed to aid minority women in pursuing nontraditional careers; also maintains the Bethune Museum and Archives for Black Women's History.

## National Emergency Civil Liberties Committee

175 5th Ave., Rm. 814
New York, NY 10010
(212)673-2040

Founded in 1951. To reestablish in full the traditional freedoms guaranteed under the Constitution and Bill of Rights. Committee "stands uncompromisingly for civil liberties for everyone and every variety of dissent." Legal staff handles test cases in the courts, without charge to the clients. Also functions as information service.

## National Forum for Black Public Administrators

777 N. Capitol St. NE, Ste. 807
Washington, DC 20002
(202)408-9300

Founded in 1983. Works to promote, strengthen, and expand the role of blacks in public administration. Seeks to focus the influence of black administrators toward building and maintaining viable communities. Develops specialized training programs for managers and executives. Provides national public administrative leadership resource and skills bank. Works to further communication among black public, private, and academic institutions. Addresses issues that affect the administrative capacity of black managers. Maintains Executive Leadership Institute which grooms mid-level executives for higher positions in government, the Mentor Program which matches aspiring black managers with seasoned executives over an 8-month period, and the Leadership Institute for Small Municipalities, which provides intensive training for elected and appointed officials from small communities. Offers training programs for black South Africans intent on achieving public administrative positions in the post-apartheid era. Sponsors the National Minority Business Development Forum to increase the participation of small and minority businesses in local government procurement and contracting programs.

## National Hook-Up of Black Women

c/o Wynetta Frazier
5117 S. University Ave.
Chicago, IL 60615
(312)643-5866

Founded in 1975. Purpose is to provide a communications network in support of black women who serve in organizational leadership positions, especially those

486

elected or appointed to office and those wishing to elevate their status through educational and career ventures. Works to form and implement a Black Women's Agenda that would provide representation for women, families, and communities and that would help surmount economic, educational, and social barriers. Supports efforts of the Congressional Black Caucus in utilizing the legislative process to work toward total equality of opportunity in society. Seeks to highlight the achievements and contributions of black women.

## National Institute Against Prejudice and Violence

31 S. Greene St.
Baltimore, MD 21201
(301)328-5170

Founded in 1984. Purpose is to study and respond to the problem of violence and intimidation motivated by racial, religious, ethnic, or anti-gay prejudice. Collects, analyzes, produces, and disseminates information and materials on programs of prevention and response. Conducts research on the causes and prevalence of prejudice and violence and their effects on victims and society; provides technical assistance to public agencies, voluntary organizations, schools, and communities in conflict; analyzes and drafts model legislation; conducts educational and training programs; sponsors conferences, symposia, and other forums for information exchange among experts.

## National Institute for Women of Color

1301 20th St. NW, Ste. 202
Washington, DC 20036
(202)296-2661

Founded in 1981. Research and advocacy organization interested in issues of concern to women of color, including: demographic trends, education, sex equity, and reproductive freedom. Assists in the formulation and implementation of public policy.

## National Minority AIDS Council

300 I St. NE, Ste. 400
Washington, DC 20002
(202)544-1076

Founded in 1986. Public health departments and AIDS organizations. Serves as a clearinghouse for information on AIDS as it affects minority communities in the United States.

## National Minority Health Association

PO Box 11876
Harrisburg, PA 17108
(717)234-3254

Founded in 1987. Health care providers and associations, consumers, executives and administrators, educators, pharmaceutical and health insurance companies, and other organizations with an interest in health. Seeks to focus attention on the health needs of minorities.

## National Office for Black Catholics

3025 4th St. NE
Washington, DC 20017
(202)635-1778

Founded in 1970. Participating organizations include National Black Sisters' Conference; National Black Catholic Clergy Caucus. Serves as a "foundation for the renewal of the credibility of the church in the black community." Works to coordinate actions designed "to liberate black people and to serve as a unifying strength." Plans to: have specialists and technicians working within the black community to coordinate community organization and development; provide leadership training for youth; attack problems of poverty and deprivation; sensitize blacks to their heritage through historical, cultural, and liturgical experience. Seeks cooperation with groups working toward black liberation. Concerns include: training black and white clergy and religious, Catholic, and non-Catholic laity; influencing decisions involving race and the church; monitoring, in order to prevent, manifestations of racism. Sponsors Pastoral Ministry Institute and Afro-American Culture and Worship Workshop; provides workshops and leadership training for parish councils and parochial schools.

## National Organization for the Professional Advancement of Black Chemists and Chemical Engineers
525 College St. NW
Washington, DC 20059
(202)667-1699

Founded in 1972. Seeks to aid black scientists and chemists in reaching their full professional potential; encourages black students to pursue scientific studies and employment; promotes participation of blacks in scientific research. Provides volunteers to teach science courses in selected elementary schools; sponsors scientific field trips for students; maintains speakers' bureau for schools; provides summer school for students of the U.S. Naval Academy. Conducts technical seminars in Africa.

## National Organization of Black College Alumni
Four Washington Square Village, No. 15E
New York, NY 10012
(212)982-7726

Founded in 1982. Works to ensure the survival of black colleges by addressing their concerns and needs and providing resources to meet these needs. Coordinates and focuses alumni support for black colleges; strengthens existing alumni associations; urges black youth to obtain a college education.

## National Organization of Black County Officials
440 1st St. NW, Ste. 500
Washington, DC 20001
(202)347-6953

Founded in 1982. Black county officials organized to provide program planning and management assistance to selected counties in the U.S. Acts as a technical information exchange to develop resolutions to problems on the local and national levels. Promotes the sharing of knowledge and methods of improving resource utilization and government operations. Conducts seminars and training sessions. Plans to maintain resource file on the achievements and history of black county officials.

## National Organization of Black Law Enforcement Executives
908 Pennsylvania Ave. SE
Washington, DC 20003
(202)546-8811

Founded in 1976. Goals are: to provide a platform from which the concerns and opinions of minority law enforcement executives and command-level officers can be expressed; to facilitate the exchange of programmatic information among minority law enforcement executives; to increase minority participation at all levels of law enforcement; to eliminate racism in the field of criminal justice; to secure increased cooperation from criminal justice agencies; to reduce urban crime and violence. Seeks to develop and maintain channels of communication between law enforcement agencies and the community; encourages coordinated community efforts to prevent and abate crime and its causes.

**National Rainbow Coalition, Inc.**
1110 Vermont Ave. NW
Washington, DC 20005
(202)728-1180

Founded in 1984 by the Reverend Jesse L. Jackson. Works to build a consensus in the area of civil rights, government, politics, labor, education, and business. Provides a platform for debate; encourages the development of a new political leadership committed to progressive domestic and international policies and programs.

**National Society of Black Engineers**
1454 Commerce St.
Alexandria, VA 22306
(703)549-2207

Founded in 1975. Seeks to increase the number of minority graduates in engineering and technology.

**National Society of Black Physicists**
Memphis State University
Dept. of Physics
Manning Hall
Memphis, TN 38152
(901)678-2620

Addresses the needs of black physicists; works to create opportunities for minorities in the field. Sponsors mentor program and lectures on research findings.

**Nation Urban Coalition**
8601 Georgia Ave. Ste. 500
Silver Spring, MD 20910
(301)495-4999

Founded in 1967. The National Urban Coalition seeks to improve the quality of life for the disadvantaged in urban areas through the combined efforts of business, labor, government, and community leaders. Operates programs which work to increase the partic-

ipation by minority students in science, math, and computer education; operates the Say Yes to a Younger's Future program.

**National Urban League**
500 E. 62nd St.
New York, NY 10021
(212)310-9000

Founded in 1910. Aims to eliminate racial segregation and discrimination in the United States and to achieve parity for blacks and other minorities in every phase of American life. Works to eliminate institutional racism and to provide direct service to minorities in the areas of employment, housing, education, social welfare, health, family planning, mental retardation, law and consumer affairs, youth and student affairs, labor affairs, veterans' affairs, and community and minority business development.

**Negro Airmen International**
PO Box 1340
Tuskegee, AL 36088
(205)727-0721

Founded in 1967. Seeks greater participation of blacks in the field of aviation through the encouragement of broader job opportunities. Encourages black youth to remain in school and enter the field. Maintains a Summer Flight Academy for teenagers at Tuskegee Institute in Alabama.

**Office for Advancement of Public Black Colleges of the National Association of State Universities and Land Grant Colleges**
1 Dupont Circle NW, Ste. 710
Washington, DC 20036-1191
(202)778-0818

Founded in 1968. Collects, organizes, interprets, and disseminates data on thirty-five predominantly black public colleges. The colleges, located in 18 states, enroll over 135,000 students.

**Omega Psi Phi**
2714 Georgia Ave. NW
Washington, DC 20001
(202)667-7158

Founded in 1911. Social fraternity.

**Operation Crossroads Africa**
475 Riverside Dr., Rm. 242
New York, NY 10115
(212)870-2106

Founded in 1958. Students and professionals, mostly from the U.S., who live and work with African counterparts during July and August on selfhelp community development projects in Africa. Opportunities are provided for interaction with village elders, educators, and political and other community leaders. Emphasizes community growth from within a "Third World" structure. Before departure, participants make an intensive study of Africa; after their return, they give speeches about their experiences. Participants pay part of the cost of the project. Organizes workcamp projects for U.S. high school students in the Caribbean and programs the visits of African and Caribbean leaders to the U.S. Sponsors training and exchange programs.

**Operation PUSH (People United to Save Humanity)**
930 E. 50th St.
Chicago, IL 60615
(312)373-3366

Founded in 1971 by the Reverend Jessie Jackson. National and international human rights organization directed toward education and economic equity and parity for all,

particularly black, Hispanic, and poor people. Seeks to create an ethical atmosphere; encourages self and community motivation and social responsibility. Sponsors PUSH for Education Program to aid the nation's public schools and restore academic excellence and discipline.

**Organization of Black Airline Pilots**
4 W. Palisade Ave.
Englewood, NJ 07631
(201)568-8145

Founded in 1976. Seeks to enhance minority participation in the aerospace industry. Maintains liaison with airline presidents and minority and pilot associations. Conducts lobbying efforts, including congressional examinations into airline recruitment practices. Provides scholarships; cosponsors Summer Flight Academy for Youth at Tuskegee Institute in Alabama.

**Phi Beta Sigma**
145 Kennedy St. NW
Washington, DC 20011
(202)726-5424

Founded in 1914. Service fraternity. Sponsors the Sigma Beta Club for high school aged males.

**Phylaxis Society**
PO Box 75680
Washington, DC 20013

Founded in 1973. Prince Hall Masonic writers and editors of Masonic publications.

**Planning and the Black Community**
Department of the Army
PO Box C-3755
Seattle, WA 98124-2255
(206)764-3614

Founded in 1980. Members of the American Planning Association interested in issues related to planning in the black community. Objectives are to: formulate and articulate positions on national, regional, and statewide policy issues related to blacks for presentation to the APA and the public; provide a forum for exchange of practical experience and knowledge among black planners; establish and strengthen liaison with black professionals and groups such as social workers, economists, lawyers, public administrators, International City Management Association, National Association for the Advancement of Colored People, and National League of Cities.

## Project Equality
1020 E. 63rd St., Ste. 102
Kansas City, MO 64110
(816)361-9222

Founded in 1965. A nationwide interfaith program enabling religious organizations, institutions, and others to support equal opportunity employers with their purchasing power. Services include: validation of hotels for conventions and meetings of organizations, validations of suppliers to member organizations and institutions, and consultant and educational services to assist employers in affirmative action and equal employment opportunity programs.

## Quality Education for Minorities
Network
1818 N St. NW, Ste. 350
Washington, DC 20036
(202)659-18118

Founded in 1987. Created to implement the plan developed by the Quality Education for Minorities Project. Believes that minorities are underserved by the educational system and thus disproportionately lack the skill needed to participate effectively in a society increasingly based on high technology. Plans to work with school systems, communities, universities, and public and private sector institutions to ensure that minority students have equal access to educational opportunities.

## Sigma Pi Phi
920 Broadway, Ste. 703
New York, NY 10010
(212)477-5550

Founded in 1904. Social fraternity. Maintains the Boule Foundation. Sigma Pi Phi is the oldest black Greek letter society in the United States.

## Southern Christian Leadership Conference
334 Auburn Ave. NE
Atlanta, GA 30312
(404)522-1420

Founded in 1957. Nonsectarian coordinating and service agency for local organizations seeking full citizenship rights, equality, and the integration of African-Americans in all aspects of life in the U.S. and subscribing to the Ghandian philosophy of nonviolence. Works primarily in sixteen southern and border states to improve civic, religious, economic, and cultural conditions. Fosters nonviolent resistance to all forms of racial injustice, including state and local laws and practices. Conducts leadership training program embracing such subjects as registration and voting, social protest, use of the boycott, picketing, nature of prejudice, and understanding politics. Sponsors citizenship education schools to teach reading and writing, help persons pass literacy tests for voting, and provide information about income tax forms, tax-supported resources, aid to handicapped children, public health facilities, how government is run, and social security. Conducts Crusade for the Ballot, which aims to double the black vote in the South through increased voter registrations.

## Southern Coalition for Educational Equity

PO Box 22904
Jackson, MS 39225-2904
(601)366-5351

Founded in 1978. Coalition of parents, students, teachers, and administrators that operates in Alabama, Georgia, Louisiana, Mississippi, and North Carolina, with plans to include eight additional states. Works toward developing more efficient educational programs and eliminating racism and sexism within southern schools. Has organized projects including: Arkansas Career Resources Project, which provides minorities and single heads of households with marketable skills and jobs; New Orleans Effective Schools Project, which attempts to increase school effectiveness through high expectations, stressing academic achievement, and quality instruction; Project MiCRO, which seeks to provide computer access for, and sharpen analytical skills of, minority students; Summer Program, which focuses on students' reading comprehension skills.

## Southern Poverty Law Center

PO Box 2087
Montgomery, AL 36102
(205)264-0286

Founded in 1971. Seeks to protect and advance the legal and civil rights of poor people, regardless of race, through education and litigation. Does not accept fees from clients. The center is currently involved in several lawsuits representing individuals injured or threatened by activities of

the Ku Klux Klan and related groups. Attempts to develop techniques and strategies that can be used by private attorneys. Operates Klanwatch.

## Southern Regional Council

1900 Rhodes Haverty Bldg.
134 Peachtree St. NW
Atlanta, GA 30303-1925
(404)522-8764

Founded in 1944. Leaders in education, religion, business, labor, the community, and the professions interested in improving race relations and combatting poverty in the South. Comprises an interracial research and technical assistance center that addresses issues of social justice and political and economic democracy. Seeks to engage public policy as well as personal conscience in pursuit of equality. Develops educational programs; provides community relations consultation and field services when requested by official and private agencies. Distributes pamphlets pertaining to desegregation of various public facilities and fosters elimination of barriers to black voting registration. Acts as official sponsor of overseas government officials, leaders, and other visitors who wish to view race relations in the South.

## Special Committee on the Situation With Regard to the Implementation of the Declaration on the Granting of Independence to Colonial Countries and Peoples

United Nations, Rm. S-3341
New York, NY 10017
(212)963-5429

Founded in 1961. United Nations committee comprising representatives of twenty-five nations concerned with the progress of people under colonial rule toward self-determination and independence. Considers situations in 18 territories based on information received from administering powers or local governments, nongovernmental organizations, published sources, and observations of the committee's visiting missions. Reviews military activities and activities of foreign economic interests in colonial territories; enlists support of United Nations specialized agencies and international institutions to assist decolonization efforts, especially through aid to colonial people; seeks to mobilize public opinion in support of decolonization by disseminating information.

### 369th Veteran's Association

369th Regiment Armory
1 369th Plaza
New York, NY 10037
(212)281-3308

Founded in 1953. Seeks to support all patriotic endeavors of the United States, and to assist members and their families through charitable programs and community activities. Donates funds, equipment, and other supplies to children's camps, need families, religious institutions, Veterans Administration Hospitals, and community and senior citizen centers. Conducts seminar and counseling sessions to assist unemployed veterans, and offers study classes to adults for preparation in Civil Service examinations.

### Trade Union Leadership Council

8670 Grand River Ave.
Detroit, MI 48204
(313)894-0303

Founded in 1957. Seeks to eradicate injustices perpetrated upon people because of race, religion, sex, or national origin. Seeks increased leadership and job opportunities for blacks.

### TransAfrica

545 8th St. SE, Ste. 200
Washington, DC 20003
(202)547-2550

Founded in 1977. Concerned with the political and human rights of people in Africa and the Caribbean, and those of African descent throughout the world. Attempts to influence U.S. foreign policy in these areas by informing the public of violations of social, political, and civil rights, and by advocating a more progressive attitude in the U.S. policy stance. Supports the work of the United Nations in Africa. Sponsors TransAfrica Action Alert to mobilize black opinion nationally on foreign policy issues by contacting influential policymakers.

### TransAfrica Forum

545 8th St. SE, Ste. 200
Washington, DC 20003
(202)547-2550

Founded in 1981. Research and education arm of TransAfrica. Seeks to provide an independent review of differing perspectives on political, economic, and cultural issues affecting black communities globally through its publications. Conducts seminars with scholars and government officials.

### Tuskegee Airmen, Inc.

65 Cadillac Sq. 3200
Detroit, MI 48226
(313)965-8858

Founded in 1972. Former airmen who flew in the segregated U.S. Army Air Corps during World War II, men and women involved in military aviation, service academies, and ROTC units. Seeks to maintain a relationship among those who fought and served in World War II. Provides information about the contributions black Americans have made to aviation history. Operates a museum at Historic Fort Wayne in Detroit, MI.

**Try Us Resources**
2105 Central Ave. NE
Minneapolis, MN 55418
(612)781-6819

Founded in 1968. Compiles and publishes minority business directories. Sponsors minority purchasing seminars.

**Union of Black Episcopalians**
National Cathedral
St. Alban
Washington, DC 20016
(804)848-2680

Founded in 1968. Objectives are: to remove racism from church and community and to achieve equal participation in policy-making, decision-making, programming, and staffing on parochial, diocesan, and national levels; to stimulate the growth of black membership throughout the church; to promote the placement of black professionals within the church without regard to race; to protect clergy and laymen from racist practices.

**Unitarian Universalist Association Black Concerns Working Group**
25 Beacon St.
Boston, MA 02108
(617)742-2100

Founded in 1985. Attempts to raise denominational public awareness of racism as a current justice issue. Works to implement recommendations regarding racial justice that were adopted by the Unitarian Universalist General Assembly in 1985. Conducts local and regional workshops in an effort to coordinate racial justice work among Unitarian Universalist congregations.

**United Black Christians**
1380 E. Hyde Park Blvd., No. 815
Chicago, IL 60615

Founded in 1970. Seeks to increase the relevance of United Church of Christ in the struggle for liberation and justice.

**United Black Church Appeal**
c/o Christ Church
860 Forest Ave.
Bronx, NY 10456
(212)665-6688

Founded in 1980. Objective is to awaken the power of the black clergy and the black church to provide leadership for the liberation of the black community. Is concerned with black economic development and political power, and the strengthening of black families and churches. Believes pastors in black churches should reestablish legitimate leadership roles within the black community. Works with troubled black youths in the community; rallies against drugs in urban areas. Supports community betterment projects including surplus food programs and distribution of food to needy families.

**United Black Fund of America**
1012 14th St. NW, Ste. 300
Washington, DC 20005
(202)783-0430

Founded in 1969. Nonprofit agencies that provide human care services to low-income or disabled blacks and other minorities. Assists disadvantaged blacks and other minorities in becoming self-sufficient by providing funding to member agencies for the establishment of health and welfare programs.

**United Church of Christ Commission for Racial Justice**
700 Prospect Ave. E., 7th Fl.
Cleveland, OH 44115-1110
(216)736-2168

Founded in 1965. Works to ensure racial justice and social equality for ethic and racial minorities worldwide. Maintains higher education program to provide scholarships to minority college students.

**United Negro College Fund**
500 E. 62nd St.
New York, NY 10021
(212)326-1100

Founded in 1944. Fundraising agency for historically black colleges and universities which are private and fully accredited. Provides information on educational programs. Sponsors college fairs for high school and community college students. Administers scholarship awards and corporate and foundation programs.

**Universal Masonic Brotherhood**
15 Vose Ave.
South Orange, NJ 07079
(201)763-1780

**Universal Masonic Order of the Eastern Star**
95 N. 18th St.
East Orange, NJ 07017

**Universal Negro Improvement Association and African Communities League of the World**
1611 W. Columbia Ave.
Philadelphia, PA 19151
(215)236-6063

**Washington Office on Africa**
110 Maryland Ave. NE, Ste. 112
Washington, DC 20002
(202)546-7961

Founded in 1972. Established to monitor and analyze developments in U.S. policy toward southern Africa and work with national and local groups which support the attainment of majority rule. Lobbies on congressional legislation affecting southern Africa.

**World Africa Chamber of Commerce**
PO Box 33144
Washington, DC 20033

Founded in 1973. Sponsors trade missions to Africa and seminars to assist members with personal contacts and in gaining knowledge in the market and the needs of the countries they service. Conducts research and development studies on the changing economic developments and attitudes in specific countries and on the continent as a whole. Provides professional consulting in areas including market development, export promotion, joint venture projects, trade finance counseling, and market research studies. Operates trade center to provide facilities for exhibits, meetings, and other activities. Additional services include: assistance with visas and business trip planning; job referrals; clearinghouse on business, political, and cultural information; office and secretarial aid for businessmen and dignitaries traveling abroad. Maintains the Continental Africa Chamber Foundation.

**World Institute of Black Communications/CEBA Awards**
463 7th Ave.
New York, NY 10018
(212)714-1508

Founded in 1978. Objectives are to broaden opportunities for blacks in the communications industry; recognize black communications contributions; and establish and quantify the value of the black consumer market to the national advertising community. Sponsors annual Communications Excellence to Black Audience Awards to patronizing corporations and creative entities for most creative, relevant, and professionally executed media efforts. Operates library on advertising directed toward the black consumer market over the last 14 years and slides on black American lifestyles. Compiles demographic and marketing research on the black consumer market.

**Young Black Programmers Coalition**
PO Box 1051
Vicksburg, MS 39181
(601)631-7191

Founded in 1976. Provides professional training and offers technical assistance to black entrepreneurs in the broadcast and music industries. Conducts lobbying activities pertaining to legislation affecting the music industry. Provides scholarships to attend black colleges and universities.

**Zeta Phi Beta**
1734 New Hampshire Ave. NW
Washington, DC 20009
(202)387-3103

Founded in 1920. Service and social sorority. Maintains the Zeta Phi Beta Sorority Educational Foundation.

# 10

# *Law*

# 🔟

# *Law*

The Legal Status of African-Americans: 1790–1883 ■ African Americans on the United States Supreme Court ■ African Americans and the Criminal Justice System ■ Major Federal Legislation ■ Major United States Supreme Court Decisions ■ Attorneys, Judges, and Legal Scholars

**Essays by George R. Johnson, Jr. and Marilyn Hortense Mackel**

## *The Legal Status of African-Americans: 1790–1883*

### by George R. Johnson, Jr.

Race always has been the most intractable social problem of American life, the indelible stain on the American body politic. The United States of America was born with the declaration that "all men are created equal" (The Declaration of Independence, 1776); yet, the reality of equality in America never has equalled its promise. Nowhere is that truer than on questions of equality between the races—that is, between white Americans and African Americans.

The legal treatment of African Americans during the period 1790 to 1883, like their treatment in most other periods in American history, was one of decided ambivalence. Consequently, no useful discussion of the Supreme Court's treatment of African Americans can begin in 1790. An understanding of the period 1790–1883 must begin with 1787

and the adoption of the American Constitution. Moreover, the Supreme Court's treatment of African Americans during this period in the nation's history must be viewed in context—in the context of the history and of the events which gave shape to the period.

In 1776 the nation began with a declaration of universal equality. But that promise ended at the color line. The ringing testimony to equality in the Declaration of Independence had its limits: it did not include the African American. In short, America began with a contradiction that centered on race. The constitutional debates of the 1780s highlight the nation's contradictory, confusing positions on race questions: this was a nation founded on the principle of individual liberty, but that liberty did not extend to the African slaves and their progeny. In the 1790s, as in the 1990s, the ambivalence persisted: Should the slaves be counted for purposes of representation? Should Congress be empowered to prohibit slavery and the slave trade? Should an escaped slave be "free" to live among the rest of us? These were some of the issues that dominated much of the discussion among the framers of the new constitution.

Perhaps one should not be surprised by this ambivalence on matters of race and equality in this country. It always has been present. The history of Constitution and the Supreme Court reveals dramatic instances of the nation's tortuous history on matters of racial equality (see Solby, ed. 1958. *The Federal Convention and the Formation of the Union,* New York: Bobbs-Merrill). The "race" problem has a long history in the United States, a history as long as the history of the nation itself.

This country's inability squarely to face the "race" question can trace its origins to the institution of African slavery. That blot on the national history still clouds the country's ability to discuss issues of race with candor. It cannot be surprising: slavery itself was never discussed with candor, either in the Constitution or in the country. As far as the Constitution was concerned, slavery was the shame "that dare not speak its name."

At the outset, the United States was mired in a debate over the question of slavery. While the debates about the composition of the national legislature were openly about the number of representatives to be accorded each state, the institution of human slavery and what to do about it clearly were major subtexts. Underneath those lofty discussions, however, lay the real issue: how to count the black slaves, who were to be found largely in the planting regions of the South? The problem of race predated the Constitution, and it would persist into the 1790s and beyond.

Even though the institution of human slavery vexed members of the constitutional convention, not once was the word itself used in the document that they submitted to the convention for ratification. Perhaps in their own minds they recognized that their championing of equality was vitiated and debased by the specter of slavery that they silently tolerated. Even though their document alluded to slavery's existence, it failed to acknowledge its presence.

In setting forth the number of representatives to be accorded each state in the lower house of Congress, the Constitution originally counted the African slaves as "three-fifths of all other persons." The "three-fifths" clause augured the history of the African American in the United States: the black American would share less in the promise of the new nation. That clause, though no longer effective, proved to be prophetic.

The original Constitution also forbade the new federal government from abolishing the slave trade or otherwise affecting matters of race before the year 1808. Again, however, the language is so abstract: "The Migration or Importation of such Persons as any of the States now existing shall think proper to admit, shall not be prohibited by the Congress prior to the Year one thousand eight hundred and eight . . ." (Art. 1, §9, ¶1).

Runaway slaves were referred to as "person[s] held to service or labour in one state . . . escaping into another. . . ." This fugitive-slave clause sought to ensure that the slave-owners' "escaped" property, when found, would be returned to him. Despite these deliberately neutral and innocuous-sounding provisions, there was no mistaking their purpose: to enshrine and ensure by law the political superiority of white Americans over the African slaves and their progeny. At the time of the Constitution's framing, one thing was certain: the African slaves and their descendants would be politically inferior to white people.

Even though the framers of the Constitution recognized the peculiar dilemma of racial discrimination as it then existed, they nonetheless decided that they could postpone a decision on the "race question," that its resolution could wait. So may have developed the recurrent American idea that matters of racial justice and racial equality can always be put off, postponed, to be decided at some other time.

With such constitutional antecedents, it is not surprising that the Supreme Court has been enormously conflicted on matters of race. The Court takes its cases as it finds them, and cases on race have never been easily or calmly settled in this country. They are not now. They were not in the period 1790–1883.

### The Early Days: *Prigg v. Pennsylvania*

Before the 1800s the Court had very few opportunities to render a decision directly on the question of slavery, so accepted was the institution as a feature of American life. Not that it was universally supported, but the law clearly recognized slaves as species of property and therefore subject to regulation as other real property might be. This regulation was often justified by citing the fugitive-slave clause of the Constitution (Art. 4, §2). One of the few pre-Civil War cases to address the slavery question and state regulatory powers in any degree was *Prigg v. Pennsylvania* (41 US [16 Peters] 539, 1842).

Pennsylvania had enacted a statute prohibiting any person from removing blacks from the state by force or violence with the intention of detaining them as slaves. The Court explained that the fugitive-slave clause "contemplates the existence of a positive, unqualified right on the part of the owner of the slave, which no state law or regulation can in any way qualify, regulate,

control, or restrain." The statute was declared invalid with respect to an escaped slave because, in the words of the Court, "any state law which interrupts, limits, delays, or postpones the right of the owner to the immediate possession of the slave, and the immediate command of his service and labor, operates pro tanto, a discharge of the slave therefrom." The Court further held that the clause implicitly vested Congress with the power to assist owners in securing the return of escaped slaves, that Congress had exercised that power by enacting the Fugitive Slave Act of 1793, that this national power was exclusive, and that any state laws regulating the means by which slaves were to be delivered up were unconstitutional.

*Prigg* announced no landmark policy in 1842. It simply affirmed the social and political realities of its time. However, during the period 1790 to 1883, two major cases involving African Americans and the issues of race did reach the Supreme Court. These two cases—*Dred Scott v. Sandford* (60 US [19 Howard] 393, 1856), *The Civil Rights Cases*, (109 US 18, 1883)—and a third relatively minor case, *Strauder v. West Virginia* (100 US 303, 1880), reveal the abiding ambivalence that consistently has characterized American racial relations.

### *Dred Scott v. Sandford*

The 1800s were consumed with sectional strife, primarily strife about race. And that period gave the nation *Dred Scott* and an irreversible impetus toward civil war (Bruce Catton. 1964. "The Dred Scott Case," in John A. Garraty, ed., *Quarrels That Have Shaped the Constitution*, New York: Harper & Row, p. 78). No other case in judicial American history has achieved as much notoriety as has *Dred Scott*. The case continues to sym-

Dred Scott

bolize the marginal status in which African-Americans often have been held in the nation's social and political order.

*Dred Scott* declared that no African American, whether free or slave, could claim United States citizenship. It also held that Congress could not prohibit slavery in the United States territories. In addition, the decision also includes what is undoubtedly the most infamous line in American constitutional history. In his opinion, Chief Justice Roger Brook Taney wrote that African-Americans had "no rights which any white man was bound to respect."

This decision—only the second in the nation's history in which the Supreme Court declared an act of Congress unconstitutional—was a clear victory for the political interests that supported slavery, particularly the South. Southerners long had argued that neither Congress nor the territorial legislature had the power to exclude slavery from a territory. Only a state could exclude slavery, they maintained.

Of course, the ruling in *Dred Scott* aroused angry resentment in the North and other parts of the country and launched the nation further along the course to civil war. It also influenced the introduction and the adoption of the fourteenth amendment to the Constitution after the Civil War. The 1868 amendment, which explicitly overruled *Dred Scott*, extended citizenship to former slaves and sought to give them full civil rights.

Dred Scott was the slave of a United States Army surgeon, John Emerson of Missouri, a state that permitted slavery. In 1834, Scott traveled with Emerson to live in Illinois, where slavery was prohibited. They later lived in the Wisconsin Territory, where slavery was prohibited by the Missouri Compromise. In 1838 Scott returned to Missouri with Emerson. Emerson later died there in 1843, and three years later Scott sued Emerson's widow for his freedom.

Scott's claim was based on the argument that his former residence in a free state and a free territory—Illinois and Wisconsin, respectively—made him a free man. A Missouri state circuit court ruled in Scott's favor, but the Missouri supreme court later reversed that decision. Meanwhile, Scott had become legally regarded as the property of John F.A. Sanford of New York. Because Sanford did not live in Missouri, Scott's lawyers were able invoke the diversity of citizenship jurisdiction to transfer the case to a federal court. The lower federal court ruled against Scott, and his lawyers appealed to the Supreme Court of the United States. By a vote of seven to two, the Supreme Court ruled that Scott could not bring a suit in federal court. The decision was announced on March 6, 1857, two days after the inauguration of President James Buchanan.

Each justice in the majority wrote a separate opinion. However, Chief Justice Taney's opinion is most often cited because of its far-reaching implications for sectional crisis and for the monumentally horrible view of the rights of African Americans that it announced. Speaking for the majority, Chief Justice Taney declared that Scott was not entitled to rights such as the right to vote or to sue in a federal court, because, as an African American, he was not a citizen of the United States (60 US 393, 1856).

The Court did not dismiss the case after ruling on Scott's citizenship, as it could easily have done. Because there was a growing national desire for a ruling on the constitutionality of such laws as the Missouri Compromise of 1820, the Taney court seized the opportunity to express its views on both congressional power and the legal status of African Americans (Catton. p. 86).

The Missouri Compromise had forbidden slavery in that part of the Louisiana Territory north of the latitude 36°30', except for Missouri. Instead of dismissing the suit, the Court discussed this issue as a part of its decision in *Dred Scott*. By the same seven to two margin, it ruled that the Missouri Compromise, which had been repealed in 1854, was unconstitutional. Taney argued that because slaves were property, Congress could not forbid slavery in territories without violating a slaveowner's right to own property under the fifth amendment. As for Scott's temporary residence in the free state of Illinois, the majority ruled that Scott then had still been subject to Missouri law.

Dred Scott was sold shortly afterward, and his new owner gave him his freedom two months after the decision.

The *Dred Scott* decision could have been a mortal blow to the newly created Republi-

can Party, which had been formed to curb the expansion of slavery into the western territories (Catton. p. 86). The decision forced Stephen A. Douglas, an advocate of popular sovereignty to devise a system that would enable settlers to ban slavery in their jurisdictions. President Buchanan, the South, and a majority of the Supreme Court had hoped that the decision would end the antislavery agitation that consumed the country. Instead, the decision increased antislavery sentiment in the North, strengthened the Republican Party, and fed the sectional antagonisms that finally exploded into war in 1861 (Catton. p. 88).

### Strauder v. West Virginia and the *Civil Rights Cases*

Between the time of the Civil War and the *Civil Rights Cases*, there was one exception to the otherwise bleak and ambivalent record of the United States Supreme Court in the civil-rights area. That was in the case of *Strauder v. West Virginia* (100 US 303, 1880). The state of West Virginia permitted only "white male persons who are twenty-one years of age" to serve on juries in the state. This, of course, meant that it was impossible for African Americans brought before West Virginia courts ever to have another African American serve on a jury deliberating in their cases. The Supreme Court invalidated this provision as a violation of the fourteenth amendment's guarantee of equal protection.

Ironically, the Civil War, caused in part by Justice Taney's dictum in *Dred Scott* that Congress could not bar slavery in the territories, actually resulted in the destruction of slavery (Allan F. Westin. 1964. "The Case of the Prejudiced Doorkeeper," [hereinafter, Westin] in John A. Garraty, ed., *Quarrels that Have Shaped the Constitution*, New

York: Harper & Row. p. 128). Moreover, the war also resulted in a completely new balance of power between the national and the state governments. Federalism, unlike it had been understood prior to the Civil War, now would function with a totally new calculus, a calculus in which the federal government was the defining constant.

The years following the war produced the Civil War amendments—the thirteenth, the fourteenth, and the fifteenth—with their concerted purpose completely to emancipate and empower the former slaves. These three amendments are compelling evidence of the new calculus which operated on federalism.

In fact, the text of the Fourteenth Amendment, overturning *Dred Scott*, emphasized the significance of this new relationship and the new power realignments that now obtained: "All persons born or naturalized in the United States and subject to the jurisdiction thereof are citizens of the United States and of the state wherein they reside . . ." (United States Constitution, Amendment 14, §1).

There now could be no dispute that citizenship in the United States was defined and protected by the national constitution and that state citizenship derived from national citizenship and was not independent of it. Augmented by Congress's enforcement powers, these amendments were the constitutional foundations that supported reconstruction, where the recently freed slaves were affirmatively supported and protected by the federal government.

A principal legislative result of this period was the passage of the Civil Rights Act of 1875 (18 Stat. 335). According to the statute, its purpose was "to protect all citizens in their civil and legal rights." Even though couched in disarmingly general terms, it was clear that the statute was designed with particular solicitude for the recently emancipated slaves, whose fate otherwise might largely have remained in the hands of people who generally were not favorably disposed to them and their new status.

The 1870s became unique years for testing race relations in the United States (Westin. p. 128). Interestingly, during this period, no state had laws requiring the separation of the races in places of public accommodation. Whatever the practice in a particular establishment or a particular jurisdiction, it was a matter of local custom, individual choice, or personal preference. An earlier statute, the Civil Rights Act of 1866, and the ratification of the fourteenth amendment in 1868 had spawned several test suits throughout the country—among them suits for denying sleeper accommodations to African Americans on a Washington-to-New York train, for refusing to sell theater tickets to blacks in Boston, for restricting blacks to front platforms in Baltimore streetcars, and for barring African-American women from the waiting rooms and parlor cars of railroads in Virginia, Illinois, and California. There also had been massive resistance on the part of whites to the social integration of the races.

Faced with these challenges, Congress, controlled by the republicans, enacted a new civil-rights act in 1875. The 1875 statute sought to invalidate all racially motivated interference by individuals with other individuals' exercise of the right to make use of "the accommodations, advantages, facilities, and privileges of inns, public conveyances and theatres . . ." (109 US 9–10). In short, the statute sought to provide legislative specificity to the constitutional norms embodied in the thirteenth and fourteenth amendments.

The *Civil Rights Cases* (109 US 3, 1883) were actually six different cases: *United States v. Singleton, United States v. Stanley, United States v. Nichols, United States v.*

*Ryan*, *United States v. Hamilton*, and *Robinson v. Memphis & Charleston Railroad*. Five of these cases were criminal prosecutions, which directly challenged the constitutionality of the 1875 statute.

The first of these cases, *United States v. Singleton*, involved the refusal of Samuel Singleton, doorkeeper of New York's Grand Opera House to honor the tickets of William R. Davis, Jr. and his fiance. On November 22, 1879, the pair had attempted to see a matinee performance of Victor Hugo's *Ruy Blas*, starring Edwin Boothe. Davis, business agent of the African-American newspaper, *The Progressive-American*, was obviously black. However, Davis's fiance, who without incident, had purchased the tickets earlier that day was described as "a bright octoroon, almost white" (Westin. p. 129). When the couple returned for the performance, they were told by Singleton that "these tickets are no good."

*Stanley* presented the refusal of hotelier, Murray Stanley, to serve a meal to Bird Gee, an African American, in Murray's Topeka, Kansas, hotel. *Nichols* involved the refusal of owner of Nichols House in Jefferson City, Missouri, to accept an African-American as a guest. In *Ryan*, the doorkeeper at Maguire's Theater in San Francisco denied a black man named George M. Tyler entry to the dress circle at Maguire's. In *Hamilton*, the conductor of the Nashville Chattanooga & St. Louis Railroad denied an African-American woman with a first-class ticket access to the ladies' car. Instead, she was relegated to "a dirty, disagreeable coach known as a smoking car."

The sixth of these cases, *Robinson v. Memphis & Charleston Railroad*, was different. This case involved travel on the Memphis & Charleston Railroad by a young African-American woman, Mrs. Sallie Robinson, and her nephew, Joseph C. Robinson. Mr. Robinson was described as a young African American "of light complexion, light hair, and light blue eyes." The train's conductor attempted forcibly to refuse the two passengers entry to the first-class parlor car for which they had purchased tickets. The conductor mistook the pair for a white man and his paramour, whose association he had thought to be for "illicit purposes." In fact, he testified at trial that these couples usually "talked, drank, smoked and acted disorderly, and were objectionable to the other passengers" in the first-class section."

The railroad conceded the constitutionality of the 1875 statute, but argued that it did not apply to the conductor's actions. The trial judge ruled that motive was dispositive under the act. So, if the conductor believed Mrs. Robinson to be a prostitute, whether reasonable or not in that assumption, the exclusion was not based on race and, therefore, the railroad was not liable. The jury found for the railroad and the Robinsons appealed.

The United States, represented before the Supreme Court by Solicitor General Samuel F. Phillips, argued strongly that the act should be upheld in all these cases. In addition, the government's brief discussed the history of the American race relations and the genesis of the Civil War amendments and their statutory descendants. The government stressed particularly the importance of equal access to public accommodations. The Solicitor General emphasized that this act was one of several enacted by "a Congress led by men who had fought in the Civil War and had framed the war amendments." Implicit in the Solicitor General's position was the idea that Congress understood, as clearly as anyone could, that it was not sufficient to outlaw slavery and to declare equal protection to be the law of the land. More was needed: specific statutory protection was necessary to ensure that every vestige of slavery and every reminder of its stigma were eliminated from public life.

The government's arguments, however, did not persuade the high court. The Court announced its decision on October 15, 1883. The Court ruled against the United States, dashing the hopes of these African-American petitioners and other citizens who believed the Civil War had eliminated racial discrimination in the United States.

The vote in the *Civil Rights Cases* was eight to one. The majority included Chief Justice Waite and Associate Justices Blatchford, Bradley, Fields, Gray, Matthews, Miller, and Woods. Justice Bradley wrote the opinion of the court, which asserted two simplistically devastating conclusions: (1) the Fourteenth Amendment is prohibitory upon the states only (101 US at 11), and (2) the Thirteenth Amendment relates only to slavery and involuntary servitude (101 US at 21).

Bradley and his colleagues maintained that the fourteenth amendment operated only as a prohibition and restriction against the states. Because the Civil Rights Act of 1875 sought to outlaw acts of private individuals, shopkeepers, and other businesses, it violated the constitution. This "state action" doctrine holds that, because the government was not the actor in these cases, the Fourteenth Amendment did not empower Congress to outlaw these practices. Also, Bradley's opinion held that, while Congress was empowered by the Thirteenth Amendment to eliminate slavery and all its vestiges, the denial of access to accommodations in commercial establishments, public conveyances, and public amusements was not a "badge or incident of slavery" (109 US at 21).

Bradley's opinion effectively halted the progress of civil rights and limited the ability of the federal government, acting through its legislature, to eliminate and eradicate racial

discrimination in this country for almost ninety years.

A single justice on the Court dissented—John Marshall Harlan. At the time, Harlan was the court's only southerner and a former slaveholder himself (Westin. p. 138). Ironically, he had also been a bitter critic of the civil war amendments during the 1860s. Between that time and the time of the decision in the case, Harlan had undergone a radical transformation. (His transformation was to achieve its fullest development thirteen years later when he dissented again in another famous civil-rights case, *Plessy v. Ferguson*).

Justice Harlan's dissent was not announced on the day of the majority's decision. In fact, the dissent probably was not written until early November 1883 (Westin. p. 141). Justice Harlan's dissent proceeds directly to attack the central failing of the majority's assertions: the grounds for the decision were "too narrow and artificial" (109 US at 26). According to Harlan, the majority have refused to embrace both "the substance and the spirit" of the Civil Rights Act. "It is not the words of the law but the internal sense of it that makes the law. The letter of the law is the body; the sense and reason of the law is the soul." And, in Justice Harlan's view, the purpose of the act "was to prevent *race* [emphasis in original] discrimination." The majority, as Harlan develops the dissent, betrayed this purpose "by a subtle and ingenious verbal criticism."

Justice Harlan's voice was eloquent, but it was a lone one, crying in the wilderness. Neither the majority of the Supreme Court nor the nation it represented cared to do much else to promote the civil rights of its new black citizens. Harlan's dissent in the *Civil Rights Cases* forecasted his more famous one in *Plessy v. Ferguson* (163 US 537, 1896), because the decision in the *Civil Rights Cases* led inexorably to the black codes, Jim Crow, and other examples of *de jure* segregation that came to define race relations in the United States.

*The Civil Rights Cases* starkly revealed the nation's ambivalence on the questions of race. On the one hand, Congress had sought to guarantee the rights of the recently freed slaves by proposing constitutional amendments that were ultimately ratified, even if some coercion was necessary. Congress went further and augmented the constitutional guarantees with additional legislative protections and safeguards. The Supreme Court, however, frustrated these constitutional and legislative initiatives with a cold and constricted reading of the thirteenth and the fourteenth amendments. An ancient pattern had reasserted itself.

# African Americans on the United States Supreme Court

### Thurgood Marshall

Thurgood Marshall, a graduate of Lincoln University and Howard University Law School, was admitted to the Maryland Bar in 1933. In 1936 he joined the National Association for the Advancement of Colored People staff as assistant to special counsel Charles Hamilton Houston. In 1938 Marshall succeeded Houston as special council, and in 1950 he became director of the NAACP Legal Defense and Education Fund. While working the NAACP and the NAACP Legal Defense and Education Fund, Marshall

Thurgood Marshall, 1958.

played a major role in some of Supreme Court history's most important cases, including *Smith v. Allwright* (1944), *Morgan v. Virginia* (1946), *Shelley v. Kraemer* (1948), *Sweatt v. Painter* (1950), and *Brown v. Board of Education of Topeka*. Between 1938 and 1961, Marshall argued thirty-two cases before the United States Supreme Court, winning twenty-nine.

In 1961 Marshall became the second African American to serve on the United States Circuit Court of Appeal, when President John F. Kennedy named him to fill a vacancy. In 1965 President Lnydon B. Johnson appointed Marshall to the post of United States Solicitor General. With the retirement of Associate Justice Tom Campbell Clark in 1967, Marshall was nominated to fill the vacancy. Marshall's nomination was met with objections from Southern Senators. Nevertheless, he was confirmed, becoming the first African-American justice in Unites States history. While on the Court, Marshall served as a supporter of affirmative action, free speech, and the rights of workers. He wrote few famous decisions, but his dissenting opinions in such cases as *Milliken v. Bradley* (1974) and *Regents of the University v. Bakke* (1978).

On June 27, 1991, Justice Marshall announced his plan to retire, due to advancing age and poor health, after some twenty-four years on the nation's highest court. On July 1 President George Bush announced that he had chosen Clarence Thomas, a black, conservative appeals court judge, as his choice to fill the vacancy created by Marshall's retirement.

### Clarence Thomas

In 1981 President Ronald Reagan appointed Clarence Thomas, a graduate of a Holy Cross College and Yale University Law School, to head the civil rights division of the Department of Education. A year later, Thomas was appointed to head the Equal Employment Opportunity Commission. In 1990 Thomas was appointed by President Bush to fill a vacancy on the United States Court of Appeals for the District of Columbia.

In a flurry of controversy, Clarence Thomas was appointed an associate justice of the United States Supreme Court in 1991, after being nominated by President George Bush. Besides Thomas's relative youth and judicial inexperience, his nomination hearings were marred by the accusations from Anita Hill that she had suffered from sexual harassment while under his employ at the Equal Employment Opportunity Commission. The nomination committee chose to approve Thomas's nomination despite the serious accusations from Hill.

Anita Hill, a relatively unknown law professor at the University of Oklahoma, became a household name when she came for-

Clarence Thomas

Anita Hill testifies before the Senate Judiciary Committee.

ward with charges of sexual harassment against Judge Thomas, purportedly committed when both had worked for the Equal Employment Opportunities Commission. Hill claimed that Thomas repeatedly pressured her to date him, told her plots of pornographic movies, and bragged about his sexual exploits. When asked why she didn't quit her job or report Thomas when the incidents occurred during the early 1980s, Hill answered that she feared she wouldn't be able to get another job.

The nation, as well as the Senate, seemed divided by the shocking testimony. Thomas denied the allegations and had many of his former co-workers testify for him. The case became highly politicized as conservatives and liberals fought for ground. Thomas, who was nominated by President George Bush, was supported by the conservatives in the Republican party because his appointment would mean an African American on the court who would uphold conservative policies. Therefore, Hill's case was taken up by many Democrats.

After the confirmation votes were counted, Thomas was nominated by the narrow margin of fifty-two to forty-eight, one of the closest margins in Supreme Court history. Apparently, the American public mirrored the pro-Thomas view. In a poll taken soon after the hearings, sixty percent sided with Thomas and only twenty percent with Hill. A year later, however, only thirty-eight percent of those Americans polled agreed with Thomas, while an equal number supported Hill's version.

## African Americans and the Criminal Justice System

### by Marilyn Hortense Mackel

Criminal justice system in America consists of three major components, law enforcement, judicial and legal services, and corrections. In the past twenty years, African Americans have assumed significant leadership roles in both law enforcement and correctional services. Although, the

PRESIDENT FRANKLIN D. ROOSEVELT

| 1937 | William H. Hastie* | District Court, Virgin Islands |
| 1939 | Harnian E. Moore* | District Court, Virgin Islands |

PRESIDENT HARRY S. TRUMAN

| 1945 | Irvin C. Mollison* | United States Customs Court |
| 1949 | William H. Hastie* | Court of Appeals, 3rd Circuit |
| 1949 | Hernian E. Moore (a)* | District Court Virgin Islands |

PRESIDENT DWIGHT D. EISENHOWER

| 1957 | Scovel Richardson* | United States Customs Court |
| 1958 | Walter Gordon* | District Court, Virgin Islands |

PRESIDENT JOHN F. KENNEDY

| 1961 | James B. Parsons | Senior Judge, District Court, Illinois |
| 1961 | Wade M. McCree** | District Court, Michigan |
| 1961 | Thurgood Marshall** | Court of Appeals, 2nd Circuit |

PRESIDENT LYNDON B. JOHNSON

| 1964 | Spottswood Robinson** | District Court, District of Columbia |
| 1964 | A. Leon Higginbotham** | District Court, Pennsylvania |
| 1965 | William B. Bryant | Senior Judge, District Court, District of Columbia |
| 1966 | Wade H. McCree**/* | Court of Appeals, 6th Circuit |
| 1966 | James L. Watson | United States Customs Court |
| 1966 | Constance B. Motley | Senior Judge, District Court, New York |
| 1966 | Spottswood Robinson | Senior Judge, Court of Appeals for the Federal Circuit |
| 1966 | Aubrey E. Robinson | Chief Judge, District Court, District of Columbia |
| 1967 | Damon Keith** | District Court, Michigan |
| 1967 | Thurgood Marshall | Associate Justice, Supreme Court |
| 1967 | Joseph C. Waddy* | District Court, District of Columbia |

PRESIDENT RICHARD M. NIXON

| 1969 | Almeric Christian*** | District Court, Virgin Islands |
| 1969 | David W. Williams | Senior Judge, District Court, California |
| 1969 | Barrington D. Parker | Senior Judge, District Court, District of Columbia |
| 1971 | Lawrence W. Pierce** | District Court, New York |
| 1971 | Clifford Scott Green | District Court, Pennsylvania |
| 1972 | Robert L. Carter | Senior Judge, District Court, New York |
| 1972 | Robert M. Duncan** | Military Court of Appeals |
| 1974 | Robert M. Duncan | District Court, Ohio |

PRESIDENT GERALD R. FORD

| 1974 | Henry Bramwell | Senior Judge, District Court, New York |
| 1976 | George N. Leighton | Senior Judge, District Court, Illinois |
| 1976 | Matthew Perry** | Military Court of Appeals |
| 1976 | Cecil F. Poole** | District Court, California |

PRESIDENT JIMMY CARTER

| 1978 | Almeric Christian (a) | Chief Judge, District Court, Virgin Islands |
| 1979 | U.W. Clemon | District Court, Alabama |
| 1978 | Robert F. Collins | District Court, Louisiana |
| 1978 | Julian A. Cook, Jr. | District Court, Michigan |
| 1978 | Damon J. Keith | Court of Appeals, 6th Circuit |
| 1978 | A. Leon Higginbotham | Court of Appeals, 3rd Circuit |

African-American Federal Judges

| 1978 | Mary Johnson Lowe | District Court, New York |
|------|-------------------|--------------------------|
| 1978 | Theodore McMillian | Court of Appeals, 8th Circuit |
| 1978 | David S. Nelson | District Court, Massachusetts |
| 1978 | Paul A. Simmons | District Court, Pennsylvania |
| 1978 | Jack E. Tanner | District Court, Washington |
| 1979 | Harry T. Edwards | Court of Appeals for the Federal Circuit |
| 1979 | J. Jerome Farris | Court of Apeals, 9th Circuit |
| 1979 | Joseph W. Hatchett | Court of Appeals, 11th Circuit |
| 1979 | Terry J. Hatter | District Court, California |
| 1979 | Joseph C. Howard | District Court, Maryland |
| 1979 | Benjamin T. Gibson | District Court, Michigan |
| 1979 | James T. Giles | District Court, Pennsylvania |
| 1979 | Nathaniel R. Jones | Court of Appeals, 6th Circuit |
| 1979 | Amalya L. Kearse | Court of Appeals, 2nd Circuit |
| 1979 | Gabrielle Kirk McDonald** | District Court, Texas |
| 1979 | John Garrett Penn | District Court, District of Columbia |
| 1979 | Cecil F. Poole | Court of Appeals, 9th Circuit |
| 1979 | Matthew J. Perry | District Court, South Carolina |
| 1979 | Myron H. Thompson | District Court, Alabama |
| 1979 | Anne E. Thompson | District Court, New Jersey |
| 1979 | Odell Horton | District Court, Tennessee |
| 1979 | Anna Digs Taylor | District Court, Michigan |
| 1979 | Horace T. Ward | District Court, Georgia |
| 1979 | Alcee L. Hastings**** | District Court, Florida |
| 1980 | Clyde S. Cahill, Jr. | District Court, Missouri |
| 1980 | Richard C. Erwin | District Court, North Carolina |
| 1980 | Thelton E. Henderson | District Court, California |
| 1980 | George Howard, Jr. | District Court, Arkansas |
| 1980 | Earl B. Gilliam | District Court, California |
| 1980 | Norma Holloway Johnson | District Court, District of Columbia |
| 1980 | Consuela B. Marshall | District Court, California |
| 1980 | George White | District Court, Ohio |

## PRESIDENT RONALD REAGAN

| 1981 | Lawrence W. Pierce | Court of Appeals, 2nd Circuit |
|------|--------------------|-------------------------------|
| 1982 | Reginald Gibson | United States Court of Claims |
| 1984 | John R. Hargrove | District Court, Maryland |
| 1984 | Henry Wingate | District Court, Mississippi |
| 1985 | Ann Williams | District Court, Illinois |
| 1986 | James Spencer | District Court, Virginia |
| 1987 | Kenneth Hoyt | District Court, Texas |
| 1988 | Herbert Hutton | District Court, Pennsylvania |

## PRESIDENT GEORGE BUSH

| 1990 | Clarence Thomas | Court of Appeals for the Federal District | |
|------|-----------------|--------------------------------------------|---|
| 1990 | James Ware | District Court, California | |
| 1991 | Saundra Brown Armstrong | District Court, California | |
| 1991 | Fernando J. Giatan | District Court, Missouri | |
| 1991 | Donald L. Graham | District Court, Florida | |
| 1991 | Sterling Johnson | District Court, New York | |
| 1991 | J. Curtis Joyner | District Court, Pennsylvania | |
| 1991 | Timothy K. Lewis | District Court, Pennsylvania | |
| 1991 | Joe B. McDade | District Court, Illinois | (a) Reappointment |
| 1991 | Clarence Thomas | Associate Justice, Supreme Court | * Deceased |
| 1992 | Garland E. Burrell, Jr. | District Court, California | ** Resigned |
| 1992 | Carol Jackson | District Court, Missouri | *** Retired |
| 1992 | Timothy K. Lewis | Court of Appeals, 3rd Circuit | **** Impeached |

African-American Federal Judges, continued

number of African-American judges, prosecutors, and defense attorneys has increased since 1970, employment of African Americans as judges and prosecutors has not increased at the rate necessary to give an appearance, if not the presence, of justice in the system. As a result, courts in large metropolitan areas have begun a critical examination of the impact of low numbers of African-American judges on the perpetuation of racism in the court system—particularly on the disproportionate arrest rate, and the harsher sentences imposed on African Americans.

### The Creation of Twentieth Century Slave Ships

Criminal justice statistics published by the United States Department of Justice provide documentation of the widespread perpetuation of discrimination in America. It is indeed not difficult to argue that the American system of criminal justice is giving birth to "Twentieth Century Slave Ships." (Little Rock, Arkansas artist, Alice Ayers, provides, in her work entitled "20th Century Slave Ship" perceptual impetus to the author for this phrase.)

The incarceration rate of African-American males is alarming—such that a common expression in the African-American community is that on any given day, there are more African-American males of college age in prisons and jails than in colleges or universities. African-American males generally have been sentenced to long mandatory minimum sentences, including life without parole, for such offenses as drug possession, while white importers of drugs are seldom arrested or are able to negotiate a lessor charge and plea bargain a for lighter sentence.

### Law Enforcement

In a sense, the roles of participants in criminal justice system can be compared to the roles players in the institution of slavery. For example, the role of law enforcement officers (the police) compares to that of the slave traders. (See John Hope Franklin, 1988. *From Slavery to Freedom, A History of Negro Americans*, 6th ed., New York: McGraw-Hill. Also see, Alex Nicholas. 1969. *Black in Blue, A Study of the Negro Policeman*, New York: Appleton-Century-Crofts. pp. 16–113.)

The largest, and to some extent, the most formidable arm of the criminal justice system, the police have the greatest visibility, and as the first point of contact for persons entering the system, make discretionary, quasi-judicial decisions to whether to arrest when an offense is alleged to have occurred. As implementors of local and national legal and political policy, police officers are agents of interest groups with power to effectuate their interest in our politically organized society "Behind the formulation of all laws is an enterprising group that stands to benefit in some way from a particular law. . . . Research on criminal law has demonstrated that criminal laws are formulated within a social context that involves the promotion of the interests of certain groups in society." (Richard Quinney. 1969. "Toward a Sociology of Criminal Law," *Crime and Justice in Society*. Boston: Little Brown and Company. pp. 1–3). The police, as enforcers of law, are organized and empowered to support the interest of those with means to shape law, a factor which may have significant bearing on why African Americans have had a particularly duplicitous relationship with the police.

On the one hand, the African-American community looks to law enforcement for protection from "criminal elements" in their communities; on the other hand, the African-American community has been aware that law enforcement officers have historically had little regard for their humanity, and have, in the exercise of their discretionary authority failed to enforce the law or to respond, when protection is sought, as it does in Anglo communities.

Law and law enforcement is a form of social engineering, providing security for the dominant political, economic, individual, and religious interests against actions that threaten their social group. (Roscoe Pound. 1942. *Social Control Through Law*, New Haven: Yale University Press. Similarly, see, Roscoe Pound, "A Survey of Social Interests," *Harvard Law Review*, 57 (October 1943), and Quinney, supra, 1–30.) African Americans have for some time been perceived and treated as a race of people whose very existence threatens the dominant social group—the fact that the African-American community has this duplicitous relationship with law enforcement is consistent with the purpose of law and law enforcement. "The slave trade became a tremendously important factor in European economic life . . ." (Franklin). Likewise, law and law enforcement in Anglo-American economic and political life.

### Judicial and Legal Services

In the comparison of the criminal justice system and the institution of slavery, judges and prosecutors can be viewed as slave owners, or masters. Although the writer is not suggesting that the offenders conduct is not the impetus for the intervention of the criminal justice system, prosecutors control the charges (offenses) and the plea that is negotiated, while judges control the resultant sentence and the fate and future of the defendant.

Prosecutors have sole discretionary authority over the charges (if any) that are filed

against offenders. Discrimination in charging occurs, when an African-American offender is subjected to multiple charges, including all possible lessor offenses, for one act, while a white offender is charged with one lessor offense for a similar criminal act (Alexander B. Smith and Harriet Pollack. 1972. *Crime and Justice in a Mass Society*, Lexington, Massachusetts: Xerox College Publishing. See also, Abraham S. Blumberg (ed.), 1970, *The Scales of Justice*, New York: Transaction Books.)

### The Correctional System

The American correctional system bears an equally close resemblance to the plantation system. There are as many African-American jailers, holders of the keys to the prison gates, as there were slaves who assured the masters and overseer of the obedience of slaves (Charles E. Owens and Jimmy Bell (eds.) 1981. *Blacks and Criminal Justice*, Mass: Lexington Books). Analogous also is the oppressive reality that, like the freed slaves, offenders released from prison, and no parole or probation, often are unable to pursue meaningful careers—rewarding work, and even menial work, is forever closed to them despite their genuine efforts to reform and to conform to the expectations of law abiding citizenship.

To examine the statistical data demonstrating the likelihood that the criminal justice system is fostering twentieth century slave ships in the African-American community, one need only examine the numerous statistical bases annually distributed by the United States Department of Justice. When viewing these statistics, it is important that the reader keep in mind that African Americans comprise 12 percent of the population of this country, approximately thirty million people. (Barbara Everitt Bryant. 1993. "The United States Population: A Typical American as seen through the Eyes of the Census Bureau," *World Almanac, 1993*, New York: Pharos Books).

In 1990, 3,224,060 African Americans were arrested, compared to 7,712,339 whites (U.S. Department of Justice, Office of Justice Programs, Bureau of Justice Statistics. 1992. *Sourcebook of Criminal Justice Statistics—1991*, Washington, DC: U.S. Government Printing Office. p. 444). An examination of selected juvenile justice data shows that in 1990, whites and Hispanics under the age of eighteen constituted 71.3 percent of the arrests made, while African-Americans constituted 26.2 percent. Of adult offenders (those age eighteen and older), whites constitute 68.8 percent of persons arrested, while African-Americans constitute only 29.4 percent (*Sourcebook of Justice Statistics—1991*).

African-American youth between the ages of fourteen and eighteen, are being removed from the juvenile courts where rehabilitation and treatment is available, at least theoretically, and subjected at a young age to the harsh world of adult corrections. In 1989 7,500 whites and Hispanics were transferred from the juvenile court to be tried as adults, while 8,500 African-Americans were similarly transferred. In 1990, the number of whites and Hispanics in the system decreased to 7,400, while the number of African Americans increased to 9,200 (National Center for Juvenile Justice, National Institute of Justice, Juvenile Justice Clearing House). In addition, increased numbers of juvenile offenders are being subjected to life sentences without possibility of parole, and to the death penalty.

African-Americans do not commit crimes in larger numbers. However, African-Americans are treated more harshly by the criminal justice system. (A recent study at the University of Washington found that, when compared to whites, African American juveniles fared worse in the juvenile justice system. The study found the African American youth were almost twice as likely to be arrested as whites, and were referred to juvenile court twice as often as whites for felonies or misdemeanors. Once arrested, African American youth were twice as likely to be detained, were less likely to be diverted into treatment or counseling, and more likely to be prosecuted.) An examination of persons under correctional supervision is equally revealing. At public juvenile facilities in 1989, whites comprise 40 percent of the population, African-Americans 42 percent, and Hispanics 16 percent (*Sourcebook of Criminal Justice Statistics*). African-Americans, in 1991 made up 43.4 percent of the jail population, whites 41.1 percent. In 1988 African-Americans constituted 46.9 percent of the state prison population, whites 49.7 percent. In 1988 African Americans constituted 22.7 percent of the federal prison population, while whites constituted 75.2 percent.

Significant is the fact that 53.8 percent of the African-American male population and 68.4 percent of the female population of the federal prisons are incarcerated for drug offenses.

Because of the ravages of slavery, African Americans have long been placed". . .well outside of the pale" of American life (Arthur M. Schlesinger, Jr. 1992. *The Disuniting of America, Reflections on a Multicultural Society*, New York: W.W. Norton & Company. p. 14). During slavery, and thereafter, African-Americans were hung, castrated, raped, and otherwise physically and mentally devastated. Today, the same psychological and physical devastation occurs at the hands of the criminal justice system, which affords them little or no protection from crime, and removes them in large numbers from their communities to be barred upon return from reasonable opportunities in American life.

## ■ MAJOR FEDERAL LEGISLATION

### Emancipation Act (April 1862)
ch.54, 12 Stat. 376

This act, abolishing slavery in the District of Columbia, was enacted April 16, 1862.

### Emancipation Act (June 1862)
ch. 111, 12 Stat. 432

This act, abolishing slavery in all other territories of the United States, was enacted June 19, 1862.

### Amendment Thirteen to the United States Constitution (1865)

This amendment, abolishing slavery and involuntary servitude in all of the United States, was ratified December 16, 1865.

### Civil Rights Act (1866)
ch. 31, 14 Stat. 27

This act was enacted April 9, 1866, to provide all citizens, especially recently freed slaves, with basic civil rights, including the right to make and enforce contracts, to bring suits in court, to purchase and sell real and personal property, and to enjoy security of person and property.

### Amendment Fourteen to the United States Constitution (1868)

This Amendment defined United States and state citizenship, and provided all citizens with the privileges and immunities of citizenship, the right to life, liberty and property, and equal protection under the law. It was ratified July 20, 1868.

### Amendment Fifteen to the United States Constitution (1870)

This Amendment was designed to protect the right of all citizens to vote. It was ratified March 30, 1870.

Engraving depicting blacks celebrating the abolition of slavery in the District of Columbia.

Engraving depicting the trial of a freedman, Florida, 1867.

### Civil Rights Act (1870)
ch. 114, 16 Stat. 140

This act was enacted May 31, 1870, to carry-out the provision of the Fifteenth Amendment. It established penalties for violations of the provisions of the amendment.

### Civil Rights Act (February 1871)
ch. 99, 16 Stat. 433

This act was enacted February 28, 1871, to further define the protections established in the Fifteenth Amendment.

### Civil Rights Act (April 1871)
ch. 22, 17 Stat. 13

This act was enacted April 20, 1871 to further outline the protections provided for by the Fourteenth Amendment. It provides for the vindication of crimes committed under the act in federal court.

### Civil Rights Act (1875)
ch. 114, 18 Stat. 335

This act was designed to provide all citizens with equal access to public places. Ruling in 1883 in a set of cases known as the *Civil Rights Cases*, the United States Supreme court invalidated the act.

### Civil Rights Act of 1957
Pub.L. No. 85-315, 71 Stat. 634

This act created the Commission on Civil Rights and empowered it to investigate allegations of deprivation of a United States citizen's right to vote, and to appraise laws and policies of the federal government with respect to equal protection of the law, and to submit a report to the President and to the Congress within two years.

### Civil Rights Act of 1960
Pub.L. No. 86-449, 74 Stat. 86

Guaranteed the provision of criminal penalties in the event a suspect crosses state lines to avoid legal process for the actual or attempted bombing or burning of any vehicle or building, and provided penalties for persons who obstructed or interfered with any order of a federal court.

### Civil Rights Act of 1964
Pub.L. No. 88-352, 78 Stat. 241

This act prohibited discrimination in the use of public accommodations whose operations involve interstate commerce, and provided enforcement measures to ensure equal access to public facilities. Also the Civil Rights Act of 1964 prohibited racial discrimination in any program receiving federal aid and prohibited discrimination in most areas of employment.

### Voting Rights Act of 1965
Pub.L. No. 89-110, 79 Stat. 437

The Voting Rights Act of 1965 struck down requirements such as literacy and knowledge tests and poll tax payments which had been used to restrict black partic-

Entrance to a segregated waiting room in Jackson, Mississippi.

ipation in voting, and provided for federal registrars to register voters should state registrars refuse to do so. It further stipulated that registered voters could not be prohibited from voting.

### Civil Rights Act of 1968
Pub.L. No. 90-284, 82 Stat. 73

This act provided for open housing by prohibiting discrimination based on race, color, religion, or national origin.

President Lyndon B. Johnson

### Equal Employment Opportunity Act of 1972
Pub.L. No. 92-261, 86 Stat. 103

This act provided the Equal Employment Opportunity Commission (which was established by the Civil Rights Act of 1964) with the authority to issue judicially enforceable cease and desist orders in cases involving discriminatory employment practices.

### Public Works Employment Act of 1977
Pub.L. No. 95-28, 91 Stat. 116, Title I

The Public Works Employment Act of 1977 provided that ten percent of funds expended as a result of federal grants be earmarked for and paid to minority business enterprises.

### Voting Rights Act of 1965 Amendment (1982)
Pub.L. No. 97-205, 96 Stat. 131

This amendment was a congressional response to the Supreme Court's ruling in *City of Mobile v. Bolden* that required proof of discriminatory intent in voting rights cases. Section 2 of the voting rights Act prohibits any voting practice or procedure "imposed or applied by any state or political subdivision in a manner which results in a denial or abridgement of the right of any citizen of the United States to vote on account of race or color. . . ."

### Civil Rights Commission Act of 1983
Pub.L. No. 98-183, 87 Stat. 1301

This act created an eight-member bipartisan commission with four members appointed by the president, and two by the Senate and House, respectively. The Commissioners are appointed to four or six year terms and can be fired only for neglect of duty or malfeasance in office. The statute was enacted after President Reagan attempted to fire Commissioners who did not express his views on civil rights. The Act extended the life of the Civil Rights Commission Authorization Act of 1978, which was scheduled to expire in 1983.

### Civil Rights Restoration Act of 1988
Pub.L. No. 100-259, 102 Stat. 31

Ruling in 1984 in the case *Grove City College v. Bell*, the United States Supreme Court ruled that not all programs and activities of an institution were covered by Title IX of the Education Amendments of 1972 (Public Law 89-10, 79 Stat. 27) and that discrimination can be barred only in programs that directly receive federal funds. Section 6 of Public Law 100-259 amended portions of the Civil Rights Act of 1964, refined the definition of programs and activities which are covered by the Civil Rights Act and other legislation. Specifically the amendment addressed Title IX of the Education Amendments of 1972, which prohibits discrimination in educational programs receiving federal financial assistance.

### Fair Housing Amendments Act of 1988
Pub.L. No. 100-430, 102 Stat 1619

The Fair Housing Amendments Act of 1988 strengthens laws that resulted from passage of the Fair Housing act of 1968. The Act of 1988 gives the Department of Housing and Urban Development (HUD) the authority to issue discrimination charges, allows administrative law justices the ability to review housing discrimination cases, and removed the $1000 limit on punitive damages that a victim of discrimination may receive.

### Civil Rights Act of 1991
Pub.L. 102-166, 105 Stat. 1071

This act is designed to provide additional remedies to deter harassment and intentional discrimination in the workplace, to provide guidelines for the adjudication of cases arising under Title VII of the Civil Rights Act of 1964, and to expand the scope of civil rights legislation weakened by Supreme Court decisions, particularly the Court's ruling in *Wards Cove Packing Co. v. Antonio*, 490 US 642 (1989).

Newspaper illustration depicting white opposition to black suffrage.

**Glass Ceiling Act of 1991**
Pub.L. 102-166, 105 Stat. 1081

Title II of the Civil Rights Act of 1991, designed to establish a means for studying and addressing the underrepresentation of women and minorities at management and decision making levels in the workforce.

## ■ MAJOR UNITED STATES SUPREME COURT DECISIONS

### Access to the Polls

#### *United States v. Reese*
92 US 214 (1876)

Prior to the Fifteenth Amendment, states regulated all details of state and local elections; states prescribed the qualifications of voters, and the manner in which those desiring to vote at an election should make their qualifications known to the election officers. Thus, the Fifteenth Amendment interferes with the past sovereignly practice and provides rules not prescribed by state law. However, this court restricted the scope of the Fifteenth Amendment and the ability of Congress to enforce it by not punishing election officials who unlawfully interfere and prevent the free exercise of the elective franchise.

The federal government indicated two Kentucky election inspectors for refusing to receive and count the vote of a black citizen. The Supreme Court held, that Congress had not yet provided "appropriate legislation'" for the punishment of the offense charged under any sections of the Fifteenth Amendment.

#### *Guinn v. United States*
238 US 347 (1915)

In 1910 an amendment to the constitution of Oklahoma, restricted the franchise according to a "grandfather clause" which provided that no illiterate person could be registered to vote. The clause, however, granted an exemption for persons who resided in a foreign country prior to January 1, 1866; had been eligible to register prior to that date, or if a lineal ancestor was eligible to vote at that time. Since no blacks were eligible to vote in Oklahoma prior to 1866, the law disenfranchised all blacks.

The United States Supreme Court in *Guinn v. United States* ruled that the grandfather clause was invalid in Oklahoma, as well as in any other state where one was in effect.

#### *Nixon v. Herndon*
273 US 536 (1927)

Dr. L. A. Nixon, an African American, was refused the right to vote in a primary election because of a State Statute that prohibited blacks from participating in Democratic Party elections in Texas. Nixon filed suit against the election officials and his case ultimately reached the United States Supreme Court. In his opinion, on *Nixon v. Herndon* Justice Oliver Wendell Holmes wrote: "It is too clear for extended argument that color cannot be made the basis of a statutory classification affecting the right set up in this case." As a result of *Nixon v. Herndon* the Texas Statute was declared unconstitutional.

#### *Nixon v. Condon*
286 US 73 (1932)

As a result of the United States Supreme Court ruling in *Nixon v. Herndon*, the Texas legislature passed a new statute. This statute empowered the state Democratic executive committee to set up its own rules regarding primary elections. The party promptly adopted a resolution stipulating that only white Democrats be allowed to participate in primaries. Dr. Nixon again filed suit, and his right to vote was again upheld by the United States Supreme Court.

### Lane v. Wilson
### 307 US 268 (1939)

In an attempt to restrict voter registration, the Oklahoma legislature stated that all Oklahomans who were already registered would remain qualified voters, but that all others would have to register within 12 days (from April 30 to May 11, 1916) or be forever barred from the polls. In 1934, I. W. Lane, an African American, was refused registration on the basis of this statute. The United States Supreme Court declared that the statute was in conflict with the Fifteenth Amendment to the United States Constitution, and, therefore was unconstitutional.

### Smith v. Allwright
### 321 US 649 (1944)

The Texas State Democratic party, during its convention in 1932, limited the right of membership to white electors. As a result, nonwhites were unable to participate in a Democratic party primary. In *Grovey v. Townsend* (295 US 45), the Supreme Court had upheld this limitation because it was made by the party in convention, not by a party executive committee. In *Smith v. Allwright*, the Supreme Court overruled *Grovey*, stating, "The United States is a constitutional democracy. Its organic law grants to all citizens a right to participate in the choice of elected officials without restriction by any state because of race." The Court noted that political party makes its selection of candidates as an agency of the state and, therefore, cannot exclude participation based on race and remain consistent with the Fifteenth Amendment.

### Gomillion v. Lightfoot
### 364 US 339 (1960)

In this case African-American citizens challenged an Alabama statute that redefined the boundaries of the City of Tuskegee. The statute altered the shape of Tuskegee and placed all but four of Tuskegee's 400 African-American voters outside of the city limits, while not displacing a single white voter.

### Baker v. Carr
### 369 US 186 (1962)

*Baker v. Carr* was brought to the Supreme Court by electors in several counties of Tennessee, who asserted that the 1901 legislative reapportionment statute was unconstitutional because the numbers of voters in the various districts had changed substantially since 1901. The plaintiffs requested that the Supreme Court either direct a reapportionment by mathematical application of the Tennessee constitutional formula to the 1960 census, or instruct the state to hold direct at-large elections. The state district court had dismissed the case on the grounds that it was a political question and, as such, did not fall within the protection of the Fourteenth Amendment. The United States Supreme Court ruled that the case involved a basic constitutional right and thereby was within court jurisdiction, and remanded the case to the state district court.

### South Carolina v. Kalzenback
### 383 US 301 (1966)

The Voting Rights Act of 1965 was designed to banish the blight of racial discrimination in voting, which has effected the electoral process for nearly a century. The act abolished literacy tests, waived accumulated poll taxes and gave the United States Attorney General vast discretionary powers to deal with areas suspected of discriminating against black voters.

The Supreme Court dismissed South Carolina's petition asserting that the act violated the United States Constitution because it encroached on an area governed by the sovereignty of the States. The Constitution holds true under Section 1 of the Fifteenth Amendment, ". . .[t]he right of citizens of the United States to vote shall not be denied or abridged by the United States or by any state on account of race, color, or previous condition of servitude."

## Allen v. State Board of Elections
393 US 110 (1969)

In *Allen v. State Board of Education*, the Supreme Court emphasized that subtle, as well as obvious state regulations, "which have the effect of denying citizens their right to vote because of their race" are prohibited. The Court confirmed that Section 5 of the Voting Rights Act covered a variety of practices other than voter registration.

## Georgia v. United States
411 US 526 (1973)

This case confirmed the propriety of the Voting Rights Act of 1965, which forbids states with a history of racial discrimination (Alabama, Georgia, Louisiana, Mississippi, North Carolina, South Carolina and Virginia) from implementing any change in voting practices and procedures without first submitting the proposed plan to the United States Attorney for approval.

## White v. Regester
412 US 755 (1973)

The Supreme Court in *White v. Regester*, struck down a Texas multi-member districting scheme that was used to prevent blacks from being elected to public office. The Court upheld a finding that even though there was no evidence that blacks faced official obstacles to registration, voting or running for office, they had been excluded from effective participation in the political process in violation of the Equal Protection Clause of the Constitution.

## City of Mobile, Alabama v. Wiley L. Bolden et al.
446 US 55 (1980)

A class action suit was filed in the United States District Court for the Southern District of Alabama on behalf of black citizens in Mobile. The suit alleged that the city's practice of electing commissioners at large by a majority vote unfairly diluted the voting strength of blacks in violation of the Fourteenth and Fifteenth amendments. The District Court, ruled that the constitutional rights of Mobile's black citizens had been violated and entered a judgment in their favor. The court also ruled that Mobile's city commissioners be replaced by a municipal government consisting of a mayor and a city council composed of persons selected from single member districts.

## Thornburg v. Gingles
478 US 30 (1986)

*Thornburg v. Gingles* was the Supreme Court's first decision interpreting the provisions of Section two of the Voting Rights Act, as amended in 1982. The amendments which prohibit voting schemes that result in a denial or abridgement of the right to vote due to race or color. In this landmark decision, the Court ruled that the redistricting plan adopted by the North Carolina legislature, which led to racially polarized voting by whites and diluted black voting strength is in violation of the Voting Rights Act. The

Voting Rights Act prohibits voting requirements that have a discriminatory effect, as well as those that are intentionally discriminatory.

### *Martin v. Wilks*
490 US 755 (1989)

In an attempt to remedy past racial discrimination in hiring and promotion practices, the City of Birmingham and its fire department consented to hiring blacks as firefighters as part of a settlement. White firefighters subsequently challenged the city, alleging that because of their race they were denied promotions in favor of less qualified blacks in violation of Title VII. Promotion decisions were made on the basis of race in reliance on the consent decree.

The Court held that a voluntary settlement between one group of employees and their employer cannot possibly settle voluntarily or otherwise, the conflicting claims of another group of employees who do not join in the agreement, on the basis that you can not deprive a person of legal rights in a proceeding to which he is not a party.

## Education

### *Missouri ex rel. Lloyd Gaines v. Canada*
305 US 339 (1938)

*Gaines v. Canada* was brought before the Supreme Court by Lloyd Lionel Gaines, an African American who had been refused admission to the School of Law of the State University of Missouri. Gaines contended that the University of Missouri's actions were a violation of his rights under the Fourteenth Amendment of the United States Constitution.

The University of Missouri defended its action by maintaining that Lincoln University, a predominantly black institution,

Lloyd Gaines

would eventually establish its own law school. The Supreme Court of Missouri dismissed Gaines' petition and upheld the university's decision to reject his application. The United States Supreme Court, however, reversed this decision, maintaining that the state of Missouri was obliged to provide equal facilities for blacks or, in the absence of such facilities, to admit them to the existing facility.

### *Sipuel v. Board of Regents of the University of Oklahoma*
332 US 631 (1948)

Ada Lois Sipuel, an African American, was denied admission to the law school of the University of Oklahoma in 1948. Sipuel requested legal assistance from the NAACP, which filed a petition in the Oklahoma courts requesting an order directing her admission. The petition was denied on the grounds that the *Gaines* decision did not require a state with segregation laws to admit a black student to its white schools. In addition, the Oklahoma court maintained that the state itself was not obligated to set up a separate school unless first requested to do so by blacks desiring a legal education. The Oklahoma court's decision was affirmed by the Supreme Court of Oklahoma. The United States Supreme Court, however, reversed this decision, and held that the state was required to provide African Americans with equal educational opportunities.

### *Sweatt v. Painter*
339 US 629 (1950)

Herman Marion Sweatt, the African-American petitioner in this case, was refused admission to the University of Texas Law School on the grounds that substantially equivalent facilities were already available in another Texas State law school open only to black students.

The United States Supreme Court ruled that Sweatt be admitted to the University of Texas Law School. Chief Justice Fred M. Vinson wrote that "in terms of number of the faculty, variety of courses and opportunity for specialization, size of the student body, scope of the library, availability of law review and similar activities, the University of Texas Law School is superior" to those in the state law school for blacks. Therefore, the refusal to admit Sweatt to the University of Texas Law School was unconstitutional.

A black schoolroom in Missouri, c.1930.

### McLaurin v. Oklahoma State Regents for Higher Education
339 US 637 (1950)

After having been admitted to the University of Oklahoma, G. W. McLaurin, an African American, was required by school officials to occupy a special seat in each classroom and a segregated table in both the library and the cafeteria because of his race.

The United States Supreme Court declared unanimously that the black student must receive the same treatment at the hands of the state as other students and could not be segregated.

### Gray v. University of Tennessee
342 US 517 (1952)

This case resulted from the refusal of a United States District Court to force the University of Tennessee to admit black students. The lone judge to whom the matter was then referred ruled that the black students were entitled to admission, but did not order the university to enforce this ruling.

The Supreme Court was asked to refer the case back to the District Court for further proceedings. Pending this appeal, however, one of the students seeking admission was enrolled at the University of Tennessee. Since the court found no suggestion that persons "similarly situated would not be afforded similar treatment," the case was dismissed as moot.

### Brown v. Board of Education of Topeka
347 US 483 (1954)

This case involved the practice of denying black children equal access to state public schools due to state laws requiring or permitting racial segregation. The United States Supreme Court unanimously held that segregation deprived the children of equal protection under the Fourteenth Amendment to the United States Constitution. The "separate but equal" doctrine of *Plessy v. Ferguson* was overturned. After reargument a year later, the case was remanded (along with its four companion cases) to the District Court, which was instructed to enter such orders as were necessary to ensure the admission of all parties to public schools on a racially nondiscriminatory basis.

### Hawkins v. Board of Control
347 US 971 (1954)

This case resulted from a ruling of the Florida Supreme Court which denied an African American the right to enter the University of Florida Law School on the grounds that he had failed to show that a separate law school for blacks was not substantively equal to the University of Florida Law School. The United States Supreme Court vacated the judgment and remanded the case to the Florida Supreme Court for a decision in light of the ruling in *Brown* which overruled the separate but equal doctrine.

After two years, the Florida Supreme Court continued to deny Hawkins the right to enter the University of Florida. Also, it had appointed a commissioner to determine when in the future Hawkins could be admitted "without causing public mischief." However, the United States Supreme Court ruled that Hawkins should be admitted to the school promptly, since there was no palpable reason for further delay.

### Turead v. Board of Supervisors
347 US 971 (1954)

This case was the result of a provisional injunction requiring the admittance of blacks to Louisiana State University. The state court of appeals reversed this action, declaring that it required the decision of a district court of three judges. The United

States Supreme Court vacated this judgment and remanded the case for consideration, again in light of *Brown*.

### Frazier v. University of North Carolina
350 US 979 (1956)

The United States Supreme Court affirmed a District Court judgment that blacks may not be excluded from institutions of higher learning because of their race or color.

### Cooper v. Aaron
358 US 1 (1958)

The impact of *Brown v. Board of Education* was very slight until the Justice Department began to initiate its own desegregation lawsuits. Arkansas state officials passed state laws contrary to the Fourteenth Amendment holdings in *Brown I* and *Brown II* forbidding states to use their governmental powers to bar children on racial grounds from attending schools where there is state participation through any arrangement, management, funds or property; and to cease and desist from desegregation practices immediately.

In *Cooper*, the Attorney General of the United States filed a petition on behalf of the United States government to enjoin the governor of Arkansas and officers of the National Guard from preventing the admittance of nine black children into Central High School September 1957 in Little Rock.

Black students being bused.

A law was passed relieving school children from compulsory attendance at racially mixed schools. The Supreme Court declared that the Fourteenth Amendment outlined in the *Brown* case is the supreme law of the land and cannot be nullified by state legislators, executive or judicial officers or evasive schemes for segregation.

### Lee v. Macon County Board of Education
389 US 25 (1967)

The United States Supreme Court in *Lee v. Macon County Board of Education*, affirmed a lower court decision ordering the desegregation of Alabama's school districts and declared state school grants to white students attending segregated private schools unconstitutional.

### Alexander v. Holmes County Board of Education
396 US 19 (1969)

The United States Supreme Court, in *Alexander v. Holmes County Board of Education*, ordered all thirty-three school districts in Mississippi to desegregate. The Department of Health, Education and Welfare (HEW) had asked that the districts be granted more time to desegregate. This was the first time HEW had sought a delay in integration, but the Court ordered that integration proceed immediately.

### North Carolina State Board of Education v. Swann
402 US 43 (1971)
&
### Swann v. Charlotte Mecklenburg Board of Education
402 US 1 (1971)

In these two cases the United States Supreme Court affirmed the use of busing and faculty transfers to overcome the effects of dual school systems—segregated school systems resulting from residential patterns.

Writing the decision, Chief Justice Warren E. Burger noted that "bus transportation has long been a part of all public educational systems and it is unlikely that a truly effective remedy could be devised without continued reliance upon it." The Court declared that segregation resulted from past misconduct and affirmed the lower court's order that the school board bus students to achieve a racial mix at each school. The ruling, however, left local district judges the authority to decide whether a desegregation plan was constitutionally adequate.

### Wright v. City of Emporia
407 US 451 (1972)
&
### Cotton v. Scotland Neck Board of Education
407 US 485 (1972)

The Supreme Court held that two towns with heavy concentrations of white students could not secede from a largely black county school system and form its own school district in an attempt to frustrate integration.

### Richmond, Virginia School Board v. State Board of Education
412 US 92 (1973)

By a four to four vote, the United States Supreme Court declined to order the integration of the predominantly black schools in Richmond with those of two white suburbs. Though the Court wrote no decision, integrationist expressed concern that permitting de facto segregation to stand in this manner would hinder corrective action in other metropolitan areas, perpetuate "neighborhood" one-race schools, and lessen the extent of integration in unitary school systems.

### Runyon v. McCrary
427 US 160 (1976)

In an unanimous decision, it was held that the Constitution places no value on discrimination, and while invidious private discrimination may be characterized as a form of exercising the freedom of association, protected by the First Amendment.

In the 1976 decision, two black children were denied admission to private schools in Virginia. The Civil Rights Act of 1866 prohibits racial discrimination in the making and enforcing of contracts. The children's parents sought to enter into a contractual relationship with the private schools on an equal basis to white and nonwhite students.

### Regents of University of California v. Allan Bakke
438 US 265 (1978)

Allan Bakke, a white male who had been denied admission to the University of California Medical School at Davis for two consecutive years, charged that the university's minority quota system—under which only disadvantaged members of certain minority races were considered for 16 of the 100 places in each year's class—denied him equal protection.

The trial court declared that the school could not take race into account in making the admissions decision and held that the challenged admissions program violated the federal and state constitutions and Title VI of the 1964 Civil Rights Act. The university appealed. Upon hearing the case, the United States Supreme Court ruled that Bakke had been illegally discriminated against and that numerical quotas based on race were unconstitutional.

### Bob Jones University v. IRS
461 US 574 (1983)

Contrary to long-standing IRS policy, the Reagan administration sought to extend tax-exempt status to schools that discriminate on the basis of race. The United States Supreme Court recognized the inability of the Justice Department to argue the case fairly, and requested former Secretary of Transportation William T. Coleman to present the argument. The Supreme Court rebuffed the Justice Department's arguments and unanimously agreed with Coleman's position that the denial of tax-exempt status to racially discriminatory schools is unconstitutional.

### Allen v. Wright
488 US 737 (1984)

Parents of African-American children instituted a nationwide lawsuit claiming that the Internal Revenue Service's failure to deny tax-exempt status to racially discriminating private schools constituted federal financial aid to racially segregated institutions and diminished the ability of their children to receive an adequate education. The United States Supreme Court refused to hear the case on the grounds that the plaintiffs did not have "standing" because they failed to show that the injury suffered was "fairly traceable" or caused by the conduct of the IRS. In addition the Court maintained that the remedy was "speculative" since there was no evidence that the withdrawal of tax-exempt status would cause schools to end their racially discriminatory practices. The Court's imposition of such an artificial and stringent standing requirement, which had not been used in other cases involving school desegregation, effectively denied the African-American parents their day in court.

## Employment

### Griggs v. Duke Power Co.
401 US 424 (1971)

Black employees challenged their employer's requirement of a high school diploma or passing of intelligence tests as a condition of employment or transfer to jobs at the plant that were previously held solely by whites prior to the enactment of Title VII of the Civil Rights Act of 1964. Blacks were employed only in the Labor Department where the highest paying jobs paid less than the lowest jobs in the other departments. When the company abandoned its policy restricting blacks to Labor in 1965, completion of high school and median scores on two aptitude tests were required to transfer from Labor to another department.

The Supreme Court found the objective of Congress in Title III was to achieve equality of employment opportunities and remove barriers that have operated in the past to favor an identifiable group of whites over other employees. Under the Act, practices, procedures, or tests neutral on their face and even neutral in their intent cannot be maintained if they operate to "freeze" the status quo of prior discrimination. The employment practice must be related to job performance.

It was determined that neither the high school diploma nor the intelligence tests were shown to bear a demonstrable relationship to successful job performance. Good intent or absence of discriminatory intent does not redeem employment procedures and practices. The employment policies had a discriminatory effect toward black employees.

### Albemarle Paper Co. v. Moody
422 US 405 (1975)

African-American employees of a paper mill in Roanoke Rapids, North Carolina successfully challenged the company's use of written tests which allegedly measured numerical and verbal intelligence. Based upon the standards enunciated in *Griggs v. Duke Power Co.*, the United States Supreme Court determined that the tests were discriminatory because they were not job-related and did not predict success on the job. More importantly, the Supreme Court held that the plaintiffs were entitled to "complete justice" and necessary relief that would "make them whole." The Court awarded the African-American employees back pay and made it clear that back pay should rarely be denied once there has been a showing of discrimination. The Court also stated that back pay cannot be denied simply because the employer acted in good faith or did not intend to discriminate.

### Hazelwood School District v. United States
433 US 299 (1977)

In this case, several African-American teachers seeking jobs in suburban St. Louis, Missouri offered statistical data indicating they had been denied employment opportunities. The plaintiffs attempted to prove their case by showing that the percentage of black students was greater than the percentage of black teachers in the school district.

Although the United States Supreme Court affirmed that "statistics can be an important source of proof in employment discrimination cases," it rejected the plaintiffs' statistical evidence as irrelevant. The Court concluded that the proper comparison was between the percentage of blacks in the relevant geographical area who were qualified to teach and the percentage of blacks in Hazelwood's teaching staff.

### *Teamsters v. United States*
431 US 324 (1977)

In enforcing the Civil Rights Act of 1964, the United States Supreme Court held that victims of past union discrimination were entitled to retroactive seniority benefits. However, the Supreme Court required proof of "intent to discriminate," in order to establish that a given seniority system is illegal. Subsequent cases in lower federal courts during the late 1970s entitled discrimination victims to retroactive back pay in addition to retroactive seniority benefits.

### *Louis Swint and Willie Johnson v. Pullman Standard and the United Steelworkers of America*
72 L.Ed 66 (1982)

African-American employees of Pullman Standard brought a lawsuit into federal district court against Pullman Standard and the United Steelworkers of America. The lawsuit alleged that Title VII of the Civil Rights Act of 1964 was violated by a seniority system. In its decision, the District Court ruled "that the difference in terms, conditions or privileges of employment resulting from the seniority system are not the result of an intention to discriminate because of race or color" and held, therefore, that the system satisfied the requirements of Section 703(h) of the Civil Rights Act. This decision was later reversed by the Court of Appeals for the Fifth Circuit which stated that, "because we find the differences in the terms, conditions and standards of employment for black workers and white workers at Pullman Standard resulted from an intent to discriminate because of race, we hold that the system is not legally valid under Section 703(h) of Title VII U.S.C. 2000e-2(h)."

### *Meritor Savings Bank, FSB v. Vinson*
106 S.Ct. 2399 (1985)

Michelle Vinson, an African-American woman employed as a teller at a bank in Washington, DC, claimed that she had been sexually harassed for more than two months by her supervisor, Sidney Taylor, a white male. Vinson alleged that employment benefits were granted or denied based upon her performance of sexual favors.

In this first United States Supreme Court ruling on sexual harassment, the Court firmly condemned sexual harassment that creates an intimidating, hostile, and offensive working environment even when the harassment does not have economic ramifications. The unanimous ruling made it clear that Title VII of the Civil Rights Act prohibits sexual harassment that involves economic reprisals or harassment that creates a hostile, sexually charged atmosphere in the workplace.

### *Watson v. Fort Worth Bank & Trust*
108 US 2777 (1987)

In the case of *Watson v. Fort Worth Bank & Trust* Clara Watson, an African-American woman, alleged that she was repeatedly denied promotion to supervisory positions which were awarded to white employees with equivalent or lesser experience. The bank contended that its promotion decisions were based on various subjective criteria including experience, previous supervisory experience, and the ability to get along with others.

The United States Supreme Court held that Watson did not have to prove intentional discrimination. The Court concluded that subjective facially neutral selection devices which disadvantage blacks in much the same way as objective criteria written tests are unlawful.

### Lorance v. AT&T Technologies
490 US 900 (1989)

This case was brought by three women employed by AT&T. A new seniority system was adopted and under the change the women were promoted from laborers to testers but lost some seniority in the process. The loss was intended to be temporary with full seniority restored in five years, but before that occurred the women were demoted. The women allege that their employer violated Title VII of the Civil Rights Act of 1964 by adopting the new seniority system with the purpose and effect of protecting incumbent testers—jobs traditionally dominated by men—from female employees who had greater plantwide seniority and who were becoming testers in increasing numbers.

Unfortunately, the claims were brought too late. The court held that the charges had not been filed within the required period after the alleged unlawful employment practice occurred and therefore were thwarted.

### Patterson v. McLean Credit Union
491 US 164 (1989)

A black female was employed as a teller and file coordinator for ten years until she was laid-off. She alleged that she had been harassed, denied promotion to accounting clerk, and later discharged because of her race. Petitioner filed suit asserting violations of Section 1981 of the Civil Rights Act.

Racial harassment relating to conditions of employment are not actionable under Section 1981 which provides, ". . .[a]ll persons . . . shall have the same right to make and enforce contracts . . . as any white citizen," because that provision does not apply to conduct which occurs after the formation of a contract including the breach of the contracts terms and enforcement thereof. Rather, the harassment asserted by the petitioner is past formation conduct of the employer which is actionable only under Title VII of the Civil Rights Act of 1964.

### Wards Cove Packing Co. v. Antonio
490 US 642 (1989)

This case was brought by a class of non-white salmon cannery workers alleging that the employer's hiring and promotion practices were responsible for the workforces racial stratification and had denied them employment opportunities as noncannery workers on the basis of race. There were two types of jobs: unskilled cannery jobs, which were filled predominately by nonwhites; and noncannery jobs, mostly classified as skilled positions held by whites and virtually all paid more. Statistics were used to show a high percentage of nonwhites in cannery jobs and a low percentage in noncannery positions, in order to show a disparate impact caused by specific identifiable employment practices.

The United States Supreme Court found that the cannery workforce did not reflect the pool of qualified job applicants or the qualified labor force population. An employer's selection methods or employment practices cannot be said to have a disparate impact on nonwhites if the absence of minorities holding such skilled jobs reflects a dearth of qualified nonwhite applicants. A mere showing that nonwhites are underrepresented in the noncannery jobs will not suffice for a Title VII violation.

## Jury Selection and Service

### Neal v. Delaware
103 US 370 (1880)

The jury commissioner's conduct was found in violation of the United States Constitution where a black criminal defendant asserted that blacks were excluded from the jury based on their race. Every citizen is afforded the right to equal protection of the laws including that the selection of jurors to pass upon his life, liberty or property shall not be hindered by the exclusion of his race based on race.

### Strauder v. West Virginia
100 US 303 (1880)

In this case the Supreme Court granted immunity to a black criminal defendant from discrimination against him in the selection process of jurors based on their race. West Virginia's state law prohibited black men from eligibility to serve as a member of a grand jury or a petit jury in the state. Thereby, denying the equal protection of the laws to a citizen based solely on their race.

### Virginia v. Rives
100 US 313 (1880)

The petitioners in *Rives* asserted that blacks had never been allowed to serve as jurors in their county in any case where a black man was interested. Virginia had no formalized or specific statute restricting black jurors from certain trials. It was held, that a mixed jury in a particular case is not essential to the equal protection of the laws, and that the right is not given by any state or federal statute.

### Hollins v. Oklahoma
295 US 394 (1935)

The defendant in this case, an African American, was charged with rape and convicted on December 29, 1931 at a trial held in the basement of the jail in Sapula, Oklahoma. Three days before the scheduled execution, the NAACP secured a stay, and later,

a reversal of his conviction by the Supreme Court of Oklahoma.

The United States Supreme Court—in a memorandum opinion—affirmed the principle that the conviction of an African American by a jury from which all blacks had been excluded was a denial of the equal protection clause of the Fourteenth Amendment to the United States Constitution.

### Hale v. Commonwealth of Kentucky
303 US 613 (1938)

In 1936 Joe Hale, an African American, was charged with murder in McCracken County, Kentucky. Hale moved to set aside the indictment on the grounds that the jury commissioners had systematically excluded blacks from jury lists.

Hale established that one out of every six residents of the county was black, and that there were at least 70 blacks out of a total of 6,700 persons qualified for jury duty. Still, there had not been a black on jury duty between 1906 and 1936. Hale's conviction and death sentence were upheld by the court of appeals of Kentucky, but both were struck down by the United States Supreme Court on the grounds that he had been denied equal protection of the law.

### Patton v. Mississippi
332 US 463 (1947)

This case involved Eddie Patton, an African American who was indicted, tried, and convicted of the murder of a white man in Mississippi. At his trial and as part of his appeal, Patton alleged that all qualified blacks had been systematically excluded from jury service solely because of race. The state maintained that, since jury service was limited by statute to qualified voters and since few blacks were qualified to vote, such a procedure was valid in the eyes of the law.

The United States Supreme Court, however, reversed Patton's conviction on the grounds that such a jury plan, resulting in the almost automatic elimination of blacks from jury service, constituted an infringement of Patton's rights under the Fourteenth Amendment.

### Shepherd v. Florida
341 US 50 (1951)

The United States Supreme Court reversed the convictions of a Florida state court involving black defendants solely on the grounds that the method of selecting the grand jury discriminated against blacks.

### Turner v. Fouche
396 US 346 (1970)

The United States Supreme Court, in *Turner v. Fouche*, affirmed the right of defendants to bring an action in federal court to end discrimination in jury selection.

### Castanda v. Partida
430 US 482 (1977)

The United States Supreme Court in *Castanda v. Partida*, upheld the use of statistical evidence demonstrating that Mexican-Americans had been systematically excluded from jury selection, and that such discrimination on the basis of race or color violated the equal protection clause of the Constitution. The principle established in this case, that statistical evidence can be used to prove intentional discrimination, has been used in later cases involving employment, housing, voting and education.

### Batson v. Kentucky
476 US 79 (1986)

In the United States Supreme Court ruling on *Batson v. Kentucky*, Justice Lewis F. Powell writing for the majority, held that the prosecution in a criminal case may not use its "preemptory challenge", those challenges to an individual juror for which no cause need be stated, to exclude black jurors in a case involving a black defendant.

### Turner v. Murray
106 US 1683 (1986)

The United States Supreme Court in *Turner v. Murray*, expanded the right of black defendants in capital cases to question potential white jurors to uncover their racial prejudices and biases.

## Public Accommodations

### Hall v. DeCuir
95 US 485 (1878)

This case involved an unsuccessful attempt of the Louisiana Legislature to prohibit racial desegregation in any form of transportation in the state. The statute was attacked as an interference with interstate commerce because it imposed a direct burden and control over common carriers when entering the state. The statute was declared unconstitutional and void because it required those engaged in the transportation of passengers among the states to carry black passengers in Louisiana in the same cabin with white passengers.

The congressional legislature will have to cure the defects in the existing laws, by refraining from action, Congress, in effect adopts the common or civil law; although, the State of Louisiana may see the need for adoption of new regulations for the public good concerning desegregation the enact-

Lunchcounter sit-in protesters.

ments can only come from Congress where it effects interstate trade and influences business prospects.

### Plessy v. Ferguson
163 US 537 (1896)

The *Plessy* case was a test of the constitutionality of an 1890 Louisiana statute providing for "separate but equal" railway carriages for whites and blacks.

The information filed in the criminal District Court charged in substance that Homer Plessy, being a passenger between two stations within the state of Louisiana, was assigned by officers of the company to the coach used by the race to which he did not belong.

In the majority opinion of the United States Supreme Court, "separate but equal"

accommodations for blacks constituted a "reasonable" use of state police power. Furthermore, it was said that the Fourteenth Amendment "could not have been intended to abolish distinctions based on color, or to enforce social . . . equality, or a co-mingling of the two races upon terms unsatisfactory to either."

### Civil Rights Cases
332 US 46, 332 US 784, 333 US 831, 334 US 834, 378 US 226 (1883)

This group of civil rights cases was heard before the United States Supreme Court in an effort to determine the constitutionality of the 1875 Civil Rights Act, the first piece of national legislation which attempted to guarantee people of all races "full and equal enjoyment" of all public accommodations, including inns, public conveyances, theaters, and other places of amusement. The Court ruled, however, that the 1875 Civil Rights Act was unconstitutional inasmuch as it did not spring directly from the thirteenth and fourteenth amendments to the Constitution. In the view of the Court, the Thirteenth Amendment was concerned exclusively with the narrow confines of slavery and involuntary servitude. The Fourteenth Amendment, by a comparable yardstick of interpretation, did not empower Congress to enact direct legislation to counteract the effect of state laws or policies. The effect of this ruling was to deprive blacks of the very protections which the three postwar Freedom Amendments were designed to provide.

### *Morgan v. Commonwealth of Virginia*
328 US 373 (1946)

Irene Morgan, an African American, refused to move to the rear seat of a Greyhound bus which was traveling from Virginia to Washington, DC, and was subsequently convicted in the lower Virginia courts for violating a state statute requiring segregation of the races on all public vehicles.

NAACP attorneys then carried the case through the Virginia courts and on to the United States Supreme Court, where it was decided that the Virginia statute could not apply to interstate passengers or motor vehicles engaged in such traffic.

A segregated bus station in Durham, North Carolina.

### Bob-Lo v. Michigan
333 US 28 (1948)

In this case, the operator of a line of passenger ships used to transport patrons from Detroit to an island amusement park was convicted of violating the Michigan Civil Rights Act for refusing passage to an African American.

The United States Supreme Court upheld the application of the Michigan Civil Rights Act.

### Rice v. Arnold
340 US 848 (1950)

This case involved the successful attempt to abolish segregation on a Miami, Florida golf course owned and operated by the city. The United States Supreme Court granted a writ of certiorari and overturned the judgment of the Florida Supreme Court which authorized the segregated use of the course.

### District of Columbia v. John R. Thompson
346 US 100 (1952)

The Supreme Court unanimously held that a restaurant owner had violated federal law, which made it a crime to discriminate against a person on account of race or color, or to refuse service to him on those grounds.

### Muir v. Louisville Park Theatrical Association
347 US 971 (1954)

In 1954 several African Americans were refused admission to an amphitheater located in a Louisville city park, leased and operated by a privately owned group not affiliated in any way with the city. The Kentucky court of appeals found no evidence of unlawful discrimination, but the United States Supreme Court overturned this judg-

ment and remanded the case for consideration in the light of the prevailing legal climate as articulated in *Brown v. Board of Education.*

### Mayor and City Council of Baltimore v. Dawson
350 US 377 (1955)

The United States Supreme Court affirmed a judgment that the enforcement of racial segregation in public beaches and bathhouses maintained by public authorities is unconstitutional.

### Holmes v. Atlanta
350 US 859 (1955)

This case involved a suit brought by African Americans to integrate a city-owned and city-operated golf course in Atlanta, Georgia. The segregated arrangements were ordered sustained by a lower court, but that order was overturned by the United States Supreme Court and the case remanded to the District Court with directions to enter a decree for plaintiffs in conformity with the Baltimore case above.

### Flemming v. South Carolina Electric
351 US 901 (1956)

This case involved a suit brought by an African-American passenger against a bus company for damages due to the bus driver's having required her to change seats in accordance with South Carolina's segregation law. The trial judge dismissed the case on the grounds that the statute in question was valid, but the court of appeals reversed this decision, holding that the "separate but equal" doctrine was no longer valid. The United States Supreme Court upheld the court of appeals.

Black bus riders in Montgomery, Alabama.

### Gayle v. Browder
352 US 114 (1956)

This case challenged the constitutionality of state statutes and ordinances in effect in the city of Montgomery, Alabama, which required the segregation of whites and blacks on public buses.

These statutes were first declared unconstitutional by the decision of a three-judge federal district court. The United States Supreme Court then affirmed this judgment.

### Katzenbach v. McClung
379 US 802 (1964)
&
### Heart of Atlanta v. United States
379 US 803 (1964)

Both cases were decided on the same day.

In the *Katzenbach* case, the Attorney General of the United States sued Ollie's Barbecue Restaurant in Birmingham, Alabama for its refusal to serve blacks in its dining accommodations, a direct violation of the anti-discriminatory public accommo-

dations clause of the 1964 Civil Rights Act. The United States District Court, Northern District of Alabama, held that the Civil Rights Act could not be applied under the Fourteenth Amendment to the United States Constitution, inasmuch as there was no "demonstrable connection" between food purchased in interstate commerce and sold in a restaurant that would affect commerce. The

Lunch counter protesters in Raleigh, North Carolina, 1960.

Plaintiffs Woodrow Lewis, Albert Dunn, and George Willis meet with attorneys William Alexander and D.L. Hollowell, in a suit against an Atlanta restaurateur, 1965.

United States Supreme Court, however, held that "the Civil Rights Act of 1964, as here applied, [is] plainly appropriate in the resolution of what. [Congress has]. found to be a national commercial problem of the first magnitude."

The *Heart of Atlanta* case dealt with a Georgia motel which solicited patronage in national advertising and had several out-of-state residents as guests from time to time. The motel had already instituted the practice of refusing to rent rooms to African Americans prior to the passage of the 1964 Civil Rights Act, and stated thereafter that it intended to continue this practice. The motel owner filed suit, maintaining that the 1964 Civil Rights Act violated both the Fifth and the Thirteenth Amendments. The United States countered with the argument that the refusal to accept blacks interfered

with interstate travel, and that the Congress in voting to apply nondiscriminatory standards to interstate commerce was not violating either amendment. The United States Supreme Court upheld the right of congressional regulation, stating that the power of Congress was not confined to the regulation of commerce among the states. "It extends to those activities intrastate which so affect interstate commerce, or the exercise of the power of Congress over it, as to make regulation of them appropriate means to the attainment of a legitimate end."

### Bell v. Maryland
378 US 226 (1964)

The United States Supreme Court ordered a Maryland district court to reconsider its affirmation of a state court conviction of twelve African Americans for trespassing, when they refused to leave a restaurant that refused to serve them entirely on the basis of their color.

### Evans v. Newton
382 US 296 (1966)

The United States Supreme Court ruled that transfer of a city park from municipal ownership to a board of private trustees does not remove its obligations under the Fourteenth Amendment.

### Shuttlesworth v. Birmingham
394 US 147 (1969)

The United States Supreme Court invalidated Birmingham's Parade-Permit law which had been used in 1963 to harass participants in an Easter March organized by Dr. Martin Luther King, Jr.

### New York State Club Association v. City of New York
108 S.Ct. 2225 (1988)

In a unanimous decision, the United States Supreme Court upheld the constitutionality of a New York City ordinance that forbids so-called private clubs from discriminating against women and minorities.

## Racial Intermarriage

### Loving v. Virginia
388 US 1 (1967)

This case virtually nullified the antimiscegenation laws, many of which remain in southern state constitutions and legal codes. It concerned a white man and black woman, residents of Virginia, who married in Washington, DC. The state of Virginia indicted and convicted them of violating its laws against racial intermarriage when the couple returned to Virginia and attempted to reside there, but released them when the couple agreed not to reside in the state for 25 years. The Lovings, however, decided to challenge the agreement and the law. Their appeal was rejected by the Virginia courts but upheld by the United States Supreme Court, which ruled the Virginia law unconstitutional. Soon thereafter, federal district courts in other states which forbade intermarriage were ordering local officials to issue marriage licenses to interracial couples applying for them.

## Requirements for Legislative Membership

### Powell v. McCormack
395 US 486 (1969)

According to the Constitution, only three basic factors govern eligibility to serve as a legislator in the United States House of Representatives: a minimum age requirement, the possession of United States citizenship, and the fulfillment of the state's residency requirement. When United States Representative Adam Clayton Powell, Jr. was excluded from the 90th Congress on the grounds that he had misused public funds and defied the courts of his home state, he filed suit in federal court in an attempt to force the House to review only the necessary credentials for membership.

The district court dismissed the first petition on the grounds that it lacked jurisdiction. By the time the case was finally heard before the United States Supreme Court, the 90th Congress had adjourned. Powell, however, was reelected and finally seated in the 91st Congress, a gesture which in the view of the court did not settle the case. The legal point on which the case hinged involved the distinction between "expulsion" and "exclusion." Despite the more than two-thirds ma-

Adam Clayton Powell leaves the Capitol after the House voted to take away his Education and Labor Committee chairmanship.

jority required for expulsion, the Court ruled that the intent of the House was to "exclude," not to "expel." The Court summation stated flatly that "the House was without power to exclude him from its membership."

## Right of Sale and Restrictive Covenants

### Buchanan v. Warley
245 US 60 (1917)

The plaintiff, Buchanan, brought an action in this case for the performance of a sale of certain real estate in Louisville, Kentucky. The purchaser, Warley an African American, maintained that he would be unable to occupy the land since it was located within what was defined by a Louisville ordinance as a white block. (The ordinance pro-

hibited whites from living in black districts, and vice versa.) Buchanan alleged that the ordinance was in conflict with the Fourteenth Amendment to the United States Constitution.

The United States Supreme Court maintained that the ordinance was unconstitutional.

### Shelley v. Kraemer
334 US 1 (1948)
&
### Hurd v. Hodge
334 US 26 (1948)

On August 11, 1945, an African-American family, the Shelleys, received a warranty deed to a parcel of land which, unknown to them, was subject to a restrictive covenant barring its sale to blacks. A lawsuit was subsequently brought in the Circuit Court of St. Louis seeking to divest the Shelleys of the title to the land. The Supreme Court of Missouri directed the trial court to strip the petitioners of their warranty deed.

The United States Supreme Court reversed this decision, maintaining that restrictive covenants, though valid contracts, could not be enforced by state courts. In the *Hurd v. Hodge* case, involving a similar set of circumstances, federal courts were similarly prohibited from enforcing such restrictive covenants.

### Reitman v. Mulkey
387 US 369 (1967)

In 1964 the California electorate voted in favor of a referendum granting "absolute discretion" to real estate owners in the sale and rental of real property, in effect voiding the state's fair housing laws. Lincoln Mulkey filed suit against property owners in Orange County to challenge the validity of the referendum. Mulkey's position failed in the lower courts but was sustained five to two by the California supreme court on the grounds that the California referendum violated the Fourteenth Amendment of the United States Constitution. The United States Supreme Court upheld the decision.

### Jones v. Alfred H. Mayer, Co.
392 US 409 (1968)

Joseph Lee Jones alleged that the sole reason a realtor refused to sell him a home was because he was black. The United States Supreme Court held that 42 U.S.C. 1982, a federal statute created during the Reconstruction era to eliminate the vestiges of slavery, prohibits all racial discrimination, public and private in the sale or rental of property.

### Trafficante v. Metropolitan Life Insurance
409 US 205 (1972)

The United States Supreme Court ruled that a complaint of racial discrimination in housing may be brought by parties who have not themselves been refused accommodation but who, as members of the same housing unit, allege injury by discriminatory housing practices. The suit had been filed by a black and a white resident of a housing development in San Francisco, who contended that the owner of the development, in maintaining a "white ghetto," was depriving plaintiffs of the right to live in a racially integrated community.

### Sentencing and Incarceration

### McKlesky v. Kemp
481 US 279 (1987)

In April 1987, the United States Supreme Court decided one of the most significant cases involving the imposition of the death penalty in America. Warren McKlesky, a thirty-eight-year-old African-American man accused of killing a police officer while robbing a furniture store, was sentenced to death by the State of Georgia. In support of his claim that the sentence violated his constitutional rights, McKlesky introduced a sophisticated statistical study that analyzed more than 2,000 murder cases in Georgia. The study demonstrated that there is a disparity in the imposition of the capital sentence based on the race of the victim, as well as the race of the defendant.

Defendants charged with killing white persons received the death penalty in eleven percent of the cases, but defendants charged with killing blacks received the death penalty in only one percent of the cases. The study further showed that prosecutors asked for the death penalty in seventy percent of the cases involving black defendants and white victims, and only nineteen percent of the cases involving white defendants and black victims. In sum, the analysis revealed that African Americans who kill whites are 4.3 times more likely to receive the death sentence.

In the five to four opinion, written by Justice Lewis F. Powell, the United States Supreme Court acknowledged that it had accepted statistics as proof of intent to discriminate in employment, housing and voting cases. However, despite the compelling statistical evidence the Court rejected McKlesky's claim that the death penalty in Georgia is applied in a racially discriminatory manner. The Court's reasoning was that although McKlesky showed the existence of racial discrimination in sentencing, he failed to prove that "racial considerations played a part in his sentence."

Finally, Justice Powell expressed concern that acceptance of McKlesky's argument would open the floodgates of litigation by black defendants seeking to introduce statistical evidence to demonstrate that race affected the outcome of their case.

## Slavery

### *Prigg v. Pennsylvania*
16 Peters 539 (1842)

In violation of a 1826 Pennsylvania anti-kidnapping statute, Edward Prigg, a professional slave catcher, Maryland, took captive Margaret Morgan, a fugitive slave residing in Pennsylvania, and was tried and convicted for kidnapping. Hearing the case, the United states Supreme Court ruled that the Pennsylvania law was unconstitutional, on the grounds that the statute was an interference with Congress' power under Article 4, Section 2 of the Constitution.

A newspaper depiction of a fugitive slave, 1837.

### *Strader v. Graham*
10 Howard 82 (1850)

In 1841, three slaves owned by Christopher Graham of Kentucky, boarded a steamboat owned by Jacob Strader and traveled to Cincinnati, from where they ultimately escaped to freedom in Canada. Graham sued Strader for the value of the slaves and the expenses incurred while trying to recover them.

Graham won the case, however, Strader appealed, claiming that the slaves had become free under Ohio law and provisions of the Northwest Ordinance

The United States Supreme Court ruled unanimously that each state had the right to determine the status of slaves within its jurisdiction, that the status of these slaves was to be determined by the state of Kentucky, and that the Northwest Ordinance was no longer in force, since those territories had become states.

### *Dred Scott v. Sandford*
19 Howard 393 (1857)

In 1835, Dred Scott, born a slave in Virginia, became the property of John Emerson, an Army doctor, in the slave state of Missouri. From there, he was taken into the free state of Illinois and later to the free territory of Minnesota.

In 1847, Scott instituted suit in the circuit court of the St. Louis County, Missouri, arguing that he should be given his freedom by virtue of his having resided on free soil. After nine years, his case was certified to the United States Supreme Court, where five of the nine justices, were Southerners.

In delivering his opinion, Chief Justice Roger Brook Taney declared that, by virtue of both the Declaration of Independence and the Constitution, African Americans could not be regarded as citizens of the

Poster advertising a public hearing on the *Dred Scott v. Sanford* case.

United States. Moreover, the Court could not deprive slaveholders of their right to take slaves into any part of the Union, North or South. In effect, therefore, the Missouri Compromise, as well as other antislavery legislation, was declared to be unconstitutional.

### Ableman v. Booth
21 Howard 506 (1859)

The United States Supreme Court upheld Congress' fugitive slave law and all its provisions; but, more importantly upheld the supremacy of federal law over state law. Booth was held in a state jail for violating the federal fugitive slave laws. Booth secured a writ of habeas Corpus from a state judge who declared the federal laws unconstitutional and the Wisconsin Supreme Court affirmed.

The state court had stepped beyond its sphere of authority. The federal court held

Booth guilty, although the State of Wisconsin is a sovereign within its territorial limits, it is limited and restricted by the United States Constitution.

## State and Local Affirmative Action Requirements

### United States Steelworkers of America v. Brian Weber
433 US 193 (1979)

The United Steelworkers of America and Kaiser Aluminum Company entered into a collective bargaining agreement including a voluntary affirmative action plan designed to eliminate conspicuous racial imbalances in Kaiser's almost exclusively white skilled workforce. The plant in Gramercy, Louisiana agreed to reserve 50 percent of the openings in the skilled job training programs for blacks until the percentage of African-American skilled workers was equal to the percentage of blacks in the local labor force. Brian Weber, a white production worker, who was turned down for the training program although he had more seniority than many accepted blacks, sued the United Steelworkers of America, claiming that the affirmative action program discriminated against whites.

The United States Supreme Court limited the issue to the narrow question of whether Title VII prohibited private employers and unions from establishing voluntary affirmative action plans. In a five to two decision, the Court upheld the affirmative action plan and established three factors to determine the validity of racial preference. The Court approved the plan because it was designed to break down Kaiser's historic patterns of racial segregation; did not unnecessarily diminish the rights of white employees since it did not require the firing of white employees; and was a temporary measure not intended to maintain racial balance but simply to eliminate an imbalance.

### Fullilove v. Klutznick
448 US 448 (1980)

The United States Supreme Court upheld a provision of the Public Works Employment Act of 1977 that required a ten percent set-aside of federal funds for minority business enterprises on local public work projects. The provision had been challenged as violation of the equal protection clause of the Fifth Amendment.

### Firefighters Local Union No. 1784 v. Stotts
467 US 561 (1984)

In May 1981, for the first time in its history, the City of Memphis announced layoffs of city employees, due to a projected budget deficit. The layoffs, which included the fire department, were to be made on a "last hired, first fired" city-wide seniority system that had been adopted in 1973. Carl Stotts, an African-American firefighter, sued to stop the layoffs, claiming that since African Americans had been hired pursuant to the affirmative action provisions of a 1980 court decree, they would be laid off in far greater numbers than their white co-workers.

In a six to three decision the United States Supreme Court held that since the 1980 court decree did not say that African Americans had special protection during a layoff, the layoffs had to be made according to the 1973 seniority system.

### Wygant v. Jackson Board of Education
476 US 267 (1986)

The United States Supreme Court dealt a tremendous blow to affirmative action in this case involving a public school system's affirmative action plan. The record reflected that the first African-American school teacher was not hired in Jackson, Michigan until 1953. By 1969, only 3.9 percent of the teachers were African American although 15.2 percent of the students were African American. In response, the school board developed an affirmative action plan which protected African-American faculty members during layoffs.

Although the United States Supreme Court had approved affirmative action plans in prior cases, it rejected the Jackson plan. The Court found that the goal of the plan, to remedy societal discrimination and afford positive role models to black students, was nebulous and not sufficiently compelling.

African Americans are now represented on most city fire and police forces.

### Local No. 93, International Association of Firefighters v. City of Cleveland
106 S.Ct. 3063 (1986)

The city of Cleveland, which had a long history of racial discrimination, negotiated a consent decree with African-American firefighters who had filed a lawsuit alleging that they had been unlawfully denied jobs and promotions. The decree included an affirmative action plan with numerical goals for promotion of African Americans to the position of supervisor.

In response to the union's challenge on behalf of white firefighters, the United States Supreme Court ruled that the lower courts had broad discretion to approve decrees in which employers settle discrimination suits by agreeing to preferential promotions of African Americans, in spite of the objections of white employees.

### Local No. 28, Sheet Metal Workers International Association v. EEOC
106 S.Ct. 3019 (1986)

After finding that the all-white union had discriminated against African Americans and Hispanics seeking to enter the sheet metal trades for more than a decade, the trial court ordered the union to establish a 29 percent non-white membership goal. The court also ruled that the union would have to pay substantial fines if the union failed to meet the goals. After the union failed to reach the goal, the court found the union in contempt and established a new goal of 29.3 percent. The union challenged the court's order.

In a complex opinion, the United States Supreme Court upheld the affirmative action goal in light of the union's "persistent or egregious discrimination" and to eliminate "lingering effects of pervasive discrimination." This was the first time the Court expressly approved the use of race conscious relief to blacks and Hispanics who were not identified victims of discrimination.

### United States v. Paradise
480 US 149 (1987)

This case originated in 1972 when the NAACP sued the Alabama Department of Highways because of its long-standing history of racially discriminating employment practices. More than eleven years later, after the Department had failed to hire or promote blacks, the trial court ordered the promotion of one black trooper for every white. The United States Attorney General challenged the constitutionality of the plan. The United States Supreme Court upheld the use of strict racial quotas and found that the plan was "narrowly tailored to serve a compelling government interest"—remedying "egregious" past discrimination against blacks.

### Johnson v. Transportation Agency, Santa Clara County, California
480 US 616 (1987)

The United States Supreme Court held that the state transportation agency's voluntary affirmative action plan, under which a female had been promoted to the position of road dispatcher over a male whose score was slightly higher, was consistent with Title VII of the Civil Rights Act of 1964. The Court held that an employer does not have to admit or prove that it has discriminated in order to justify efforts designed to achieve a more racially balanced workforce. The employer only needs to demonstrate that there is a "conspicuous . . . imbalance in traditionally segregated job categories."

### City of Richmond v. J.A. Croson Co.
109 S.Ct. 706 (1989)

Richmond adopted a Minority Business Utilization Plan that was not sufficiently narrowly tailored to remedy past discrimination in the construction industry. The Plan allowed minorities a fixed thirty percent quota of the public contracts based solely on their race. The policy provided no guidance for the city's legislating body to determine the precise scope of the injury it sought to remedy except racial balancing.

## ■ ATTORNEYS, JUDGES, AND LEGAL SCHOLARS

### Clifford Alexander (1933– )
*Former Associate Counsel to the President of the United States*

Born in New York City, September 21, 1933, Clifford Alexander went to Harvard and earned a bachelor's degree cum laude in 1955, and attended Yale Law School afterwards, earning a LL.B. in 1958. After attending these prestigious universities, he went on to become the assistant district attorney of New York County, working there from 1959 to 1961. Positions as the executive director of the Hamilton Grange Neighborhood Conservation district in Manhattanville from 1961 to 1962, and as executive program director of HARYOU from 1962 to 1963, followed. In 1963, he became a member of the National Security Council.

Alexander was hired by President Lyndon Johnson as his deputy special assistant in

1964, and quickly rose to become the President's deputy special counsel in 1967. He became chairman of the Equal Employment Opportunity Commission in 1967, where he was under constant pressure from Republican Senators like Everett Dirksen, who accused him of bullying reluctant employers into complying with federal guidelines for minority employment. He left that position in 1969.

In the years between 1969 and 1976, Alexander worked for several different law offices in private practice. He also became a Harvard overseer. At Harvard, he was involved in working out details with craft unions which were obliged to offer and implement concrete proposals for improving minority employment opportunities.

President Jimmy Carter appointed Alexander as the secretary of the Department of the Army, the first African American to serve in that position. Alexander won the Outstanding Civilian Service Award from the Department of the Army in 1980, after he finished his 1977–80 appointment to that position. Since 1981, Alexander has been president of Alexander Associates, Inc., and served as a consultant to Major League Baseball, working to improve minority hiring practices.

In addition, Alexander has had his own television program, "Black on White," has been director of several Dreyfus money funds, served on the board of directors for the Mexican-American Legal Defense and Education Fund, and taught as a professor at Howard University.

### Violette Anderson (1882–19?)

*First African-American Woman to Practice Law Before the Supreme Court*

Violette Anderson was born July 16, 1882, in London, England, the daughter of Richard E. and Marie (Jordi) Neatley. When she was young, the family moved to the United States, where she attended North Division High School in Chicago, Illinois from 1895 to 1899; Chicago Athenaeum, 1903; the Chicago Seminar of Sciences from 1912 to 1915, and Chicago Law School from 1917 to 1920, earning her LL.B. in 1920. Soon after, she was wed to Albert E. Johnson. Anderson was a Republican and her church affiliation was Episcopalian.

Anderson worked as a court reporter from 1905 to 1920, a job which sparked her interest in law. She began a private practice in 1920, becoming the first African-American woman to practice law in the United States District Court Eastern Division. From 1922 to 1923, she served as the first female city prosecutor in Chicago.

After five years of practice before the high court of Illinois, by application of Judge James A. Cobb of Washington, DC, Anderson was admitted to practice for the Supreme Court of the United States, becoming the first African-American woman to obtain this post. Her admission became a precedent that allowed other African-American women to do the same.

Anderson also belonged to the Federal Colored Women's Clubs, was president of Friendly Big Sisters League of Chicago, First Vice-President of Cook County Bar Association, and secretary of Idlewild Lot Owners Association. In addition, she was the member of the executive board of Chicago Council of Social Agencies.

### Derrick Albert Bell, Jr. (1930–   )

*Professor of Law*

Derrick Albert Bell, Jr. was born in Pittsburgh, Pennsylvania, November 6, 1930, the son of Derrick and Ada Bell. He attended Duquesne University and received his LL.B.

from the University of Pittsburgh Law School. He married Jewel A. Hairston and the couple has three children. Bell is a member of the bar in Washington DC, Pennsylvania, New York, California, the United States Supreme Court, the United States Courts of Appeals for fourth, fifth, sixth, eighth, and tenth circuits and several federal district courts. Since 1969 he has been teaching law at Harvard Law School. Bell has written several important books on the law, including *Race, Racism and American Law*, second edition, 1980, and *And We Are Not Saved, The Elusive Quest for Racial Justice*, 1987. Bell also served as editor of *Desegregation Dialogue, Searching for Remedies Under Brown*.

After graduating from law school, Bell worked for the United States Department of Justice from 1957 to 1959, at the Pittsburgh Branch of the NAACP as executive secretary from 1959 to 1960, and for the NAACP Legal Defense and Education Fund as staff attorney from 1960 to 1966. In 1966 he was made deputy assistant to the secretary for civil rights for the Department of Health, Education and Welfare. He also served for a year as the director of the Western Center on Law and Poverty.

Bell began as a lecturer on law at Harvard Law School in 1969, became a professor in 1971, and left in 1980 to be Dean of the University of Oregon Law School. He returned to Harvard Law School in 1986 where he currently is a professor of law.

### Jane Matilda Bolin (1908– )
*First African-American Woman Judge*

At the relatively young age of thirty-one, Jane Matilda Bolin was honored by being chosen to be the first African-American woman judge in the United States. She presided over the Domestic Relations Court of the City of New York (subsequently called the Family Court of the State of New York) for forty years. Her first ten-year appointment came from Mayor Fiorello La Guardia in 1939. She was appointed to three more successive ten-year terms by mayors William O'Dwyer, John Lindsay, and Robert F. Wagner, Jr. After forty years of service, Bolin reached the mandatory retirement age and had to step down, but not before she became well known over the country for her work. Bolin was also known for her striking beauty. John Powers, head of a world-renowned modeling agency, named her one of the "Powers Girls" of 1949.

Born April 11, 1908 in Poughkeepsie, New York, her father was the first African-American graduate of Williams College. Bolin attended Wellesley College and Yale University School of Law, where she received her LL.B. in 1931. She worked with her father, who was also a lawyer, until she passed the New York State Bar examination; she then practiced in Poughkeepsie before moving to New York City to practice law with her husband, Ralph E. Mizelle.

In 1937, Bolin was appointed assistant corporation counsel for New York City, which she held until she received her appointment to the Domestic Relations Court. Outside of her career, Bolin has taken an active role in the Wiltwyck School for Boys, the Child Welfare League of America, the Neighborhood Children's Center, and the local and national NAACP. She has also travelled extensively and met several heads of state in Africa. She counted among her friends Eleanor Roosevelt, educator Mary McLeod Bethune and Judge Waties Waring, who ruled in the first public school desegregation case. Bolin has received honorary degrees from Morgan State University, Western College for Women, Tuskegee Institute, Hampton University and Williams College.

After her retirement, Bolin became a volunteer reading teacher for the New York

City public schools for a few years. She received an appointment to the Regents Review Committee of the New York State Board of Regents, which holds hearings involving professional discipline of more than thirty-two professions. She is currently working on this committee.

## Jerome Farris (1930– )
*United States Court of Appeals Judge, Ninth Circuit*

Jerome Farris was elected circuit judge of the United States Court of Appeals Ninth Circuit in 1979 and continues to serve in that capacity.

Judge Farris was born on March 4, 1930, in Birmingham, Alabama. Willie Joe and Elizabeth Farris were his parents. He earned his B.S. degree from Morehouse College in 1951. In 1952, he joined the United States Army Signal Corps. He received a M.S.W. from Atlanta University in 1955, and received his J.D. from the University of Washington in 1958. Farris is married to Jean Shy and has two children.

He started out in private practice with Weyer, Schroeter & Sterne in 1958, becoming a partner in 1959. He stayed in private practice until he became a Washington State court of appeals judge in 1969. He was the chairman of the State Federal Judicial Council of Washington from 1983 to 1987. In addition, he has served as president on the Washington State Jr. Chamber of Commerce from 1965 to 1966; a trustee with the Pacific Northwest Ballet from 1978 to 1983; and as a regent of the University of Washington since 1985.

Farris has been honored with the Clayton Frost Award from the Jaycees in 1966, received an honorary LL.D. from Morehouse College in 1978, and the Order of the Coif from the University of Washington Law School.

## William H. Hastie (1904–1976)
*First Black United States Court of Appeals Judge, Third Circuit*

From 1949–71, William H. Hastie served as a United States Court of Appeals Judge of the Third Circuit, the first African-American man to hold a federal appeals judicial position.

Hastie was born in Knoxville, Tennessee, November 17, 1904. He was the son of William Henry and Roberta Child Hastie. He received his A.B. from Amherst College in 1925, an LL.B. from Harvard University in 1930 and a S.J.D. from the same institution in 1933. He received honorary LL.D.s from many institutions, including Rutgers University, Howard University and Temple University. In 1943 he married Beryl Lockhart. The couple had three children.

He was admitted to the bar in 1930 and was in private practice from 1930 to 1933. In 1933, he became assistant solicitor of the Department of the Interior, where he served until 1937. In 1937, he became a judge of the District Court of the Virgin Islands, leaving in 1939 to become dean of the Howard University School of Law. In 1942, he was the first civilian aide to the secretary of war. He was governor of the Virgin Islands between 1946 and 1949, before his subsequent position as United States Circuit Court of Appeals judge.

He was also a Trustee of the Amherst College and a Fellow of the American Academy of Arts and Sciences. Hastie died April 14, 1976 in Philadelphia, Pennsylvania.

## Joseph W. Hatchett (1932– )
*United States Court of Appeals Judge, Eleventh Circuit*

Judge Joseph W. Hatchett was appointed a United States Circuit Judge of the United States Court of Appeals on October 1, 1981,

William Hastie, 1949.

and he currently retains that position. Judge Hatchett was the first black to be appointed to the highest court of a state since reconstruction, the first black to be elected to public office in a statewide election in the South, and first black to serve on a federal appellate court in the South.

Born in Clearwater, Florida, September 17, 1932, Hatchett received his A.B. from Florida A & M University in 1954 and his J.D. from Howard University in 1959. He also has certification in his specialties—a Naval Justice School Certificate in 1973, an Appellate Judge Course in 1977, and an American Academy of Judicial Education Appellate Judge Course in 1978.

Hatchett was in private practice in Florida from 1959 to 1966, and served as the contract consultant for the City of Datona Beach for three years. He became an assis-

tant United States Attorney in Jacksonville, Florida in 1966, then served as the first assistant of the United States Attorney for the Middle District of Florida. In 1971, he became the United States magistrate for the Middle District of Florida, and was a Supreme Court justice for the state of Florida from 1975 to 1979. He was a United States circuit judge for United States Court of Appeals, Fifth Circuit from 1979 to 1981, before advancing to his current position.

He was honored with a Howard University Post Graduation Achievement Award in 1977, named Most Outstanding Citizen from the Broward County National Bar Association in 1976 received a Medallion for Human Relations from Bethune-Cookman in 1975, and has been awarded several honorary doctorates. He is the author of several publications in the field of law, including *Criminal*

*Law Survey, 1978,* University of Miami Law Review; *1978 Developments in Florida Law,* 1979; *Pre-Trial Discovery in Criminal Cases,* Federal Judicial Center Library, 1974.

### A. Leon Higginbotham, Jr. (1928–   )
*Professor of Law, Former United States Court of Appeals Judge*

Leon Higginbotham, Jr. was appointed on October 13, 1977 by President Jimmy Carter to the United States Circuit Judge's position. Just prior to this appointment, he had served on the Federal Trade Commission—the first black and the youngest person ever to hold the post of commissioner.

Born in Trenton, New Jersey, on February 25, 1928, Higginbotham began as an engineering student at Purdue University, but later went to Antioch College to study liberal arts. He received his LL.B. in 1952 from Yale School of Law. This was quite a step for a man who started out as a shoe store porter.

After graduation, he became an assistant district attorney in Philadelphia, and later moved into private practice. He was sought out by Pennsylvania Governor David Lawrence to become a member of the Pennsylvania Human Rights Commission. Elected president of the Philadelphia chapter of NAACP, Higginbotham later earned the honor of "One of the 10 Outstanding Young Men in America" by the United States Junior Chamber of Commerce. He was made district judge in 1964, where he served until his appointment to the United States Circuit Court in 1977. Higginbotham was also a lecturer at Harvard Law School and an adjunct professor at the University of Pennsylvania.

Higginbotham is well known for his prolific writing. He has authored more than one hundred articles as well as an acclaimed book, *In the Matter of Color: Race and the American Legal Process; The Colonial Period.* He has also been praised for his unusual competency in logic and language. In his esteemed career, he has won over forty honorary degrees.

A. Leon Higginbotham, Jr., 1969.

### Anita Hill (1956–   )
*Professor of Law*

Born on July 30, 1956, in Morns, Oklahoma, Anita Hill was a relatively unknown law professor at the University of Oklahoma when her name became a household word virtually overnight. It was during the Senate confirmation hearings in October 1991, for United States Supreme Court Justice Clarence Thomas that Hill became famous. She came forward with sexual harassment charges against Judge Thomas that shocked the nation, and many watched as she poured out painful details of Thomas's alleged sexual harassment, purportedly committed when both had worked for the Equal Employment Opportunities Commission. Hill claimed that Thomas repeatedly pressured her to date him, told her plots of pornographic movies, and bragged about his sex-

Anita Hill

ual exploits. When asked why she didn't quit her job or report Thomas when the incidents occurred during the early 1980s, Hill answered that she feared she wouldn't be able to get another job.

Following the hearings, Hill continued to be hounded by the press. Her experience with the hearings had changed her life, as well as her career direction. She had been a professor of commercial law. She decided to take a year-long sabbatical in order to look at the possibility of founding an institute with the purpose of researching racism and sexism. Hill also made many speeches around the country about her experience.

Controversy didn't escape her on campus, either. Several lawmakers made news when they asked that Anita Hill be fired. However, her dean and other members of the faculty support her. Funding is underway to create

a University of Oklahoma professorship to study discrimination in the workplace. Most likely, Hill will be placed in that position.

### Charles Hamilton Houston (1895–1950)
*Former NAACP Legal Counsel*

Charles Hamilton Houston was born in Washington, DC, on September 3, 1895. Finishing high school at the young age of fifteen, he went on to attend Amherst College and earned his A.B. from that institution in 1915, one of six valedictorians. He taught English briefly, then enlisted in the United States Army in 1917, and served in France and Germany until 1919. He attended Harvard Law School and became the first African-American editor of the *Harvard Law Review*. He received his LL.B. in 1922, and was at the top five percent of his class. He also became the first African-American to receive a S.J.D. from Harvard University in 1923. In 1923, he received a Sheldon Fellowship and studied civil law at the University of Madrid. He was admitted to the Washington, DC bar in 1924.

Houston was in private practice with his father from 1924 to 1950. Between 1929 and 1935, he was vice dean of the school of law at Howard University. He was special counsel to the NAACP from 1935 to 1940, and a member of the national legal aid committee from 1940 to 1950. He served as the vice-president for the American Council on Race Relations from 1944 to 1950, and was a member of the President's Commission on Fair Employment Practice in 1944.

While with the NAACP, Houston teamed with the American Fund for Public Service to direct a program of legal action and education aimed at the elimination of segregation. Former student Thurgood Marshall served under Houston for several years. While in this position, Houston argued several cases before the United States Supreme

Court, including *Missouri ex rel. Gaines v. Canada*. The court ruled that Missouri could not keep an African American from attending the white state law school because there was no such school for African-Americans. This ruling was a major blow to the separate but equal rule.

Historically, Houston's major impact was in his strengthening of Howard University's Law School, as well as his work in civil rights litigation. Much of the cases he argued were instrumental in setting precedents that were to be used in the historic *Brown v. Board of Education* and *Boling v. Sharpe* cases that were to outlaw racial segregation. In addition, he was a columnist for *The Afro-American*.

Houston died April 22, 1950 of a heart ailment and was buried in Lincoln Memorial Cemetery. Five Supreme Court justices attended his funeral. He received a great deal of recognition after his death, including the Springarn Medal, awarded by the NAACP.

**Nathaniel R. Jones (1926–   )**
*United States Court of Appeals Judge, Sixth Circuit*

Nathaniel R. Jones is a distinguished judge, attorney and administrator. President Jimmy Carter appointed him to the Sixth Circuit Court of Appeals in Cincinnati, Ohio on October 15, 1979. Prior to that, he was general counsel for the NAACP from 1969 to 1979, executive director of the Fair Employment Practices Commission of the City of Youngstown, Ohio from 1966 to 1969, in private practice, and a United States Attorney for the Northern District of Ohio.

While with the NAACP, Judge Jones organized the attack against northern school segregation and also argued in the Supreme Court's Detroit school case *Bradley v.*

*Milliken*. The Dayton and Columbus, Ohio school desegregation cases heard before the Supreme Court were also organized by Jones. He has headed a three-man team which investigated grievances of black servicemen in Germany and responded to the attacks against affirmative action. He was also a national liaison for the famous "Kalamazoo Case."

He was made deputy general counsel to the President's Commission on Civil Disorders in 1967 and co-chairman of the Civilian Military Task Force on Military Justice in 1972.

Jones received a B.A. degree from Youngstown University in 1951, and his LL.B. in 1956. He has honorary degrees from Youngstown University and Syracuse University.

Nathaniel Jones, 1985.

### Amalya Lyle Kearse (1937–   )

*United States Court of Appeals Judge,
    Second Circuit*

Judge Amalya Lyle Kearse was born June 11, 1937, in Vauxhall, New Jersey. She attended Wellesley College for her B.A. in 1959, and went to the University of Michigan for her J.D. in 1962. Kearse was in private practice from 1962 to 1969, also working as an adjunct lecturer for the New York University Law School from 1968 to 1969. She was then made United States Court of Appeals Circuit Judge.

Kearse has won the Jason L. Honigman Award for Outstanding Contribution to the Law Review Editorial Board. She has also served on the board of directors for the NAACP Legal Defense and Education Fund, as well as the National Urban League. She was appointed to the President's Commission for the Selection of judges and served between 1977 and 1978. She served on the executive committee for Civil Rights Under Law for nine years, has been a member of the American Law Institute since 1977 and a fellow in the American College of Trial Lawyers since 1979.

### Damon J. Keith (1922–   )

*United States Court of Appeals Judge, Sixth
    Circuit*

Damon J. Keith was appointed to the United States District Court by President Lyndon Johnson and served there from 1967 to 1977. In 1977, he became a judge for the United States Court of Appeals, Sixth Circuit Court in Detroit, Michigan. He currently holds this position.

Born July 4, 1922 in Detroit, Keith attended West Virginia State College where he received his A.B. in 1943. Following graduation, he served in the army for three years. He returned to school to earn his LL.B. from

Damon Keith

Howard University in 1949. In 1951 Keith took a job as an attorney for the Office of the Friend of the Court in Detroit, and held that position from 1951 to 1955. He received an LL.M. from Wayne State University in 1956.

Keith worked for the Wayne County Board of Supervisors from 1958 to 1963, then went into private practice from 1964 to 1967 before being appointed a judge. He has been active in the Michigan Civil Rights Commission, a trustee in the Medical Corporation of Detroit, a member of the Citizen's Advisory Committee on Equal Educational Opportunity, first vice president emeritus of the Detroit Chapter of the NAACP, a member of the management committee of the Detroit YMCA, a member of the Detroit Council of the Boy Scouts of America, a member of the Detroit Arts Commission, and vice president of the United Negro College Fund of

Detroit. Keith is also a trustee of Interlochen Arts Academy and the Cranbrook School.

Judge Keith has been honored with many accolades, including being named one of one hundred Most Influential Black Americans by *Ebony* magazine, in 1971 and 1977; received a citizen award from Michigan State University and became a Springarn Medalist in 1974. He has received honorary degrees from the University of Michigan, Howard University, Wayne State University, Michigan State University, and New York Law School.

### Wade Hampton McCree, Jr. (1920–1987)
*Professor of Law, Former Solicitor General*

Wade Hampton McCree, Jr. was appointed to the post of solicitor general by President Jimmy Carter, where he served

Wade McCree, Jr.

from 1977 to 1981. McCree had already led a distinguished career as a judge and lawyer by the time he reached that position. He died August 30, 1987.

McCree was born in Des Moines, Iowa on July 3, 1920. He attended Fisk University to earn his A.B. in 1941, and received his LL.B. from Harvard University in 1944. In 1948, he was admitted to the bar in Michigan. He had a private law practice from 1948 to 1952. From 1952 to 1954 he was commissioner of the Michigan Workmen's Compensation Commission. He became a circuit judge for Wayne County, Michigan in 1954 until 1961, then a judge for the United States District Court Eastern District in Michigan from 1961 to 1966. McCree had the honor of being the first African-American judge in the state of Michigan. From 1966 to 1967 he presided over the United States Court of Appeals Sixth Circuit. From 1981 until his death in 1987, he was a member of the faculty at the University of Michigan Law School.

McCree was honored with over thirty honorary degrees in his lifetime, including LL.D. degrees from Howard University, Harvard University, Boston University, Brandeis University and Tuskegee Institute.

### Theodore McMillian (1919– )
*United States Court of Appeals Judge,*
    *Eighth Circuit*

Born January 28, 1919 in St. Louis, Missouri, Theodore McMillian attended Lincoln University, receiving his B.S. degree in 1941 and earned his LL.B. degree from St. Louis University Law School in 1949. He served in the Signal Corps from 1942 to 1946.

McMillian has been a lecturer at St. Louis University Law School as well as a faculty member of Webster College. He became a circuit judge for the state of Missouri and served as an assistant circuit attorney for the City of St. Louis from 1953 to 1956. From 1972 to 1978, he was a judge with the Missouri court of appeals. He became a United States Circuit Court of Appeals circuit judge for the eighth circuit in 1978. He continues to serve that capacity.

Judge McMillian has been a member of the board of trustees for Blue Cross, and a member of the Danforth Foundation Advisory Council. He served on the Presidential Council of St. Louis University, and as a board chairman for Human Development Corporation between 1964 and 1977. He has also been a member of the National Legal Aid Advisory Board.

He has been honored with an Alumni Merit Award from St. Louis University, an Award of Honor from the Lawyers Association in 1970, and a Man of the Year Award in 1970.

Carmel Carrington Marr, 1968

### Carmel Carrington Marr (1921– )
*Former Legal Advisor to the United States Mission to the United Nations*

Carmel Carrington Marr was born in Brooklyn, New York and attended Hunter College for her B.A. (cum Laude) in 1945, continuing education to earn her J.D. from Columbia University Law School in 1948. As an experienced lawyer in international law, she was appointed by President Harry Truman to the position of legal advisor to the United States Mission to the United Nations in 1953. She served that position until 1967, keeping in constant contact with missions from other parts of the world, and serving on a number of key committees of the United Nations General Assembly.

Marr began her career in private practice from 1949 to 1953. After her position as legal advisor to the United Natopms, she became the senior legal officer of the United Nations Secretariat from 1967–68, and then left to become a member of the New York State Human Rights Appeal Board from 1968 to 1971. Between 1971 and 1986 she served as commissioner of the New York State Public Service Commission. She retired from that position, becoming an energy consultant from 1987 until 1990.

Marr was also the chairperson of the advisory council of the Gas Research Institute between 1979 and 1986, the chairperson of the United States Department of Transportation Technology Pipeline Safety Standards Commission from 1979 to 1985, and the chairperson of the National Association of Regulatory Utility Commissioners Gas Commission from 1984 to 1986. She became president of NARUC's Great Lakes Conference of Public Utility Commission, and was on the board of the National Arts Stabilization Fund.

Marr has been honored as an Outstanding Community Service by the Brooklyn Urban League, and has been honored by Gas Research Institute, NYS Public Service Commission, American Red Cross, National Council of Churches, and *Mademoiselle* magazine.

### Thurgood Marshall (1908–1993)

*First African-American United States Supreme Court Associate Justice, Former NAACP Legal Counsel*

Thurgood Marshall's long and illustrious career was capped by his 1967 nomination to the highest court in the land—the United States Supreme Court—where he became the first African-American to hold the coveted position of Supreme Court Justice. At fifty-nine, the son of a sleeping-car porter and the great-grandson of a slave became a sign of progress for many. He was viewed with the utmost respect for all of his years on the bench, retiring June 27, 1991. Marshall died at the age of eighty-four in 1993. He was laid in state in the Great Hall of the Supreme Court of the United States on the same bier where Abraham Lincoln once rested. Over 20,000 mourners paid their last respects to Justice Marshall.

Born in Baltimore, Maryland on July 2, 1908, Marshall earned a B.A. degree from Lincoln University, hoping to become a dentist. He changed his mind, and instead went

Thurgood Marshall

to Howard University's law school, graduating in 1933 at the top of his class. He immediately went into private practice in Baltimore, where he remained for five years.

In 1936, he entered into what was going to be a long and illustrious career with the NAACP, starting as an assistant special counsel, and eventually becoming director-counsel of the Legal Defense and Educational fund, a position he left in 1961. In 1938, as a national special counsel, he handled all cases involving the constitutional rights of African Americans. Then, in 1950, he was named director-counsel of the organization's eleven-year-old Legal Defense and Education Fund. In 1954, as part of an imposing team of lawyers, he played a key role in the now-historic Supreme Court decision on school desegregation, *Brown v. Board of Education*, which overruled the "separate but equal" doctrine in public education. He also figured prominently in such important cases as *Sweatt v. Painter* (requiring the admission of a qualified black student to the law school of Texas University) and *Smith v. Allwright* (establishing the right of Texas blacks to vote in Democratic primaries). Of the thirty-two cases that he argued before the Supreme Court, Marshall won twenty-nine.

Marshall was also known for his lifelong support of rights for women. Constance Baker Motley commented that Marshall hired her for a NAACP counsel position when virtually every other employer had turned her down. He also encouraged her when he argued cases before the Supreme Court, and made certain he pointed out other African-American women role models.

In 1961, Marshall became a federal circuit judge for the second circuit. In 1946, he was awarded the prestigious Springarn Medal for his many achievements. He had over twenty honorary degrees to his credit, including LL.D. honors from the University of Liberia

in 1960, the University of Michigan in 1964, and University of Otago, in Dunedin, New Zealand in 1968. Marshall was also the representative for the White House Conference on Youth and Children, and a member of the National Bar Association. He was once sent by President John F. Kennedy to be a personal representative to the independence ceremonies of Sierra Leone.

**Constance Baker Motley (1921– )**
*First African-American Female Federal Judge*

Born September 14, 1921, in New Haven, Connecticut, Constance Baker Motley became the first African-American woman to become a federal judge. The child of West Indian parents was appointed in 1966 by President Johnson to the United States District Court for Southern New York. The appointment marked the high point of her long career in politics and civic affairs.

While still a law student at Columbia University, Motley began working with the

Constance Baker Motley, 1962.

NAACP Legal Defense and Educational Fund, beginning an association that was to make her famous as a defender of civil rights. In 1946, she was awarded her LL.B., and began to work full-time with the NAACP, eventually becoming an associate counsel. During her twenty-year career with the organization, Motley had argued nine successful NAACP cases before the United States Supreme Court, and had participated in almost every important civil rights case that had passed through the courts since 1954—from Autherine Lucy in Alabama to James Meredith in Mississippi.

In 1964, Motley decided to make a run for the New York State Senate, and was successful. She became the first African-American woman to hold that position. After only a year in the Senate, Motley ran for the position of Manhattan Borough President, emerging the victor by the unanimous final vote of the city council. She thus became the first woman to serve as a city borough president, and, therefore, also the first woman on the Board of Estimate.

Motley was appointed to the United States District Court in 1966. In 1982, she was named chief judge of the federal district court that covers Manhattan, the Bronx, and six counties north of New York City. In 1986 she was named senior judge. She currently holds this position.

She holds many honorary degrees from prestigious universities and was honored with the Elizabeth Blackwell Award from Hobart and William Smith College in 1965.

## George Ruffin (1834–1886)
*First African-American Law School*
*Graduate of Harvard University*

George Ruffin was born in Richmond, Virginia, in 1834, the first son of free African-Americans. In 1853, the family moved to Boston and Ruffin graduated from Chapman Hall school and joined with the Republican party. He moved for a short while to Liverpool, England after becoming disillusioned by the Dred Scott decision. Returning to Boston, Ruffin worked as a barber. But he was busy with other works, writing a review for the *Anglo-African* in 1863, and attending the National Negro Convention in 1864.

As he continued his profession, he also began to read law with a local law firm. He was admitted to the Harvard Law School, which at that time did not require a bachelor's degree, and graduated in 1869. He became the first African American to earn the LL.B. from Harvard, and perhaps the first to graduate from a university law school in the United States He joined the firm of Harvey Jewell, and then won a seat on the Massachusetts legislature in 1869, becoming the second African-American to serve in that body.

Ruffin became known as an exceptional speaker and debater as he focused his attention to the problems in the South. In 1876 and 1877 he won election to the Boston Common Council. He had the honor of presiding over the Negro convention of New Orleans in 1872. His law practice was also prospering at this time.

Frederick Douglass was a friend of Ruffin's, and Ruffin was asked to contribute to the introduction to the 1881 revision of *The Life and Time of Frederick Douglass.* Ruffin was appointed in November of 1883 as judge of a municipal court in Charlestown. He became the first African-American judge in Massachusetts, continuing his work on equality. He supported racial amalgamation, congratulating Douglass on his marriage to Helen Pitts, a white woman, despite the stormy controversy. In 1883 he was also made consul resident for the Dominican Republic in Boston.

Ruffin's other activities included president of the Wendell Phillips Club of Boston, member and president of the Banneker Literary Club of Boston, and superintendent and officer of the Twelfth Baptist Church of Boston.

Ruffin died of Bright's disease on November 20, 1886. Because of his generous giving to charities, he died a relatively poor man.

### Clarence Thomas (1948–  )
*United States Supreme Court Associate Justice*

Thomas was born June 23, 1948, in Pin Point, Georgia. His parents were poor, and when he was young his father left the family. At the age of seven, Thomas's house burned down and his mother could no longer hold the family together. With his brother, Thomas went to live with his maternal grandparents in Savannah. While his grandfather had little education, he was determined that Thomas would go to school and make something of himself. Thomas's early atmosphere was one of strict discipline. He attended various all-black and mixed-race Catholic schools. He intended to enter the priesthood, but left when he encountered a racist seminarian.

Thomas transferred to Holy Cross College and earned his B.A. He was accepted into Yale Law School in 1971, after Yale had adopted an affirmative action program. Thomas was never certain whether he was admitted for his credentials or because of his race. This is perhaps one of the reasons he has remained staunchly against affirmative action. He earned his J.D. in 1974.

After graduating, he became an assistant attorney general for the state of Missouri, working there from 1974 to 1977, then worked briefly at Monsanto Company in St. Louis as an attorney, specializing in pesti-

Clarence Thomas

cide, fungicide and rodenticide law. He also worked as a legal assistant for Senator John C. Danforth.

From 1981 to 1982 he was an assistant secretary for civil rights with the Department of Education, then moved on to chair for the Equal Employment Opportunity Commission, a position he held from until 1990. His tenure there was controversial, as he was not allied with either liberals or civil rights leaders, and he didn't feel comfortable with the white conservative hierarchy. It has been debated whether the status of African-Americans was helped or hurt by the policies he set at the EEOC.

After Robert H. Bork resigned his Circuit Court position because he had been rejected for a place on the United States Supreme Court, Thomas was appointed to the post. He served there until he was made a justice on the Supreme Court in 1991. Since then Thomas has filled his role as a conservative presence on the bench. He has voted with Justice Scalia, the court's most notorious conservative, in fifty-six of ninety cases.

In 1992, Thomas was one of ten people to receive the Horatio Alger Award.

### Robert H. Terrell (1857–1915)
*First Black Federal Judge*

Robert H. Terrell was born in Charlottesville, Virginia, on November 27, 1857. He worked in a dining hall to pay for his classes at Harvard College, where he graduated in 1884, magna cum laude, the first African-American to do so. He went to work in the Washington, DC public schools, and also attended Howard University Law School, earning his LL.B. in 1889 and his LL.M. in 1893. In 1889, he went to work as the chief clerk in the office of the auditor of the United States Treasury Department.

He was involved in the private practice of law from 1892 to 1898, leaving to become a teacher again, and later became principal of the M Street High School. He was also elected to the Board of Trade in the 1890s. In 1901, he was appointed as a justice of the peace in Washington, DC, partially due to the influence of the conservative Booker T. Washington. Like many African-Americans of his day, Terrell was torn between his strongly held civil rights beliefs and Washington's conservative ideas. Again, through Washington's influence, Terrell was nominated by President Taft for the position of judge of the Municipal Court of the District of Columbia in 1910. Despite racial protests in the Senate, Terrell signed the appointment, and held the position until his death on December 20, 1915. His tenure on the court was filled with Republican presidents. Terrell suffered from a stroke in 1911, and a second a year later. His health was also complicated with asthma.

Terrell taught at the Howard University Law School from 1910 to 1925. He was grand master of the Grand United Order of Odd Fellows of the District of Columbia. There was a Robert H. Terrell Law School in Washington, DC from August 12, 1931, to 1950, and an elementary school named after him.

# Bibliography

# Bibliography

## Compiled by Donald Franklin Joyce

*Included in this selected bibliography are titles which were published between 1990 and 1992, reviewed favorably in the reviewing media, and judged to be significant contributions to the study of black history and culture in the United States and in Africa. The titles are arranged under two major divisions: "Africana" and "African Americana." Within these two divisions titles are arranged alphabetically by author under categories indicative of their subject matter. A list of the names, addresses and telephone numbers of all publishers included follows the bibliography.*

## ■ AFRICANA

### Agriculture

Barnett, Tony, and Abbas Abdelkarim. *Sudan: The Gezira Scheme and Agricultural Transition.* London: Frank Cass, 1991.

Freeman, Donald B. *A City of Farmers: Informal Urban Agriculture in the Open Spaces of Nairobi, Kenya.* Montreal: McGill-Queen's University Press, 1991.

Gyllstrom, Bjorn. *State Administrative Rural Change: Agricultural Cooperatives in Rural Kenya.* New York: Routledge, 1991.

Kidane, Mengisteab. *Ethiopia: Failure of Land Reform and Agricultural Crisis.* Westport, CT: Greenwood Press, 1990.

### Apartheid

Burman, Sandra, and Pamela Reynolds, eds. *Growing Up In a Divided Society.* With forewords by Archbishop Desmond Tutu and Robert Coles. Evanston, IL: Northwestern University Press, 1992.

Cohen, Robin, Yvonne G. Muthien, and Abebe Zegeye, eds. *Repression and Resistance: Inside Accounts of Apartheid.* London; New York: Hans Zell Publishers, 1990.

Davis, R. Hunt, ed. *Apartheid Unravels.* Gainesville, FL: University of Florida Presses, 1991.

Dumor, E.K. *Ghana, OAU and Southern Africa: An African Response to Apartheid.* Accra: Ghana University Press, 1991.

Ellis, Stephen. *Comrades Against Apartheid: The ANC and the South African Communist Party in Exile.* London: James Currey/Indiana University Press, 1992.

Ellman, Stephen. *In a Time of Trouble: Law and Liberty in South Africa's State of Emergency.* New York: Oxford University Press, 1992.

Giliomee, Herman, and Laurence Schlemmer. *From Apartheid to Nation-Building.* Capetown, S.A.: Oxford University Press, 1990.

Grundy, Kenneth. *South Africa: Domestic Crisis and Global Challenge.* Boulder, CO: Westview Press, 1991.

Heard, Anthony Hazlett. *The Cape of Storms: A Personal History of the Crisis in South Africa.* Fayetteville: University of Arkansas Press, 1990.

Holland, Heidi. *The Struggle: A History of the African National Congress.* New York: Braziller, 1990.

Hull, Richard W. *American Enterprise in South Africa: Historical Dimensions of Engagement and Disengagement.* New York: New York University Press, 1990.

Human Rights Watch. *The Killings of South Africa: The Role of the Security Forces and the Response of the State.* New York: Human Rights Watch, 1991.

Johns, Sheridan, and R. Hunt Davis, eds. *Mandela, Tambo and the African National Congress: The Struggle Against Apartheid, 1948-1990: A Documentary Survey.* New York: Oxford University Press, 1991.

Kalley, Jacqueline A. *South Africa's Road to Change, 1987–1990.* Westport, CT: Greenwood Press, 1991.

Lemon, Anthony, ed. *Homes Apart: South Africa's Segregated Cities.* Bloomington: Indiana University Press, 1991.

Maasdorp, Gavin, and Alan Whiteside, eds. *Towards a Post-Apartheid Future: Political and Economic Relations in South Africa.* New York: St. Martin's Press, 1992.

Mallaby, Sebastian. *After Apartheid: The Future of South Africa.* New York: Times Books, 1992.

Moss, Rose. *Shouting at the Crocodile: Popo Molefe, Patrick Lekota, and the Freeing of South Africa.* Boston: Beacon Press, 1990. (Dist. by Farrar, Strauss, Giroux)

Price, Robert M. *The Apartheid State in Crisis: Political Transformation in South Africa, 1975–1990.* New York: Oxford University Press, 1991.

Shepherd, George W., ed. *Effective Sanctions on South Africa: The Cutting Edge of Economic Intervention.* Westport, CT: Greenwood Press, 1991.

Sparks, Allister. *The Mind of South Africa.* New York: Knopf, 1990.

Spink, Kathryn. *Black Sash: The Beginning of a Bridge in South Africa.* With a foreword by Archbishop Desmond Tutu. London: Methuen, 1991.

## Art

Courtney-Clarke, Margaret. *African Canvas: The Art of West African Women.* New York: Rizzoli, 1990.

Okediji, Mayo, ed. *Principles of "Traditional" African Art.* Ile Ife: Bard Book, 1992 (Dist. by Avon).

Smithsonian Institution. Libraries. National Museum of African Art Branch. *Catalog of the Library of the National Museum of African Art Branch of the Smithsonian Library.* Boston: G.K. Hall, 1991.

Vogel, Susan. *Africa Explores: Twentieth Century African Art.* New York: The Center for African Art, 1991.

Williams College Museum of Art. *Assuming the Guise: African Masks Considered and Reconsidered.* Williamstown, MA: Williams College Museum of Art, 1991.

Williamson, Sue. *Resistance Art in South Africa.* New York: St. Martin's Press, 1990.

## Autobiography and Biography

Appiah, Joseph. *Joe Appiah: The Autobiography of an African Patriot.* New York: Praeger, 1990.

Bunche, Ralph Johnson. *An African American in South Africa: The Travel Notes of Ralph J. Bunche, 28 September 1937–1 January 1938.* Edited by Roger R. Edgar. Athens: Ohio University Press, 1992.

Gastrow, Shelagh, ed., *Who's Who in South African Politics.* 3rd ed., London: Hans Zell Publishers, 1990.

Glickman, Harvey, ed., *Political Leaders of Contemporary Africa South of the Sahara: A Biographical Dictionary.* Westport, CT: Greenwood Press, 1992.

Harris, Eddy L. *Native Stranger: A Black American's Journey into the Heart of Africa.* New York: Simon & Schuster, 1992.

Isert, Paul Erdmann. *Letters on West Africa: Paul Erdmann Isert's Journey to Guinea and the Caribbean Islands in Columbia (1788).* Translated by Selena Axelrod Winsnes. New York: Oxford University Press, 1992.

Lockot, Hans Wilhelm. *The Mission: The Life, Reign and Character of Haile Selassie I.* New York: St. Martin's Press, 1990.

Mashinini, Emma. *Strikes Have Followed Me All My Life: A South African Autobiography.* New York: Routledge, 1991.

Meer, Fatima. *Higher Than Hope: The Authorized Biography of Nelson Mandela.* New York: Harper & Row, 1990.

Mendelsohn, Richard. *Sammy Marks: the Uncrowned King of the Transvaal.* Athens: Ohio University Press, 1991.

Modisan, Blake. *Blame Me on History.* New York: Simon & Schuster, 1990.

Nkrumah, Kwame. *Kwame Nkrumah: The Conakry Years: His Life and Letters.* Compiled by June Milne. New York: Zed Books, 1991. (Dist. by Humanities Press)

Rake, Alan. *Who's Who in Africa: Leaders for the 1990s.* Metuchen, NJ: Scarecrow, 1992.

Rodney, Walter. *Walter Rodney Speaks: The Making of an African Intellectual.* With introduction by Robert Hill. Foreword by Howard Dodson. Trenton, NJ: Africa World Press, 1990.

Vaillant, Janet G. *Black, French and African: A Life of Leopold Sedar Senghor.* Cambridge: Harvard University Press, 1990.

Vigne, Randolph, ed. *A Gesture of Belonging: Letters from Bessie Head, 1965–1979.* Portsmouth, NH: Heinemann, 1991.

Wiseman, John A. *Political Leaders in Black Africa: A Biographical Dictionary of the Major Politicians Since Independence.* Brookfield, VT: Gower Publishing Co., 1991.

## Economics

Blumenfield, Jesmond. *Economic Interdependence in Southern Africa: From Conflict to Cooperation.* New York: Printer/St. Martin's Press, 1991.

Chole, Eschetu, ed. *Food Crisis in Africa: Policy and Management Issues.* New Delhi: Vikas Publishing House, 1990. (Dist. by Advent House)

Claessen, Henri J.M., and Pieter van de Velde, eds. *Early State Economies.* New Brunswick, NJ: Transaction Publishers, 1991.

Cock, Jacklyn, ed. *Going Green: People, Politics and the Environment in South Africa.* New York: Oxford University Press, 1991.

Crockcroft, Laurence. *Africa's Way: A Journey from the Past.* UK: Tauris, 1990. (Dist. by St. Martin's Press)

Crush, Jonathan, Alan Jeeves, and Donald Yudelman *Africa's Labor Empire: A History of Black Migrancy to the Gold Mines.* Boulder, CO: Westview Press/D. Philip, 1991.

Edington, J.A.S. *Rubber in West Africa.* Anaheim, CA: Collings, 1991.

Henige, David, and T.C. McCaskie, eds. *West African Economic and Social History: Studies in Memory of Marion Johnson.* Madison: African Studies Program, University of Wisconsin, 1990.

Hodd, Michael. *The Economies of Africa: Geography, Population, History, Stability, Performance, Forecasts.* Boston: G. K. Hall, 1991.

Mahjoub, Azzam, ed. *Adjustment or Delinking? The African Experience.* London: Zed Press, 1990. (Dist. by Humanities Press)

Martin, Matthew. *The Crumbling Facade of African Debt Negotiations: No Winners.* New York: St. Martin's Press, 1991.

Mingst, Karen A. *Politics and the African Development Bank.* Lexington: University of Kentucky Press, 1990.

Nyango'oro, Julius, and Timothy Shaw, eds. *Beyond Structural Adjustment in Africa: The Political Economy of Sustainable and Democratic Development.* New York: Praeger, 1992.

Okolo, Julius Emeka, and Stephen Wright, eds. *West African Regional Cooperation and Development.* Boulder, CO: Westview Press, 1990.

Peckett, James, and Hans Singer, eds. *Towards Economic Recovery in Sub-Saharan Africa: Essays in Honor of Robert Gardner.* New York: Routledge, 1991.

Pradervand, Pierre. *Listening to Africa: Developing Africa from the Grassroots.* New York: Praeger, 1990.

Pryor, Frederic L. *The Political Economy of Poverty, Equity and Growth: Malawi and Madagascar.* New York: Oxford University for the World Bank, 1990.

Rau, Bill. *From Feast to Famine: Official Cures and Grassroots Remedies to Africa's Food Crisis.* New York: Zed Books, 1991 (Dist. by Humanities Press).

Riddell, Roger C. *Manufacturing Africa: Performance and Prospects of Seven Countries in Sub-Saharan Africa.* Portsmouth, NH: Heinemann, 1990.

Sarhof, Joseph A. *Hydropower Development in West Africa: A Study in Resource Development.* New York: P. Lang, 1990.

Siddle, David, and Ken Swindell. *Rural Change in Tropical Africa: From Colonies to Nation-States.* Cambridge, MA: Basil Blackwell, 1990.

Stewart, Frances, ed. *Alternative Development Strategies in Sub-Saharan Africa.* New York: St. Martin's Press, 1992.

## Education

King, Kenneth, ed., *Botswana: Education, Culture and Politics.* Edinburgh: University of Edinburgh Press, 1990.

Mungazi, Dickson A. *Colonial Education for Africana: George Starks in Zimbabwe.* Westport, CT: Praeger, 1991.

Njobe, M.W. *Education for Liberation.* Johannesburg: Skotaville, 1990.

Okeem, E.O., ed. *Education in Africa: Search for Realistic Alternatives.* London: Institute for African Alternatives, 1990.

Okunor, Shiame. *Politics, Misunderstandings, Misconceptions: The History of Colonial Universities.* New York: P. Lang, 1991.

## Folklore and Folk Culture

Berry, Jack, comp. and trans. *West African Folktales.* Edited with introduction by Richard Spears. Evanston, IL: Northwestern University Press, 1991.

Gunner, Liz, and Mafika Gwala, eds. and trans., *Musho!: Zulu Popular Praises.* East Lansing: Michigan State University Press, 1991.

McDermott, Gerald. *Zomo the Rabbit: A Trickster Tale from West Africa.* San Diego: Harcourt Brace Jovanovich, 1992.

Mohindra, Kamlesh. *Folk Tales of West Africa.* New Delhi: Sterling Pubs., 1991. (Dist. by APT Books)

Njoku, John E. Eberegbulaum. *The Igbos of Nigeria: Ancient Rites, Changes and Survival.* Lewiston, NY: Edwin Mellen Press, 1990.

Schipper, Mineke. *Source of All Evil: African Proverbs and Sayings on Women.* Chicago: Ivan R. Dee, 1991.

Smith, Alexander McCall. *Children of Wax: African Folk Tales.* New York: Interlink Books, 1991.

Ugorji, Okechukwu K. *The Adventures of Torti: Tales from West Africa.* Trenton, NJ: Africa World Press, 1991.

## General Reference

Asante, Molafi Keto *The Book of African Names.* Trenton, NJ: Africa World Press, 1991.

Blackhurst, Hector, comp. *Africa Bibliography 1989.* Manchester, UK: Manchester University Press, 1991. (Dist. by St. Martin's Press, Inc.)

Fredland, Richard. *A Guide to African International Organizations.* New York: Hans Sell Publishers, 1991.

Morrison, Donald George, Robert Cameron Mitchell, and John Naber Paden. *Black Africa: A Comparative Handbook.* 2nd ed., New York: Paragon House/Irvington, 1990.

Moss, Joyce, and George Wilson. *Peoples of the World: Africans South of the Sahara.* Detroit: Gale Research Inc., 1991.

Sarfoh, Joseph A. *Energy in the Development of West Africa: A Selected Annotated Bibliography.* New York: Greenwood Press, 1991.

Thurston, Anne. *Guide to Archives and Manuscripts Relating to Kenya and East Africa in the United Kingdom.* New York: Hans Zell Publishers, 1991.

Zell, Hans M. *The African Studies Companion: A Resources Guide and Directory.* Providence, NJ: Hans Zell Publishers, 1990.

## Government and Politics

Bowman, Larry W. *Mauritius: Democracy and Development in the Indian Ocean.* Boulder, CO: Westview Press, 1991.

Charlick, Robert B. *Niger: Personal Rule and Survival in the Sahel.* Boulder, CO: Westview Press, 1991.

Clingman, Stephen, ed. *Regions and Repertoires: Topics in South African Politics and Culture.* Johannesburg: Raven Press, 1991. (Dist. by Ohio University Press.)

Clough, Marshall S. *Fighting Two Sides: Kenyan Chiefs and Politicians, 1918–1940.* Niwot, CO: University Press of Colorado, 1990.

Cowell, Alan. *Killing the Wizards: Wars of Power and Freedom from Zaire to South Africa.* New York: Simon & Schuster, 1992.

Deng, Frances M., and I. William Zartman, eds. *Conflict Resolution in Africa.* Washington: Brookings Institution, 1991.

Forrest, Joshua B. *Guinea-Bissau: Power, Conflict and Renewal in a West African Nation.* Boulder, CO: Westview Press, 1992.

Gambari, I.A. *Political and Comparative Dimensions of Regional Integration: The Case of ECOWAS.* New York: The Humanities Press, 1991.

Hanlon, Joseph. *Mozambique: Who Calls the Shots.* Bloomington: Indiana University Press, 1991.

Hansen, Holger Bernt, ed. *Changing Uganda: The Dilemmas of Structural Adjustment and Revolutionary Change.* Athens: Ohio University Press, 1991.

Henze, Paul B. *The Horn of Africa: From War to Peace.* New York: St. Martin's Press, 1991.

Herbst, Jeffrey. *State Politics in Zimbabwe.* Berkeley: University of California, 1990.

Hughes, Arnold, ed. *The Gambia: Studies in Society and Politics.* Birmingham, UK: University of Birmingham, Centre for African Studies, 1991.

Ingham, Kenneth. *Politics in Modern Africa: The Uneven Tribal Dimension.* New York: Routledge, 1990.

Johnson, Willard R. *West African Governments and Volunteer Development Organizations: Priorities for Partnerships.* Lanham, MD: University Press of America, 1990.

Khalid, Mansour. *The Government They Deserve: The Role of the Elite in Sudan's Political Evolution.* New York: Kegan Paul International, 1990.

Kriger, Norma J. *Zimbabwe's Guerrilla War: Peasant Voices.* New York: Cambridge University Press, 1991.

Machobane, L.B.B.J. *Government and Change in Lesotho, 1800–1966: A Study of Political Institutions.* New York: Macmillan, 1990.

Moss, Glenn, and Ingrid Obery, eds. and comps. *South Africa Contemporary Analysis.* London: Hans Zell Publishers, 1990.

Nyang'oro, Julius E., and Timothy M. Shaw, eds. *Beyond Structural Adjustment in Africa: The Political Economy of Sustainable and Democratic Development.* New York: Praeger, 1992.

O'Brien, Donal B. Cruise, John Dunn, and Richard Rathbone, eds. *Contemporary West African States.* New York: Cambridge University Press, 1990.

Ogunsanwo, Alaba. *The Transformation of Nigeria: Scenarios and Metaphors.* Lagos: University of Lagos Press, 1991.

Reyna, Stephen P. *Wars Without End: The Political Economy of a Precolonial African State.* Hanover, NH: University Press of New England, 1990.

Riley, Eileen. *Major Political Events in South Africa, 1948–1990.* New York: Facts on File, 1991.

Schlosser, Dirk Berg, and Rainer Siegler. *Political Stability and Development: A Comparative Analysis of Kenya, Tanzania and Uganda.* Boulder, CO: Lynne Rienner, 1990.

Sklar, Richard L., and C. S. Whitaker. *African Politics and Problems in Development.* Boulder, CO: Lynne Rienner, 1991.

Tareke, Gebru. *Ethiopia, Power and Protest: Peasant Revolts in the Twentieth Century.* New York: Cambridge University Press, 1991.

Vines, Alex. *Renamo: Terrorism in Mozambique.* Bloomington: Indiana University Press, 1991.

Wunsch, James S., and Dele Olowu, eds. *The Failure of the Centralized State: Institutions and Self-Governance in Africa.* Boulder, CO: Westview Press, 1990.

Wylie, Diana. *A Little God: The Twilight of Patriarchy in a Southern Africa Chiefdom.* Hanover, NH: University Press of New England, 1990.

## Health

Baron, Vida C. *African Power: Secrets of the Ancient Ibo Tribe.* San Diego, Barez Publishing Co., 1992.

Falala, Toyin, ed. *The Political Economy of Health in Africa.* Athens: Ohio University for International Studies/Ohio University Press, 1992.

King, Richard D. *African Origin of Biological Psychiatry.* Germantown, TN: Seymour-Smith, Inc., 1990.

Turner, Edith L.B., et al. *Experiencing Ritual: A New Interpretation of African Healing.* Philadelphia: University of Pennsylvania Press, 1992.

Williams, A. Olufemi. *AIDS: An African Perspective.* Boca Rotan, FL: CRC Press, 1992.

Wolff, James, et. al. *Beyond Clinic Walls, Case Studies in Community-Based Distribution.* West Hartford, CT: Kumarian Press, 1990.

## History

Ayittey, George B.N. *Indigenous African Institutions.* Ardsley-on-Hudson, NY: Transnational Publishers, 1991.

Banbera, Tayiru. *A State of Intrigue: The Epic of Bamana Segu According to Tayiru Banbera.* Edited by David Conrad; transcribed and translated with the assistance of Soumaila Diakit'e. Oxford, UK: Oxford University Press, 1990.

Cammack, Diana. *The Rand at War, 1899–1902: The Witwatersrand and the Anglo-Boer War.* Berkeley: University of California Press, 1990.

Collelo, Thomas. *Angola: A Country Study* 3rd ed., Washington, DC: Government Printing Office, 1991.

Collins, Robert O. *Western African History.* New York: W. Wiener, 1990.

Crais, Clifton C. *White Supremacy and Black Resistance in Pre-Industrial South Africa: The Making of the Colonial Order in the Eastern Cape, 1770–1865.* Cambridge, UK: Cambridge University Press, 1992.

Digre, Brian. *Imperialism's New Clothes: The Repartition of Tropical Africa, 1914–1919.* New York: P. Lang, 1990.

Diop, Cheikh Anta. *Civilization or Barbarism: An Authentic Anthropology.* Translated by Yaa-Lengi Meema Ngemi; edited by Harold J. Salemson and Marjolijn de Jager. Brooklyn: Lawrence Hill Books, 1991.

Echenberg, Myron J. *Colonial Conscripts: The Tirailleurs S'en'egalais in French West Africa, 1857–1960.* Portsmouth, NH: Heinemann, 1991.

Friedman, Kajsa Ekholm. *Catastrophe and Creation: The Transformation of an African Culture.* Philadelphia: Hardwood Academic Publishers, 1991.

Gann, L.H., and Pete Duignan. *Hope for Africa.* Stanford, CA: Stanford University Press, 1991.

Gordon, April, ed. *Understanding Contemporary Africa.* Boulder, CO: Lynne Reinner Publishers, 1992.

Hair, P.E.H. *Black Africa in Time Perspective: Four Talks on Wide Historical Themes.* Liverpool, UK: Liverpool University Press, 1990. (Dist. by University of Pennsylvania Press).

Hair, P.E.H. *English Seamen and Traders in Guinea, 1553–1565: The New Evidence of their Wills.* Lewiston, NY: E. Mellen Press, 1992.

Hansen, Emmanuel. *Ghana Under Rawlings: Early Years.* Lagos: Malthouse Press, 1991.

Hassen, Mohammed. *The Oromo of Ethiopia: A History.* New York: Cambridge University Press, 1990.

Hudson, Peter. *Two Rivers: In the Footsteps of Mungo Park.* London: Chapmans Publishers, 1991.

Human Rights Watch. *Evil Days: Thirty Years of War and Famine in Ethiopia.* New York: Human Rights Watch, 1990.

Ki-Zerbo, J., ed. *UNESCO General History of Africa, Vol. 1: Methodology and African Prehistory.* Berkeley: University of California Press, 1990.

Lamphear, John. *The Scattering Time: Turkans Responses to Colonial Time.* New York: Oxford University Press, 1992.

Law, Robin. *The Slave Coast of West Africa, 1550–1750: The Impact of the Atlantic Slave Trade on African Society.* New York: Oxford University Press, 1991.

Manning, Patrick. *Slavery and African Life: Occidental, Oriental and African Slave Trades.* New York: Cambridge University Press, 1990.

Metaferia, Getchew. *The Ethiopian Revolution of 1974 and the Exodus of Ethiopia's Trained Human Resources.* Lewiston, NY: Edwin Mellen Press, 1991.

Mokhtar, G., ed. *UNESCO General History of Africa, Vol. II: Ancient History of Africa.* Berkeley: University of California Press, 1990.

Mooncraft, Paul L. *African Nemesis: War and Revolution in Southern Africa (1945–2010).* Riverside, NJ: Pergamon Press, 1990.

Morton, Fred. *Children of Ham: Freed Slaves and Fugitive Slaves on the Kenya Coast, 1873–1907.* Boulder, CO: Westview, 1990.

Mostert, Noel. *Frontiers: The Epic of South Africa's Creation and the Tragedy of the Xhosa People.* New York: Knopf, 1992.

Munford, Clarence J. *The Black Ordeal of Slavery and Slave Trading in the French West Indies, 1625–1715.* Lewiston, NY: Edwin Mellen Press, 1991.

Nasson, Bill. *Abraham Esau's War: A Black South African War in the Cape, 1899–1902.* New York: Cambridge University Press, 1991.

Obasanjo, Olusegun, and Hans d'Orville, eds. *The Impact of Europe in 1992 on West Africa.* New York: C. Russak, 1990.

Ochieng, William, ed. *Themes in Kenyan History.* Nairobi: Heinmann Kenya, 1990.

Ogot, B.A., ed. *Africa from the Sixteenth to the Eighteenth Century.* Berkeley: University of California Press, 1992.

Remmer, Douglas, ed. *Africa Thirty Years Ago.* Portsmouth, NH: Heinemann, 1991.

Shillington, Kevin. *History of Africa.* New York: St. Martin's Press, 1990.

Solow, Barbara L., ed. *Slavery and the Rise of the Atlantic System.* Cambridge, UK; New York: Cambridge University Press, 1991.

Stauton, Irene, comp. and ed. *Mothers of the Revolution: The War Experiences of Thirty Zimbabwean Women.* Bloomington: Indiana University Press, 1991.

Stedman, Stephen John. *Peacemaking in the Civil War: International Mediation in Zimbabwe, 1974–1980.* Boulder, CO: Lynne Rienner, 1991.

Temperley, Howard. *White Dreams, Black Africa: The Anti-Slavery Expedition to the River Niger, 1841–42.* New Haven: Yale University Press, 1991.

Thompson, Leonard. *A History of South Africa.* New Haven: Yale University Press, 1990.

Wyse, Akintola J.G., and H.C. Bankhole-Bight. *Politics in Colonial Sierra Leone, 1919–1958.* New York:Cambridge University Press, 1991.

Yarak, Larry W. *Asante and the Dutch, 1744–1873.* New York: Oxford University Press, 1990.

Young, John. *They Fell Like Stones: Battles and Casualties of the Zulu War, 1879.* Novato, CA: Presidio Press, 1991.

## International Relations

Kent, John. *The Internationalization of Colonialism: Britain, France and Black Africa.* New York: Oxford University Press, 1992.

Russell, Sharon Stanton, Karen Jacobsen, and William Deane Stanley. *International Migration and Development in Sub-Sahara Africa.* Washington, DC: The World Bank, 1991.

Thompson, Joseph E. *American Policy and African Famine: The Nigeria-Biafra War, 1966–1970.* New York: Greenwood Press, 1970.

Winros, Gareth M. *The Foreign Policy of GDR in Africa.* Cambridge, UK: Cambridge University Press, 1991.

## Language and Literature

Abraham, Cecils ed. *The Tragic Life: Bessie Head and Literature in South Africa.* Trenton, NJ: Africa World Press, 1990.

Achebe, Chinua. *Hopes and Impediments: Selected Essays.* New York: Doubleday, 1990.

Bjornson, Richard. *The African Quest for Freedom and Identity: Cameroonian Writing and the National Experience.* Bloomington: Indiana University Press, 1991.

Dram'e, Kandioura. *The Novel as Transformation Myth: A Study of the Novels of Mongo Beti and Ngugi wa Thiongo.* Syracuse, NY: Syracuse University, 1990.

Dunton, Chris. *Make Man Talk True: Nigerian Drama in English Since 1970.* New York: Hans Zell Publishers, 1992.

Elimimian, Isaac Iraber. *Theme and Style in African Poetry.* Lewiston, NY: E. Mellen, 1991.

February, V.A. *Mind Your Colour: The Coloured Stereotype in South African Literature.* London and New York: Kegan Paul International, 1991. (Dist. by Routledge, Chapman & Hall, Inc.).

Gikandi, Simon. *Reading Chinua Achebe: Language and Ideology in Fiction.* Portsmouth, NH: Heinemann, 1991.

Gunner, Liz, ed., and trans. *Musho!: Zulu Popular Praises.* East Lansing: Michigan State University Press, 1991.

Hale, Thomas A. *Scribe, Griot and Novelist: Narrative Interpreters of the Songhay Empire Followed by the Epic of Askia Mohammed Recounted,* Gainesville, FL: University of Florida Press/Center for African Studies, 1990.

Harrow, Kenneth, ed., *Faces of Islam in African Literature*. Portsmouth, NH: Heinemann, 1991.

Harrow, Kenneth, Jonathan Ngate, and Clarissa Zimra, eds. *Crisscrossing Boundaries in African Literatures, 1986*. Washington, DC: Three Continents Press/African Literature Association, 1991.

Ikonne, Chidi, Emelia Oko, and Peter Onwudinjo, eds. *African Literature and African Historical Experience*. New York: Heinemann, 1991.

Innes, Catherine Lynette. *Chinua Achebe*. New York: Cambridge University Press, 1990.

Innes, Catherine Lynette. *The Devil's Own Mirror: The Irishman and the African Modern Literature*. Washington, DC: Three Continents Press, 1990.

James, Adeola, ed., *In Their Own Voices: African Women Writers Talk*. Portsmouth, NH: Heinemann, 1990.

Jones, Eldred Durosimi, ed. *The Question of Language in African Literature Today: Borrowing and Carrying: A Review*. Trenton, NJ: Africa World Press, 1991.

Julien, Eileen. *African Novels and the Question of Orality*. Bloomington: Indiana University Press, 1992.

Lazarus, Neil. *Resistance in Postcolonial African Fiction*. New Haven, CT: Yale University Press, 1991.

Lindfors, Bernth. *Popular Literature in Africa*. Trenton, NJ: Africa World Press, 1991.

Liyong, Taban Lo. *Another Last Word*. New York: Heinemann, 1990.

Miller, Christopher L. *Theories of Africans: Franco-Phone Literature and Anthropology in Africa*. Chicago: University of Chicago Press, 1990.

Mortimer, Mildred. *Journey Through the French African Novel*. Portsmouth, NH: Heinemann, 1990.

Nethersole, Reingard, ed. *Emerging Literature*. New York: P. Lang, 1990.

Ngara, Emmanuel. *Ideology and Form in African Poetry: Implications for Communication*. Portsmouth, NH: Heinemann, 1990.

Obiechina, Emmanuel N. *Language and Theme: Essays on African Literature*. Washington, DC: Howard University Press, 1990.

Orisawayi, Dele, et. al., eds. *Literature and Black Aesthetics*. New York: Heinemann, 1990.

Owomoyela, Onjekan. *Visions and Revisions: Essays on African Literatures and Criticisms*. New York: P. Lang, 1991.

*Research in African Literatures: Critical Theory and African Literature*. Bloomington: Indiana University Press, 1990.

*Research in African Literature: Dictatorship and Oppression*. Bloomington: Indiana University Press, 1990.

Roscoe, Adrian A., and Hangson Msika. *The Quiet Chameleon: Modern Poetry from Central Africa*. New York: Hans Zell Publishers, 1992.

Scheub, Harold. *The African Storyteller: Stories from African Oral Traditions*. Dubuque, IA: Kendell/Hunt, 1991.

Schipper, Mineke. *Beyond the Boundaries: Text and Context in African Literature*. Chicago: Ivan R. Dee, 1990.

Sicherman, Carol. *Ngugi wa Thiong: A Source Book on Kenyan Literature and Resistance*. New York: Hans Zell Publishers, 1990.

Soyinka, Wole. *Myth, Literature, and the African World*. New York: Cambridge University Press, 1990.

Trump, Martin, ed. *Rendering Things Visible: Essays on South African Literary Culture*. Athens: Ohio University Press, 1991.

Wilentz, Gay Alden. *Binding Cultures: Black Women Writers in Africa and the Diaspora*. Bloomington: Indiana University Press, 1992.

Wylie, Hal, Dennis Brutus, and Juris Silenieks, eds. *African Literature, 1988: New Masks*. Washington, DC: Three Continents Press/The African Literature Association, 1990.

### Law, Law Enforcement, Civil and Human Rights

Ahire, Philip Terdo. *Imperial Policing: The Emergence and Role of the Police in Nigeria, 1860–1960*. Philadelphia: Open University Press, 1991.

Bazille, Susan, ed. *Putting Women on the Agenda*. Johannesburg, S.A.: Raven Press, 1991. (Dist. by Ohio University Press).

Braham, Peter, ed. *Racism and Antiracism: Inequalities in Opportunities and Policies*. Philadelphia: Sage/Open University Press, 1992.

Hansson, Desiree, and Dirk van Zyl Smit, eds. *Toward Justice? Crime and State Control in South Africa*. New York: Oxford University Press, 1990.

Mann, Kristin, ed. *Law in Colonial Africa*. Portsmouth, NH: Heinemann, 1991.

Shepherd, George W., and Mark O.G. Anikpo, eds. *Emerging Human Rights: The African Political Economy Concept*. Westport, CT: Greenwood Press, 1990.

### Media

Faringer, Gunilla L. *Press Freedom in Africa*. Westport, CT: Praeger, 1991.

Harden, Blaine. *Africa: Dispatches from a Fragile Continent*. London: Harper Collins, 1990.

Hawk, Beverly G., ed. *Africa's Media Image*. New York: Praeger, 1992.

Sturges, Paul, and Richard Neill. *The Quiet Struggle: Libraries and Information for Africa*. New York: Mansell, 1990.

### Music

Arom, Simha. *African Polyphony and Polyrhythm: Musical Structure and Methodology*. Translated by Martin Thom and Barbara Tucker. New York: Cambridge University Press, 1991.

Bender, Wolfgang. *Sweet Mother: Modern African Music*. Translated by Wolfgang Freis. Chicago: University of Chicago Press, 1991.

Collins, John. *West African Pop Roots*. Philadelphia: Temple University Press, 1992.

Gray, John. *African Music: A Bibliographic Guide to the Traditional Popular Art and Liturgical Music of Sub-Saharan Africa*. Westport, CT: Greenwood Press, 1991.

Lems-Dworkin, Carol. *African Music: A Pan-African Annotated Bibliography*. New York: Hans Zell Publishers, 1991.

Stewart, Gary. *Breakout: Profiles in African Rhythm*. Chicago: University of Chicago Press, 1992.

Waterman, Christopher Alan. *Juju: A Social History and Ethnography of an African Popular Music*. Chicago: University of Chicago Press, 1990.

### Pan-Africanism

Agyeman, Opoku. *Nkrumah's Ghana and East Africa: Pan-Africanism and African Interstate Relations*. Cranbury, NJ: Fairleigh Dickinson University Press, 1992.

Clarke, John H. *Africans at the Crossroads: Notes for an African World Revolution*. Trenton, NJ: Africa World Press, 1992.

Staniland, Martin. *American Intellectuals and African Nationalists, 1950–1970*. New Haven: Yale University Press, 1991.

### Performing Arts

Diawara, Manthia. *African Cinema: Politics and Culture*. Bloomington: Indiana University Press, 1992.

Erlman, Veit. *African Stars: Studies in Black South African Performance*. Chicago: University of Chicago Press, 1991.

Lee, Jacques K. *Sega: The Mauritius Folk Dance*. London: Nautilus Publishing Co., 1990.

Orkin, Martin. *Drama and the South African State*. Manchester, UK: Manchester University Press, 1991. (Dist. by St. Martin's Press)

## Religion and Philosophy

Dankwa, Nano O., III. *Christianity and African Traditional Beliefs.* Edited by John W. Branch. New York: Power of the World Publishing Co., 1990.

Felder, Cain Hope, ed. *Stony the Road We Trod: African American Biblical Interpretation.* Minneapolis: Fortress Press, 1991.

Gbadegesin, Segun. *African Philosophy: Traditional Yoruba Philosophy and Contemporary African Realities.* New York: Lang, 1991.

Gifford, Paul. *The New Crusaders: Christianity and the New Right in Southern Africa.* London: Pluto, 1991.

Gray, Richard. *Black Christians and White Missionaries.* New Haven: Yale University Press, 1991.

Oldfield, J.R. *Alexander Crummell (1819–1898) and the Creation of an African-American Church in Africa.* Lewiston, NY: Edwin Mellin Press, 1990.

Olupona, Jacob K. *African Traditional Religions in Contemporary Society.* New York: Paragon, 1991.

Oruka, H. O. *Trends in Contemporary African Philosophy.* Nairobi, Kenya: Shirikon Publishers, 1990.

Peek, Philip M., ed. *African Divination Systems: Ways of Knowing.* Bloomington: Indiana University Press, 1991.

Prozesky, Martin, ed. *Christianity Amidst Apartheid.* New York: London, Macmillan, 1990.

Soyinka, Wole. *The Credo of Being and Nothingness.* Ibadan: Spectrum Books, 1990.

Vanderaa, Larry A. *A Survey of Christian Reformed World Missions and Churches in West Africa.* Grand Rapids, MI: Christian Reformed World Missions, 1991.

## Sociology and Psychology

Barnes, James Franklin. *Gabon: Beyond the Colonial Legacy.* Boulder, CO: Westview Press, 1992.

Bell, Leland V. *Mental and Social Disorder in Sub-Saharan Africa: The Case of Sierra Leone, 1787–1990.* Westport, CT: Greenwood Press, 1991.

Carr-Hill, Roy A. *Social Conditions in Sub-Saharan Africa.* London; New York: Macmillan, 1991.

Cleaver, Tessa, and Marion Wallace. *Namibia: Women in War.* Foreword by Glenys Kinnock. Atlantic Highlands, NJ: Zed Books, 1990.

Cobley, Alan Gregord. *Class and Consciousness: The Black Petty Bourgeoisie in South Africa, 1924–1950.* Westport, CT: Greenwood Press, 1990.

Coles, Catherine, and Beverly Mack, eds. *Hausa Women in the Twentieth Century.* Madison: University of Wisconsin Press, 1991.

Gordon, Robert J. *The Bushman Myth: The Making of a Namibian Underclass.* Boulder, CO: Westview Press, 1992.

Hill, Martin J.D., ed. *The Harambee Movement in Kenya: Self-Help Development and Education Among the Kamba of Chat District.* Atlantic Highlands, NJ: Athlone Press, 1991.

Kilbride, Philip Leroy. *Changing Family Life in East Africa: Women and Children at Risk,* Philadelphia: Pennsylvania State University Press, 1990.

Mohammad, Duri, ed., *Social Development in Africa: Strategies, Policies and Programmes After the Lagos Plan.* Providence, NJ: H. Zell Publishers, 1991.

Moran, Mary. *Civilized Women: Gender and Prestige in Southeastern Liberia.* Ithaca, NY: Cornell University Press, 1991.

Nsamenang, A. Bame. *Human Development in Cultural Conflict.* Foreword by Michael Lamb. Newbury Park, CA: Sage Publications, 1992.

Ominde, S. H., ed. *Kenya's Population Growth and Development to the Year 2000.* Columbus: Ohio University Press, 1990.

Reynolds, Pamela. *Dance Cat: Child Labour in the Zambezi Valley.* London: Hans Zell Books, 1991.

Riseman, Paul. *First Find Your Child A Good Mother: The Construction of Self in Two African Communities.* New Brunswick, NJ: Rutgers University Press, 1992.

Robertson, Struan. *The Cold Choice: Pictures of a South African Reality.* Grand Rapids, MI: Wm. B. Erdmans Publishing Co., 1992.

## ■ AFRICAN AMERICANA

### Art, Architecture, and Photography

Bearden, Romare. *Memory and Metaphor: The Art of Romare Bearden, 1940–1987.* New York: Studio Museum of Harlem/Oxford University Press, 1991.

Durham, Michael S. *Powerful Days: The Civil Rights Photography of Charles Moore.* Introduction by Andrew Young. New York: Stewart, Tabori & Chang, 1991.

Easter, Eric, D. Michael Cheers, and Dudley M. Brooks, eds. *Songs of My People: African Americans: A Self-Portrait.* Introduction by Gordon Parks. Essays by Sylvester Monroe. Boston: Little, Brown, 1992.

McElroy, Guy C. *Facing History: The Black Image in American Art, 1710–1940.* Edited by Christopher C. French. Washington, DC: Bedford Arts/Corcoran Gallery, 1990.

Powell, Richard J. *Homecoming: The Art and Life of William H. Johnson.* New York: National Museum of American Art/Rizzoli, 1991.

Rozelle, Robert V., et. al. eds. *Black Art: Ancestral Legacy: The African-American Impulse in African-American Art.* New York: Abrams, 1990.

Thomison, Dennis, comp. *The Black Artist in America: An Index to Reproductions.* Metuchen, NJ: Scarecrow Press, 1991.

Travis, Jack, ed. *African-American Architects in Current Practice.* New York: Princeton Architecture Press, 1991.

### Autobiography and Biography

Baker, Donald P. *Wilder: Hold Fast to Dreams: A Biography of L. Douglas Wilder.* Cabin John, MD: Seven Locks, 1990.

Baldwin, Lewis V. *There Is a Balm in Gilead: The Cultural Roots of Martin Luther King, Jr.* Minneapolis: Fortress Press, 1991.

Bigelow, Barbara Carlisle, ed. *Contemporary Black Biography.* Detroit: Gale Research Inc., 1992.

Bjarkman, Peter C. *Ernie Banks.* Introduction by Jim Murray. New York: Chelsea House, 1992.

Brown, Drew T., III. *You Gotta Believe!: Education + Hard Work − Drugs = The American Dream.* New York: Morrow, 1991.

Brown, James, and Bruce Tucker. *James Brown: The Godfather of Soul.* New York: Thunder's Mouth Press, 1990.

Buchmann-Moller, Frank. *You Just Fight for Your Life: The Story of Lester Young.* New York: Praeger, 1990.

Campbell, James. *Talking at the Gate: A Life of James Baldwin.* New York: Viking, 1991.

Carson, Clayborne. *Malcolm X; The FBI File.* Introduction by Spike Lee. Edited by David Gallen. New York: Carroll & Graf Publishers, Inc., 1991.

Carson, Clayborne, ed. *The Papers of Martin Luther King, Jr.* Berkeley: University of California Press, 1991.

Chilton, John. *The Song of the Hawk: The Life and Recordings of Coleman Hawkins.* New York: St. Martin's Press, 1990.

Davis, Benjamin O., Jr. *Benjamin O. Davis, Jr., American: An Autobiography.* Washington, DC: Smithsonian Institution, 1991.

Davis, Miles, and Quincy Troupe. *Miles, The Autobiography.* New York: Simon & Schuster, 1990.

Deane, Bill. *Bob Gibson.* Introduction by Jim Murray. New York: Chelsea House, 1992.

Dees, Morris. *A Season for Justice: The Life and Times of Civil Rights Lawyer Morris Dees.* New York: Scribner, 1991.

Faser, Jane. *Walter White.* New York: Chelsea House, 1991.

Goldman, Roger, and David Gallen. *Thurgood Marshall: Justice for All.* New York: Carroll & Graf, 1992.

Hamilton, Charles V. *Adam Clayton Powell, Jr.: The Political Biography of an American Dilemma.* New York: Atheneum, 1991.

Hawkins, Walter L. *African American Biographies: Profiles of 558 Current Men and Women.* Jefferson, NC: McFarland & Co., 1992.

Hayes, Bob. *Run, Bullet, Run.* New York: Harper Collins, 1990.

Kranz, Rachel C. *The Biographical Dictionary of Black Americans.* New York: Facts on File, 1992.

Kremer, Gary R. *James Milton Turner and the Promise of America: The Public Life of a Post-Civil War Black Leader.* Columbia: University of Missouri Press, 1991.

Levi, Darrell E. *Michael Manley: The Making of a Leader.* Athens: University of Georgia Press, 1990.

McFeely, William S. *Frederick Douglass.* New York: Norton, 1990.

Mosby, Dewey F., and Darrel Sewell. *Henry Ossawa Tanner.* New York: Rizzoli, 1991.

Naughton, Jim. *Taking to the Air: The Rise of Michael Jordan.* New York: Warner Books, 1992.

Pallister, Janis L. *Aime Cesaire.* New York: Twayne, 1991.

Perry, Bruce. *Malcolm: The Life of a Man Who Changed Black America.* Barrytown, NY: Station Hill, 1991.

Pfieffer, Paula F. *A. Philip Randolph, Pioneer of the Civil Rights Movement.* Baton Rouge: Louisiana State University Press, 1990.

Phelps, J. Alfred. *Chappie: America's First Black Four-Star General.* Novato, CA: Presidio Press, 1991.

Phelps, Shirelle, ed. *Who's Who Among Black Americans, 1993–94.* 7th ed., William C. Matney, Jr., Consulting Editor. Detroit: Gale Research Inc., 1993.

Pickens, William. *Bursting Bonds: Enlarged edition (of) The Heir of Slaves: The Autobiography of a "New Negro".* Edited by William L. Andrews. Bloomington: Indiana University Press, 1991.

Rattenbury, Ken. *Duke Ellington, Jazz Composer.* New Haven: Yale University Press, 1991.

Rivlin, Benjamin, ed. *Ralph Bunche, The Man and His Times.* Foreword by Donald F. Henry. New York: Holmes & Meier, 1990.

Rose, Cynthia. *Living in America: The Soul Saga of James Brown.* London: Serpent Tale, 1990 (Dist. by Consortium Book Sales Distribution.)

Rout, Kathleen. *Eldridge Cleaver.* Boston: Twayne/G.K. Hall, 1991.

Schwartzman, Myron. *Romare Bearden: His Life and Art.* New York: Abrams, 1990.

Shapiro, Leonard. *Big Man on Campus: John Thompson and the Georgetown Hoyas.* New York: Holt, 1991.

Shapiro, Miles. *Bill Russell.* Introductory essay by Coretta Scott King. New York: Chelsea House, 1991.

Sifford, Charlie. *Just Let Me Play: The Story of Charlie Sifford: The First Black PGA Golfer.* Latham, NY: British American Publishers, 1992.

Smith, Eric Ledell. *Bert Williams: A Biography of the Pioneer Black Comedian.* Jefferson, NC: McFarland, 1992.

Stewart, James Brewer. *William Lloyd Garrison and the Challenge of Emancipation.* Arlington Heights, IL: Harlan Davidson, 1992.

Strode, Woody, and Sam Young. *Goal Dust: An Autobiography.* Lantham, MD: Madison Books, 1990.

Tucker, Ken. *Ellington: The Early Years.* Champaign: University of Illinois Press, 1991.

Urban, Wayne J. *Black Scholar: Horace Mann Bond, 1904–1972.* Athens: University of Georgia Press, 1992.

Vache, Warren W. *Crazy Fingers: Claude Hopkins' Life in Jazz.* Washington, DC: Smithsonian Institution Press, 1992.

Watts, Jill. *God, Harlem U.S.A.: The Father Divine Story.* Berkeley: University of California Press, 1992.

Weland, Gerald. *Of Vision and Valor: General O. O. Howard, A Biography.* Canton, OH: Daring Publishing Group, 1991.

Wells, Dicky. *The Night People: The Jazz Life of Dicky Wells.* As told to Stanley Dance. rev. ed., Washington, DC: Smithsonian Institution Press, 1991.

Wills, Maury, and Mike Celizic. *On the Run: The Never Dull and Often Shocking Life of Maury Wills.* New York: Carroll & Graf, 1991.

## Black Nationalism and Pan-Africanism in the United States

Crosby, Edward W., and Linus A. Hoskins, eds. *Africa for the Africans: Selected Speeches of Marcus Mosiah Garvey; Malcolm X; and Nelson Kolihlahla Mandela.* Kent, OH: The Institute for African American Affairs, Department of Pan-African Studies, Kent State University, 1991.

Crummell, Alexander. *Destiny and Race: Selected Writings, 1840–1898.* Edited with introduction by Wilson J. Moses. Amherst: University of Massachusetts Press, 1992.

Drake, St. Clair. *Black Folks Here and There: An Essay in History and Anthropology.* 2 vols. Los Angeles: University of California, Los Angeles, Center for Afro-American Studies, 1991.

Harris, Robert, et. al. *Carlos Cooks: And Black Nationalism from Garvey to Malcolm.* Dover, MA: Majority Press, 1992.

Jacques, Geoffrey. *The African-American Movement Today.* New York: Watts, 1992.

Lemelle, Sid. *Pan-Africanism for Beginners.* New York: Writers and Readers Publishing, Inc., 1992.

Lewis, Rupert, ed. *Garvey: His Work and Impact.* Trenton, NJ: Africa World Press, 1991.

Martin, Tony, comp. and ed. *African Fundamentalism: A Literary and Cultural Anthropology of Garvey's Harlem Renaissance.* Dover, MA: Majority Press, 1991.

Moses, Wilson J. *Alexander Crummell: A Study of Civilization and Discontent.* Amherst: University of Massachusetts Press, 1992.

## Civil Rights, Law, and Civil Protests

*Administrative History of the Civil Rights Division of the Department of Justice During the Johnson Administration.* 2 vols., New York: Garland Publishing Co., 1991.

Aguirre, Adalberto, Jr., and David V. Baker. *Race, Racism and the Death Penalty in the United States.* Barrien Springs, MI: Vande Vere Publishers, 1992.

Belknap, Michal. *Racial Violence and Law Enforcement in the South.* New York: Garland Publishing Co., 1991.

Belknap, Michal. *Securing the Enactment of Civil Rights Legislation, 1965–1968.* New York: Garland Publishing Co., 1991.

Belknap, Michal. *Urban Race Riots.* New York: Garland Publishing Co., 1991.

Belknap, Michal. *Voting Rights.* New York: Garland Publishing Co., 1991.

Belz, Herman. *Equality Transformed: A Quarter-Century of Affirmative Action.* New Brunswick, NJ: Transaction, 1991.

Blumberg, Rhoda L. *Civil Rights, the Freedom Struggle.* rev. ed., Boston: Twayne G.K. Hall, 1991.

Bolick, Clint. *Unfinished Business: A Civil Rights Strategy for America's Third Century.* San Francisco: Research Institute of Public Policy, 1990.

Cagin, Seth, and Philip Dray. *We Are Not Afraid: The Story of Goodman, Schwerner and Chaney and the Civil Rights Campaign for Mississippi.* New York: Bantam Books, 1991.

Capeci, Dominic, and Martha Wilkerson. *Layered Violence: the Detroit Rioters of 1943.* Jackson: University Press of Mississippi, 1991.

Carson, Clayborne, et. al. eds. *"The Eyes on the Prize" Civil Rights Reader: Documents, Speeches, and Firsthand Accounts from the Black Freedom Struggle, 1954–1990.* New York: Viking, 1991.

Cashman, Sean Dennis. *African-Americans and the Quest for Civil Rights, 1900–1990.* New York: New York University Press, 1991.

Cashmore, Ellis, and Eugene McLaughlin, eds. *Out of Order?: Policing Black People.* New York: Routledge, 1991.

Cone, James H. *Martin and Malcolm and America: A Dream or a Nightmare.* New York: Orbis Books, 1991.

Cook, Anthony. *Law, Race and Social Theory.* Boston: New England School of Law, 1991.

Detefsen, Robert R. *Civil Rights Under Reagan.* San Francisco: ICS Press, 1991.

*Encyclopedia of African American Civil Rights: From Emancipation to the Present.* Westport, CT: Greenwood Press, 1992.

Epstein, Richard Allen. *Forbidden Grounds: The Case Against Employment Discrimination Laws.* Cambridge: Harvard University Press, 1992.

Ezorsky, Gertrude. *Racism and Justice: The Case for Affirmative Action.* Ithaca, NY: Cornell University Press, 1991.

Fendrich, James Max. *Ideal Citizens: The Legacy of the Civil Rights Movement.* Albany: State University of New York Press, 1993.

Finkelman, Paul, ed. *African Americans and the Law.* New York: Garland Publishing Co., 1991 (*Race, Law and American History, 1700–1900. The African American Experience.*)

Finkelman, Paul, ed. *African-Americans and the Legal Profession in Historical Perspective.* New York: Garland Publishing Co., 1991 (*Race, Law, and American History, 1700–1990. The African American Experience,* vol. 10).

Finkelman, Paul, ed. *African-Americans and the Right to Vote.* Edited by Paul Finkelman. New York: Garland Publishing Co., 1992. (*Race, Law, and American History, 1700–1900. The African-American Experience,* vol. 6).

Finkelman, Paul, ed. *Lynching, Racial Violence, and Law.* New York: Garland Publishing Co., 1992. (*Race, Law, and American History, 1700–1990. The African-American Experience,* vol. 9.)

Finkelman, Paul, ed. *Race and Criminal Justice.* New York: Garland Publishing Co., 1992. (*Race, Law, and American History, 1700–1900. The American Experience,* vol. 8.)

Finkelman, Paul, ed. *Race and Law Before Emancipation.* New York: Garland Publishing Co., 1992. (*Race, Law and American History, 1700–1990. The African American Experience,* vol. 2.)

Finkelman, Paul, ed. *The Era of Integration and Civil Rights, 1930–1990.* New York: Garland Publishing Co., 1992. (*Race, Law, and American History, 1700–1990. The African American Experience,* vol. 5).

Fiscus, Ronald Jerry. *The Constitutional Logic of Affirmative Action.* Edited by Stephen Wasby. Durham, NC: Duke University Press, 1992.

Fisher, Sethard. *From Margin to Mainstream: The Social Progress of Black Americans.* 2nd ed., Savage, MD: Rowman & Littlefield, 1992.

Goings, Kenneth W. *The NAACP Comes of Age: The Defeat of Judge Parker*. Bloomington: Indiana University Press, 1990.

Goldwin, Robert A. *Why Blacks, Women and Jews Are Not Mentioned in the Constitution, and Other Unorthodox Views*. Washington, DC: American Enterprise Institute, 1990.

Graetz, Robert S. *Montgomery, A White Preachers Memoir*. Minneapolis: Fortress Press, 1991.

Grafman, Bernard, ed. *Controversies in Minority Voting: The Voting Rights Act in Perspective*. Washington, DC: Brookings Institute, 1992.

Graham, Hugh Davis. *The Civil Rights Era: Race, Gender and National Policy, 1960–1972*. New York: Oxford University Press, 1990.

Hampton, Henry, and Steve Fayer, comps. *Voices of Freedom: An Oral History of the Civil Rights Movement from the 1950s Through the 1980s*. New York: Bantam Books, 1990.

Harding, Vincent. *Hope and History: Why We Must Share the Story of the Movement*. Maryknoll, NY: Orbis Books, 1990.

Harris, Jacqueline. *A History of the NAACP*. New York: Watts, 1992.

Jackson, James E. *The Bold Bad '60s: Pushing the Point for Equality Down South and Out Yonder*. New York: International Publishers, 1992.

James, Hunter. *They Didn't Put That on the Huntley-Brinkley Report!: A Vagabound Reporter Encounters the New South*. Athens: University of Georgia, 1993.

*Justice Department Briefs in Crucial Civil Rights Cases*. 2 vols., New York: Garland, 1991.

Kapur, Sudarshan. *Raising Up a Prophet: The African-American Encounter with Gandhi*. Boston: Beacon, 1992.

King, Richard. *Civil Rights and the Idea of Freedom*. New York: Oxford University Press, 1992.

Kull, Andrew. *The Color-Blind Constitution*. Cambridge: Harvard University Press, 1992.

Levy, Peter B., ed. *Dictionary History of the Modern Civil Rights Movement*. New York: Greenwood Press, 1992.

Levy, Peter B., ed. *Let Freedom Ring: A Documentary History of the Modern Civil Rights Movement*. New York: Praeger, 1992.

Lyon, Danny. *Memories of the Civil Rights Movement*. Text and photographs by Danny Lyon; foreword by Julian Bond. Chapel Hill: University of North Carolina Press, 1992.

Meier, August, et. al. eds. *Black Protest in the Sixties*. New York: M. Wiener, 1991.

Meier, August. *A White Scholar and the Black Community, 1945–1965: Essays and Reflections*. Afterword by John H. Bracey, Jr. Amherst: University of Massachusetts Press, 1992.

Mills, Nicolaus. *Like a Holy Crusade: Mississippi, 1964—The Turning of the Civil Rights Movement in America*. Chicago: I.R. Dee, 1992.

Nieli, Russell, ed. *Racial Preference and Racial Justice: The New Affirmative Action Controversy*. Washington, DC: Ethics and Public Policy Center, 1991 (Dist. by National Book Network.)

Nieman, Donald G. *Promises to Keep: African Americans and the Constitutional Order, 1776 to the Present*. New York: Oxford University Press, 1991.

O'Reilly, Kenneth. *Racial Matters: The FBI's Secret File on Black America, 1960–1972*. New York: Free Press, 1991.

Powledge, Fred. *Free At Last?: The Civil Rights Movement and the People Who Made It*. Boston: Little, Brown, 1990.

Reed, Merl E. *Seedtime for the Modern Civil Rights Movement: The President's Committee on Fair Employment Practice, 1941–1946*. Baton Rouge: Louisiana State University Press, 1991.

Robinson, Amelia Boynton. *Bridge Across Jordan*. rev. ed., Washington, DC: Schiller Institute, 1991.

Robinson, Armistead L., and Patricia Sullivan, eds. *New Directions in Civil Rights Studies*.

Charlottesville: University Press of Virginia, 1991.

Sigelman, Lee, and Susan Welch. *Black Americans' Views of Racial Inequality: The Dream Deferred.* New York: Cambridge University Press, 1991.

Sikora, Frank. *Until Justice Rolls Down: The Birmingham Church Bombing Case.* Tuscaloosa: University of Alabama Press, 1991.

Stern, Mark. *Calculating Visions: Kennedy, Johnson and Civil Rights.* New Brunswick, NJ: Rutgers University Press, 1992.

Swift, Jeanne, ed. *Dream and Reality: The Modern Black Struggle for Freedom and Equality.* New York: Greenwood Press, 1991.

Thomas, Clarence. *Clarence Thomas: Confronting the Future: Selections from the Senate Confirmation Hearing and Prior Speeches.* Washington, DC: Regnery Gateway, 1992.

Urofsky, Melvin I. *A Conflict of Rights: The Supreme Court and Affirmative Action.* New York: Scribners, 1991.

Watson, Denton L. *Lion in the Lobby: Clarence Mitchell, Jr.'s Struggle for the Passage of Civil Rights Laws.* New York: Morrow, 1990.

Wright, Roberta Hughes. *The Birth of the Montgomery Bus Boycott.* Southfield, MI: Charro Book Co., 1991.

## Economics, Entrepreneurship, and Labor

Broadnax, Derek. *The Black Entrepreneurs Guide to Million Dollar Business Opportunities.* Austin, TX: Black Entrepreneurs Press, 1990.

Broadnax, Derek. *The Black Entrepreneurs Guide to Money Sources: How to Get Your Share.* Austin, TX: Black Entrepreneurs Press, 1990.

Butler, John Sibley. *Entrepreneurship and Self-Help Among Black Americans: A Reconsideration of Race and Economics.* Albany: State University of New York Press, 1991.

Dewart, Janet, ed. *The State of Black America, 1991.* New York: National Urban League, 1991.

Duncan, Mike. *Reach Your Goals In Spite of the Old Boy Network: A Guide for African American Employees.* Edgewood, MD: M.E. Duncan and Co., 1990.

Grant, Nancy L. *TVA and Black Americans: Planning for the Status Quo.* Philadelphia: Temple University Press, 1990.

Green, Shelley, and Paul Pryde. *Black Entrepreneurship in America.* Brunswick, NJ: Transactions Publishers, 1990.

Greenberg, Jonathan D. *Staking a Claim: Jake Simmons and the Making of an African-American Oil Dynasty.* New York: Atheneum, 1991.

Reed, Wornie, ed. *Social, Political and Economic Issues in Black America.* Amherst: University of Massachusetts, William Monroe Trotter Institute, 1990.

Rosen, George H. *Black Money.* Chelsea, MI: Scarborough House, 1990.

## Education

Allen, Walter R., Edgar Epps, and Nesha Z. Haniff, eds. *College in Black and White: African American Students in Predominately White and Historically Black Public Universities.* Albany: State University of New York Press, 1991.

Altbach, Philip G., and Kofi Lomotey, eds. *The Racial Crisis in American Higher Education.* Albany: State University of New York Press, 1991.

Bowman, J. Wilson. *America's Black Colleges.* South Pasadena, CA: Sandcastle Publishing Co., 1992.

Fife, Brian L. *Desegregation in American Schools: Comparative Intervention Strategies.* New York: Praeger, 1992.

Finkelman, Paul, ed. *The Struggle for Equal Education.* New York: Garland Publishing Co., 1992. (*Race, Law, and American History, 1700–1990. African-American Experience,* vol. 7.)

Formisano, Ronald P. *Boston Against Busing: Race, Class, and Ethnicity in the 1960s and 1970s.* Chapel Hill: University of North Carolina Press, 1991.

Harmon, Marylen E. *The Infusion of African and African American Studies into the Curriculum.* Roanoke, VA: Absolute Writings Ltd., 1991.

Irvine, Jacqueline Jordan. *Black Students and School Failure: Policies, Practices, and Prescriptions.* Westport, CT: Greenwood Press, 1990.

Lomotey, Kofi, ed. *Going to School: The African-American Experience.* Albany: State University of New York Press, 1990.

Lusane, Clarence. *The Struggle for Equal Education.* New York: F. Watts, 1992.

Margo, Robert A. *Race and Schooling in the South, 1880–1950.* Chicago: University of Chicago Press, 1991.

National Afro-American Museum and Cultural Center. *From Victory to Freedom: The African American Experience: Curriculum Guide, Secondary School Course of Study.* Wilberforce, OH: National Afro-American Museum and Cultural Center, 1991.

Neufeldt, Harvey G., and Leo McGee, eds. *Education of the African American Adult: An Historical Overview.* Westport, CT: Greenwood, 1990.

Pratt, Robert A. *The Color of Their Skin: Education and Race in Richmond, Virginia, 1954–89.* Charlottesville: University of Virginia Press, 1992.

Sachar, Emily. *Shut Up and Let the Lady Teach: A Teacher's Year in a Public School.* New York: Poseidon Press, 1991.

Thompkins, Susie Powers. *Cotton-Patch Schoolhouse.* Tuscaloosa: University of Alabama Press, 1992.

Willie, Charles V., Antoine M. Garibaldi, and Wornie L. Reed, eds. *The Education of African Americans.* Westport, CT: Auburn House/Greenwood Publishing Group, 1991.

## Folklore and Folk Culture

Abrahams, Roger D. *Singing the Master: The Emergence of African American Culture in the Plantation South.* New York: Pantheon Books, 1992.

Hall, Gwendolyn Midlo. *Africans in Colonial Louisiana: The Development of Afro-Creole Culture.* Baton Rouge: Louisiana State University Press, 1992.

Hazzard-Gordon, Katrina. *Jookin': The Rise of Social Dance Formation in African-American Culture.* Philadelphia: Temple University Press, 1990.

Hill, James L., ed. *Studies in African and African American Culture.* New York: P. Lang, 1990.

Holloway, Joseph E., ed. *Africanisms in American Culture.* Bloomington: Indiana University Press, 1990.

Njeri, Itabari. *Every Good-Bye Ain't Gone: Family Portraits and Personal Escapades.* New York: Times Books, 1990.

Roberts, John W. *From Trickster to Badman: The Black Folk Hero in Slavery and Freedom.* Philadelphia: University of Pennsylvania Press, 1990.

Spalding, Henry D., comp. and ed. *Encyclopedia of Black Folklore and Humor.* Introduction by J. Mason Brewer. Middle Village, NY: Jonathan David Publishers, 1990.

Sundquist, Eric J. *The Hammers of Creation: Folk Culture in Modern African-American Culture.* Athens: University of Georgia Press, 1992.

Twining, Mary A., and Keith E. Baird, eds. *Sea Island Roots: African Presence in Carolina and Georgia.* Trenton, NJ: Africa World Press, 1991.

## General Reference

Asante, Molefi K. *The Historical and Cultural Atlas of African Americans.* New York: Macmillan, 1991.

*The Black Resource Guide, 1990–1991 Edition.* Washington, DC: Black Resource Guide, Inc., 1991.

Bogle, Donald, ed. *Black Arts Annual, 1988/89.* New York: Garland, 1990.

Donovan, Richard X. *Black Scientists of America.* Portland, OR: National Book Co., 1990.

Fitzpatrick, Sandra, and Maria Godwin. *The Guide to Black Washington: Places and Events of Historical and Cultural Significance in the Nation's Capital.* New York: Hippocrene, 1990.

Furtaw, Julia C., ed. *Black American Information Directory.* 2nd ed., Detroit: Gale Research Inc., 1992.

Hancock, Sybil. *Famous Firsts of Black Americans.* Gretna, LA: Pelican Publishing Co., 1991.

Horton, Carrell Peterson, and Jessie Carney Smith, comps. and eds. *Statistical Record of Black America.* 2nd ed., Detroit: Gale Research Inc., 1991.

Smithsonian Institution. *African and African American Resources at the Smithsonian.* Washington, DC: Smithsonian Institution, 1991.

Southern, Eileen, and Josephine Wright, comps. *African American Traditions in Song, Sermon, Tale, and Dance, 1600s–1920: An Annotated Bibliography of Literature, Collections, and Artworks.* Westport, CT: Greenwood Press, 1990.

Thum, Marcella. *Hippocrene U.S.A. Guide to Black America: A Directory of Historic and Cultural Sites Relating to Black America.* New York: Hippocrene Books, 1992.

## Health

Bailey, A. Peter. *The Harlem Hospital Story: 100 Years of Struggle Against Illness.* Richmond, VA: Native Sun Publishers, 1991.

Bailey, Eric J. *Urban African American Health Care.* Lantham, MD: University Press of America, 1991.

*The Black Women's Health Book: Speaking for Ourselves.* Seattle: Seal Press, 1990.

Duh, Samuel V. *Blacks and AIDS: Genetic or Environmental Causes.* Newbury Park, CA: Sage Publications, 1991.

*Health of Black Americans from Post Reconstruction to Integration, 1871–1960: An Annotated Bibliography of Contemporary Sources.* Westport, CT: Greenwood Press, 1990.

McBride, David. *From TB to AIDS: Epidemics Among Urban Blacks Since 1900.* Albany: State University of New York Press, 1991.

*National Black Health Leadership Directory, 1990–91.* Washington, DC: NRW Associates, 1991.

## History

*The African American Experience: A History.* Sharon Harley, Stephen Middleton, and Charlotte Stokes, Consultants. Englewood Cliffs, NJ: Prentice-Hall, 1992.

America, Richard, ed. *The Wealth of Races: The Present Value of Benefits from Past Injustices.* Westport, CT: Greenwood Press, 1991.

Anderson, Eric, and Alfred Moss, Jr., eds. *The Facts of Reconstruction: Essays in Honor of John Hope Franklin.* Baton Rouge: Louisiana State University Press, 1991.

Andrews, George Reid. *Blacks and Whites in Sao Paulo Brazil, 1888–1988.* Madison: University of Wisconsin Press, 1992.

Aptheker, Herbert. *Anti-Racism in U.S. History: The First Hundred Years.* New York: Greenwood Press, 1992.

Aptheker, Herbert. *To Be Free: Pioneering Studies in Afro-American History.* Introduction by John Hope Franklin. New York: Citadel Press, 1991.

Bailey, Richard. *Neither Carpetbaggers Nor Scalawags: Black Officeholders During the Re-*

*construction in Alabama.* Montgomery, AL: R. Bailey Publishers, 1991.

Beeth, Howard, and Cary E. Wintz, eds. *Black Dixie: Afro-Texan History and Culture in Houston.* College Station, TX: Texas A&M University Press, 1992.

Berlin, Irs, and Philip D. Morgan, eds. *The Slaves' Economy: Independent Production by Slaves in the Americas.* London: F. Cass, 1991.

Berlin, Irs, et. al., eds. *Slaves No More: Three Essays on Emancipation and the Civil War.* New York: Cambridge University Press, 1992.

*The Black Abolitionist Papers, Vol. 3: The United States, 1830–1846.* Chapel Hill: University of North Carolina Press, 1991.

Boney, F.N., Richard L. Hume, and Rafia Zafar. *God Made Man, Man Made the Slave.* Macon, GA: Mercer University Press, 1990.

Bryan, Patrick. *The Jamaican People, 1880–1902: Race and Social Control.* New York: Macmillan, 1991.

Bush, Barbara. *Slave Women in Caribbean Society, 1650–1838.* Bloomington: University of Indiana Press, 1990.

Campbell, Randolph B. *An Empire for Slavery: The Peculiar Institution in Texas, 1821–1865.* Baton Rouge: Louisiana State University Press, 1991.

Cantor, George. *Historic Landmarks of Black America.* Detroit: Gale Research Inc., 1991.

Cohen, William. *At Freedom Edge: Black Mobility at the Southern Quest for Racial Control, 1861–1915.* Baton Rouge: Louisiana State University Press, 1991.

Cornelius, Janet Duitsman. *"When I Can Read My Title Clear": Literacy, Slavery, and Religion in the Antebellum South.* Columbia: University of South Carolina Press, 1991.

Counter, S. Allen. *North Pole Legacy: Black, White and Eskimo.* Amherst: University of Massachusetts Press, 1991.

Crouch, Berry A. *The Freedmen's Bureau and Black Texans.* Austin: University of Texas Press, 1992.

Davis, Lenwood G. *A Travel Guide to Black Historical Sites and Landmarks in North Carolina.* Winston-Salem, NC: Bandit Books, 1991.

*Deromantizing Black History: Critical Essays and Reappraisals.* Knoxville: University of Tennessee Press, 1991.

Dillon, Merton L. *Slavery Attacked: Southern Slaves and Their Allies, 1619–1865.* Baton Rouge: Louisiana State University Press, 1990.

Downey, Dennis B., and Raymond M. Hyser. *No Crooked Death: Coatsville, Pennsylvania, and the Lynching of Zachariah Walker.* Champaign: University of Illinois Press, 1991.

Drago, Edmund L., ed. *Broke by the War: Letters of a Slave Trader.* Columbia: University of South Carolina Press, 1991.

Dykstra, Robert. *Bright Radical Star: Black Freedom and White Supremacy on the Hawkeye Frontier.* Cambridge: Harvard University Press, 1993.

Fede, Andrew. *People Without Rights: An Interpretation of the Fundamentals of the Law of Slavery in the U.S. South.* New York: Garland Publishing Co., 1992.

Ferguson, Leland G. *Uncommon Ground: Archaeology and Early African America, 1650–1800.* Washington, DC: Smithsonian Institution Press, 1992.

Finkelman, Paul, ed. *The Age of Jim Crow: Segregation from the End of Reconstruction to the Great Depression.* New York: Garland Publishing Co., 1992. (*Race, Law, and American History, 1760–1990. The African American Experience*, vol. 4.)

Finkelman, Paul, ed. *Emancipation and Reconstruction.* New York: Garland Publishing Co., 1992. (*Race, Law and American History, 1700–1990. The African American Experience*, vol. 3.)

Franklin, Vincent P. *Black Self-Determinism: A Cultural History of African-American Resistance.* 2nd ed., Brooklyn, NY: Lawrence Hill Books, 1992.

Frey, Sylvia. *Water from the Rock: Black Resistance in a Revolutionary Age.* Princeton, NJ: Princeton University Press, 1992.

Gatewood, Willard B. *Aristocrats of Color: The Black Elite, 1880–1920.* Bloomington: Indiana University Press, 1990.

Genovese, Eugene D. *The Slaveholders' Dilemma: Freedom and Progress in Southern Conservative Thought, 1820–1860.* Columbia: University of South Carolina Press, 1992.

Greenberg, Cheryl Lynn. *"Or Does It Explode?": Black Harlem in the Great Depression.* New York: Oxford University Press, 1991.

Hamilton, Kenneth Marvin. *Black Towns and Profit, Promotion and Development in the Trans-Appalachian West, 1877–1915.* Champaign: University of Illinois Press, 1991.

Harley, Sharon. *The African American Experience: A History.* Englewood Cliffs, NJ: Globe, 1992.

Harris, Richard S. *Politics & Prejudice: A History of Chester, Pennsylvania Negroes.* Apache Junction, AZ: Relmo Pubs., 1991.

Harrison, Alfredteen, ed. *Black Exodus: The Great Migration from the American South.* Oxford: University Press of Mississippi, 1991.

Henry, Paget, and Paul Buhle, eds. *C.L.R. James' Caribbean.* Durham, NC: Duke University Press, 1992.

Hornsby, Jr., Alton. *Chronology of African-American History: Significant Events and People from 1619 to the Present.* Detroit: Gale Research Inc., 1991.

Horton, James Oliver. *Free People of Color: Inside the African American Community.* Washington, DC: Smithsonian Institution, 1993.

Inikoroi, Joseph E., and Stanley L. Engerman, eds. *The Atlantic Slave Trade: Effects on Economic Societies, and Peoples in Africa, the Americas and Europe.* Durham, NC: Duke University Press, 1992.

Jackson, Terrance. *Putting It All Together: World Conquest, Global Genocide and African Liberation.* Bronx, NY: AKASA, 1991.

Jones, Howard. *The Red Diary: A Chronological History of Black Americans in Houston and Some Neighboring Harris County Communities-122 Years Later.* Austin, TX: Nortex Press, 1992.

Jones, Norrece T. *Born a Child of Freedom, Yet A Slave: Mechanisms of Control and Strategies of Resistance in Antebellum South Carolina.* Middletown, CT: Wesleyan University Press, 1990.

Jordan, Winthrop. *Tumult and Silence at Second Creek: An Inquiry into a Civil War Slave Conspiracy.* Baton Rouge: Louisiana State University Press, 1993.

Katz, William Loren. *Breaking the Chains: African American Slave Resistance.* New York: Atheneum, 1990.

Lane, Roger. *William Dorsey's Philadelphia and Ours: On the Origins and Future Prospects of Urban Black America.* New York: Oxford University Press, 1991.

Lesko, Kathleen M., ed. *Black Georgetown Remembered: A History of Its Black Community from the Founding of "The Town of George" in 1751 to the Present Day.* Washington, DC: Georgetown University Press, 1991.

Malone, Ann Patton. *Sweet Chariot: Slave Family and Household Structure in Nineteenth Century Louisiana.* Chapel Hill: University of North Carolina Press, 1992.

McLaurin, Melton A. *Celia, a Slave.* Athens: University of Georgia Press, 1991.

McMillen, Sally Gregory. *Southern Women: Black and White in the Old South.* Arlington Heights, IL: Harlan Davidson, 1992.

Meillassaux, Claude. *The Anthropology of Slavery: The Womb of Iron and Gold.* Translated by

Alide Dasnois. Chicago: University of Chicago Press, 1991.

Meyer, Mary K. *Free Blacks in Hartford, Somerset, and Talbort Counties, Maryland.* Mt. Airy, MD: Pipe Creek Publications, 1991.

Middleton, Stephen. *The Black Laws in the Old Northwest: A Documentary History.* New York: Greenwood Press, 1992.

Munford, Clarence J. *The Black Ordeal of Slavery and Slave Trading in the French West Indies, 1625–1715.* Lewiston, ME: Edwin Mellen, 1991.

Nash, Gary B. *Freedom by Degrees: Emancipation in Pennsylvania and Its Aftermath.* New York: Oxford University Press, 1991.

Nash, Gary B. *Race and Revolution.* Madison, WI: Madison House, 1990.

Oakes, James. *Slavery and Freedom: An Interpretation of the Old South.* New York: Knopf, 1990.

Pearson, Edward. *Slave Work and Culture in Town and Country.* Williamsburg, VA: Institute of Early American History and Culture, 1991.

Perdue, Charles L., ed. *Weevils in the Wheat: Interviews with Virginia Ex-Slaves.* Charlottesville: University Press of Virginia, 1992.

Reidy, Joseph. *From Slavery to Agrarian Capitalism in the Cotton Plantation South: Central Georgia, 1800–1880.* Chapel Hill: University of North Carolina Press, 1992.

Richardson, Bonham C. *The Caribbean in the Wide World, 1492–1922.* New York: Cambridge University Press, 1992.

Richter, William L. *Overreached on All Sides: The Freedmen's Bureau Administrators in Texas, 1865–1868.* College Station: Texas A&M University Press, 1991.

Schwartz, Stuart B. *Slaves, Peasants, and Rebels: Reconsidering Brazilian Slavery.* Champaign: University of Illinois Press, 1992.

Schweninger, Loren. *Black Property Owners in the South, 1790–1915.* Champaign: University of Illinois Press, 1990.

Slaughter, Thomas P. *Bloody Dawn: The Christiana Riot and Racial Violence in Antebellum North.* New York: Oxford University Press, 1991.

Solow, Barbara L., ed. *Slavery and the Rise of the Atlantic System.* New York: Cambridge University Press/W.E.B. DuBois Institute for Afro-American Research, 1991.

Stanisland, Martin. *American Intellectuals and African Nationalists; 1955–1970.* New Haven, CT: Yale University Press, 1991.

Stevenson, Lisbeth Gant. *African-American History: Heroes in Hardship.* Cambridge, MA: Cambridgeport Press, 1992.

Stone, Albert E. *The Return of Nat Turner: History, Literature, and Cultural Politics in Sixties America.* Athens: University of Georgia, 1992.

Stone, Frank Andrews. *African American Connecticut: African Origins, New England Roots.* Storrs, CT: Isaac N. Thut World Education Center, 1991.

Terry, Ted. *American Black History: Reference Manual.* Tulsa, OK: Myles Publishing Co., 1991.

Thomas, Richard W. *Life for Us: Building Black Community in Detroit, 1915–1945.* Bloomington: Indiana University Press, 1992.

Thornton, John. *Africa and Africans in the Making of the Atlantic World, 1400–1680.* New York: Cambridge University Press, 1992.

White, Shane. *Somewhat More Independent: The End of Slavery in New York City 1770–1870.* Athens: University of Georgia Press, 1991.

Williams, Jacob C. *Lillie: Black Life in Martins Ferry, Ohio During the 1920s and 1930s.* Ann Arbor, MI: Braun-Brumfield, 1991.

Williams, Lee E. *Post-War Riots in America, 1919 and 1946: How the Pressures of War Exacerbated American Urban Tensions to the Breaking Points.* Lewiston, NY: E. Mellen, 1991.

## Language, Literature, and Drama

Babb, Valerie Melissa. *Ernest Gaines.* Boston: Twayne/G.K. Hall, 1991.

Bailey, Guy, Natalie Maynor, and Patricia Cukor-Avila, eds. *The Emergence of Black English: Text and Commentary*. Philadelphia: J. Benjamins Publishing Co., 1991.

Baker, Houston A., and Patricia Redmond, eds. *Afro-American Literary Study in the 1990s*. Chicago: University of Chicago Press, 1990.

Baraka, Imamu Amiri. *The Leroi Jones/Amiri Baraka Reader*. Edited William J. Harris. New York: Thunder's Mouth Press, 1991.

Barksdale, Richard K. *Praisesong of Survival: Lectures and Essays, 1957–1989*. Introduction by R. Baxter Miller. Urbana: University of Illinois, 1992.

Bassett, John E. *Harlem in Review: Critical Reactions to Black American Writers, 1917–1939*. Selinsgrove, PA: Susquehanna University Press, 1992.

Benitoz-Rojo, Antonio. *The Repeating Island: The Caribbean and the Postmodern Perspective*. Durham, NC: Duke University Press, 1992.

Blackshire-Belay, Carol Aisha, ed. *Language and Literature in the African American Imagination*. Westport, CT: Greenwood Press, 1992.

Bloom, Harold, ed. *Bigger Thomas*. New York: Chelsea House, 1990.

Brown, Stewart, ed. *The Art of Derek Walcott*. UK: Seren Books, 1992. (Dist. by Dufour Editions, Inc.)

Busby, Mark. *Ralph Ellison*. Boston: Twayne/G.K. Hall, 1991.

Butler, Robert. *Native Son: The Emergence of a New Black Hero*. Boston: Twayne/G.K. Hall, 1991.

Cartey, Wilfred. *Whispers from the Caribbean: I Going Away, I Going Home*. Los Angeles: University of California, Los Angeles, Center for Afro-American Studies, 1991.

DeJongh, James. *Vicious Modernism: Black Harlem and the Literary Imagination*. New York: Cambridge University Press, 1990.

Dieke, Ikenna. *The Primordial Image: African, Afro-American, and Caribbean Mythopoetic Text*. New York: P. Lang, 1991.

Draper, James P., ed. *Black Literature Criticism: Excerpts from Criticism of the Most Significant Works of Black Authors over the Past 200 Years*. 3 vols., Detroit: Gale Research Inc., 1992.

Edwards, Walter F., and Donald Winford, eds. *Verb Phrase Patterns in Black English and Creole*. Detroit: Wayne State University Press, 1991.

Fabre, Michel. *Richard Wright: Books and Writers*. Oxford: University Press of Mississippi, 1990.

Gates, Henry Louis, Jr. *Loose Canons: Notes on the Culture Wars*. New York: Oxford University Press, 1992.

Hamalian, Leo, and James V. Hatch, eds. *The Roots of African American Drama: An Anthology of Early Plays, 1858–1938*. Detroit: Wayne State University Press, 1991.

Hord, Fred L. *Reconstructing Memory: Black Literary Criticism*. Chicago: Third World Press, 1991.

Johnson, Dianne. *Telling Tales: The Pedagogy and Power of African American Literature for Youth*. New York: Greenwood Press, 1990.

Jones, Gayl. *Liberating Voices: Oral Tradition in African American Literature*. Cambridge, MA: Harvard University Press, 1991.

Joseph, Margaret Paul. *Caliban in Exile: The Outsider in Caribbean Fiction*. New York: Greenwood Press, 1992.

Kinnamon, Kenneth, ed. *New Essays on Native Son*. New York: Cambridge University Press, 1990.

Metzger, Linda, Hal May, Deborah A. Straub, and Susan M. Trosky, eds. *Black Writers*. Detroit: Gale Research Inc., 1989.

Mikolyzk, Thomas A. comp. *Langston Hughes: A Bio-Bibliography*. Westport, CT: Greenwood Press, 1990.

Miller, R. Baxter. *The Art and Imagination of Langston Hughes*. Lexington: University of Kentucky Press, 1990.

Morrison, Toni. *Playing in the Dark: Whiteness and the Literary Imagination*. Cambridge, MA: Harvard University Press, 1992.

Newby, James Edwards. *Black Authors: A Selected Annotated Bibliography*. New York: Garland, 1990.

Ntire, Daphne Williams, ed., and comp. *Roots and Blossoms; African American Plays for Today*. Troy, MI: Bedford Publishers, 1991.

Peterson, Bernard L. *Early Black American Playwrights and Dramatic Writers: A Biographical Dictionary and Catalog of Plays, Films and Broadcasting Scripts*. Westport, CT: Greenwood Press, 1990.

Rajiv, Sudhi. *Forms of Black Consciousness*. New York: Advent Books, 1992.

Rollock, Barbara. *Black Authors and Illustrators of Children's Books: A Biographical Dictionary*. 2nd ed., New York: Garland, 1992.

Smith, Valerie. *Self-Discovery and Authority in Afro-American Narrative*. Cambridge, MA; Harvard University Press, 1991.

Stepto, Robert B. *From Behind the Veil: A Study of Afro-American Narrative*. 2nd ed., Urbana: University of Illinois Press, 1991.

Thurman, Wallace. *Infants of the Spring*. With foreword by Amritjit Singh. Boston: Northeastern University Press, 1992.

Toomer, Jean. *Essentials*. Edited by Rudolph P. Bird. Athens: University of Georgia Press, 1991.

Washington, Mary Helen, ed. *Memory of Kin: Stories About Family by Black Writers*. New York: Doubleday, 1991.

Wilson, August. *Two Trains Running*. New York: Dutton, 1992.

## Media, Publishing, and Book Collecting

Chester, Thomas Morris. *Thomas Morris Chester, Black Civil War Correspondent: His Dispatches from the Virginia Front*. With Biographical Essay and Notes by R.J.M. Blackett. New York: DeCapo Press, 1991.

Dates, Jannette L., and William Barlow. *Split Image: African Americans in the Mass Media*. Washington, DC: Howard University Press, 1990.

Hill, George. *Black Women in Television: An Illustrated History and Bibliography*. New York: Garland Publishing Co., 1990.

Joyce, Donald Franklin. *Black Book Publishers in the United States: A Historical Dictionary of the Press, 1817–1990*. Westport, CT: Greenwood Press, 1991.

Schuyler, George S. *Black Empire: George S. Schuyler Writing As Samuel I. Brooks*. Edited by Robert A. Hill and R. Kent Rasmussen. Boston: Northeastern University, 1991.

Silk, Catherine, and John Silk. *Racism and Anti-Racism in American Popular Culture: Portrayals of African-Americans in Fiction and Film*. Manchester, UK: Manchester University Press, 1990. (Dist. by St. Martin's Press)

Sinnette, Elinor Des Verney, W. Paul Coates, and Thomas C. Battle, eds. *Black Bibliophiles and Collectors: Preservers of Black History*. Washington, DC: Howard University Press, 1990.

## Military Participation

Collum, Danny Duncan, ed. *African Americans in the Spanish Civil War: "This Ain't Ethiopia, but It'll Do"*. New York: G.K. Hall, 1992.

Cox, Clinton. *Undying Glory: The Story of the Massachusetts 54th Regiment*. New York: Scholastic, Inc., 1991.

Donaldson, Gary. *The History of African-Americans in the Military: Double V*. Malabar, FL: Krieger Publishing Co., 1991.

Gooding, James Henry. *On the Altar of Freedom: A Black Soldier's Civil War Letters from the Front*. Edited by Virginia Matzke Adams. Amherst: University of Massachusetts Press, 1991.

Johnson, Charles. *African American Soldiers in the National Guard: Recruitment and Deploy-*

*ment During Peacetime and War.* New York: Greenwood Press, 1992.

Redkey, Edwin S., ed. *A Grand Army of Black Men: Letters from African-American Soldiers in the Union Army.* New York: Cambridge University Press, 1992.

### Music

Allen, Ray. *Singing in the Spirit: African-American Sacred Quartets in New York City.* Philadelphia: University of Pennsylvania Press, 1991.

Boggs, Vernon W. *Salsiology: Afro-Cuban Music and the Evolution of Salsa in New York City.* Westport, CT: Greenwood Press, 1992.

Booth, Stanley. *Rhythm Oil: A Journey Through the Music of the American South.* New York: Pantheon, 1991.

Cantor, Louis. *Wheelin' on Beale.* Foreword by B.B. King. New York: Pharos, 1992.

Costello, Mark, and David Foster Wallace. *Signifying Rappers: Rap and Race in the Urban Present.* New York: Ecco Press, 1990.

Donovan, Richard X. *Black Musicians of America.* Portland, OR: National Book Co., 1991.

Finn, Julio. *The Bluesman: The Musical Heritage of Black Men and Women in the Americas.* New York: Interlink Books, 1991.

Floyd, Samuel A., ed. *Black Music in the Harlem Renaissance: A Collection of Essays.* Westport, CT: Greenwood Press, 1990.

Friedwall, Will. *Jazz Singing: America's Great Voices from Bessie Smith to Bebop and Beyond.* New York: Scribner's, 1990.

Harris, Michael W. *The Rise of Gospel Blues: The Music of Thomas Andrew Dorsey in the Urban Church.* New York: Oxford University Press, 1992.

Horne, Aaron, comp. *Keyboard Music of Black Composers: A Bibliography.* Westport, CT: Greenwood Press, 1992.

Horne, Aaron, comp. *String Music of Black Composers: A Bibliography.* Westport, CT: Greenwood Press, 1991.

Horne, Aaron. comp. *Woodwind Music of Black Composers* Westport, CT: Greenwood Press, 1990.

Jackson, John A. *Big Beat Heat: Alan Freed and the Early Years of Rock & Roll.* New York: Schirmer/Macmillan, 1991.

Merrill, Hugh. *The Blues Route.* New York: Morrow, 1990.

Morgan, Thomas L. *From Cakewalk to Concert Hall: An Illustrated History of African American Popular Music from 1895 to 1930.* Washington, DC: Elliott & Clark Publishers, 1992.

Morton, David C. and Charles K. Wolfe. *DeFord Bailey: A Black Star in Early Country Music.* Knoxville: University of Tennessee Press, 1991.

Peretti, Burton W. *The Creation of Jazz: Music, Race and Culture in Urban America.* Urbana: University of Illinois Press, 1992.

Perry, Frank. *Afro-American Vocal Music: A Select Guide to Fifteen Composers.* Berrien Springs, MD: Vande Verde Publishers, 1991.

Porter, Lewis, ed. *A Lester Young Reader.* Washington, DC: Smithsonian Institution Press, 1991.

Price, Sammy. *What Do They Want: A Jazz Autobiography.* Edited by Caroline Richmond. Chronological discography compiled by Bob Weir. Urbana: University of Illinois Press, 1990.

Roach, Hildred. *Black American Music Past and Present: Pan-African Composers.* 2nd ed., Malabar, FL: Kruger, 1992.

Rosenthal, David H. *Hard Bop: Jazz and Black Music, 1955–1965.* New York: Oxford University Press, 1992.

Scott, Frank. *The Down Home Guide to the Blues.* Pennington, NJ: A Capella Books, 1990.

Spencer, Jon Michael, ed. *The Emergency Black and the Emergence of Rap.* Durham: Duke University Press, 1991.

Spencer, Jon Michael, ed. *Sacred Music of the Secular City: From Blues to Rap.* Durham: Duke University Press, 1992.

Story, Rosalyn. *And So I Sing: African American Divas of Opera and Concert.* New York: Warner Books, 1990.

Tate, Greg. *Flyboy in the Buttermilk: Essays on Contemporary America.* New York: Simon and Schuster, 1992.

Turner, Patricia. *Dictionary of Afro-American Performers: 78 RPM and Cylinder Recordings of Opera, Choral Music and Song, ca. 1900–1949.* New York: Garland, 1990.

Walker-Hill, Helen. *Piano-Music by Black Women Composers: A Catalogue of Solo and Ensemble Works.* New York: Greenwood Press, 1992.

Wright, Josephine, and Samuel A. Floyd, Jr., eds. *New Perspectives on Music: Essays in Honor of Eileen Southern.* Warren, MI: Harmonie Park Press, 1992.

## Performing Arts

Adamczke, Alice J. *Black Dance: An Annotated Bibliography.* New York: Garland Publishing Co., 1990.

Ely, Melvin Patrick. *The Adventures of Amos 'n' Andy: A Social History of an American Phenomenon.* New York: Free Press, 1991.

Gray, John, comp. *Black Theatre and Performance: A PanAfrican Bibliography.* Westport, CT: Greenwood Press, 1990.

Gray, John, comp. *Blacks in Film and Television: A Pan-African Bibliography of Films, Filmmakers, and Performers.* Westport, CT: Greenwood Press, 1990.

Hansberry, Lorraine. *A Raisin in the Sun: The Unfilmed Original Screenplay.* Edited by Robert Nemiroff. Foreword by Jewell Gres. Afterword by Spike Lee. New York: Dutton, 1992.

Hughes, Langston, and Zora Neale Hurston. *Mule Bone: A Comedy of Negro Life.* Edited by George H. Bass and Henry L. Gates. New York: Harper Collins, 1991.

Jhally, Sut, and Justin Lewis. *Enlightened Racism: The Cosby Show, Audiences, and the Myth of the American Dream.* Boulder, CO: Westview Press, 1992.

Jones, G. William. *Black Cinema Treasurey: Lost and Found.* Denton, TX: University of North Texas Press, 1991.

Klotman, Phyllis Rauch, ed. *Screenplays of the African American Experience.* Bloomington: Indiana University Press, 1991.

Mapp, Edward. *Directory of Blacks in the Performing Arts.* 2nd ed., Metuchen, NJ: Scarecrow Press, 1990.

## Politics

Barker, Lucius J., ed. *Ethnic Politics and Civil Liberties.* New Brunswick, NJ: Transaction Books, 1992.

Clavel, Pierre, and Wim Wiewel, eds. *Harold Washington and the Neighborhoods: Progressive City Government in Chicago, 1983–1987.* New Brunswick, NJ: Rutgers University Press, 1991.

Gomes, Ralph C., and Linda Faye Williams eds. *From Exclusion to Inclusion: The Long Struggle for African American Political Power.* Westport, CT: Greenwood Press, 1992.

Henry, Charles P. *Culture and African American Politics.* Bloomington: Indiana University Press, 1990.

Henry, Charles P. *Jesse Jackson: The Search for Common Ground.* Oakland, CA: Black Scholar Press, 1990.

Jennings, James. *The Politics of Black Empowerment: The Transformation of Black Activism in Urban America.* Detroit: Wayne State University Press, 1992.

Joint Center for Political and Economic Studies. *Black Elected Officials: A National Roster.* Washington, DC: Joint Center for Political and Economic Studies Press, 19–.

Kimball, Penn. *Keep Hope Alive: Super Tuesday and Jesse Jackson's 1988 Campaign for the Presidency.* Washington, DC: Joint Center for Political and Economic Studies, 1992.

Lawson, Steven. *Running for Freedom: Civil Rights and Black Politics in America Since 1941.* Philadelphia: Temple University Press, 1990.

Marable, Manning. *The Crisis of Color and Democracy: Essays on Race, Class and Power.* Monroe, ME: Common Courage Press, 1992.

McCartney, John T. *Black Power Ideologies: An Essay in African American Political Thought.* Philadelphia: Temple University Press, 1992.

Natanson, Nicholas. *The Black Image in the New Deal: The Politics of FSA.* Knoxville: University of Tennessee Press, 1992.

Orfield, Gar, and Carole Ashkinaze. *The Closing Door: Conservative Policy and Black Opportunity.* Chicago: University of Chicago Press, 1991.

Parker, Frank R. *Black Votes Count: Political Empowerment in Mississippi After 1965.* Chapel Hill: University of North Carolina Press, 1990.

Rees, Matthew. *From the Deck to the Sea: Blacks and the Republican Party.* Wakefield, NH: Longwood Press, 1991.

Rivlin, Gar. *Fire on the Prairie: Chicago's Harold Washington and the Politics of Race.* New York: Holt, 1992.

Van DeBurg, William L. *New Day in Babylon: The Black Power Movement and American Culture.* Chicago: University of Chicago Press, 1992.

## Race Relations

Brady, Paul L. *A Certain Blindness: A Black Family's Quest for the Promise of America.* Atlanta: ALP Publishers, 1990.

Brooks, Roy L. *Rethinking the American Race Problem.* Berkeley: University of California, 1991.

Collier, Peter, ed. *Second Thoughts About Race in America.* Lanham, MD: Madison Books, 1991.

Crouch, Stanley. *Notes of a Hanging Judge: Essays and Reviews.* New York: Oxford University Press, 1990.

Davis, F. James. *Who Is Black: One Nation's Definition.* University Park: Pennsylvania State University Press, 1991.

DeSantis, John. *For the Color of His Skin: The Murder of Yusuf Hawkins and the Trial of Bensonhurst.* Introduction by Alan M. Dershowitz. New York: Pharos Books, 1991.

Essed, Philomena. *Understanding Racism: An Interdisciplinary Theory.* Newbury Park, CA: Sage, 1991.

Hacker, Andrew. *Two Nations: Black and White, Separate, Hostile, Unequal.* New York: Scribner's, 1992.

Horowitz, Irving Louis. *Daydreams and Nightmares: Reflections on a Harlem Childhood.* Jackson: University Press of Mississippi, 1990.

Hynes, Charles J., and Bob Drury. *Incident at Howard Beach: The Case for Murder.* New York: Putnam, 1990.

Leiman, Melvin M. *Racism in the U.S.A.: History and Political Economy.* Concord, MA: Paul & Co., 1992.

Lewis, Earl. *In Their own Interests: Race, Class, and Power in Twentieth-Century Nolf, Virginia.* Berkeley: University of California Press, 1991.

McFadden, Robert, et. al. *Outrage: The Story Behind the Tawana Brawley Hoax.* New York: Bantam, 1990.

Pemberton, Gayle. *The Hottest Water in Chicago: One Family, Race, Time and American Culture.* Winchester, MA: Faber & Faber, 1992.

Perlmutter, Philip. *Divided We Fall: A History of Ethnic, Religious, and Racial Prejudice in America.* Ames: Iowa State University Press, 1992.

Rasberry, William. *Looking Backward at Us.* Jackson: University Press of Mississippi, 1991.

Salzman, Jack, ed. *Bridges and Boundaries: African Americans and American Jews.* New York: Braziller, 1992.

Steele, Shelby. *The Contest of Our Character: A New Vision of Race in America.* New York: St. Martin's Press, 1990.

Stepan, Nancy Leys. *The Hour of Eugenics: Race, Gender, and Nation.* Ithaca, NY: Cornell University Press, 1991.

Terkel, Studs. *Race: How Blacks and Whites Think and Feel About the American Obsession.* New York: New Press/Norton, 1992.

Welch, Susan, and Lee Sigelman. *Black America's Views of Racial Equality: The Dream Deferred.* New York: Cambridge University Press, 1991.

Zegeye, Abebe, ed. *Exploitation and Exclusion: Race and Class in Contemporary U.S. Society.* London: Hans Zell Publishers, 1991.

Zweigenhaft, Richard L., and G. William Domhoff. *Blacks in the White Establishment: A Study of Race and Class in America.* New Haven, CT: Yale University Press, 1991.

## Religion and Philosophy

Baer, Hans, and Merrill Singer. *African-American Religion in the Twentieth Century: Varieties of Protest and Accommodation.* Knoxville: University of Tennessee, 1992.

Davis, Lenwood G. *Daddy Grace: An Annotated Bibliography.* New York: Greenwood Press, 1992.

Dvorak, Katherine L. *An African-American Exodus: the Segregation of Southern Churches.* With preface by Jerald C. Brauer. Brooklyn, NY: Carlson Publishing Co., 1991.

Harris, Leonard, ed. *The Philosophy of Alain Locke.* Philadelphia: Temple University Press, 1990.

Haynes, Lemuel. *Black Preacher to White America: the Collected Writings of Lemuel Haynes, 1774–1833.* Edited by Richard Newman. New York: Carlson Publishing Co., 1990.

Hopkins, Dwight N., and George C.L. Cummings, eds. *Cut Loose Your Stammering Tongue: Black Theology in the Slave Narratives.* Maryknoll, NY: Orbis Books, 1991.

Howard, Victor B. *Conscience and Slavery: the Evangelistic Calvinistic Domestic Missions, 1837–1861.* Kent, OH: Kent State University Press, 1990.

Irvin, Dona L. *The Unsung Heart of Black America: A Middle-Class Church at Midcentury.* Columbia: University of Missouri Press, 1992.

Jacobs, Claude F., and Andrew J. Kaslow. *The Spiritual Churches of New Orleans: Origins, Beliefs and Rituals of an African-American Religion.* Knoxville: University of Tennessee Press, 1991.

Johnson, John L. *Black Biblical Heritage.* Nashville: Winston-Derek Publishers, 1990.

Lincoln, C. Eric, and Lawrence H. Mamiya. *The Black Church in the American Experience.* Durham, NC: Duke University Press, 1990.

Martin, Sandy D. *Black Baptists and African Missions: the Origins of a Movement, 1880–1915.* Macon, GA: Mercer University Press, 1990.

Ochs, Stephen J. *Desegregating the Altar: The Josephites and the Struggle for Black Priests, 1871–1960.* Baton Rouge: Louisiana State University Press, 1990.

Payne, Wardell J., ed. *Directory of African American Religious Bodies: A Compendium by the Howard University School of Divinity.* Prepared under the auspices of the Research Center on Black Religious Bodies, Howard University School of Divinity. Washington, DC: Howard University Press, 1991.

Seymour, Robert E. *Whites Only: A Pastor's Retrospective on Signs of a New South.* Valley Forge, PA: Judson Press, 1991.

Spencer, Jon Michael. *Black Hymnody: A Hymnological History of the African-American Church.* Knoxville: University of Tennessee Press, 1992.

Spencer, Jon Michael. *Protest and Praise: Sacred Music of Black Religion.* Minneapolis: Augsburg Fortress Publishers, 1990.

Walker, Theodore, Jr. *Empower the People: Social Ethics for the African-American Church.* Maryknoll, NY: Orbis Books, 1991.

Walker, Wyatt Tee. *Spirits That Dwell in Deep Woods III: The Prayer and Praise Hymns of the Black Religious Experience.* New York: Martin Luther King Press, 1991.

Wood, Forrest G. *The Arrogance of Faith: Christianity and Race in America from the Colonial Era to the Twentieth Century.* New York: Knopf, 1990.

## Sociology and Psychology

Andersen, Margaret L. *Race, Class and Gender: An Anthology.* Belmont, CA: Wadsworth Publishing Co., 1992.

Anderson, Elijah. *Streetwise: Race, Class and Social Change in an Urban Community.* Chicago: University of Chicago Press, 1990.

Baer, Hans, and Yvonne Jones, eds. *African Americans in the South: Issues of Race, Class and Gender.* Athens: University of Georgia Press, 1992.

Benjamin, Lois. *The Black Elite: Facing the Color Line in the Twentieth Century.* Chicago: Nelson-Hall, 1991.

Billingsley, Andrew. *Climbing Jacob's Ladder: The Future of the African-American Family.* New York: Simon and Schuster, 1991.

Blackwell, James Edward. *The Black Community: Diversity and Unity.* 3rd ed., New York: Harper Collins, 1991.

Bowser, Benjamin, ed. *Black Male Adolescents: Parenting and Education in Community Context.* Latham, MD: University Press of America, 1991.

Consortium for Research on Black Adolescence Staff and Patricia Bell-Scott. *Black Adolescence: Current Issues and Annotated Bibliography.* Boston: G.K. Hall, 1990.

Edelman, Marian Wright. *The Measure of Our Success: A Letter to My Children and Yours.* Boston: Beacon Press, 1992.

Hay, Fred J. *African-American Community Studies from North America. A Classified, Annotated Bibliography.* New York: Garland, 1991.

Hopson, Darlene, and Derek Hopson. *Different and Wonderful: Raising Black Children in a Race Conscious Society.* New York: Simon and Schuster, 1992.

Jones, Howard, and Wanda Jones. *Heritage and Hope: The Legacy and Future of the Black Family in America.* Wheaton, IL: Victor Books, 1992.

Kunjufu, Jawanza. *Countering the Conspiracy to Destroy Black Boys.* Chicago: African American Images, 1990.

Leigh, Wilhelmina A., ed. *The Housing Status of Black Americans.* New Brunswick, NJ: Transaction Books, 1992.

Lemann, Nicholas. *The Promised Land: The Great Black Migration and How It Changed America.* New York: Knopf, 1991.

Platat, Anthony M. *E. Franklin Frazier Reconsidered.* New Brunswick, NJ: Rutgers University Press, 1991.

Trotter, Joe William, ed. *The Great Migration in Historical Perspective: New Dimensions of Race, Class and Gender.* Bloomington: Indiana University Press, 1991.

## Sports

Cooper, Michael L. *Playing America's Game: The Story of Negro League Baseball.* New York: Lodestar Books, 1993.

Page, James A. *Black Olympian Medalists.* Englewood, CO: Libraries Unlimited, 1991.

## Women

Alexander, Adele Logan. *Free Women of Color in Rural Georgia, 1789–1879.* Fayetteville: University of Arkansas Press, 1991.

Baker, Houston A. *Working of the Spirit: The Poetics of Afro-American Women's Writings.* Chicago: University of Chicago Press, 1991.

The Black Women Oral History Project. *Guide to the Transcripts.* Edited by Ruth E. Hill. Westport, CT: Meckler, 1991.

Braxton, Joanne M. *Black Women Writing Autobiography: A Tradition Within a Tradition.* Philadelphia: Temple University Press, 1990.

Braxton, Joanne M., and Andree Nicola McLaughlin, eds. *Wild Women in the Whirlwind: Afro-American Culture and the Contemporary Literary Renaissance.* New Brunswick, NJ: Rutgers University Press, 1990.

Brown, Karen McCarthy. *Mama Lola: A Voodoo Priestess in Brooklyn.* Berkeley, University of California Press, 1991.

Brown-Guillory, Elizabeth, ed., and comp. *Wines in the Wilderness: Plays by African American Women from the Harlem Renaissance to the Present.* Westport, CT: Greenwood Press, 1990.

Bundles, A'Lelia Perry. *Madam C. J. Walker.* New York: Chelsea House, 1991.

Busby, Margaret, ed. *Daughters of Africa: An International Anthology of Words and Writings by Women of African Descent; From the Ancient World to Present.* New York: Pantheon, 1992.

Butler-Evans, Elliott. *Race, Gender, and Desire: Narrative Strategies in the Fiction of Toni Cade Bambara, Toni Morrison, and Alice Walker.* Philadelphia: Temple University Press, 1990.

Caraway, Nancie. *Segregated Sisterhood: Racism and the Politics of American Feminism.* Knoxville: University of Tennessee Press, 1991.

Celsi, Teresa N. *Rosa Parks and the Montgomery Bus Boycott.* Brookfield, CT: Millbrook Press, 1991.

Crawford, Vicki L., Jacqueline Anne Reese, and Barbara Woods, eds. *Women in the Civil Rights Movement: Trailblazers and Torchbears, 1941–1965.* Brooklyn, NY: Carlson Publishing Co., 1990. (*Black Women in United States History,* vol. 16.)

Davis, Michael D. *Black American Women in Olympic Track and Field: A Complete Illustrated Reference.* Jefferson, NC: McFarland, 1992.

Gates, Henry Louis, Jr. *Reading Black, Reading Feminist.* New York: Meridan, 1991.

Glassman, Steve, and Kathryn Lee Seidel, eds. *Zora in Florida.* Gainesville: University Presses of Florida, 1991.

Guy-Sheftall, Beverly. *Daughters of Sorrow: Attitudes Toward Black Women.* New York: Carlson Publishing Co., 1990. (*Black Women in United States History,* vol. 11.)

Harris, Trudier. *Fiction and Folklore: The Novels of Toni Morrison.* Knoxville: University of Tennessee Press, 1991.

Hine, Darlene Clark, ed. *Black Women in American History, From Colonial Times Through the Nineteenth Century.* Brooklyn, NY: Carlson Publishing Co., 1990.

Hooks, Bell. *Black Looks: Race and Representation.* Boston: South End Press, 1992.

Ihle, Elizabeth L., ed. *Black Women in Higher Education: An Anthology of Essays, Studies and Documents.* New York: Garland Publishing Co., 1992.

Jackson, Carlton. *Hattie: The Life of Hattie McDaniel.* Lantham, MD: Madison Books, 1990.

Jones, Adrienne Lash. *Jane Edna Hunter: A Case Study of Black Leadership.* Brooklyn, NY: Carlson Publishing Co., 1990. (*Black Women in United States History,* vol. 12)

Jones, Beverly Washington. *Quest for Equality: The Life and Writing of Mary Eliza Church Terrell, 1863–1954.* Brooklyn, NY: Carlson Publishing Co., 1990. (*Black Women in United States History,* vol. 13.)

Kent, George E. *A Life of Gwendolyn Brooks.* Lexington: University of Kentucky Press, 1990.

King, Joyce Elaine, and Carolyn Ann Mitchell. *Black Mothers to Sons: Juxtaposing African American Literature and the Social Practice.* New York: Peter Lang, 1990.

Kubitschek, Missy Dehn. *Claiming the Heritage: African-American Women Novelists and History.* Oxford: University Press of Mississippi, 1991.

Mabalia, Dorethea Drummond, *Toni Morrison's Developing Class Consciousness.* Cranbury, NJ: Susquehanna University Press/Associated University Presses, 1991.

Morton, Patricia. *Disfigured Images: The Historical Assault on Afro-American Women.* Westport, CT: Greenwood Press, 1991.

Nathiri, N.Y., ed. *Zora! Zora Neale Hurston: A Woman and Her Community.* Orlando, FL: Sentinel Books, 1991.

Neverdon-Morton, Cynthia. *Afro-American Women of the South and the Advancement of the Race, 1895–1925.* Knoxville: University of Tennessee Press, 1990.

Otfinoski, Steven. *Marian Wright Edelman—Defender of Children's Rights.* New York: Rosen Publishing Group, 1991.

Reckley, Ralph. *Twentieth Century Black Women in Print: Essays.* Acton, MA: Copley Publishers, 1991.

Roses, Lorraine Elena, and Ruth Elizabeth Randolph. *Harlem Renaissance and Beyond: Literary Biographies of 100 Black Women Writers, 1900–1945.* Boston: G.K. Hall, 1990.

Salem, Dorothy. *To Better Our World: Black Women in Organized Reform.* Brooklyn, NY: Carlson Publishing Co., 1990. (*Black Women in United States History,* vol. 14.)

Samuels, Wilfred D., and Clenora Hudson-Weems. *Toni Morrison.* Boston: G.K. Hall, 1990.

Scott, Kesho Yvonne. *The Habit of Surviving: Black Women's Strategies for Life.* New Brunswick, NJ: Rutgers University Press, 1991.

Smith, Jesse Carney, ed. *Notable Black American Women.* Detroit: Gale Research Inc., 1991.

Smith, Rita Webb, and Tony Chapelle. *The Woman Who Took Back Her Streets: One Woman Fights the Drug Wars and Rebuilds Her Community.* Far Hill, NJ: New Horizon, 1991.

Thompson, Mildred I. *Ida B. Wells-Barnett: An Exploratory Study of An American Black Woman, 1893–1930.* Brooklyn, NY: Carlson Publishing Co., 1990. (*Black Women in United States History,* vol. 15)

Walker, Melissa. *Down From the Mountaintop: Black Women's Novels in the Wake of the Civil Rights Movement, 1966–1989.* New Haven, CT: Yale University Press, 1991.

Walker, Robbie Jean, ed. *The Rhetoric of Struggle: Public Addresses by African American Women.* New York: Garland Publishing Co., 1992.

Werner, Craig. *Black American Women Novelists: An Annotated Bibliography.* Englewood Cliffs, NJ: Salem Press, 1990.

Williams, Constance Willard. *Black Teenage Mothers: Pregnancy and Child Rearing from Their Perspective.* Lexington, MA: Lexington Books, 1991.

Woody, Bette. *Black Women in the Workplace: Impacts of Structural Change in the Economy.* Westport, CT: Greenwood Press, 1992.

Yee, Shirley J. *Black Women Abolitionists: A Study in Activism, 1828–1860.* Knoxville: University of Tennessee Press, 1992.

## ■ NAMES AND ADDRESSES OF PUBLISHERS OF BOOKS WHICH APPEAR IN THIS BIBLIOGRAPHY

### A

A cappella Books, PO Box 380, Pennington, NJ 08534, Tel.: (609)737-6525.

ABC-Clio, Inc., PO Box 1911, Santa Barbara, CA 93116-1911, Tel.: (800)422-2546.

Harry N. Abrams, Inc., 100 5th Ave., New York, NY 10011, Tel.: (800)345-1359.

AKASA Press, 2440-10 Hunter Ave., Ste. 1OG, Bronx, NY 10475, Tel.: (212)671-9639.

Advent Books, Inc., 141 E. 44th St., Ste. 511, New York, NY 10017, Tel.: (212)697-0887.

Africa World Press, PO Box 1892, Trenton, NJ 08607, Tel.: (609)771-1666.

African Studies Association, Emory University, Credit Union Bldg., Atlanta, GA 30322, Tel.: (404)329-6410.

Algonquin Books, PO Box 2225, Chapel Hill, NC 27515, Tel.: (919)933-0108.

American Enterprise Institute for Public Policy Research, 1150 17th St. NW, Washington, DC 20036, Tel.: (202)862-5800.

Apt Books, Inc., 141 E. 44th St., Ste. 511, New York, NY 10017, Tel.: (212)697-0887.

Associated University Presses, 440 Forsgate Dr., Cranbury, NJ 08512, Tel.: (609)655-4770.

Atheneum, c/o MacMillan Publishing Co., 866 3rd Ave., New York, NY 10022, Tel.: (800)257-5755.


**B**

Backwards & Backwards Press, 7561 Pearl Rd., Cleveland, OH 44130, Tel.: (216)243-5335.

Richard Bailey, Box 1264, Montgomery, AL 36102, Tel.: (205)271-6565.

Bandit Books, Inc., PO Box 11721, Winston-Salem, NC 27106, Tel.: (919)785-7414.

Bantam Books, 666 5th Ave., New York, NY 10103, Tel.: (212)765-6500.

Barez Publishing Co., 8690 Aero Dr., Ste. M-332, San Diego, CA 92123-1734, Tel.: (800)247-5900.

Beacon Press, 25 Beacon St., Boston, MA 02108, Tel.: (617)742-2110.

Bedford Arts/Corcoran Gallery of Art, 301 Brannon St., Ste. 410, San Francisco, CA 94107, Tel.: (415)882-7870.

Bedford Publishers, Inc., 779 Kirts, Troy, MI 48084, Tel.: (313)362-0369.

John Benjamins North America, Inc., 821 Bethlehem Pike, Philadelphia, PA 19118, Tel.: (215)836-1200.

Black Entrepreneurs Press, 4502 S. Congress Ave., Ste. 254, Austin, TX 78744, Tel.: (512)444-9962.

The Black Resources Guide, Inc., 501 Oneida Pl. NW, Washington, DC 20011, Tel.: (202)291-4373.

George Braziller, Inc., 60 Madison Ave., Ste. 1001, New York, NY 10010, Tel.: (212)889-0909.

British American Publishing Ltd., 19 British American Blvd., Latham, NY 12148, Tel.: (518)786-6000.


**C**

Calyx Books, PO Box B, Corvalis, OR 97339, Tel.: (503)753-9384.

Cambridge University Press, 40 W. 20th St., New York, NY 10011, Tel.: (212)924-3900.

Cambridgeport Press, 15 Chalk St., Cambridge, MA 02139, Tel.: (617)497-4437.

Carlson Publishing Co., 52 Remsen St., Brooklyn, NY 11201, Tel.: (718)875-7460.

Carol Publishing Group, 600 Madison Ave., New York, NY 10022, Tel.: (212)486-2200.

Carroll & Graf Publishers, Inc., 260 5th Ave., New York, NY 10001, Tel.: (212)889-8772.

The Center for African-Art, 560 Broadway, Ste. 206, New York, NY 10012-3945, Tel.: (212)966-1313.

Charro Books Co., Inc., 29777 Telegraph Rd., No. 2500, Southfield, MI 48034, Tel.: (313)356-0950.

Chelsea House Publishers, 95 Madison Ave., New York, NY 10011, Tel.: (212)683-4400.

Christian Reformed World Missions, 2850 Kalamazoo SE, Grand Rapids, MI 49560.

Citadel Press, c/o Carol Publishing Group, 600 Madison Ave., New York, NY 10022, Tel.: (212)486-2220.

Adam Randolph Collings, Inc., PO Box 8658, Anaheim, CA 92812, Tel.: (714)534-7976.

Common Courage Press, Box 702, Jackson Rd. and Rte. 19, Monroe, ME 04951, Tel.: (207)525-0900.

Consortium Book Sales & Distribution, 287 E. 6th St., Ste. 365, St. Paul, MN 55101, Tel.: (612)221-9035.

Copley Publishing Group, 138 Great Rd., Acton, MA 01720, Tel.: (508)263-9090.

Cornell University Press, 124 Roberts Pl., PO Box 250, Ithaca, NY 14851, Tel.: (607)257-7000.

CRC Press, Inc., 2000 Corporate Blvd. NW, Boca Raton, FL 33431, Tel.: (407)994-0555.

**D**

Daring Publishing Group, 913 Tuscarawas St. W., Canton, OH 44702, Tel.: (216)454-7519.

Ivan R. Dee, Inc., 1332 N. Halsted St., Chicago, IL 60622, Tel.: (312)787-6262.

Doubleday, 666 5th Ave., New York, NY 10103, Tel.: (800)223-6834.

Dufour Editions, Inc., PO Box 449, Chester Springs, PA 19425-0449, Tel.: (215)458-5005.

Duke University Press, PO Box 6697, College Sta., Durham, NC 27108, Tel.: (919)684-2173.

**E**

ECA Associates, PO Box 15004, Great Bridge Sta., Chesapeake, VA 23320, Tel.: (804)547-5542.

William B. Eerdmans Publishing Co., 255 Jefferson Ave. SE, Grand Rapids, MI 49503, Tel.: (800)253-7521.

**F**

Faber & Faber, Inc., 50 Cross St., Winchester, MA 01890, Tel.: (617)721-1427.

Facts on File, Inc., 460 Park Ave. S., New York, NY 10016, Tel.: (212)683-2214.

Fairleigh Dickinson University Press, 440 Forsgate Dr., Cranbury, NJ 08512, Tel.: (609)655-4770.

Farrar, Straus & Giroux, Inc., 19 Union Sq. W., New York, NY 10003, Tel.: (800)631-8571.

Augsburg Fortress, Publishers, 426 S. 5th St., PO Box 1209, Minneapolis, MN 55440, Tel.: (800)848-2738.

Free Press, 866 3rd Ave., New York, NY 10022, Tel.: (212)702-3130.

**G**

Gale Research Inc., 835 Penobscot Bldg., Detroit, MI 48226-4094, Tel.: (800)877-4253.

Garland Publishing, Inc., 717 5th Ave., New York, NY 10016, Tel.: (212)751-7447.

Georgetown University Press, Intercultural Center, Rm. 111, Washington, DC 20057, Tel.: (202)687-6063.

Gower Publishing Co., Old Post Rd., Brookfield, VT 05036, Tel.: (802)276-3162.

Greenwood Publishing Group, Inc., 88 Post Rd. W., PO Box 5007, Westport, CT 06881, Tel.: (203)226-3571.

Grove Weidenfeld, 841 Broadway, 4th Fl., New York, NY 10003-4793, Tel.: (212)614-7850.

Guilford Publications, Inc., 72 Spring St., New York, NY 10012, Tel.: (212)431-9800.

**H**

G.K. Hall & Co., Inc., 70 Lincoln St.1, Boston, MA 02111, Tel.: (617)423-3990.

Harlan Davidson, Inc., 110 N. Arlington Heights Rd., Arlington Heights, IL 60004, Tel.: (708)253-9720.

Harmonie Park Press, 23630 Pinewood, Warren, MI 48091, Tel.: (313)755-3080.

Harmony Books, c/o Crown Publishers, Inc., 201 E. 50th St., New York, NY 10022, Tel.: (212)572-6120.

HarperCollins Inc., 10 E. 53rd St., New York, NY 10022, Tel.: (800)331-3761.

Harvard University Press, 79 Garden St., Cambridge, MA 02138, Tel.: (617)495-2600.

Bibliography

Heinemann Educational Books, Inc., 361 Hanover St., Portsmouth, NH 03801-3912, Tel.: (603)431-7894.

Hemisphere Publishing Corp., 1900 Frost Rd., Ste. 101, Bristol, PA 19007, Tel.: (215)785-5000.

Hippocrene Books, Inc., 171 Madison Ave., New York, NY 10016, Tel.: (212)685-4371.

Holmes & Meier Publishers, Inc., 30 Irving Pl., New York, NY 10003, Tel.: (212)254-4100.

Holt, Rinehart & Winston, Inc., 6277 Sea Harbor Dr., Orlando, FL 32887, Tel.: (407)345-2500.

Hoover Institute Press, Stanford University, Stanford, CA 94305-6010, Tel.: (415)723-3373.

Howard University Press, 2900 Van Ness St. NW, Washington, DC 20008, Tel.: (202)806-8450.

Human Rights Watch, 485 5th Ave., New York, NY 10017-6104, Tel.: (212)972-8400.

Humanities Press International, Inc., 165 1st Ave., Atlantic Highlands, NJ 07716-1289, Tel.: (908)872-1441.


**I**

ICS Press, 243 Kearny St., San Francisco, CA 94108, Tel.: (415)981-5353.

Independent Publishers Group, 814 N. Franklin St., Chicago, Il 60610, Tel.: (312)337-0747.

Indiana University Press, 601 N. Morton St., Bloomington, IN 47404-3797, Tel.; (8l2)855-4203.

Institute of Early American History and Culture, PO Box 220, Williamsburg, VA 23187, Tel.: (804)221-1110.

Interlink Publishing Group, Inc., 99 7th Ave., Brooklyn, NY 11215, Tel.: (718)797-4292.

International Publishers Co., Inc., 239 W. 23rd St., New York, NY 10011, Tel.: (212)366-9816.

International Specialized Book Services, 5602 NE Hassalo St., Portland, OR 97213-3640, Tel.: (503)287-3093.

Ivy Books, 201 E. 50th St., New York, NY 10022, Tel.: (212)572-2573.


**J**

Joint Center for Political and Economic Studies, Inc., 1301 Pennsylvania Ave. NW, Ste. 400, Washington, DC 20041-1797, Tel.: (202)626-3500.

Jonathan David Publishers, Inc., 68-22 Eleat Ave., Middle Village, NY 11379, Tel.: (718)456-8611.

Judson Press, PO Box 851, Valley Forge, PA 19482-0851, Tel.: (800)331-1053.

Just Us Books, Inc., 301 Main St., Ste. 22-24, Orange, NJ 07050, Tel.: (800)762-7701.


**K**

Kendell/Hunt Publishing Co., 2460 Kerper Blvd., Dubuque, IA 52001, Tel.: (319)588-1451.

Kent State University Press, 101 Franklin Hall, Kent, OH 44242, Tel.: (800)666-2211.

Kluwer Academic Publishers, 101 Philip Dr., Assinippi Park, Norwell, MA 02061, Tel.: (617)871-6600.

Alfred A. Knopf, Inc., 201 E. 50th St., New York, NY 10022, Tel.: (212)572-2103.

Krieger Publishing Co., Inc., PO Box 9542, Melborne, FL 32902, Tel.: (407)724-9542.

Kumarian Press, Inc., 630 Oakwood Ave., Ste. 119, West Hartford, CT 06110-1505, Tel.: (203)953-0214.


**L**

Lexington Books, 125 Spring St., Lexington, MA 02173, Tel.: (617)862-6650.

Little, Brown & Co., Inc., 34 Beacon St., Boston, MA 02108, Tel.: (800)343-9204.

Louisiana State University Press, Highland Rd., Baton Rouge, LA 70893, Tel.: (504)388-6294.

Lynne Rienner Publishers, Inc., 1800 30th St., Ste. 314, Boulder, CO 80301, Tel.: (303)444-6684.

# M

McFarland & Co., Inc., Publishers, Box 611, Jefferson, NC 28640, Tel.: (919)246-4460.

MacMillan Publishing Co., 866 3rd Ave., New York, NY 10022, Tel.: (800)257-6509.

Madison Books, 4720 Boston Way, Lantham, MD 20706, Tel.: (800)462-6420.

Madison House Publishers, Inc., PO Box 3100, Madison, WI 53704, Tel.: (608)244-6210.

Majority Press, PO Box 538, Dover, MA 02030, Tel.: (617)828-8450.

Martin Luther King Press, 132 W. 116th St., New York, NY 10026, Tel.: (212)866-0301.

Meckler Corp., 11 Ferry Ln. W., Westport, CT 06880, Tel.: (203)226-6967.

Edwin Mellen Press, PO Box 450, Lewiston, NY 14092, Tel.: (716)754-2266.

Mercer University Press, 1400 Coleman Ave., Macon, GA 31207, Tel.: (912)752-2880.

Michigan State University Press, 1405 S. Harrison Rd., East Lansing, MI 48824, Tel.: (517)355-9543.

Millbrook Press, Inc., Old New Milford Rd., Brookfield, CT 06804, Tel.: (203)740-2220.

Myles Publishing Co., 436 E. Ute St., Tulsa, OK 74106, Tel.: (918)663-7701.

# N

NRW Associates Directory, 1315 Hamlin St. NE, Washington, DC 20017, Tel.: (202)635-4808.

National Academy Press, 2101 Constitution Ave. NW, Washington, DC 20418, Tel.: (800)624-6242.

National Afro-American Museum and Cultural Center, PO Box 578, Wilberforce, OH 45384, Tel.: (513)376-4944.

National Book Co., PO Box 8795, Portland, OR 97207-8795, Tel.: (503)228-6345.

National Book Network, 4720 Boston Way, Lanham, MD 20706-4310, Tel.: (301)459-8696.

National Urban League, Inc., 500 E. 62nd St., New York, NY 10021, Tel.: (212)310-9000.

Native Sun Publishers, Inc., PO Box 13394, Richmond, VA 23225, Tel.: (804)233-8249.

New York University Press, 70 Washington Sq. S., New York, NY 10012, Tel.: (212)998-2575.

Northeastern University Press, 360 Huntington Ave., 272 Huntington Plaza, Boston, MA 02115, Tel.: (617)437-5480.

Northwestern University Press, 625 Colfax St., Evanston, IL 60201, Tel.: (708)491-5315.

W.W. Norton & Co., Inc., 500 5th Ave., New York, NY 10110, Tel.: (212)354-5500.

# O

Ohio University Press, 220 Scott Quadrangle, Athens, OH 45701, Tel.: (614)593-1155.

Open University Press, c/o Taylor & Francis, Inc., 79 Madison Ave., Ste. 1106, New York, NY 10016, Tel.: (212)725-1999.

Orbis Books, Fathers & Brothers of Maryknoll, Walsh Bldg., Maryknoll, NY 10545, Tel.: (800)258-5838.

Oxford University Press, Inc., 200 Madison Ave., New York, NY 10016, Tel.: (800)334-4349.

# P

Pacific Research Institute for Public Policy, 177 Post St., Ste. 500, San Francisco, CA 94108, Tel.: (415)989-0833.

Pantheon Books, Inc., 201 E. 50th St., New York, NY 10022, Tel.: (212)872-8238.

Paragon House Publishers, 90 5th Ave., New York, NY 10011, Tel.: (212)620-2820.

Pathfinder Press, 410 West St., New York, NY 10014, Tel.: (212)741-0690.

Paul & Co. Publishers, Consortium, Inc., PO Box 442, Concord, MA 01742, Tel.: (508)369-3049.

Pelican Publishing Co., Inc., 1101 Monroe St., Gretna, LA 70053, Tel.: (800)843-4558.

Pennsylvania State University Press, 820 N. University Dr., Ste. C, University Park, PA 16802, Tel.: (814)865-1327.

Pergamon Press, Inc., Front & Braun Sts., Riverside, NJ 08075-1197, Tel.: (609)461-6500.

Peter Lang Publishing, Inc., 62 W. 45th St., New York, NY 10036, Tel.: (212)302-6740.

Pharos Books, 200 Park Ave., New York, NY 10166, Tel.: (212)692-3830.

Power of the Word Publishing Co., 176-03 Jamaica Ave., Jamaica, NY 11432, Tel.: (718)949-1987.

Praeger Publishers, c/o Greenwood Press Publishing Group, Inc., 88 Post Rd., W., Box 5007, Westport, CT 06881, Tel.: (203)226-3571.

Presidio Press, 31 Pamaron Way, Novato, CA 94949, Tel.: (415)883-1373.

Princeton Architectural Press, 37 E. 7th Ave., New York, NY 10003, Tel.: (800)458-1131.

Princeton University Press, 41 William St., Princeton, NJ 08540, Tel.: (800)777-4726.

Putnam Publishing Group, 200 Madison Ave., New York, NY 10016, Tel.: (800)631-8571.

**R**

Raintree Steck-Vaughn Publications, 11 Prospect St., Madison, NJ 07940, Tel.: (800)531-5015.

Regnery Gateway, Inc., 1130 17th Ave. NW, Ste. 600, Washington, DC 20036, Tel.: (202)457-0978.

Rizzoli International Publications, Inc., 300 Park Ave. S., New York, NY 10010, Tel.: (800)462-2387.

Rosen Publishing Group, Inc., 29 E. 21st St., New York, NY 10010, Tel.: (212)777-3017.

Routledge, Chapman & Hall, Inc., 29 W. 35th St., New York, NY 10001-2291, Tel.: (212)244-3336.

Rowman & Littlefield, Publishers, Inc., 4720 Boston Way, Lanham, MD 20706, Tel.: (301)459-3366.

Russell Sage Foundation, 112 E. 64th St., New York, NY 10021, Tel.: (415)931-6000.

Rutgers University Press, 109 Church St., New Brunswick, NJ 08901, Tel.: (201)932-7764.

**S**

Sage Publications, Inc., 2455 Teller Rd., Newbury Park, CA 91320, Tel.: (805)499-0721.

St. Martin's Press, Inc., 175 5th Ave., New York, NY 10010, Tel.: (800)325-5525.

Salem Press, Inc., PO Box 1097, Englewood Cliffs, NJ 07632, Tel.: (201)871-3700

Sandcastle Publishing Co., PO Box 3070, South Pasadena, CA 91031-6070, Tel.: (213)255-3616.

K.G. Saur, 121 Chanlon Rd., New Providence, NJ 07974, Tel.: (908)665-2828.

Scarborough House, PO Box 459, Chelsea, MI 48118, Tel.: (313)475-1210.

Scarecrow Press, Inc., 52 Liberty St., Box 4167, Metuchen, NY 08840, Tel.: (800)537-7107.

Schiller Institute, Inc., PO Box 66082, Washington, DC 20005, Tel.: (202)628-0272.

Scholastic, Inc., 730 Broadway, New York, NY 10003, Tel.: (212)505-3000.

Charles Scribner's Sons, c/o MacMillan Publishing Co., 866 3rd Ave., New York, NY 10022, Tel.: (212)702-2000.

Seal Press-Feminist, 3131 Western Ave., No. 410, Seattle, WA 98121-1028, Tel.: (206)283-7844.

Seven Locks Press, PO Box 27, Cabin John, MD 20818, Tel.: (800)537-9359.

Seymour-Smith, Inc., PO Box 381063, Germantown, TN 38138-1063, Tel.: (901)754-4418.

Simon & Schuster, Inc., 1230 Avenue of Americas, New York, NY 10020, Tel.: (212)698-7000.

Smithsonian Institution Press, 470 L'Enfant Plaza, Ste. 7100, Washington, DC 20560, Tel.: (202)287-3748.

South Asia Books, PO Box 502, Columbia, MO 75205, Tel.: (314)474-0116.

South End Press, 116 St. Botolph St., Boston, MA 02115, Tel.: (617)266-0629.

State University of New York Press, State University Plaza, Albany, NY 12246-0001, Tel.: (800)666-2211.

Station Hill Press, Station Hill Rd., Barrytown, NY 12507, Tel.: (914)758-5840.

Steward, Tabori & Chang Publishers, 575 Broadway, New York, NY 10012, Tel.: (212)941-2929.

Summit Books, 1230 Avenue of the Americas, New York, NY 10020, Tel.: (212)698-7501.

Syracuse University Foreign & Comparative Studies Program, 321 Sims Hall, Syracuse, NY 13244, Tel.: (315)443-4667.

## T

Temple University Press, 1601 N. Broad St., University Services Bldg., Rm. 305, Philadelphia, PA 19122, Tel.: (800)447-1656.

Texas A&M University Press, Drawer C, College Stat., TX 77843, Tel.: (800)826-8911.

Third World Press, 7524 S. Cottage Grove Ave., PO Box 730, Chicago, IL 60619, Tel.: (312)651-0700.

Three Continents Press, 1901 Pennsylvania Ave. NW, Ste. 407, Washington, DC 20006, Tel.: (202)223-2554.

Thunder's Mouth Press, 54 Greene St., Ste. 45, New York, NY 10013, Tel.: (212)226-0277.

I.N. Thut World Education Center, University of Connecticut, School of Education, Box U-93, Storrs, CT 06269-2093, Tel.: (203)486-4812.

Times Books, c/o Random House, Inc., 201 E. 50th St., New York, NY 10022, Tel.: (800)726-0600.

Times Change Press, PO Box 1380, Ojai, CA 93023, Tel.: (800)488-8595.

Transaction Publishers, Rutgers University, New Brunswick, NJ 08903, Tel.: (201)932-2280.

Transnational Publishers, Inc., PO Box 7282, Ardsley-on-Hudson, NY 10503, Tel.: (914)693-0089.

Turman Publishing Co., 1319 Dexter Ave. N., Ste. 30, Seattle, WA 98119, Tel.: (206)282-6900.

Twayne, c/o G.K. Hall, 70 Lincoln St., Boston, MA 02111, Tel.: (617)423-3990.

Tycooly Publishing USA, PO Box 2178, Riverton, NJ 08077, Tel.: (509)486-1755.

## U

University of Alabama Press, PO Box 870380, Tuscaloosa, AL 35487-0380, Tel.: (205)348-5180.

University of Arkansas Press, 201 Ozark St., Fayetteville, AR 72701, Tel.: (509)575-5647.

University of California, Los Angeles, Center for Afro-American Studies, 160 Haines Hall, 405 Hilgard Ave., Los Angeles, CA 90024-1545, Tel.: (213)825-3528.

University of California Press, 2120 Berkeley Way, Berkeley, CA 94720, Tel.: (415)642-4247.

University of Chicago Press, 5801 S. Ellis Ave., Chicago, IL 60637, Tel.: (800)621-2736.

University of Illinois Press, 54 E. Gregory Dr., Champaign, IL 61820, Tel.: (217)333-0950.

University of Massachusetts, William Monroe Trotter Institute for the Study of Black Culture, Harbor Campus, Boston, MA 02125, Tel.: (617)287-5880.

University of North Carolina Press, PO Box 2288, Chapel Hill, NC 27515-2288, Tel.: (800)848-6224.

University of North Texas Press, PO Box 13856, Denton, TX 76203, Tel.: (817)565-2142.

University of Pennsylvania Press, 418 Service Dr., Philadelphia, PA 19104-6097, Tel.: (215)898-6261.

University of South Carolina Press, 1716 College St., Columbia, SC 29208, Tel.: (803)777-5243.

University of Tennessee Press, 293 Communications Bldg., Knoxville, TN 37996-0325, Tel.; (615)974-3321.

University Press of America, Inc., 4720 Boston Way, Lanham, MD 20706, Tel.: (301)459-3366.

University Press of Kentucky, 663 S. Limestone St., Lexington, KY 40508-4008, Tel.: (606)257-2951.

University Press of Mississippi, 3825 Ridgewood Rd., Jackson, MS 39211, Tel.: (601)982-6205.

University Press of New England, 17 1/2 Lebanon St., Hanover, NH 03755, Tel.: (603)646-3340.

University Press of Virginia, PO Box 3608, University Sta., Charlottesville, VA 22903, Tel.: (804)924-3468.

University Presses of Florida, 15 NW 15th St., Gainesville, FL 32611, Tel.: (904)392-1351.

University Publications of America, 4520 E. West Hwy., Ste. 600, Bethesda, MD 20814-3319, Tel.: (301)657-3200.

Urban Research Press, Inc., 840 E. 87th St., Chicago, IL 60619, Tel.: (312)994-7200.

## V

Vande Vere Publishing, Ltd., 8744 College Ave., Berrien Springs, MI 49103, Tel.: (616)473-1510.

Vantage Press, Inc., 516 W. 34th St., New York, NY 10001, Tel.: (212)736-1767.

Victor Books, 1825 Wheaton Ave., Wheaton, IL 60187, Tel.: (800)323-9409.

Virago Press, c/o Trafalgar Square, PO Box 257, North Comfort, VT 05053, Tel.: (800)423-4525.

## W

Wadsworth Publishing Co., 10 Davis Dr., Belmont, CA 94002, Tel.: (415)595-2350.

Warner Books, Inc., 666 5th Ave., New York, NY 10103, Tel.: (800)733-3000.

Franklin Watts, Inc., 387 Park Ave., New York, NY 10016, Tel.: (212)686-7070.

Wayne State University Press, 5959 Woodward Ave., Detroit, MI 48202, Tel.: (313)577-4601.

Wesleyan University Press, c/o University Press of New England, 17 1/2 Lebanon St., Hanover, NH 03755, Tel.: (603)646-3340.

Westview Press, 5500 Central Ave., Boulder, CO 80301-2847, Tel.: (303)444-3541.

Wiener, Moshe, 854 Newburg Ave., N., Woodmere, NY 11581.

Winston-Derek Publishers, Inc., PO Box 90883, Nashville, TN 37209, Tel.: (800)826-1888.

## Y

Yale University Press, 92A Yale Sta., New Haven, CT 06520, Tel.: (203)432-0825.

## Z

Hans Zell (UK), c/o K.G. Saur, 121 Chanlon Rd., New Providence, NJ 07974, Tel.: (908)665-2828.

# Picture and Text Credits

# *Picture and Text Credits*

## *Pictures*

*Cover:* Colin Powell: AP/Wide World Photos; Three men: S.B. Burns M.D. and the Burns Archive; Firefighter: UPI/Bettmann.

*Chronology:* p. 4: The Bettmann Archive; p. 5: Library of Congress; p. 6: Library of Congress; p. 7: Library of Congress; p. 8: Library of Congress; p. 9: New York Public Library; p. 11: Library of Congress; p. 12: Archive Photos; p. 17: Library of Congress; p. 18: Library of Congress; p. 19: Library of Congress; p. 20: Library of Congress; p. 22: The Bettmann Archive; p. 23: Library of Congress; p. 24: Library of Congress; p. 25: National Archives; p. 26: Library of Congress; p. 28: Library of Congress; p. 30: National Archives; p. 32: AP/Wide World Photos; p. 33: UPI/Bettmann; p. 34: Library of Congress; p. 35: UPI/Bettmann; p. 37: Library of Congress; p. 38: Library of Congress; p. 40: AP/Wide World Photos; p. 41: Library of Congress; p. 42: UPI/Bettmann; p. 43: AP/Wide World Photos; p. 45: UPI/Bettmann; p. 46: UPI/Bettmann; p. 46: Library of Congress; p. 47: National Archives; p. 48: UPI/Bettmann; p. 49: UPI/Bettmann; p. 50: UPI/Bettmann; p. 51: UPI/Bettmann; p. 54: UPI/Bettmann; p. 55: AP/Wide World Photos; p. 57: AP/Wide World Photos; p. 58: AP/Wide World Photos; p. 59: UPI/Bettmann; p. 63: AP/Wide World Photos; p. 67: AP/Wide World Photos; p. 70: AP/Wide World Photos; p. 73: AP/Wide World Photos; p. 74: UPI/Bettmann; p. 77: UPI/Bettmann; p. 77: AP/Wide World Photos; p. 78: AP/Wide World Photos; p. 82: AP/Wide World Photos; p. 90: AP/Wide World Photos; p. 93: AP/Wide World Photos; p. 96: UPI/Bettmann; p. 97: UPI/Bettmann; p. 98: UPI/Bettmann; p. 99: AP/Wide World Photos; p. 100: AP/Wide World Photos.

*African-American Firsts:* p. 106: Library of Congress; p. 110: United States Army; p. 111: AP/Wide World Photos; p. 112: AP/Wide World Photos; p. 114: AP/Wide World Photos; p. 116: AP/Wide World Photos; p. 117: National Association for the Advancement of Colored People; p. 118: AP/Wide World Photos; p. 119: AP/Wide World Photos; p. 120: UPI/Bettmann; p. 120: AP/Wide World Photos; p. 121: AP/Wide World Photos.

*Significant Documents in African-American History:* p. 131: Library of Congress; p. 134: Library of Congress; p. 137: Library of Congress; p. 141: Library of Congress; p. 145: Library of Congress; p. 147: The Bettmann Archive; p. 148: AP/Wide World Photos; p. 155: Library of Congress; p. 165: AP/Wide World Photos; p. 171: AP/Wide World Photos; p. 177: Consulate General of Jamaica; p. 182: Library of Congress; p. 187: AP/Wide World Photos; p. 188: Eisenhower Library; p. 193: National Broadcasting Corporation; p. 197: UPI/Bettmann; p. 203: Tex Harris, *Amsterdam News*; p. 207: UPI/Bettmann.

*African-American Landmarks:* p. 215: AP/Wide World Photos; p. 216: AP/Wide World Photos; p. 220: AP/Wide World Photos; p. 221: National Park Service; p. 225: UPI/Bettmann; p. 232: AP/Wide World Photos; p. 231: Burton Historical Collection, Detroit Public Library; p. 239: AP/Wide World Photos; p. 242: AP/Wide World Photos; p. 244: AP/Wide World Photos; p. 253: Denver Public Library; p. 254: Schomburg Center for Research in Black Culture, New York Public Library; p. 258: UPI/Bettmann; p. 259: AP/Wide World Photos.

***Africa and the Western Hemisphere:*** p. 263: United Nations; p. 265: National Museum of African Art; p. 270: United Nations; p. 270: National Museum of African Art; p. 271: National Museum of African Art; p. 274: United Nations; p. 276: United Nations; p. 278: United Nations; p. 280: United Nations; p. 281: United Nations; p. 282: United Nations; p. 283: United Nations; p. 287: United Nations; p. 289: National Museum of African Art; p. 290: National Museum of African Art; p. 292: United Nations; p. 294: United Nations; p. 295: National Museum of African Art; p. 296: National Museum of African Art; p. 300: United Nations; p. 301: United Nations; p. 302: United Nations; p. 304: United Nations; p. 306: United Nations; p. 307: National Museum of African Art; p. 308: National Museum of African Art; p. 310: National Museum of African Art; p. 313: Bahama News Bureau; p. 317: United Nations; p. 319: United Nations; p. 320: Judy Gurovitz, The Clement-Petrolik Co.; p. 321: United Nations; p. 322: Jamaica Tourist Board; p. 323: United Nations; p. 324: United Nations.

***Africans in America: 1600–1900:*** p. 334: New York Public Library; p. 335 Library of Congress; p. 336 Library of Congress; p. 337: Library of Congress; p. 338: Library of Congress; p. 341: Library of Congress; p. 342: Library of Congress; p. 343: New York Historical Society; p. 343: Library of Congress; p. 346: Library of Congress; p. 347: National Portrait Gallery; p. 348: Library of Congress; p. 350: Library of Congress; p. 353: The Bettmann Archive; p. 354: Library of Congress; p. 355: Library of Congress; p. 356: Library of Congress; p. 357: New York Public Library; p. 358: AP/Wide World Photos; p. 360: New York Public Library; p. 362: Archive Photos; p. 362: Library of Congress.

***Civil Rights:*** p. 370: Library of Congress; p. 371: Schomburg Center for Research in Black Culture, New York Public Library; p. 371: UPI/Bettmann; p. 372: AP/Wide World Photos; p. 373: AP/Wide World Photos; p. 374: AP/Wide World Photos; p. 374: Library of Congress; p. 376: UPI/Bettmann; p. 377: AP/Wide World Photos; p. 379: AP/Wide World Photos; p. 380: AP/Wide World Photos; p. 381: UPI/Bettmann; p. 383: AP/Wide World Photos; p. 384: AP/Wide World Photos; p. 387: AP/Wide World Photos; p. 388: UPI/Bettmann; p. 389: AP/Wide World Photos;p. 390: Library of Congress; p. 391: *Amsterdam News*; p. 392: UPI/Bettmann; p. 394: AP/Wide World Photos; p. 396: Library of Congress.

***Black Nationalism:*** p. 406: Library of Congress; p. 408: The Bettmann Archive; p. 409: Archive Photos; p. 411: Library of Congress; p. 412: Library of Congress;p. 414: AP/Wide World Photos; p. 417: UPI/Bettmann; p. 418: Archive Photos; p. 418: Library of Congress.

***National Organizations:*** p. 424: The Bettmann Archive; p. 425: National Association for the Advancement of Colored People; p. 426: Library of Congress; p. 427: AP/Wide World Photos; p. 428: Library of Congress; p. 429: Ace Creative Photos; p. 430: AP/Wide World Photos; p. 431: AP/Wide World Photos; p. 432: AP/Wide World Photos; p. 433: UPI/Bettmann; p. 434: AP/Wide World Photos; p. 435: AP/Wide World Photos; p. 437: Library of Congress; p. 438: UPI/Bettmann; p. 438: AP/Wide World Photos; p. 440: AP/Wide World Photos; p. 441: AP/Wide World Photos; p. 442: AP/Wide World Photos; p. 443: UPI/Bettmann; p. 444: A. Philip Randolph Institute; p. 445: AP/Wide World Photos; p. 446: UPI/Bettmann; p. 447: Bill Sparow, *Encore*; p. 448: National Urban League.

***Law:*** p. 502: New York Public Library; p. 507: UPI/Bettmann; p. 508: AP/Wide World Photos; p. 509: AP/Wide World Photos; p. 515: Library of Congress; p. 516: Library of Congress; p. 517: AP/Wide World Photos; p. 517: UPI/Bettmann; p. 522: National Association for the Advancement of Colored People; p. 523: UPI/Bettmann; p. 525: UPI/Bettmann; p. 533: UPI/Bettmann; p. 524: Library of Congress; p. 536: AP/Wide World Photos; p. 537: AP/Wide World Photos;

p. 539: AP/Wide World Photos; p. 544: UPI/Bettmann; p. 549: AP/Wide World Photos; p. 550: UPI/Bettmann; p. 551: AP/Wide World Photos; p. 552: AP/Wide World Photos; p. 553: AP/Wide World Photos; p. 554: AP/Wide World Photos; p. 555: AP/Wide World Photos; p. 556: UPI/Bettmann; p. 557: UPI/Bettmann; p. 559: AP/Wide World Photos.

**Politics:** p. 563: UPI/Bettmann; p. 567: UPI/Bettmann; p. 568: UPI/Bettmann; p. 569: AP/Wide World Photos; p. 570: AP/Wide World Photos; p. 571: UPI/Bettmann; p. 573: AP/Wide World Photos; p. 574: UPI/Bettmann; p. 575: United States Senate Historical Office; p. 577: AP/Wide World Photos; p. 578: AP/Wide World Photos; p. 579: AP/Wide World Photos; p. 580: AP/Wide World Photos; p. 581: AP/Wide World Photos; p. 582: AP/Wide World Photos; p. 583: AP/Wide World Photos; p. 584: Archive Photos; p. 585: AP/Wide World Photos; p. 586: UPI/Bettmann; p. 587: AP/Wide World Photos; p. 588: AP/Wide World Photos; p. 590: AP/Wide World Photos; p. 592: AP/Wide World Photos; p. 593: AP/Wide World Photos; p. 594: UPI/Bettmann; p. 597: AP/Wide World Photos; p. 598: AP/Wide World Photos; p. 601: United States Senate Historical Office; p. 602: United Nations; p. 603: AP/Wide World Photos; p. 604: Library of Congress; p. 605: AP/Wide World Photos; p. 606: AP/Wide World Photos; p. 607: AP/Wide World Photos; p. 609: AP/Wide World Photos; p. 610: AP/Wide World Photos.

**Population:** p. 618: Kenneth Estell; p. 619: Kenneth Estell; p. 620: S.B. Burns and the Burns Archive; p. 621: Library of Congress; p. 621: National Archives; p. 626: Kenneth Estell; p. 627: Kenneth Estell.

**Employment and Income:** p. 644: UPI/Bettmann; p. 647: Sue Steller; p. 649: Kenneth Estell; p. 653: UPI/Bettmann; p. 654: National Aeronautics and Space Administration; p. 655: Sue Steller; p. 656: Kenneth Estell.

**Entrepreneurship:** p. 668: Library of Congress; p. 670: Walker Collection of A'Lelia Perry Bundles; p. 672: Andy Roy; p. 674: AP/Wide World Photos; p. 675: Kenneth Estell; p. 676: AP/Wide World Photos; p. 677: Superb Manufacturing,

Inc.; p. 678: AP/Wide World Photos; p. 679: AP/Wide World Photos; p. 680: UPI/Bettmann; p. 681: AP/Wide World Photos; p. 683: Fisk University Library.

**The Family:** p. 694: Faustine Jones-Wilson; p. 694: Library of Congress; p. 695: Brain V. Jones; p. 696: Brain V. Jones; p. 700: Brain V. Jones; p. 702: Kenneth Estell; p. 703: Kenneth Estell; p. 709: Kenneth Estell; p. 710: Edwin L. Wilson, Sr.

**Education:** p. 724: Library of Congress; p. 725: Schomburg Center for Research in Black Culture, New York Public Library; p. 726: Library of Congress; p. 726: South Carolina Historical Society; p. 727: Library of Congress; p. 443: Library of Congress; p. 727: The Bettmann Archive; p. 728: The Bettmann Archive; p. 729: Library of Congress; p. 730: AP/Wide World Photos; p. 729: AP/Wide World Photos; p. 731: UPI/Bettmann; p. 733: UPI/Bettmann; p. 735: AP/Wide World Photos; p. 736: Bruce Griffin; p. 737: Beverly Hardy; p. 730: Molefi Kete Asante; p. 739: Surlock Photographers; p. 741: AP/Wide World Photos; p. 742: AP/Wide World Photos; p. 743: AP/Wide World Photos; p. 744: AP/Wide World Photos; p. 746: John F. Kennedy Library; p. 748: AP/Wide World Photos; p. 749: AP/Wide World Photos; p. 750: AP/Wide World Photos.

**Religion:** p. 774: New York Public Library; p. 776: Archive Photos; p. 777: SB. Burns and the Burns Archive; p. 779: Archive Photos; p. 780: AP/Wide World Photos; p. 782: AP/Wide World Photos; p. 783: AP/Wide World Photos; p. 784: AP/Wide World Photos; p. 786: AP/Wide World Photos; p. 787: *New York Daily News*; p789]791: AP/Wide World Photos; p. 790: UPI/Bettmann; p. 791: AP/Wide World Photos; p. 795: AP/Wide World Photos; p. 797: AP/Wide World Photos; p. 797: New York Public Library; p. 798: UPI/Bettmann; p. 800: UPI/Bettmann; p. 802: AP/Wide World Photos; p. 802: The Bettmann Archive; p. 804: AP/Wide World Photos; p. 807: AP/Wide World Photos.

**Literature:** p. 813: Schomburg Center for Research in Black Culture, New York Public Library; p. 814: AP/Wide World Photos; p. 816: AP/Wide World Photos; p. 817: AP/Wide World Pho-

tos; p. 818: AP/Wide World Photos; p. 821: UPI/
Bettmann; p. 823: AP/Wide World Photos; p. 828:
AP/Wide World Photos; p. 830: UPI/Bettmann;
p. 833: AP/Wide World Photos; p. 834: Springer/
Bettmann Film Archive; p. 835: AP/Wide World
Photos; p. 839: AP/Wide World Photos; p. 840:
AP/Wide World Photos; p. 841: AP/Wide World
Photos; p. 842: AP/Wide World Photos; p. 843:
New York Historical Society; p. 844: AP/Wide
World Photos; p. 845: AP/Wide World Photos;
p. 846: AP/Wide World Photos.

***The Media:*** p. 856: AP/Wide World Photos;
p. 858: AP/Wide World Photos; p. 859: AP/Wide
World Photos; p. 861: American Broadcasting
Company; p. 862: AP/Wide World Photos; p. 864:
AP/Wide World Photos; p. 865: Tony Brown Pro-
ductions, Inc.; p. 866: Black Entertainment Tele-
vision; p. 867: AP/Wide World Photos; p. 869: AP/
Wide World Photos; p. 870: Turner Broadcasting
System Management; p. 871: Black Enterprise
Magazine; p. 872: AP/Wide World Photos; p. 874:
UPI/Bettmann; p. 875: Associated Publishers;
p. 876: AP/Wide World Photos; p. 877: Washing-
ton Post; p. 878: AP/Wide World Photos; p. 880:
AP/Wide World Photos; p. 881: AP/Wide World
Photos; p. 882: AP/Wide World Photos; p. 883:
AP/Wide World Photos.

***Performing Arts:*** p. 941: Library of Congress;
p. 944: AP/Wide World Photos; p. 946: AP/Wide
World Photos; p. 947: AP/Wide World Photos;
p. 948: Ron Scherl; p. 950: AP/Wide World Pho-
tos; p. 951: WABC-TV, New York; p. 952: AP/
Wide World Photos; p. 953: New York City
Ballet; p. 954: UPI/Bettmann; p. 955: AP/Wide
World Photos; p. 957: AP/Wide World Photos;
p. 958: AP/Wide World Photos; p. 959: AP/Wide
World Photos; p. 962: AP/Wide World Photos;
p. 963: AP/Wide World Photos; p. 965: AP/Wide
World Photos; p. 966: AP/Wide World Photos;
p. 967: AP/Wide World Photos; p. 969: AP/Wide
World Photos; p. 971: AP/Wide World Photos;
p. 972: AP/Wide World Photos; p. 973: AP/Wide
World Photos; p. 974: AP/Wide World Photos;
p. 975: AP/Wide World Photos; p. 976: Tri-Star
Pictures; p. 979: Matha Swope Associates;
p. 980: UPI/Bettmann; p. 980: AP/Wide World
Photos; p. 981: AP/Wide World Photos; p. 982:
AP/Wide World Photos; p. 982: Archive Photos;
p. 983: Island Pictures; p. 984: UPI/Bettmann;

p. 985: Archive Photos; p. 990: AP/Wide World
Photos; p. 991: AP/Wide World Photos; p. 993:
Archive Photos; p. 994: AP/Wide World Photos;
p. 995: AP/Wide World Photos; p. 997: AP/Wide
World Photos; p. 998: Archive Photos; p. 999:
AP/Wide World Photos; p. 1000: UPI/Bettmann;
p. 1000: AP/Wide World Photos; p. 1001: AP/
Wide World Photos; p. 1003: Darlene Hammond/
Archive Photos.

***Classical Music:*** p. 1008: Schomburg Center
for Research in Black Culture, New York Public
Library; p. 1009: Schomburg Center for Research
in Black Culture, New York Public Library;
p. 1010: AP/Wide World Photos; p. 1011: AP/
Wide World Photos; p. 1012: AP/Wide World
Photos; p. 1014: AP/Wide World Photos; p. 1015:
Hurok Attractions; p. 1017: AP/Wide World Pho-
tos; p. 1020: The Bettmann Archive; p. 1022: AP/
Wide World Photos; p. 1027: AP/Wide World
Photos; p. 1033: The Bettmann Archive; p. 1034:
Archive Photos; p. 1036: UPI/Bettmann; p. 1038:
AP/Wide World Photos; p. 1041: AP/Wide World
Photos; p. 1043: AP/Wide World Photos; p. 1044:
AP/Wide World Photos; p. 1045: Archive Photos;
p. 1046: AP/Wide World Photos.

***Jazz Music:*** p. 1055: AP/Wide World Photos;
p. 1055: The Bettmann Archive; p. 1057: UPI/
Bettmann; p. 1059: AP/Wide World Photos;
p. 1060: *Downbeat*; p. 1061: AP/Wide World Pho-
tos; p. 1063: AP/Wide World Photos; p. 1068:
Shaw Artists Corporation; p. 1070: William Mor-
ris; p. 1073: National Archives; p. 1073: AP/Wide
World Photos; p. 1075: AP/Wide World Photos;
p. 1076: AP/Wide World Photos; p. 1076: S.B.
Burns and The Burns Archive; p. 1077: AP/Wide
World Photos; p. 1078: Springer/Bettmann Film
Archive; p. 1080: The Bettmann Archive; p. 1082:
Columbia Records; p. 1085: Ron Rogers; p. 1088:
AP/Wide World Photos; p. 1089: UPI/Bettmann;
p. 1090: AP/Wide World Photos; p. 1091: The
Bettmann Archive; p. 1093: AP/Wide World Pho-
tos; p. 1094: AP/Wide World Photos; p. 1096: AP/
Wide World Photos; p. 1101: UPI/Bettmann.

***Popular Music:*** p. 1108: AP/Wide World Photos; p. 1109: Archive Photos; p. 1112: AP/Wide
World Photos; p. 1113: AP/Wide World Photos;
p. 1114: AP/Wide World Photos; p. 1116: AP/
Wide World Photos; p. 1119: AP/Wide World

Photos; p. 1121: Archive Photos; p. 1122: AP/Wide World Photos; p. 1123: AP/Wide World Photos; p. 1124: AP/Wide World Photos; p. 1126: AP/Wide World Photos; p. 1127: AP/Wide World Photos; p. 1130: AP/Wide World Photos; p. .1133: AP/Wide World Photos; p. 1134: AP/Wide World Photos; p. 1135: Archive Photos; p. 1137: AP/Wide World Photos; p. 1138: AP/Wide World Photos; p. 1141: AP/Wide World Photos; p. 1142: AP/Wide World Photos; p. 1144: UPI/Bettmann; p. 1146: AP/Wide World Photos; p. 1147: AP/Wide World Photos; p. 1149: AP/Wide World Photos; p. 1151: AP/Wide World Photos.

**_Fine and Applied Arts:_** p. 1157: National Museum of American Art/Art Resource; p. 1161: Galbreath Photo Service; p. 1162: Whitney Museum of American Art; p. 1165: Whitney Museum of American Art; p. 1167: Fairchild Publications; p. 1169: AP/Wide World Photos; p. 1171: Art Resource; p. 1173: AP/Wide World Photos; p. 1174: AP/Wide World Photos; p. 1177 AP/Wide World Photos; p. 1183: National Museum of American Art/Art Resource; p. 1185: Whitney Museum of American Art; p. 1186: UPI/Bettmann; p. 1189: UPI/Bettmann; p. 1190: UPI/Bettmann; p. 1191: AP/Wide World Photos; p. 1195: National Museum of American Art/Art Resource; p. 1197: UPI/Bettmann; p. 1198: National Museum of American Art/Art Resource; p. 1199: AP/Wide World Photos; p. 1201: General Motors, Public Relations; p. 1202: AP/Wide World Photos; p. 1205: United Nations.

**_Science and Medicine:_** p. 1224: The Bettmann Archive; p. 1224: AP/Wide World Photos; p. 1225: AP/Wide World Photos; p. 1227: The Bettmann Archive; p. 1229: AP/Wide World Photos; p. 1230: Library of Congress; p. 1233: The Granger Collection, New York; p. 1235: UPI/Bettmann; p. 1236: AP/Wide World Photos; p. 1236: AP/Wide World Photos; p. 1237: Library of Congress; p. 1239: AP/Wide World Photos; p. 1240: AP/Wide World Photos; p. 1241: AP/Wide World Photos; p. 1242: The Bettmann Archive.

**_Sports:_** p. 1254: UPI/Bettmann; p. 1255: UPI/Bettmann; p. 1257: AP/Wide World Photos; p. 1258: AP/Wide World Photos; p. 1259: AP/Wide World Photos; p. 1260: AP/Wide World Photos; p. 1261: AP/Wide World Photos; p. 1262: AP/Wide World Photos; p. 1263: AP/Wide World Photos; p. 1265: Carl Nesfield; p. 1266: AP/Wide World Photos; p. 1266: Archive Photos; p. 1268: AP/Wide World Photos; p. 1269: AP/Wide World Photos; p. 1270: AP/Wide World Photos; p. 1273: UPI/Bettmann; p. 1274: AP/Wide World Photos; p. 1275: AP/Wide World Photos; p. 1276: National Broadcasting Co.; p. 1276: UPI/Bettmann; p. 1277: AP/Wide World Photos; p. 1278: AP/Wide World Photos; p. 1279: AP/Wide World Photos; p. 1280: AP/Wide World Photos; p. 1281: UPI/Bettmann; p. 1284: AP/Wide World Photos; p. 1286: AP/Wide World Photos; p. 1288: AP/Wide World Photos; p. 1289: AP/Wide World Photos; p. 1290: AP/Wide World Photos; p. 1291: AP/Wide World Photos; p. 1299: AP/Wide World Photos; p. 1300: AP/Wide World Photos.

**_Military:_** p. 1304: AP/Wide World Photos; p. 1304: Library of Congress; p. 1305: Library of Congress; p. 1306: AP/Wide World Photos; p. 1307: National Archives; p. 1308: Library of Congress; p. 1310: National Archives; p. 1312: National Archives; p. 1314: United States Army; p. 1316: United States Air Force; p. 1319: United States Army; p. 1323: United States Army; p. 1324: United States Marine Corps; p. 1325: AP/Wide World Photos; p. 1325: United States Marine Corps; p. 1326: United States Navy; p. 1328: United States Air Force: p. 1328: United States Army; p. 1329: National Archives; p. 1331: AP/Wide World Photos; p. 1332: AP/Wide World Photos; p. 1332: United States Navy; p. 1333: UPI/Bettmann; p. 1334: AP/Wide World Photos.

# _Text_

**_Significant Documents in African-American History:_** "Lift Every Voice and Sing," p. 176: Used by permission of Edward B. Marks Music Company. "I Have a Dream," pp. 192–95: Reprinted by arrangement with The Heirs to the Estate of Martin Luther King, Jr., c/o Joan Daves Agency as agent for the proprietor; copyright 1963 by Martin Luther King, Jr., copyright renewed 1991 by Coretta Scott King.

# Index

# Index

# N

# X

# Y